FEELING
WOMEN'S
LIBERATION

NEXT WAVE
New Directions in Women's Studies
*A series edited by Inderpal Grewal,
Caren Kaplan, and Robyn Wiegman*

FEELING
WOMEN'S
LIBERATION

VICTORIA HESFORD

Duke University Press   Durham and London   2013

© 2013 Duke University Press. All rights reserved. Printed in the United States of America on acid-free paper ∞. Designed by Courtney Baker. Typeset in Arno Pro by Keystone Typesetting, Inc.

Library of Congress Cataloging-in-Publication Data
Hesford, Victoria.
Feeling women's liberation / Victoria Hesford.
pages cm—(Next wave : new directions in women's studies)
Includes bibliographical references and index.
ISBN 978-0-8223-5376-8 (cloth : alk. paper)
ISBN 978-0-8223-5390-4 (pbk. : alk. paper)
1. Feminism—United States—History—20th century. 2. Lesbian feminism—United States—History—20th century. I. Title. II. Series: Next wave.
HQ1421.H47 2013
305.420973'0904—dc23
2012048667

CONTENTS

ACKNOWLEDGMENTS

The 1970s was the time of my childhood. I remember it fondly but also as a different time, a time out of step. In my world three events cut the 1970s off from the 1980s: the death of my father, moving from primary school to high school, and the election of Margaret Thatcher. None of these changes made my life happier or less complicated, and perhaps for this reason a dreamworld of the 1970s has tended to set the scene for my flights of fancy and imagination. In the 1980s, in England, feminism was a public activity—one that was a visible and active participant in the various political protests against what we now routinely call the neoliberalism of Margaret Thatcher's Conservative government's foreign and domestic policies. From the miners' strike in 1984, to the long encampment of the Greenham Common antinuclear, antimilitarization women's peace camp, which began in 1981 and lasted in some form until 2000, to the organized and widespread resistance to Clause 28 of the Local Government Act of 1988, forbidding local authorities to "promote" homosexuality, feminism was part of the everydayness of British national public life. It was in the news and on the TV: it helped create the atmosphere—the structure of feeling—of that time. My interest in the feminisms of the 1970s is structured through this sense of its manifest presence in "my" 1980s, as well as the distinction of affect that make the 1970s, for me, a different time from the 1980s.

This affective distinction between one decade and another—a distinction that is both personal and public—was mediated, for me, through a longing for, and fascination with, "America." The America I fell in love with was the fictional version on British TV, and it was the aesthetics of the American mass culture of the 1970s—the jerky, heady, campy energy of its racial and sexual masquerade—that also set the scene for my interest in feminism in the 1970s. For me, "women's liberation" first functioned as part of this mediated landscape—a landscape that suggested, at least on first viewing, a playful excess of gendered, sexual, and racial genres of being. *Women's liberation* became a term that incited complex and diffuse imaginings that were neither wholly "political," in the strong sense of the word, nor particularly coherent as an attitude or position from which to argue for or against the kinds of feminism it was supposed to represent. Instead, it tended to operate as a metaphor for something not representable: it was both a promise and a mystery.

Now, of course, I don't think of women's liberation that way. And that is no bad thing. To stay stuck in a nostalgic longing for the thereness of its imagined promise is precisely what I have tried to resist in this book. We owe the complexity of its historical manifestations a much more rigorously confrontational and skeptical response than that. But I offer this bit of "me-ness" here as a reminder of how political projects and movements operate as constellations of imagined and actualized goals and achievements, as well as holding spaces for often diverse, contradictory, and unthought-through aspirations for something other than what we already know. In other words, women's liberation allowed me to think and feel myself a feminist before I knew what that might mean.

There are others who have also allowed me that holding space, and who have offered the kinds of intellectual inspiration and support that have made this book possible. First and foremost, I have to thank my mother, Patricia Bullock, for keeping us going, for unconditional love, and for allowing me the space to imagine otherwise. She was also the first really, really smart woman I met, and the person who set in motion what happened next. Thanks too go to my sisters, Zoë and Kate Hesford, for their love and support as well as their notoriety on their too infrequent visits to the United States. I owe a lot to my friends back home—they have been generous hosts, made me laugh, and kept me up with everything Brit side: a big thank you to Ness and Paul Wilson, Phillippa Maye, Esther Oxford, Andrew Kaye, and, a little closer to New York, Anne O'Byrne.

This book's life started when I was an undergraduate in Maria Lauret's two-term course on Women in American Society at Sussex University. It was in that class that I first experienced the intellectual and erotic excitement of studying and thinking about feminist movements and theory. It was also in Maria's class that I first read Kate Millett's *Sexual Politics* and *Flying*. At Emory University I was fortunate to receive the support, intellectual generosity, and exacting expectations of Amy Schrager Lang. Julie Abraham and Angelika Bammer were also inspirational teachers and readers of the very early drafts of this book. A special thank you must go to Cindy Patton, whom I was lucky enough to encounter in my final years at

Emory. There are a lot of us out there who owe a great deal to Cindy's brilliance, as well as to her willingness to be a mentor in all the ways that word promises.

I must also thank my colleagues at Stony Brook University for their comradeship and smarts, especially Celia Marshik, Sara Lipton, Nancy Tomes, Ritch Calvin, Mary Jo Bona, Mary Rawlinson, Joanne Davila, Shirley Lim, Francoise Cromer, Melissa Forbis, Nerissa Balce, E. K. Tan, and Peter Manning. Thanks too to my fellow Transmissions of Culture reading group, led by the phenomenal E. Ann Kaplan, and enjoyable precisely because I get to think out loud with Susan Scheckel, Katherine Sugg, Jeff Santa Ana, Adrián Peréz Melgosa, Melissa Forbis, and Iona Man-Cheong. Thanks too to Kelly Oliver for her advice and support while at Stony Brook. I owe a great deal to Laura Micham, the Merle Hoffman Director of the Sallie Bingham Center for Women's History and Culture in the David M. Rubenstein Rare Book and Manuscript Library at Duke University for her help with my research questions and for acquiring the Kate Millett Papers (among many other incredible queer and feminist collections). More recently, as a postdoctoral fellow in the Women's Studies Program at Duke University, I have had the great pleasure of working with and benefitting from the intellectual vitality of Ranjana Khanna, Kimberly Lamm, Kathy Rudy, Kathi Weeks, Robyn Wiegman, and Ara Wilson. I want to especially thank Ranji, who, as director of the program, was a generous mentor and host during my year at Duke. I would also like to thank the staff in Women's Studies at Duke for their practical support during the finishing of this book: Lillian Spiller, Melanie Mitchell, Gwen Rogers, and Marialana Weitzel.

I am also indebted to my publisher, Duke University Press, and especially Ken Wissoker, who shepherded me through the revision process with a firm hand and insightful advice. Thanks too to Leigh Barnwell and Susan Albury for their guidance during the preparing of the manuscript for publication. I was also the beneficiary of three incredibly constructive and thoughtful reader reports. Thank you dear anonymous readers: your suggestions improved the book immeasurably. Finally, I need to say a huge thank you to two people. First, I must thank Robyn Wiegman, whose insightful, brilliant reading of the manuscript made *Feeling Women's Liberation* a much better book than it would otherwise have been. Thank you for inspiring me to become a better thinker and writer. I can't think of anyone better at reading reparatively. And lastly, I thank Lisa Diedrich, who made me believe that finishing was possible, who read every draft, and who continues to be at the center of everything. This book is for you.

Parts of chapter 3 were first published in the article "The Politics of Love: Women's Liberation and Feeling Differently," *Feminist Theory* 10, no. 1 (2009): 5–33, and an earlier version of chapter 5 first appeared as "Feminism and Its Ghosts: The Spectre of the Feminist-as-Lesbian," *Feminist Theory* 6, no. 3 (2005): 227–50.

AROUND 1970

*The Feminist-as-Lesbian and a
Movement in the Making*

Women's liberation is a term that draws some people toward it and repels others.[1] As a name for a particular moment and style of feminist protest, *women's liberation* both evokes and elides the complex array of feminist movements that emerged in the United States and beyond in the late 1960s and early 1970s. The name has come to stand, variously, for a radical as opposed to liberal form of feminism, grassroots rather than centrally organized feminism, a white middle-class rather than women of color feminism, a transnational postwar feminism, a nationalist and provincial form of feminism, a hopeful and exciting feminist moment, and a depressingly racist and essentializing feminist moment. That women's liberation stands for all of these things and more attests to the complexity and unsettledness of its historical moment. It also attests to the asymmetry of power in the production of history as an account of what happened and why. In this book I argue two things at once: that the women's liberation movement was a historical event of great significance, but what that significance was and is remains subject to intense feelings of attachment and disidentification that occlude its historical complexity. *Feeling Women's Liberation* addresses those feelings as key to any understanding of the movement as a significant historical event. Hence my organizing claim: the women's liberation movement was an upsetting event in postwar American history, and its upsetting eventfulness has had repercussions for how its archive has since been read by those within and without the so-called second wave of feminism.

In particular I argue that subsequent accounts of the movement by academic and popular feminism, queer theory, and mainstream public culture have tended to locate the meaning of the movement in developmental narratives of success or failure that depend on a reading of its archive as both origin and blueprint for its ensuing manifestation as a specific kind of feminism. That is, instead of approaching the archive as an array of rhetorical materials that sought to persuade and enact a new political constituency and world into being, it has instead largely been read as evidence of specific and coherent theoretical and ideological standpoints, which are then defended or criticized in a more knowing present. The consequences of such narrativizations, I suggest, are a tendency to naturalize the whiteness of women's liberation and to make its so-called bourgeois preoccupations—its revolt against marriage, the vaginal orgasm, and housework, along with its fight for the legalization of abortion and for sexual harassment laws—seem inevitable and uncontested political goals of the movement. One of the main contentions of this book, therefore, is that it is the failure to historicize the *production* of women's liberation as a *white* women's movement that has led to the reductive and incomplete readings of its archive and the feelings of attachment or disidentification that animate those readings.

Most of the happenings, position papers, manifestoes, essays, and media coverage I analyze in *Feeling Women's Liberation* either took place in or were written around 1970. I return to 1970 because that was the year "women's liberation" exploded into the national public sphere. Although groups of women had been meeting within the context of the New Left and black freedom movements and calling themselves women's liberationists since at least 1967, and although the Miss America protest, the first nationally recognized public action of the nascent movement, took place in 1968, it wasn't until 1970 that women's liberation became a dominant story in the national press.[2] The "watershed" year for the women's liberation movement was 1970, not only because of the media's increased coverage of its events and people but also because of the explosion in mainstream publishing of feminist position papers, manifestoes, and anthologies.[3] Books like Robin Morgan's anthology *Sisterhood Is Powerful* and Kate Millett's *Sexual Politics* were published in 1970 and became best sellers with an international audience. Other works, like Shulamith Firestone's *The Dialectic of Sex* and Toni Cade's *The Black Woman*, were also published in 1970 by mainstream publishers and to widespread media attention. The year 1970 was also when the Equal Rights Amendment (ERA) was not only brought, once again, before the congressional subcommittee responsible for constitutional amendments but it was also rushed through congressional committees and debated in both houses, something not seen in the fifty years the ERA had been a political goal of feminists and largely the result of effective feminist lobbying of Congress.[4] While the ERA fight became one of the news stories of the year, other defining events that became part of the emergence into the national public sphere of women's liberation—the persecution and arrest of Angela Davis by the FBI, the sit-in and subsequent takeover of the *Ladies' Home Journal* by New York radical feminists, the nationally organized Women's Strike for Equality, and the zap action by the Lavender Menace at the Second Congress to Unite Women—all took place in 1970 and received widespread media coverage and movement recognition.[5]

Most of the few historical studies and memoirs of women's liberation also highlight 1970 as a major turning point in the trajectory of the movement. Two of the most influential histories of the movement, Alice Echols's *Daring to Be Bad: Radical Feminism in America, 1967–1975* and Ruth Rosen's *The World Split Open: How the Modern Women's Movement Changed America*, locate the fragmentation and ultimate dissolution of women's liberation as a social movement in the "gay/straight split" that erupted in 1970. Alice Echols, for example, locates the breakdown of the movement from a radical, politically activist movement to a cultural, lifestyle-oriented movement in the "eruption of difference" caused by the controversy over lesbianism that began in the New York chapter of the National Organization for Women (NOW) in 1970.[6] While Benita Roth, Kimberly Springer, and Barbara Ryan, in their sociological analyses of the Chicana, black, and women's liberation movements, note the emergence of the "lesbian issue," in and around 1970, as one of the major reasons for the tensions within and subsequent factionalism of the various feminist movements of the era.[7]

I also turn to 1970 because it was the year that Kate Millett became, for a moment, the most famous feminist in America. In its provocative assertions that sexuality was a primary site for the reproduction of social power, along with its passionate and, at that time, unique critique of the portrayal of heterosexuality by writers like Norman Mailer and Henry Miller, Millett's *Sexual Politics* was probably the first explicitly feminist PhD dissertation in the American academy, as well as one of the first cultural and intellectual products of the women's liberation movement.[8] Just one month after publication, the book went into its fourth printing with over fifteen thousand copies sold. *Life* magazine even went so far as to call it the *Das Kapital* of the women's movement, and *Time*, as part of its extensive analysis of the women's liberation movement in the summer of that year, called Millett the Mao Tse-tung of the movement and put her on the front cover.[9] In 1970 Kate Millett also figured in a related public drama: in December she was accused by *Time* of being bisexual and, therefore, of harming the credibility and legitimacy of the then fledgling women's movement. At the same time, some within the movement accused her of simultaneously pretending straightness to the media while claiming lesbian sisterhood in private.[10] In the short space of one year Millett had gone from radical feminist icon of the mainstream media to designated betrayer of an entire movement.

For these reasons, Kate Millett plays a central and recurring role in *Feeling Women's Liberation*. Her notoriety in 1970 as both the media-anointed leader and lesbian betrayer of the movement meant she became a figure around which, to use Alan Sinfield's phrase in relation to Oscar Wilde's public notoriety in 1895, "contest and change" occurred, both in the movement and in the national public sphere.[11] Her outing as bisexual by *Time* and the attendant crisis over lesbianism in the women's liberation movement were part of a series of events that marked the emergence of a new figure—the feminist-as-lesbian—which, in turn, has had a defining effect on the way in which women's liberation in particular and feminism in general has been remembered and represented, in both the supercultural domain of the mass media and in the subcultural domains of popular and academic feminism and queer theory. By following the figure back to that moment— a beginning, but just one, of women's liberation—this book analyzes the "disconcerting nexus" out of which Kate Millett became, if only for a moment, a representative figure of women's liberation. This return to 1970 is conducted not as an attempt to reconstruct some hidden, originary truth of the movement, nor as a biographical resurrection of Millett as a (lost) heroine of that era. It is conducted in order to access some of the forces, both social and cultural, that not only produced the issues and shape of the U.S. women's liberation movement but also the images and narrative accounts through which the movement has since been constructed as an object of knowledge and memory.

Of course, other media events happened both before and after 1970 that have since formed part of how women's liberation is known and remembered in the public sphere. Shirley Chisholm's run for the Democratic nomination for president in 1972 and the Bobby Riggs versus Billy Jean King tennis match in 1973 were both directly associated with women's liberation. The King versus Riggs tennis match was billed as a battle of the sexes, received prime-time TV coverage with an estimated fifty million viewers, and drew thirty thousand people into the Houston Astrodome to witness King's easy win over Riggs. A debate on feminism in 1971 at Manhattan's Town Hall, organized as "a dialogue on women's liberation" and featuring Germaine Greer, Diana Trilling, Jacqueline Ceballos, and Jill Johnston, also became a notorious media event when Johnston, the dance critic of the *Village Voice* and agent provocateur for an absurdist form of lesbian feminism, recited a feminist lesbian manifesto and proceeded to roll around on the stage kissing with two friends, much to the horror of the event's moderator Norman Mailer.[12] Similarly, the Miss America protest of 1968 received TV and print media coverage of its boardwalk protests and, indirectly, of its attempt to disrupt the pageant itself, while several prime-time TV series, including *Maude* (1972–78) and *The Mary Tyler Moore Show* (1970–77), can be included in the archive of film and TV shows that made women's liberation a nationally mediated event in the 1970s. However, while other things happened both before and after 1970, it was the events of 1970 that have had a defining effect on how second-wave feminism, and women's liberation in particular, has been remembered and narrativized by academic and popular feminism, queer theory, and mainstream public culture. I argue that it is from the conjunction of mainstream media coverage of the movement and the simultaneous eventfulness of the movement's revolt and claims to political and social agency during 1970 that the feminist-as-lesbian first emerged as a figure of and for women's liberation, and it is through this figure that many of the metaphors, phrases, and terms of the movement circulated—even if they also connect with, as they no doubt do, events that happened prior to or after 1970.

THE ARCHIVE OF WOMEN'S LIBERATION
What is found at the historical beginning of things is not the inviolable identity of their origin; it is the dissension of other things, it is disparity.
—Michel Foucault, "Nietzsche, Genealogy, History"

One of the primary motivations for writing this book was my desire to seek a way out of what had become, by the late 1990s and early 2000s, a debilitating and profoundly distorting set of theoretical, institutional, and political antagonisms in the United States between feminist and queer studies.[13] The debates seemed so fraught with feeling that I wanted to figure out where the antagonism had come from—a question that led me back toward the women's liberation movement. It seemed to me that so much of the suspicion between feminist and queer studies rested on divergent convictions about the historical effects and meanings of the women's liberation movement within their respective fields and related subcultures. While feminist historians and scholars have attempted to provide new historical narratives and archives that would prove in emphatic fashion the insurgent radicalism of women's liberation and its transformative effect on U.S. postwar history,[14] much of the recent "queer desire for history," while offering a rich repertoire of theoretical and methodological concepts for thinking about what a queer historiography might look like, has almost completely bypassed the second-wave era.[15] Like ships passing in the night, a feminist concern with its own history and the queer desire for history have left each untouched and often unnoticed by the other.

Feeling Women's Liberation intervenes in this political, theoretical, and historical impasse in two ways. First, rather than simply claim the movement's historical importance and centrality to postwar social transformations at the outset and then try to prove it, I ask: How has the history of women's liberation been produced; what stories have been constructed and disseminated as memories of women's liberation, in the mass-mediated public sphere as well as the subcultural worlds of feminist and queer studies? In order to answer that question I return to the emergent moments of the women's liberation movement by "read[ing] along the grain" of its archive.[16] Such attention to the *productive detail* of the women's liberation movement is vitally important at this historic juncture precisely because it can render explicit some of the overdetermined and reductive ways in which the movement has become an object of knowledge in contemporary memoirs, conventional historical studies, subcultural memory, and collective cultural memory. By conducting an immersion analysis of the mainstream media coverage of the movement in 1970, combined with archival research in women's movement collections, including a wide-ranging reading of the movement's position papers and early published collections, I follow along the production of the women's liberation archive in order to track the conditions of possibility through which ideas of the movement and its political imaginary were shaped.

Although Ann Laura Stoler's subject is the formal and institutionalized archive of the colonial state rather than the more ephemeral, scattered, and disorderly archive of a movement like women's liberation, her methodological emphasis on focusing on the archive's production, on reading for "its regularities, for its logic of recall, for its densities and distributions," is pertinent to the question of how feminist and queer scholars and activists in the United States might read the documentary remainders of a protest movement like women's liberation.[17] Changing our conception of the archive from a repository of things to a process of knowledge production, as Stoler argues for, is to read the documentations of the past for the "evidentiary paradigms" that make claims to truth and for political action intelligible "at a particular time, for a particular contingent and in a particular way." The point of such an approach to the archive is less to establish the falsity of the powerful's claims to epistemological authority than to emphasize the effectivity of those claims—an effectivity that lies beyond or in excess of the claims made on its behalf by the powerful: "The task is less to distinguish fiction from fact than to track the production and consumption of those facticities themselves."[18] For Stoler, this kind of tracking work allows us to map "the conditions of possibility which shaped what could be written, what warranted repetition, what competencies were rewarded in archival writing, what stories could not be told and what could not be said."[19]

In contrast to Stoler's methodological emphasis on how particular histories are constructed through conventions of knowledge production and arrangement, the published histories and memoirs of women's liberation have, for the most part, tended to tell the same story. They have employed a narrative that might be called, for convenience's sake, "from simplicity to complexity." Positing a particular, singular origin of the movement, namely the experiences of young, white, middle-class women in postwar America, they then either trace or assume a burgeoning complexity as the movement realized the disparateness of other women's experiences. Sara Evans's groundbreaking historical study *Personal Politics: The Roots of Women's Liberation in the Civil Rights Movement and the New Left* asserts the cataclysmic influence of the civil rights movement on the women's movement but in a way that reinscribes the separation of issues of race from those of gender. The story she writes is, as she acknowledges, a partial one—that of young, white, middle-class women's rise to political consciousness through the political resistance of African Americans in the civil rights movement. For Evans, the beginnings of women's liberation can be located in the journey many young, white women took from the respectable neighborhoods of their southern or northeastern childhoods to the outposts of rural Mississippi in the summer of 1964. By regarding the civil rights movement as inspiration and analogy for the women's movement, Evans cannot easily incorporate the participation of black women in the women's movement more generally, though she does acknowledge the separate directions black and white women took out of organizations like the Student Nonviolent Coordinating Committee (SNCC) into feminism. Instead, through an adherence to a coherent, unified narrative, the beginnings of the women's movement are fixed, inadvertently perhaps, in a singular origin: the politicization of young, middle-class, white women through the example of the civil rights movement.[20]

In *Daring to Be Bad*, perhaps the most influential history of women's liberation, Alice Echols takes up the story where Evans leaves it. While Evans narrates the origins of the women's liberation movement, Echols describes its emergence and subsequent decline as a distinct movement. And like Evans, Echols has a particular story to tell: "This book analyzes the trajectory of the radical feminist movement from its beleaguered beginnings in 1967 through to its ascendance as the dominant tendency within the movement to its decline and supplanting by cultural feminists in the mid 1970s."[21] While Echols's concentration on the life span of one wing of the movement offers an incredibly rich and illuminating account of radical feminism—one to which this book is indebted—it also tends to force the ferment of disparate views and "cohorts" constitutive of the larger movement into an overly schematic presentation of its history.[22] The radical feminists become the instigators and crusaders of women's liberation, and those groups on the margins of women's liberation disappear from view. This problematic schema occurs as a consequence of the developmental causality intrinsic to the telling of any story, having less to do with any intentional exclusion or oversight on Echols's part. Because her history of women's liberation is told as a story—with a beginning, middle, and end—cultural feminism, lesbian feminism, and women of color feminism, are all presented as descriptive terms of a discrete array of feminisms that came after the initial insurgencies of radical feminism. Echols's story of radical feminism creates, in its wake, the implicit, if not explicit, idea that the diversity of feminisms today is a marker of the failures of the women's liberation movement in the mid- to late 1970s.[23]

More problematic, perhaps, than the narrativization of history exemplified in the texts above is the tendency in *The Feminist Memoir Project: Voices from Women's Liberation* (1998), edited by Rachel Blau DuPlessis and Ann Snitow, to present personal accounts of the movement as transparent conduits of real historical truth. In their introduction, DuPlessis and Snitow assert that the goal of their collection is to "stand against the belittling and demonizing, not only of feminism but of many of the political struggles of the sixties."[24] By collecting reminiscences from women active during the era of the second wave, the editors hope that the historical importance of the movement's actions and accomplishments will be made more manifest in a present that has largely "relegated" it "to the footnotes and the margins" of the history of that time.[25] While the intention to connect past and present in our historicizations of the women's liberation movement is important and necessary in a contemporary world that prefers its feminism to be over and done with, the question of why the women's liberation movement has been relegated to the margins of the historiography of the 1960s and belittled (to a much greater degree than other protest movements of the 1960s, as the editors state) is never directly addressed. Moreover, the choice of contributors in conjunction with the introductory remarks of the editors tend, as a whole, to restage some of the problems endemic to the "remembering" of the women's movement—the same problems they are attempting to counteract.[26] As Beverly Guy-Sheftall writes in her contribution to *The Feminist Memoir Project*, she was "not surprised by the predictable picture of 'second-wave' feminists being mostly white." Nor could she have been surprised by her "disappointment at the small number of narratives by African-American women" in the collection.[27] And yet, Guy-Sheftall is surprised, "startled" even, at coming across mimeographed documents from the National Black Feminist Organization (NBFO) while researching her contribution. Guy-Sheftall's surprise comes from remembering her participation in women's groups at Spelman in the late 1960s, seeing the publication date of the documents as being in 1973, and realizing that her participation in the women's movement began long before written histories of the movement have recognized the participation of African American women. Her surprise is a moment when the "ruse of history" breaks down,[28] a moment when she realizes that her memories and the documentary remains of the past have diverged. Guy-Sheftall's moment of surprise reminds us that the women's movement has been remembered, even by its participants, in a particular way, one that *The Feminist Memoir Project*, rather than critiquing, tends to reenact.

In *The World Split Open*, a more recent historical study and one I draw on throughout this book, Ruth Rosen attempts to argue against a singular origin for the movement, locating its beginnings in the changing political, social, and cultural contexts of the United States in the twentieth century. As she writes in her introduction:

> Many readers, I suspect, probably know that American feminism was shaped by the political culture of the fifties and sixties. But it also developed out of much longer and deeper political traditions—such as the disestablishment of religion as a state force and a profound distrust of centralized government; the celebration of individual enterprise and initiative; a class politics expressed mostly through race and gender; a long evangelical tradition that has existed outside political parties and government; and a deep and abiding belief that in America, one can always reinvent oneself.[29]

Here, Rosen explicitly claims the second-wave women's movement as a particularly American phenomenon and simultaneously embeds the movement in the general sweep of "American history." And yet, while the intention is to reveal the inextricable influence and constitutive effect of the women's movement on American history—to reclaim its importance to and for American history—Rosen's perspective also tends to suggest that the movement was, in some sense, inevitable. As a result, any analysis of feminism as a dissident movement becomes difficult, for the "shape" of the movement has already been prescribed by historical trends greater than its own, heterogeneous particularity.

The problem, as Joan Scott, among others, has noted, is a historiographical one.[30] The history of the second wave is told as a story—one that tends to efface the very heterogeneity and threat Rosen is trying to account for.

Indeed, the structure of Rosen's book follows a trajectory similar to the other published histories of the movement: the first chapter begins with the "Dawn of Discontent" and the last chapter with the "Proliferation of Feminism." Like Evans, Rosen locates the "discontent" mainly in the lives of white, middle-class women, and like Echols, she understands the "proliferation" of feminisms to be something—as the order of her chapters suggests—that happened after the initial eruption of women's liberation. Rosen's history, like the other texts noted above, engages in what I would call a project of recovery, one that re-remembers a history that has been lost or submerged by a hegemony that has repeatedly made feminism disappear from the social and political landscapes of American history. And in the attempt to recover what has been forgotten, Rosen wants to restate the seriousness of the movement and claim its rightful place in the historical record. But by restating that history in the form of a narrative, which intrinsically depends upon a progressive development (even if that development ends in the unhappiness of a disintegrating movement in the 1980s), Rosen's account, like those of Evans's, Echols's, and the collected memoirs in DuPlessis and Snitow's book, inevitably presupposes what the origin, and the success, of the women's movement's "story" is.

There are ironies to this story. In the desire to order and account for the movement's rise and fall, the very real presence of racism, heterosexism, and classism in the movement becomes calcified into a unified account of the movement that tends to cement, rather than bring into question, the ahistorical assumptions that women's liberation—and the women's movement in the late 1960s and early 1970s more generally—was a racist and classist movement. The presence of other voices, groups, and political affiliations at the beginnings of the movement are elided and covered over in the attempt to account for the movement's limitations and failures. This kind of narrative straightjacketing leads to historical oversights that, as Guy-Sheftall's moment of surprise suggests, produce major shifts in the perceptions and memories of historical reality. The consequences for how the women's movement is remembered can be startling. Flora Davis in *Moving the Mountain: The Women's Movement in America since 1960* writes about the early 1980s as a period when "feminists were thrown on the defensive. They lost some battles and won others, and overall progress for women stalled. Nevertheless, new feminist groups kept emerging, many of them now being formed by women of color."[31] And yet, two hundred pages later, she writes, "in 1973, with black militancy fading and male chauvinism rampant, the National Black Feminist Organization was founded. Within a year, NBFO had spawned ten chapters and spawned a conference."[32] The presence of historical facts that contradict the story Davis wants to tell about the movement does not produce a reevaluation of the story. Rather, it goes unremarked upon, as if the fact of black women's feminist activism in the early years of the second wave belongs to another story. What counts as history ultimately is not the complex, contradictory, heterogeneous mess of any moment or era but a story that is already familiar.

Katie King, in her analysis of U.S. feminist discourses titled *Theory in Its Feminist Travels: Conversations in U.S. Women's Movements*, brings the deployment of such singular narratives of the past into critical view. She reveals the inevitable implicatedness and partial perspective of all attempts to write the history of a political movement by the participants themselves or by others, like me, who are invested in that movement as a consequence of our relationship to feminism.[33] For King, such histories are "origin stories," which are "interested stories, all of them. They construct the present moment, and a political position in it, by invoking a point in time out of which that present moment unfolds—if not inevitably, then at least with a certain coherence."[34] King's critique is meant to be neither reductive nor dismissive; her intention is not to argue against the necessity of historical inquiry but to problematize the way stories of the second-wave era tend to elide the contingency of their production in the present. By analyzing moments and events that were "instances of contests for meaning within U.S. feminism," when "whole systems of signifiers are reduced to one," King interrogates moments where the ferment of the early women's liberation movement gets fixed into a dominant account.[35]

One of the moments King traces is the construction of lesbianism as a magical sign for feminism within women's liberation. Employing Foucault's method of descriptive comparison, King traces the discursive travels of the term *lesbian* within the early writing of the movement, charting the way it came to stand for feminism at the expense of either an analysis of heterosexuality as a set of discourses and social relations or the constitution of relationships between feminism and other structures of social differentiation and ordering, like race and class. King's analysis of the production of feminist histories of the women's liberation movement, and her analysis of the changing signification of lesbianism in the movement in particular, has influenced my work. But whereas King focuses entirely on the competing discourses within the women's movement itself, I want to situate the emergence of the lesbian as a figure of and for second-wave feminism both within and outside the movement. The moment when the "shit hit the *Time* fan"—when Kate Millett was outed by *Time* magazine, and lesbians were being kicked out of various feminist groups and organizations in 1970—was a moment when feminism and lesbianism became explosively conjoined for those outside as well as inside the movement.[36] The emergence of the feminist-as-lesbian figure (rather than just the internal discursive "travels" of the term *lesbian*) was a moment, I argue, when the phenomenon of the women's liberation movement was apprehended through a limited set of associations that still define, to a large degree, the way in which the movement is known and remembered today.

Unlike the histories and memoirs discussed above, my interest in this moment, and in its relation to the history of American feminism and women's liberation in particular, is based less on restating the importance of the women's liberation movement to postwar American history than on attending to the productive detail of its claims to political, social, and cultural presence. Reading along the grain of the movement's archive opens up the complexity of the movement's eventfulness to a scrutiny that does not reduce or foreclose the possibilities of meaning inherent to it; it also invites us to pay the kind of loving attention to a past that might make us want to turn away from it, rather than toward it. Here, then, *Feeling Women's Liberation* intervenes in the burgeoning field of queer historiography by drawing attention to the danger, rather than (just) the pleasure, of a loving look backward at the past. The queer desire for history as a practice of producing loving attachments to what has often remained marginal or discarded in the writing of history, while capable of generating archives that can be world and community making in the present, tends to elide or downplay the implicatedness of any putatively queer history in cultural and social regimes of normalization. With a kind of fascinated myopia, the queer desire for history can too often settle on the ephemera and marginalia of queer lives and subcultures rather than asking what Wendy Brown calls "the more difficult questions about the bearing of the past on the present."[37] By analyzing the conjuncture of feminist *and* mass cultural representations of the women's liberation movement, I try to avoid the risk of too quickly substituting the pleasures of thinking otherwise for the continuing practice of a necessary, active, yet always interested estrangement from the past. Methodologically, then, I am concerned with the predicament we are all—feminist and queer—faced with when we want to articulate the forgotten or diminished history of the subjugated, marginalized, or simply dismissed to the possibilities of a future that will take into account what happened and offer something different and perhaps better. How do we keep the knotty achievements, as well as the difficulties and failures, of a movement like women's liberation—a movement that forms part of the conditions of possibility for queer and feminist theory and studies in the present—in critical sight while paying it the kind of loving attention needed to conjure up its complex eventfulness?

THE EMERGENCE OF THE FEMINIST-AS-LESBIAN AND THE EVENT OF WOMEN'S LIBERATION

Rather than produce another story of women's liberation, or conduct a loving look backward at its lost possibilities as something to be recuperated in the present, I understand my return to the movement's beginnings as an attempt to enact a responsibility toward its eventfulness by mapping a relationship between what, in Wendy Brown's terms, "we have inherited" from that era and "what is not yet born."[38] Drawing upon recent theorizations of the event in feminist history and cultural studies, I approach women's liberation as a surprising eruption of action and thought that coalesced into a feminism that was generative of new meanings and practices—of feminism but also of femininity, sexuality, race, and so on.[39] To understand women's liberation as an eruption of the new is not, however, to approach it as something unconnected to older forms of feminist protest and to other protest movements of the era; instead, it is to see the movement as having effects that exceeded its immediate context and continue to infuse and constrain the present in ways that we are more and less knowing about. To understand women's liberation as an event is to approach it as both possibility and legacy.

The primary vehicle for this mapping between historical inheritance and imaginative projection is the feminist-as-lesbian, a figure who appeared at the beginning of the twentieth century, when feminism rather than women's rights became a social and political force, and a figure who reappeared, in a different form, during the momentous days of the early women's liberation movement in the late 1960s and early 1970s, when dyke baiting became a prominent tactic of antifeminists and anti-lesbian feminists and lesbian feminism came into being partly as a response to that baiting.[40] Defined as the "ball-busting, selfish, hairy extremist," we all know,

now, what a feminist is.[41] Susan Douglas's succinct description denotes the figure through which popular cultural conceptions of feminism have been organized in mainstream culture since the 1970s. Yet I would argue that the feminist-as-lesbian, as I call her in order to delimit her from the historical specificity of lesbian feminism, has also tended to be the figure through which generalized perceptions of second-wave feminism have been organized as memory in the academy and in queer and feminist subcultures. As the "flannel shirt androgyne[,] closeminded, antisex puritan[,] humorless moralist[,] racist and classist ignoramus[, and] essentialist utopian," to use Bonnie Zimmerman's portrait of the stereotypical lesbian feminist, she often stands for the perceived essentialism of second-wave feminism and for the limits of its cross-class and cross-race alliances.[42] The exaggerated terms by which both Douglas and Zimmerman describe the feminist-as-lesbian can be read as an effect of her hypervisible presence across the borders between mass culture and subcultures, as well as those between feminist and queer studies and theories. She's a monster; she's ridiculous; she's laughable, contemptuous, shameful or fearless, joyful, and full of hubris. As a repository for a complex array of affect and emotion, the figure draws us to a sense, a practical knowledge, of women's liberation that often goes unacknowledged or unaccounted for.

Indeed, it is through such overfamiliarity or hypervisiblity that the figure of the feminist-as-lesbian operates in the present as a ghost rather than as an icon or symbol of second-wave feminism.[43] Avery Gordon offers an example of hypervisibility in her reading of Ralph Ellison's *Invisible Man* in *Ghostly Matters*. For Ellison, the visibility of the African American male's blackness blinds the white onlooker to the complexity of the man's individual personhood while also maintaining the (empowering) ignorance of the white onlooker's partial vision. According to Gordon, it is precisely the way in which visibility can become "a type of invisibility" that "apparitions and hysterical blindness[es]" are produced.[44] The feminist-as-lesbian, in her hypervisibility, blinds us to the complex forces that first produced her while also blinding us to our own *interest* in her; she is de-realized—made to appear insubstantial and anterior to history—in a way that echoes the vaporization of the black man in Ellison's *Invisible Man*.

Today the feminist-as-lesbian is everywhere and nowhere. Sometimes she appears in classroom discussions when students are asked to describe their understanding of feminism. At other times she appears in movies and television shows about modern young women and in magazine and newspaper articles about the apparent demise of feminism in the late twentieth and early twenty-first century. And sometimes she appears in the work of scholars eager to differentiate queer from lesbian and lesbian feminism or one kind of feminist theory from another.[45] This everywhere and nowhere characteristic of the feminist-as-lesbian is itself a sign of her spectrality: she floats from discursive domain to discursive domain, present yet without substance; she is necessary to the discussion or representation but never its subject. The spectrality of the feminist-as-lesbian works in complex ways to screen us from the multiple ways in which the various feminisms of the early second-wave era challenged the postwar American social and cultural hegemony, and in her continuing hypervisibility, the figure also reminds us that those challenges are not yet over.

As a spectral remainder of the women's liberation movement, the feminist-as-lesbian is both an effect and affective repository of the movement's engagement with the world, and as such, she is a product of forces neither entirely internal nor external to women's liberation as a movement and as a counterpublic sphere. The manifestation of power that produced the apparition of the feminist-as-lesbian has to be understood, therefore, in a doubling sense: as an imposition (it was, for example, *Time* magazine who publicly outed Kate Millett, not the women's movement or Millett herself) and as agency (a significant minority within the movement would go on in the early 1970s to propose a form of lesbianism as the *only* credible feminist position). It is in this moment of conjunction, rather than as the outcome of any developing political position or designed repression, that the feminist-as-lesbian emerged in the way that she did, looking the way she did, and representing the things she did. *Feeling Women's Liberation* attempts to examine this fundamental ambivalence in the production of the feminist-as-lesbian by first diagnosing the moment of the figure's arising—the "eruption of forces" from which she emerged.[46] I then trace out from that moment the economies of emotion, feminist and nonfeminist, from which she was fashioned, if not always deliberately, as a figure of and for women's liberation.

While operating as a clue, a remainder, of what is unknowable and unrepresentable about the movement's emergence onto the scene of political contestation and revolt in the late 1960s and early 1970s, the figure of the feminist-as-lesbian also operates as a screen memory that works to contain and displace our knowledge, not just of the women's liberation movement but of the second-wave era more generally. The ambivalence of the feminist-as-lesbian also has to be understood, then, as intrinsic to her legibility as a *shorthand notation* for women's liberation.[47] While she screens us from the multiplicity and possibilities of the early years of the second-wave era, she is also a remnant of those possibilities. An excavation of the ways in which feminists thought, if not always acted, their resistance to heterosexuality in the early years of the women's liberation movement also forms part of my return to the documentary remainders of women's liberation. Though it might be common knowledge in the corridors of women's studies programs that women's liberation challenged the institutions and cultural norms of heterosexuality, how that challenge was enacted in the movement's manifestoes and position papers is less obvious, and so I ask: What rhetorical forms, metaphors, and phrases were deployed and accrued meaning as part of women's liberation's political revolt against what at the time was called sexism? And how did lesbianism become a "domain of active and intense problematization" in the early years of the movement in ways that both did and did not change the conceptual and experiential parameters of female sexuality?[48]

And, finally, by returning to the details of her production, *Feeling Women's Liberation* asks how the feminist-as-lesbian figure covers over or, perhaps more appropriately, "whites-out," the complex ways in which the histories and practices of racism shaped the movement itself and accounts of it.[49] That women's liberation was formally recognized as a movement by the recorders and commentators of mainstream America when white, middle-class women picketed the Miss America Pageant in Atlantic City in 1968 and marched down Fifth Avenue holding up placards demanding their liberation in the summer of 1970, is hardly surprising in a society stratified by race and class hierarchies. However, this process of publicity whereby some women (young, white, and middle class) and not others are seen as political activists, as feminists, and recorded as such by the national media has very real repercussions for what we know of the women's liberation movement in the present. The moment the movement became "history"—was taken note of and its events recorded—was also the moment when that history was formed through distortion and elision. The hypervisibility of the feminist-as-lesbian figure, as an image memory of the women's liberation movement, emerged out of this process of representation through distortion and elision.

At the same time I understand the whiteness of women's liberation as something in need of historicization. My return to the emergent moments of women's liberation is also, then, an attempt to trace the contours of its thought as productive of an economy of emotion that marked the movement as white. While the rhetoric of the political movements of the era traveled across the borders of constituency and geography that made them distinct from each other, the circulation of affect and emotion it enacted changed dramatically depending on the political constituency addressed. The images and metaphors of anger in the Black Power movement, for example, conjured starkly different histories of social injustice and objects of resistance than those in the women's liberation movement, even if some of the words and phrases remained the same. To feel an emotion, as Alison M. Jaggar writes, "presupposes the existence of a social group" that feels things the same way. Conversely, an emotional appeal will only work if it makes you feel recognized as part of the group the appeal presumes in its address.[50] The emotional economy of women's liberation rhetoric presumed, in Lauren Berlant's terms, "a commonality of experience for people marked by femininity" based on the ideas and images of an "ordinary" or "normal" femininity—even if the appeal was made in order to reject those ideas and images.[51] The materials of women's liberation I read in this book —the best-selling and/or widely distributed essays first published in the alternative press or anthologized in mainstream publishing venues—offer an "archive of feelings" through which women's liberation became a name and a movement that some women, and not others, could identify with and invest in as a political and social possibility.[52] The whiteness of women's liberation, in other words, was not simply a social fact of women's liberation but was actively produced, in part, by the movement's rhetorical self-invention.

Here, then, I understand race, like gender, to be performative in the Butlerian sense: as a habit of iteration that reproduces a continuity of social and cultural effects but in ways that simultaneously opens up the possibility of deviation or contradiction. Butler's notion of performativity resonates with recent theorizations of race in social theory and performance studies and is useful for thinking about race as something people enact and reproduce in their everyday lives.[53] In addition, the reproduction of race— in this case the reproduction of women's liberation as a white women's feminism—also depends upon the capacity to recall previous ways of doing and thinking whiteness or, more specifically, white femininity, even if those recollections are, at the same time, always an active reinvention of the past that lead, potentially, to deviant or contradictory ways of doing white womanhood. Here, then, the dynamic historicity of Butler's notion of performativity as something that both recalls and invents the past gives me a way to think about how women's liberation became a movement of and for white women, rather than to simply assume it or state it as fact and leave it at that. It also enables me to think about how women's liberation may have reproduced white femininity in ways that both conformed to and deviated from the norm. What exactly did the performance of whiteness in women's liberation consist of? How was the whiteness of women's liberation continuous with that of mainstream American culture and society, and how was it not?

ECONOMIES OF EMOTION AND SHORTHAND NOTATIONS
But social thought is not abstract. Even when they correspond to and express
the present, the ideas of society are always embodied in persons or groups.
—Maurice Halbwachs, *On Collective Memory*

In order to track the economies of emotion from which the feminist-as-lesbian was fashioned as a figure of and for women's liberation, I employ a method of reading the archive that depends upon approaching particular terms and phrases as "access points" to the contingencies of the movement's moment of invention.[54] The emphasis of my analysis is on the creativity of the movement's rhetorical enactment as a distinct feminist movement—on the newness of its beginnings—rather than on an evaluation of the relative merits of its particular practice of feminism. In this sense my project echoes the work of other scholars interested in returning to the social movements of the 1970s in order to ask what was novel or inaugural about the politics of those movements.[55] But at the same time my project is not simply one of recuperation of a lost or misinterpreted feminist moment. Instead, I attempt to counter overly reductive or monolithic accounts of the movement by reading its textual archive as an effect of the movement's entanglement in its historical context, that is, as a product of the movement's involvement in mass cultural and subcultural public spheres and social worlds not of its own making. My reading of the widely circulated phrases and terms of the early years of the movement is also an attempt to track the way in which the newness, contingent and compromised, of the movement can only be apprehended in relation to what was already known at the time of its emergence as a distinct form of feminism.

Sara Ahmed's understanding of the social and cultural productivity of emotion will be helpful in my reading of the archive precisely because she provides a model for conceptualizing the rhetorical enactment of women's liberation as a political idea and constituency made manifest through circuits of feeling that are, in turn, the effects of past forms of social struggle and political contest. Drawing upon various schools of thought on the emotions, Ahmed argues that emotions reside neither in objects or bodies but "take the shape" of the contact between different bodies or between bodies and objects.[56] Operating through "affective economies" that are the result of previous histories of contact, emotions are produced through the association of signs, figures, and objects "in relationships of difference and displacement," which shape our social worlds.[57] For example, in the United States in the 2000s fear, hate, and sometimes both circulate through the association of "the terrorist" with "Muslim" and "Arab," which produces relations of difference between "American" and "Arab" or "Muslim" that, while full of present geopolitical tensions, are also infused with, and thereby given meaning by, the histories of European and American colonialism and anticommunism.

Although Ahmed's argument that emotions are social processes rather than innate biophysical phenomena makes both phenomenological and sociological claims, the material of her analysis is rhetoric, and in this sense, her work converges in interesting ways with Daniel Gross's work on seventeenth-century political rhetoric. Taking up the Aristotelian notion of rhetoric as "a theoretical art that contrives human affairs," Gross argues that passions and emotion were, prior to the emergent hegemony of modern science, understood as the "unnatural" product of human interaction and social organization.[58] In his readings of thinkers from Hobbes to Adam Smith to the political pamphlets of the English Civil War, Gross demonstrates that emotion is, in effect, "a function of social difference" that works precisely through an uneven distribution across the relationships between different social actors and locations.[59] The passions we associate with some social figures (for example, the shame of the poor man) in contradistinction to those we associate with others (the reasonableness of the professional) are neither evidence of human nature nor the social effect of some inner psychic failure or success on the part of one individual over another. Instead, for Gross as for Ahmed, emotions are the makers of social distinction and a function of publicity. Rhetoric, in other words, as the communication of sentiment not only organizes social distinctions but also actively makes us more invested in, and sympathetic to, some performances of social presence rather than others.

Ahmed's and Gross's concern with reestablishing the interdependency of politics and emotion through the constitutive presence of rhetoric in the making of social worlds frames my attempt to track the political appeal of women's liberation as a world-making force, which generated its own creatures of publicity and forms of social presence. What both Ahmed and Gross demonstrate, in convincing detail, is that emotions *do* a lot of social and political work, and they cannot be separated from the historical or social as something private or biological. Indeed, emotions shape the social and political worlds in which we live and are infused by a history that makes them work—have meaning—in the present.

To think about the production of women's liberation as an effect of the circulation of emotions at the time of the movement's arising is to also realize the difficulty feminists face in changing their own and others' perceptions—feelings—about a movement like women's liberation. As Baxandall and Gordon state in the introduction to their illuminating collection of women's liberation documents, *Dear Sisters: Dispatches from the Women's Liberation Movement*, there are long-standing "widespread misconceptions" about the women's liberation movement in both the historical record and popular memory.[60] Thinking about the social and cultural work emotions do helps us to realize why those misconceptions are not easily corrected by an increased documentation of the movement's achievements and writings, as Baxandall and Gordon hope, nor by education, as Ruth Rosen hopes in *The World Split Open*. Rather, those "misconceptions" will only disappear once the affective economies of fear, contempt, and shame (to name just three of the negative emotions associated with feminism and women's liberation more particularly), which so effectively produce and reproduce feminism in the social imaginary, have little or no claim on our feelings. A project for the long term surely, but one for which we need to confront the emotions that shaped the figures of women's liberation and our responses to them.

In addition to drawing upon theories of emotion and rhetoric in my reading of the women's liberation archive, I also look to public sphere theory and theories of collective memory as a way to think about the entangling of the U.S. national public sphere and the counterpublic sphere of feminism in the production of women's liberation as an event that could be named and thought into being in and around 1970. In particular I draw on Maurice Halbwachs's field-forming work on collective memory and his conception of social thought as, in effect, a memory that in "its entire content consists only of collective recollections or remembrances" of people and groups.[61] As collective memory, social thought contains "social frameworks" and notions of people and groups through which we understand ourselves and our relation to the world. These frameworks "confine and bind our most intimate remembrances": we cannot think of ourselves and others without them.[62] One of Halbwachs's primary examples of a social framework was the notional practice of family life. As a social framework that provides ideas of persons and their relations, "the family" works to meld the particular with the general. While each individual family remembers through the particular events that mark and orientate its history, those events are also, simultaneously, general—weddings, birthdays, funerals—or experienced through general genres of emotional response (the scripts of normative feeling or sentiment that people are disposed to follow when something extraordinary or unexpected happens, as in a child's death or infidelity). This melding of the general with the particular leads to the figures of the family, like the mother, expressing "an entire character," just as each event "recapitulates an entire period in the life of the group."[63] For Halbwachs, this representativeness embedded in the work of the family as social framework leads to specific scenarios and figures becoming shorthand notations for complex social lives and histories.

Although, as Andreas Huyssen and others have argued, Halbwachs's paradigm for conceptualizing social and group memories is less able to explain the fragmentation and multiplication of collective memories in today's mass-mediated age, Halbwachs's assertion that societies remember through people and scenarios that are, in turn, "contained" by generalized notions and images nevertheless remains a useful way of understanding why collective memories and historical accounts of political events and social movements revolve around recurring names, phrases, and figures, which act as shorthand notations for complex political contestations and struggles.[64] For this reason, Halbwachs's understanding of the reproduction of social thought through generalized notions resonates with Lauren Berlant's recent work on the "intimate public" of women's culture. Rather than social life and memory, Berlant looks to mass culture as a form of public life that invites us to invest a sense of belonging to a commonality of experience in commodified "genres of intimacy."[65] Despite the obvious differences of object and theoretical paradigms, both Halbwachs and Berlant are interested in the ways in which people become invested in conventionality and its byproduct: the reproduction of the normal as social continuity.

For Berlant, as for Halbwachs, stereotypes (and in Berlant's case mass cultural genres) become forms through which people feel and imagine themselves part of the everyday world of the present. Rather than offering fantasies of the exceptional, the mass-mediated, intimate public spheres Berlant examines offer people the fantasy of being ordinary, which is to say, they offer people, and in Berlant's case of "women's culture" all those who identify with and invest a sense of self in the category "women," the fantasy of being part of a generalizable—white and middle-class—notion of what it means to be a woman. Unlike Halbwachs's overly monolithic understanding of collective memory, Berlant makes clear the distinction between protopolitical forms of publicity and those that traffic in commodified forms of affective belonging, and for this reason her work adds to Halbwachs's insights about the inheritance of the past in the present: she demonstrates that social thought is made in multiple domains of communal and public life and that, in the twentieth and twenty-first centuries, the relationship between the political and the mass cultural is both overly enmeshed and complicated by the mediating capacity of consumer capitalism. How women's liberation became a style of protest with its own forms of feminist subjectivity and collectivity, in other words, was not made in an exclusive domain of politics nor in the mass-mediated public sphere but through their entanglement with each other.

Women's liberation, in becoming a political movement, drew upon and saw its objects in the intimate public spheres of mass-mediated women's culture, as well as in the everyday experiences of women's supposedly ordinary "private" lives. It was precisely "the affective and emotional attachments located in fantasies of the common, the everyday, and a sense of ordinariness" that were the source of feminist collectivity and belonging in women's liberation and also the grounds of its political struggle.[66] One of the hypotheses of Feeling Women's Liberation is that the cultural struggle over the meaning of second-wave feminisms, and of who second-wave feminists were, was fought over and through the perceived ordinariness of the lives and bodies of middle-class white women, and this struggle has had effects not only on how the women's liberation movement constituted itself as a movement but also on how the movement is remembered and felt today. That the women's liberationist was most often seen and imagined as a white, middle-class woman has repercussions for how she operates as a shorthand notion or what I would call, in this mass-mediated age, an image memory of women's liberation.[67] The figure of the women's liberationist or her sister figure, the feminist-as-lesbian, is recognizable through the knowledge of what she is not and through the already established cultural preconceptions of what she "looks" like. And as an image memory of women's liberation, she continues the legacy of thinking —remembering—feminism as a white woman's cause. She is one example among many of how the history of racism (as well as of class and sexuality) is thought and felt through generalizable bodies and characters rather than through the abstractions of historical exegesis and argument. Indeed, part of the insidious and enduring power of racism—in both feminism and society in general— can be located in the way in which social memory binds us to a past thought and is felt through the enduring shorthand notations, or image memories, of particular types of bodies and collectivities.

The emergence of the feminist-as-lesbian figure as a shorthand notation for women's liberation eclipsed the heterogeneity and subversive force of the movement in its emergent moment. It has also tended to condemn second-wave feminists, who constructed a feminist cultural imaginary through the articulation of a transformed and transformative meaning of lesbianism, to the twilight world of a "wrong" or "embarrassing" feminism. In taking up Drucilla Cornell's call for an "ethical investigation" of the "historical meaning given to the category feminism,"[68] I hope not to reveal "what really happened" during the rise of the women's liberation movement, nor claim the rightfulness of those who took up "women's liberation" or, indeed, lesbian feminism as a political identity, but to open up the complexity of the movement's emergence as an event of second-wave feminism and to lay bare some of the processes of elision, reduction, and displacement through which we have come to know of that event and those feminists.

FROM LADY PROTESTORS
TO URBAN GUERRILLAS

*Media Representations of the
Women's Liberation Movement in 1970*

On December 14, 1970, *Time* magazine published an editorial titled "Women's Lib: A Second Look" under the heading of the magazine's Behavior section.[1] The editorial focused on what had been one of the mainstream news stories of the year: the women's liberation movement. Drawing upon a posse of "experts" comprising journalists and one anthropologist, the second look was aimed at Kate Millett, author of the movement's best seller from that year, *Sexual Politics*, in which Millett had made the argument that "coitus" was the "charged microcosm" through which the "patriarchal" social system maintained its power.[2] At a November discussion on gay liberation and sexuality at Columbia University, Millett had, at the insistent behest of an audience member, disclosed her bisexuality and called herself a lesbian.[3] It was this declaration, by the "high priestess" of the movement no less, that *Time* saw as an opportune occasion for taking a second look at the movement. Millett's "disclosure," *Time* asserted, was "bound to discredit her as a spokeswoman for her cause, cast further doubt on her theories, and reinforce the views of those skeptics who routinely dismiss all liberationists as lesbians."[4]

Time begins its second look at women's liberation by quoting from Irving Howe's review of *Sexual Politics* for *Harper's* magazine.[5] Titled "The Middle-Class Mind of Kate Millett," Howe's review was less a considered analysis of the book's argument and more an attack on Millett's bourgeois failings as a scholar and writer. *Sexual Politics*, Howe claimed, displayed "a farrago of blunders, distortions, vulgarities and plain nonsense" that revealed Millett to be "guilty of 'historical reductionism,' 'crude simplification,' 'middle-class parochialism,' 'sexual monism,' 'methodological sloppiness,' 'arrogant ultimatism' and 'comic ignorance.'" Howe's dismissal of *Sexual Politics* reeks of a class-inflected misogyny. Yet, ironically and revealingly, it is precisely for not writing like a woman that Howe ultimately finds fault with Millett. Her writing, he informs the reader, reads like that of a "female impersonator," and the sloppiness and ignorance of the book can be put down to her "blindness" to the charms and specificity of womanhood.[6] In Howe's paradoxical accusation that Millett's "feminine" failures as a writer (middle-class parochialism, sexual monism, methodological sloppiness) are due to her *pretending* to be a woman, the terms of *Time's* review of women's liberation are revealed. Rather than an analysis of the political arguments and goals of the movement, the second look would be concerned with redrawing the boundaries between a proper femininity and its many upsetting alternatives—a potentially treacherous exercise, as Howe's paradoxical accusations suggest, in its demand that there be a coherent and legible femininity available for public display.

Evoking Cold War paranoia about the "enemy within"—the second look after all, is a look that distrusts what it sees—the article deploys Howe's accusation that Millett was not a woman but pretending to be one, as evidence of the now clearly suspect sexuality of the movement as a whole. Echoing McCarthy's congressional witch hunts of the early 1950s, the magazine asks the "provocative questions" put by other critics of the movement: "Can the feminists think clearly? Do they know anything about biology? What about their maturity, their morality, their sexuality?"[7] What began as an attack on one woman and her book becomes a broadside directed at the entire movement. Millett's faults are the movement's faults, and the real fault of Millett is her sexuality, a fault that suggests not only the presence in the women's liberation movement of foggy thinking, immaturity, and immorality but also the lack of "real" women.

The rest of the second look, through the comments of various "experts," is an elaboration of this accusation. Lionel Tiger, a Rutgers anthropologist and popular media talking head on the women's movement in 1970, finds fault with women liberationists because they refuse to accept the fact of biological difference between men and women. Midge Decter and Janet Malcolm, both highbrow journalists and respected social commentators, echo Tiger's analysis by arguing that liberationists are women who refuse to grow up and take responsibility for their future lives as wives and mothers. Drawing on the scientism and crude Freudianism of midcentury American popular psychology, the comments of Decter and Malcolm evoke postwar notions of the lesbian as suffering from emotional immaturity and a propensity to immorality wrought by an arrested development. Stuck at the stage of Oedipal outrage at the father, women's liberationists, as Helen Lawrenson, another "expert" quoted in the article argues, are consumed by a "splenetic frenzy of hatred" for men.[8] The women who make up the ranks of the women's liberation movement are, according to Lawrenson, who gets to have the last word, "sick and silly creatures."[9]

What is most striking about *Time*'s second look at the women's liberation movement is the unabashed viciousness of its tone.[10] The display of vitriol, even after nearly forty years, is shocking. The repetitiveness and excessiveness of the accusations—women's liberationists don't just express a hatred of men but a "splenetic" hatred; they're not just "silly" but "sick and silly"—work as a kind of incantation of condemnation. The article doesn't want to persuade through argument or analysis, it wants to move its readers and impress on them an image of women's liberation that will disgust or horrify and make them turn away from the movement as a significant political event. The attack is focused on the women of women's liberation—their psyches, emotions, and sexuality. From Howe's condemnation of Millett as a female impersonator to Decter's, Malcolm's, and Lawrenson's portrait of women's liberationists as sexually and emotionally immature, the accusations of the article constantly return to, and evoke, the figure of the lesbian. Explicitly named at the beginning of the article in relation to Millett and her "disclosure," the lesbian becomes the figure through which the emotive force of the attack on women's liberation is generated.

That *Time* structured its second look at women's liberation as an exposé of the movement's inherent, hidden, lesbianism is also striking. Although the article suggests that critics of the movement "routinely" dismissed all liberationists as lesbians, it presents Millett's disclosure as revelation, as a shocking discovery that also simultaneously reveals a different, less known, and more troubling women's liberation movement. There is no attempt at the subtle allusion to or insinuation of lesbianism that had, historically, structured most mainstream commentary on feminism in the twentieth century. The silences surrounding the relation of lesbianism to feminism, which, as Eve Sedgwick has artfully argued, are not so much evidence of a lack of knowledge but an effect of the deployment of ignorance in the discourse on sexuality, are no longer able, it seems, to contain and fix the meanings of either feminism or lesbianism.[11] Indeed, rather than the insinuation of a strategically deployed silence, the article explodes with comments and statements that work repeatedly to create a relation between lesbianism and women's liberation. Encoded as an exposé, *Time*'s disclosure of Millett's bisexuality performs a different kind of discursive containment: it restates lesbianism as out of bounds, as something anterior to "normal" sexuality and, therefore, as something anterior to "normal" women. As a consequence, women's liberationists are marked as anterior to normal women, with the lesbian the boundary figure through which that separation is made. Exposure or "outing" as cultural encoding also works to efface the social and historical context of the disclosure; the past, and the social world in which the women's liberation movement operates, is thrown into shadow by the bright light of revelation. The effect is to reduce the complex historicity of the women's liberation movement—and of lesbianism, feminism, political struggle, and the workings of power—to particular types of people who are at once transformed into mythical rather than historical figures.

The article's concern with producing a portrait of the typical women's liberationist—with making her a visible and legible figure—is further evidenced by the drawing placed at the center of the page on which the article appears (fig. 1.1). The drawing stands as the embodiment of the article's critique of women's liberation and works as a visual prompt for the kinds of emotions the second look is designed to evoke. Standing with one arm held high in front of her, a burning bra hanging from her hand, the drawing depicts a strong-thighed, loose-bosomed Amazon in a summer dress. With her other hand on a hip that juts to the side in a pose of insouciant disdain, the figure stares defiantly beyond the gaze of the reader. Her face is stern

FIG. 1.1. *The Women's Liberationist, Time,*
"Women's Lib: A Second Look," December 14, 1970, 50.

and humorless; her unsmiling, unseeing stare standing in stark contrast to the women in the advertizing images of the magazine that invite the reader to project or invest desires and dreams in their appearance. Instead, the staring eyes, screened by glasses, reflect back to the reader a blankness—an unreadability that denies any possibility of communication other than confrontation. The effect of the figure's posture and look is to keep the reader at a distance—the jutting hip pushing the reader away—and to provoke resistance. She demands the reader's disidentification. She doesn't want to appeal to us or to persuade us; she wants to confront us with her difference. Signaling this difference is the WITCH badge nestling between her breasts and the burning bra held high in her right hand. The burning bra animates the entire image, infusing it with an affective power that radiates beyond the encoding work of the article.

The burning bra had emerged as a magical sign of women's liberation during the Miss America protest in Atlantic City in September 1968. Although the protest involved the Freedom Trash Can, into which women were encouraged to throw "instruments of torture to women," like bras and girdles, no bra was actually burned. Alice Echols notes, however, that a protest organizer, in order to generate media interest in the event, had "leaked" a story to the press suggesting that bras were burned as part of the protest.[12] Through a conjunction of media and movement interests, the burning bra became an object that circulated between the media and the movement, generating associations that suggested the meaning of women's liberation in different ways to different publics. As a signifier of women's liberation in the drawing, the burning bra evokes both the threat of the movement—that it was "playing with fire" by stoking the flames of women's anger—and also the idea that the movement was engaged in an irreverent, disrespectful dismissal of normative femininity. The flames suggest the passion of that dismissal but also a fury toward femininity and its paraphernalia of constraint and artifice. Taken within the context of the article's attack on women's liberation, the reader is invited to interpret this passion and fury as evidence of emotional and sexual immaturity and, therefore, as evidence of the lesbian tendencies of women's liberation. Yet that passion and fury, along with the irreverent unconcern for a respectable femininity the public display of a (burning) bra suggests, might also inspire different feelings. Rather than disgust and fear, readers might feel wonder and excitement when looking at the figure of a woman so unconcerned with male approval and social norms.

This potential ambivalence in the cultural legibility of the drawing, despite the encoding work of the article as a whole, is further suggested by the figure's uneasy mixture of feminine and masculine physical qualities. Her long hair and glasses along with her rounded but not soft figure invoke the pictures of Millett that had appeared in the press the previous summer, while her hippie dress, woolen bag, and Roman sandals suggest her resemblance to the many white, middle-class women who populated the ranks of the New Left in the 1960s.[13] Yet the masculine set of her grim-lined jaw, solid frame, and well-muscled physique also suggest, in their incongruity with the overtly feminine summer dress, an unease with femininity and a desire to expand beyond its shapeliness. The conflation of the hard and muscular with the soft and shapely make the figure neither feminine nor masculine but an incoherent, strange mixture of the two. In this drawing cultural memories of the lesbian as mannish, as butch, as immature, as sick, and as possibly contagious are conjured *in relation* to the image of the white, female political protestor of the 1960s. What emerges from this association, and the cultural memories that infuse it with affect, is a new and therefore potentially troubling cultural figure: not the lesbian or the feminist but the feminist-as-lesbian.

In this chapter I examine the press coverage of the women's liberation movement in 1970—the year the movement exploded into the national public sphere—by mainstream publications like *Time*. The force of that magazine's attack in its second look at the movement—its vitriolic and unabashed attempt to reject and dismiss the movement—suggests that women's liberation had become an upsetting and discomforting phenomena by the winter of 1970. Other publications were also explicitly critical of the movement by the end of 1970, and like *Time*, their criticisms were also often made through accusations of lesbianism. I am interested in exploring mainstream press coverage of the movement in order to excavate the representational forms through which that upset and discomfort took shape and was given meaning. I am much less interested in adjudicating the relative merits and accuracies of the coverage. Instead, I look to the media as a primary domain for the production of collective memory in postwar U.S. culture, and the emphasis of my analysis will be on how the mainstream press produced and circulated images and narrative frameworks through which women's liberation became known—thought and felt—in the national public sphere in 1970. I focus on those moments of uncertainty and ambivalence in the press coverage, when the narrative frameworks and cultural images become, as in *Time*'s "Women's Lib: A Second Look," strange and incoherent. It is in these moments of representational disquiet, I argue, that we can begin to excavate how the women's liberation movement disturbed the cultural imaginings of the postwar American national public sphere.

In my analysis of the media coverage of the movement I concentrate on the portraits of feminists that increasingly appeared in the press in 1970. This strategy of personification became the dominant framework for representing the movement by the end of 1970, and, although this representational strategy was not new to the press coverage of women's liberation or, indeed, of feminism—women's social presence in general, as John Berger so succinctly puts it, is dependent on her "appearance" rather than on her actions[14]—I explore the ways in which this strategy produced what Sara Ahmed calls an "affective economy" in which particular objects (the burning bra) and figures circulated in the press coverage and worked to shape certain emotional responses to the movement.[15] In Ahmed's terms, emotions do not "reside positively" in bodies, signs, or objects but "work as a form of capital." They shape our relations with others precisely because they are an accumulative effect of the circulation of different objects, figures, and signs through which we inhabit and apprehend our social worlds. These circuits or economies of feeling are, in turn, the product of past associations and relations of "difference and displacement,"[16] such that the figure of the lesbian evokes feelings and impressions that are an effect of older associations, like those between prostitution and lesbianism in the early years of the twentieth century and those between the raced and classed female bodies of nineteenth-century eugenics and social purity movements. It is through such affective economies that past political and cultural struggles for social power infuse and shape the struggles of the present and give them meaning. Tracing the affective economy through which particular impressions and images of women's liberation were conjured in 1970 leads us to confront the historicity of that movement's political challenge and the continuities and discontinuities of collective cultural memory through which the movement was thought and known in the public sphere.

In this chapter, then, I want to think about how the press coverage of women's liberation, and the portraits of women liberationists in particular, act as affective repositories and disseminators of collective memories of past events and movements that then produce the women's liberation movement as a nameable phenomenon in 1970. How do these portraits and the collective cultural memories they evoke lead us to particular, often conflicting, cultural fantasies of who feminists are, who lesbians are, and who women are? What do these portraits reveal about how a national femininity is inscribed on particular raced and classed bodies? And what do these fantasies tell us about the challenges posed by the women's liberation movement to the imagined community of the American public sphere? In its rejection of Cold War notions of the privatized, middle-class home as the space of good citizenship, women's liberation made the ideological parameters of normative femininity a primary site of cultural struggle in the late 1960s and early 1970s. The mainstream media participated in and became a venue for that cultural struggle by deploying a discourse of respectability—a discourse redolent with the histories of race and class exclusions from the imagined community of American citizenship—in which the images of women's liberation were fashioned in intimate relation to a national femininity defined as white and middle class.

THE MASS MEDIA AS NATIONAL PUBLIC SPHERE

In the late twentieth and early twenty-first century, as Andreas Huyssen has argued, our sense of social belonging and historical continuity is as dependent, if not more so, on the "imagined memories" of the media as it is on the "relatively stable" collective memories enacted through locally situated social groups and people.[17] The increasing dependence on mass-mediated cultural memories has had a profound impact on the way in which people experience their social worlds. The stability of local and familial affiliations can be superseded by our attachments to, and investments in, less manifest and more virtual domains of belonging. We are now much more likely to think of ourselves as part of a public full of people we have never met than part of a hereditary line or kinship network. This more virtual quality of social existence places a different kind of "burden" on us, as Michael Warner has argued. Instead of social status being determinative of our place in the world irrespective of our desires and fantasies, the virtual worlds of a mass-mediated public sphere "makes us believe our consciousness to be decisive" and that the "direction of our glance can constitute our social world." As Warner carefully makes clear, the qualitative shift in how people in late modernity experience their sociality lies as much in their beliefs—what they think and feel—as it does with any significant structural transformation of the social domain. Yet this shift in thought and belief has a profound effect on the function of the public sphere. In their multiplicity and inventedness (as opposed to emerging from socially and geographically located groups and events), the imagined memories of the public sphere function less to reproduce the stable diachronic continuity of the social world as to maintain a synchronic discursive space for conjuring publics. These publics and their constant conjuring depend on what Warner calls an "appellative energy," and our sense of belonging in these mediascapes comes not through kinship or local affiliation but through our attentiveness and responsiveness to the appeal of particular publics.[18]

In the case of the dominant public sphere of the mainstream U.S. media, that work of interpellation also involves the constitution and maintenance of a hegemonic "America"—an imagined homogeneity of nationness through which its citizens think of themselves as belonging to the same collective "we." The public imagined through the mainstream media, then, is also one that is dependent on an active forgetting, or "whiting-out," of the inequalities and marginalizations of social difference.[19] Contests or struggles for power are, if they happened in the past, reimagined through what Benedict Anderson calls the "narrative of nation with its strange antigenealogical teleology."[20] In this narrative, the past is always read as a necessary outcome of the present such that, for example, slavery is rewritten as the inevitable origin for the progress story of American multiculturalism. If the contests for power are happening in the present, a collective forgetting is enacted through a cultural struggle over forms of representation through which those contests become historical events. In the national public sphere of the late twentieth century, history doesn't simply happen elsewhere and then get recorded by the media; it is enacted through, and in relation to, the media.

The world-making possibilities of the public sphere played a constitutive role in how the new social movements of the 1960s and 1970s understood what politics was and how it was done. As Todd Gitlin argues, political movements in the late twentieth century "feel called upon to rely on large-scale communications in order to matter, to say who they are and what they intend to publics they want to sway." Movements become "newsworthy only by submitting to the implicit rules of newsmaking, by conforming to journalistic notions (themselves embedded in history) of what a 'story' is, what an 'event' is, what a 'protest' is. The processed image then tends to become 'the movement' for wider publics and institutions."[21] As with the New Left, the women's movement was reliant on the power of the mass media to make the movement visible to people who had yet to identify themselves with the goals and views of the movement, and also like the New Left, it soon found itself depicted in the media's representational frames. The image of women's liberation that appealed to the not-yet-liberationists was largely promulgated by the print and television media.

Gitlin's analysis of the media's participatory role in the making of the New Left draws on a Habermasian understanding of the twentieth-century public sphere as a domain usurped by a consumer capitalist mass media and dominated by the spectacle. Publicity, rather than debate, determines political action and contest in the twentieth century.[22] Unlike Habermas, Gitlin does not view this transformation as necessarily undemocratic. Like many scholars who were also active in the social movements of the 1960s, Gitlin is appreciative of the powerful protodemocratic possibilities of being able to fashion a political identity and movement through the publicity-generating machine of the mass media. However, like Habermas, Gitlin also argues that the mass media plays a crucial role in the production and maintenance of social and political hegemonies. Run by companies and conglomerates that serve the interests of powerful elites, the mass media circulates information and cultural narratives that secure the economic and political interests of the powerful. For Gitlin, as for Habermas, the late twentieth-century public sphere does not so much provide a discursive space for the interaction and serious discussion of citizens as provide a domain for the circulation of represented "realities." In this view, the mass media, with the news media as a primary mode for the dissemination of information and the production of authoritative or legitimate knowledge, serves as "technologies for managing consensus" rather than as "organs of public information."[23] These technologies, according to Gitlin, are evident in the journalistic notions of the mainstream press. Journalistic traditions and paradigms participate in the production of hegemony in that they force the eventfulness of a particular uprising or movement into already constituted "frames" of understanding that determine what a political event or story is. In Gitlin's analysis, the failures of the New Left—its inability to effect a significant transformation of the national political public sphere—can at least in part be attributed to the ability of the media to contain its revolutionary intentions through the deployment of reductive and distorting representational frames.

Gitlin's reading of the media's containment and distortion of the New

Left's political agenda and practices is an important and necessary one, but as a number of feminist media scholars have argued, his analysis of the relation between the mass media and social movements of the 1960s does not go far enough. The transformation of the national public sphere into a mass-mediated, market-driven domain of publicity leads to a more profound change in the constitution of political constituencies and social movements than Gitlin's argument allows for.[24] Implicit in Gitlin's understanding of the relation of the mass media to the emergence of the New Left is the assumption of an initial separation between the two. For Gitlin, the media imposed a view of the New Left onto the movement and the public and, as a result, distorted its political aims and objectives. Yet the new social movements—whether the New Left or women's liberation—weren't so much forced into conforming to journalistic notions (and demonstrations like the Miss America protest in 1968 certainly reveal a knowingness on the part of the women's movement about what would make a good news-making spectacle) as they were themselves made possible through the dynamics of a late twentieth-century public sphere.

The political community of the New Left, as envisioned by the Port Huron Statement issued by the Students for a Democratic Society (SDS) in 1962, for example, was not defined in terms of local affiliations or an assumed class identification. The "we" evoked by the statement consisted of a "generation" of white, middle-class college students who felt themselves connected to millions of "abstract others" and "Negroes" by the common threat of nuclear annihilation and the witnessing, through TV initially, of the racist oppression of southern and urban black Americans.[25] It was a we "imagined," in Benedict Anderson's terms, as a community that went beyond the local and the particular and relied for its conception on the information technologies of late capitalism, those "representational modes that promise to depict otherwise unseeable totalities to ordinary citizens."[26] The New Left defined in the Port Huron Statement, while spoken of from one particular perspective, was based on the perception that people who were strangers to each other—white college students, black Americans in the rural south and northern cities, and "abstract others" beyond national borders—had common concerns and common goals.[27] Through their televisions, movie screens, and daily newspapers, the authors of the statement could envision the "unseeable totalities" of nuclear annihilation, national or institutional racism, and colonial wars and imagine themselves in relation to millions of strangers and abstract others as a consequence.

The community of the New Left (and of "the movement" in general) was also imagined by the Port Huron Statement to consist of individuals, rather than classes or groups.[28] As Marianne DeKoven writes in her analysis of the statement, "the 'we' of the New Left and the counterculture was always an aggregate of consenting, actively participating individuals."[29] The emphasis of the statement's introductory section, "Agenda for a Generation," was on these individuals and their coming to political consciousness. Imagined first and foremost in the likeness of the statement's authors, the individuals of the New Left were white, middle-class students whose comfortable lives had been "penetrated by events too troubling to dismiss." These events—the black freedom movement, imperialist political violence, and nuclear threat of the Cold War—were "too immediate and crushing in their impact, too challenging in the demand that we as individuals take the responsibility for encounter and resolution."[30] Here, the political identity of the proto–New Left activist is articulated not in terms of their social or class status, nor is it based on their membership in a particular political party, but rather it is based on their being called upon by events—seen primarily if not entirely through the media—that were too "crushing" to ignore. The political appeal and sense of belonging expressed in the statement came from an attentiveness and responsiveness to the "appellative energy" of the public sphere—precisely the same sphere that, in Gitlin's analysis, was constraining and distorting the emancipatory politics of the movement.

By the end of the 1960s the political communities of the new social movements were also being imagined and enacted through the mobilization of particular styles of self-fashioning. The Black Power, women's liberation, and gay liberation movements of the late 1960s articulated their politics in relation to subcultural fashions and ways of living that publicized their presence and enacted "stranger relationality" with others who did not yet think of themselves as feminists, gay, or black revolutionaries.[31] The crafting of a particular style or public identity as a form of political appeal depended on, and was enacted through, the ability of the mass media to circulate images and narrative frameworks. The prototypical feminist that Betty Friedan called on in the early 1960s was the lonely housewife trapped in a suburb in the Midwest—a woman Friedan herself had long ceased to be and who had no obvious connection to her activism in the labor movement. Later in the 1960s, the Black Power movement, especially the Black Panther Party, fashioned a particular aesthetic style based on an urban, cool look that, through its circulation in the public spheres of the African American and mainstream press, became a way for other African Americans to recognize themselves as "black" and to express their identification with the movement's black nationalist and Pan-Africanist politics. By 1970 gay liberation addressed its imagined community through an appeal to "come out," an address that depended on a sense that gay people "are everywhere" and could be communicated with where ever they were—in New York and San Francisco but also in Spartanburg, South Carolina, and Peoria, Illinois (perhaps even next door to Friedan's prototypical feminist). Like the Black Power and women's movements, gay liberation did not simply "rely on large-scale communications in order to matter, to say who they are," as Gitlin argues. Rather, the media made it possible to imagine gay liberation and to enact a political movement through those imaginings.

The production and representation of women's liberation did not emerge, therefore, out of a dichotomous clash between movement intentions and media practices, although there was a divergence, inevitably, between the two. Rather, it was the result of a crisis of imagination in which the dictates of a public sphere, dependent upon the spectacle as its primary form of publicity, created the need for a feminism that could be looked at and identified with. *Time*'s depiction of the typical women's liberationist in their second look at women's liberation was not simply the product of a regime of repression but was the result of a convergence of the unknown that depended, paradoxically, on a reworking of already known and familiar representations of women and feminists in order for that unknowability to be present. Who women liberationists were, what they wanted, and how they imagined women at the time and in the future were questions the women's liberation movement was struggling to answer—through the imagined community of a public sphere that demanded an imagistic representativeness—just as much as the mass media.

The crisis of imagination that marked the emergence of women's liberation as a national phenomenon in 1970 had less to do with the movement's stated political goals and more to do with the wider social and political context in which it operated. The last years of the 1960s had increased the sense of an impending "race war" and a social breakdown in American society. After the assassination of Martin Luther King Jr. in 1968 there was widespread racial unrest in cities across the United States as African Americans expressed their anger and frustration at the violence, both state organized and private, directed at their communities and political leaders. The FBI's murderous crackdown on the Black Panthers in 1968 and 1969, the escalation of the Vietnam War with the invasion of Cambodia in 1970, and the disintegration of the New Left and emergence of violent splinter groups like the Weathermen by the end of the 1960s exacerbated widespread feelings of despair and paranoia in American society. The trial and imprisonment of Huey P. Newton, the cofounder of the Oakland-based Black Panther Party in 1968, and police assassinations of the Chicago-based Black Panthers Fred Hampton and Mark Clark in late 1969 were national news events that generated a groundswell of public support for the besieged Panthers. By the late 1960s the Black Panthers had become the most visible incarnation of a decade long fermenting of a Black Power movement intent on confronting the institutional and systematic racism of American society. In contrast to the integrationist politics of the civil rights movement, the Black Power movement explicitly connected the struggle of African Americans to wars of liberation in the Third World. Whether argued for in terms of a Pan-Africanism or class struggle, the Black Power movement demanded a revolution in race relations and often invoked the specter of that revolution through guerrilla warfare.[32]

In conjunction with the rise of the Black Power movement, Angela Davis, along with Stokely Carmichael and Huey P. Newton, had become a national symbol of black militancy by 1970. Forced from her job in the philosophy department at UCLA for being a member of the American Communist Party and falsely accused of participating in a violent attempt to free Black Panther prisoners from a courthouse in California, Davis was, by 1970, in the news, on the FBI's Ten Most Wanted list, and on the run. Shadowing the newsworthiness of the emergent women's liberation movement in 1970, then, and providing the counterpoint to images of the movement in the American mass media, was the specter of an increasingly radicalized and brutalized Black Power movement that was both the focus and scapegoat for national fears of social breakdown and chaos. The representational forms through which the meaning of women's liberation was constructed in the mass media in 1970 would be forged in relation to the national presence of Black Power and its confrontations with the bourgeois order of white America.[33]

In 1970 there was no consensus about what women's liberation was, both within and outside of the movement. As Susan Brownmiller notes in her memoir, *In Our Time*, 1970 was the "watershed year," the moment when women's liberation was defined through internal conflict and its simultaneous emergence onto the national scene.[34] The year 1970 was also when the Equal Rights Amendment (ERA) was debated in both houses of Congress, something not seen in the fifty years the ERA had been a political goal of feminists and largely the result of effective feminist lobbying of Congress.[35] While the ERA fight became one of the news stories of the year, the flurry of publications emanating from a broadly feminist perspective in 1970 also suggested the newsworthiness of the movement.[36] But like the fight over the ERA, these publications also revealed a lack of consensus not only over the idea of equality but also over the idea of liberation. Books like Kate Millett's *Sexual Politics*, Robin Morgan's *Sisterhood Is Powerful*, and Toni Cade's *The Black Woman*, for example, had very different and even opposing stories to tell about the need for feminism and its goals. Similarly, during the ERA fight, feminists lined up on all sides of the debate, some arguing for an equality of sameness between men and women, some arguing for an equality through the acceptance of difference (this was the argument of many union women who argued that labor laws needed to take into account the "double shift" domestic burdens of women), and some arguing against the concept of equality itself as inherently biased toward a (male) standard.

So, while women's liberation became increasingly newsworthy in 1970, it also became increasingly apparent that the movement was not homogeneous or unified in its political positions. For the news media, this lack of homogeneity—the explosive proliferation of the movement into myriad groups and interests—presented a problem of representation. That *Time*'s "Women's Lib: A Second Look" in December was markedly different in tone and content from the *Time* article on Kate Millett in August of the same year suggests that the media was struggling to find a story in 1970 through which to fix the movement as a representable reality.[37] It is precisely because of this lack of consensus, and the struggle within the mainstream media to find *the* story or *the* image of women's liberation, that 1970 becomes a significant moment for understanding how and why collective memories of women's liberation look and feel the way they do. As the year the movement emerged into the national public sphere, the moment it entered history—its events taken note of and recorded by the "official" historians and documenters of American social and political life—1970 was

also the moment when public knowledge and memories of women's liberation were formed through distortion and elision. By following the media's
coverage of the movement throughout 1970, the process of hegemony in
the making can be tracked. As 1970 progressed, the media covered a range
of stories and events and struggled to come to a representable consensus
on what and who the women's liberation movement was. In other words,
1970 was a "moment of indeterminacy," when the media could be seen at
work, not simply managing consensus but constructing it.

The focus of my analysis of the media in 1970 is the *New York Times*'s
coverage of the movement, although I supplement this with analyses of
other media sources like national news magazines and group-specific publications like *Ebony*, directed at middle-class African Americans, and *Playboy*, directed at middle-class white men (for the most part).[38] I concentrate
on the *New York Times* for three reasons. First, the *New York Times* is the
only truly national paper in the United States, having the largest circulation by far of all the daily broadsheets. Second, and in relation, the *New
York Times* in 1970 served as a resource for most other news services (including network television news), which tended to set their news agendas
on what the *New York Times* found most newsworthy.[39] Related to the *New
York Times*'s national reach and stature, then, was its ability to influence
other news services and to define, as a result, what was and wasn't deemed
worthy of coverage. The paper was also a resource, through the reporting
of leaks and its access to the political establishment, for government communications about policy and for setting its political agenda, and as a
result, the *New York Times* played a significant role in the shaping of the
American public sphere in 1970.[40]

As a leading national newspaper and player in the production of the
national public sphere, the *New York Times* was, in 1970, a primary organ
for "managing consensus" and for the representation of an imagined national community. With power and influence in the domain of politics as
well as the mass media, the paper functioned as a purveyor and barometer
of cultural and social hegemony in the United States. Focusing on the *New
York Times*, therefore, allows me to analyze how mainstream representations of sociocultural events are made and become the standard by which
we remember a national past. In relation to the women's movement in
particular, by taking up this particular slice of the media coverage, I can
analyze the ways in which the movement entered into a collective historical
consciousness and the moment when the cultural authorities recognized

the movement as an event worthy of record. Indeed, it is at least in part through the representative work done by media institutions like the *New York Times* that we come to know today who and what women's liberation was then.

Although there was no one perspective offered by the *New York Times* in its coverage of the movement—the editorial page shifted its viewpoint quite markedly over the course of the year, and the articles offered in the News section of the paper were different in tone and content from those offered in the Magazine and Features sections—the deployment of a discourse of respectability is evident throughout. For example, Eileen Shanahan, in her reporting of the ERA fight in Congress draws upon the idea of political actors as reasonable citizens, a notion remembered collectively through the bodies of those citizens most at home in the traditional institutions of American political life—white, middle-class men—and depicts the women arguing both for and against the amendment as rational political actors engaged in serious political debate. In contrast, the features articles and stories on movement protests, where political action takes place on the street and outside of the traditional domains of power, draws upon a discourse of respectability for precisely opposite ends. In these articles the women activists are, for the most part, depicted as irrational fanatics and "exhibitionists." The Jekyll and Hyde portrait of women political activists offered by the paper is evidence of what was at stake in media representations of women's liberation and what constrained the activists as they attempted to fashion themselves as political actors in the public sphere. From "lady protestors" hovering in the traditional corridors of American power to "street fighting urban guerrillas" out to destroy men and families alike, movement activists were drawn in terms of a contrast between middle-class respectability and its socially marginalized others. It was a contrast that conjured the specters of American social abjection—the morally suspect and degenerate figures that have historically marked the boundaries between whiteness and blackness, civilization and unruliness—and who infuse the twentieth-century American public discourses on gender and sexuality. The struggle to represent women's liberation in the United States was, and is, a struggle over the making and unmaking of the internal frontiers of American social exclusion and marginalization.

As 1970 drew to a close and the ERA fight dropped out of the news, the *New York Times*'s coverage of the movement becomes almost exclusively concerned with portraying the "liberationists" themselves. The fact that, by the end of 1970, "human interest" stories, composed largely of portrayals of the activists, outnumbered all the other types of coverage is not only a testament to the tradition of representing women in terms of the domestic and the (low) cultural but also, I argue, a testament to the crux of the problem for both the media in its need to represent the movement and the women's movement in its need to represent itself to other women. Who women were and what they wanted to be, especially when related to calls for social transformation, were questions central to the appeal and the threat of the women's liberation movement and became, unlike questions of legislation or public policy, the defining themes of the women's movement in 1970.

LADY PROTESTORS

In her *Village Voice* article, "The Next Great Movement in History Is Theirs," published in 1969, Vivian Gornick anticipated the impact the newly emergent women's liberation movement would have on the American public sphere in the coming decade. Gornick's unabashed enthusiasm for the cause (Susan Brownmiller quotes Gornick in her memoir as saying her experience researching the article became something of a "conversion" to "the truth, the beauty, the shining whiteness of it all")[41] marked the beginnings of a distinctly different attitude from the one previously adopted by the press in its coverage of "women's rights." As Sharon Howell has noted in her rhetorical analysis of the second-wave women's movement and the mass media, the press, and specifically the *New York Times*, had, prior to the late 1960s, tended to adopt an attitude that ranged from outright vilification to "amusement."[42] But by 1970 and the emergence of women's liberation, stories on or about feminism had moved from the realm of the occasional, eyebrow-raising news piece tucked in the back pages of the *New York Times* News section, to the heady heights of the front page.[43]

Evidence of women's liberation's newsworthiness in 1970 can be found in every section of the *New York Times*, from the editorial page to the sports pages and, perhaps most notably, in the paper's coverage of congressional politics. The paper's reporting of the proposed nomination of G. Harrold Carswell to the Supreme Court in January, and the opening of the ERA hearings in Congress in May, is often framed in terms of "women's rights" and includes commentary from feminists active in the movement. The headline for an article on Carswell's nomination, "Carswell Called Foe of

Women's Rights," published on January 30, suggests that the paper regarded the women's movement as a worthy participant in national debates over significant political decisions. And, indeed, the article begins with feminist objections to Carswell put forth by Representative Patsy Mink of Hawaii and Betty Friedan, founding member and president of the National Organization for Women (NOW). Yet the framing of the article as being about "women's rights" is misleading. Although the objections to the nomination voiced by Friedan and Mink are the subject of the article's first paragraph, the vast majority of the article is devoted to accusations of racism and the objections of civil rights activists to the Carswell nomination. The discrepancy between the headline and first paragraph and the rest of the article suggests that the real reason for the headline is to play on the currency of women's liberation as a topic of interest rather than to engage in any serious discussion of Carswell's potentially problematic views on women. The article's willingness to acknowledge the existence and claims of the women's movement and its refusal, at the same time, to address those claims as substantive political issues displays an ambivalent attitude toward the women's movement, an attitude that runs through much of the New York Times's coverage of the movement in the first months of 1970. What was an "amused stance" in the 1960s becomes a much more uneasy mixture of acknowledgment of the movement's existence and political claims and a desire to resist the implications of their presence on the national political scene.

The first paragraph of "Carswell Called Foe of Women's Rights" begins with a quote from Betty Friedan in which she links the fight against sexism with the fight against racism: "G. Harrold Carswell was accused today of harboring not only racist beliefs but also 'sexist' views in opposition to equal rights for women. 'Racism and sexism often go hand in hand,' Betty Friedan, author of 'The Feminine Mystique' and president of the National Organization for Women, told the Senate Judiciary Committee."[44] By putting quotation marks around the word *sexist* in the introduction to Friedan's comment, the report creates a distinction between *sexist* and *racist* that sets up the article's implicit evaluative comparison between the two terms. On the one hand, the quotation marks suggest the newness of the word in 1970 and can be interpreted as conveying the originality of Friedan's criticism of Carswell—a perspective accentuated by the article's subsequent quote from a senator surmising that Friedan's and Mink's accusations of sexism were "the first time that a nominee had been challenged because of his supposed views on the legal rights of women."[45] On the other hand, the quotation marks suggest that, unlike the accusation of racism (a word with no need of attendant quotation marks), the validity of being criticized for sexism is open to question—a reading invited by the senator's reference to the lack of historical precedent for Friedan's and Mink's criticisms. Here, then, the use of quotation marks shifts the signifying work of *sexist* from *Carswell* to *women's rights*, and the subject of the opening paragraph also shifts as a consequence from the validity of Carswell's nomination to the validity of women's rights as a political cause and participant in public political discourse

The production of women's rights as the true subject of the article's opening paragraph is further brought into focus by its comparison of the relative merits of the accusations of racism and sexism directed at Carswell. While the criticisms by Friedan and Mink are articulated in terms of a determining link between sexism and racism—Representative Mink's remarks are even more forceful than Friedan's: "male supremacy, like white supremacy, is equally repugnant to those who really believe in equality"[46]— the article's intentions lie in precisely the opposite direction. By devoting the majority of the article to remarks by senators and civil rights activists (none of whom, unlike Friedan, have their criticisms commented on by other sources) on the segregationist past of Carswell, the article suggests a distinction between racism and sexism, implying that while one is worthy of consideration as a criticism of Carswell (and society as a whole) the other is not. In other words, contrary to Friedan's and Mink's comments, racism is used in the article to evoke the history of segregation and the civil rights movement not in order to confront or address that history but in order to efface the historicity of "sexism" and the validity of the fight for women's rights in the present.

The article's attempt to separate racism as a serious historical and social problem that nevertheless needs no examination from the "novelty" of sexism is undone, however, by the photograph used to accompany the article. Set in the center of the page and directly below the headline is a large headshot of Representative Mink. The use of a photograph of Mink, rather than, say, Judge Carswell, further enacts the article's attempt to make women's rights, rather than Carswell, its subject. The image of Mink works as a signifier of the women's movement's meaningfulness, which, in turn, invites the reader to think of women's rights in terms of the bodiliness and feminine quality of women rather than as a movement with a political agenda and perspective. In its deployment of the photograph, the article exemplifies Habermas's argument that the function of the public sphere in the twentieth century is to produce "represented realities" rather than act as a medium for the exchange of opinions and arguments. The concern of the article, in relation to its coverage of feminist objections to Judge Carswell's nomination, is not to provide access to a discussion about the effects of sexism in society, its relation to the history of racism, and its effects on the Supreme Court in particular, but to reduce women's liberation to an image of femininity through which the meaning of the movement is evoked.

What undoes this cultural encoding is the visceral presence of the image of Representative Mink. As a congressional representative, Mink disrupts the private/public distinctions through which femininity is made meaningful in the American public sphere. And as a mixed-race American whose congressional district is in Hawaii—a contact zone of American colonialism—she also disrupts the social taxonomy of American racism. Instead of fixing and thereby containing the meaning of women's rights in an image of familiar femininity, the photograph of Mink acts to implode the borders between race and sex, history and the present, and feminism and civil rights that the article is trying to reassert. The embodiment of women's rights in the figure of Mink works to reduce the historical force of both sexism and racism to particular bodies and groups. Yet the image of Mink also acts as a haunting reminder of miscegenation—precisely the national fear, and desire, that brings the historicity of sexism into intimate contact with that of racism. The article works to distinguish women's rights from the "serious" political work of civil rights and the history of racism in America, only for the image of Mink to act as a reminder of the imbricative relations between them.

The practice of figuring the meaning of the women's movement through images of femininity and the bodies of particular women worked in disruptive tandem with the paper's coverage of political events, including its coverage of the ERA hearings. In its reporting of the ERA's journey through Congress, the *New York Times* does manage to be less the producer of a represented reality and more a mediator of informative reflection on society—an achievement that only adds to the incoherency of the paper's coverage of the movement in the first half of 1970. Most of the articles on the ERA fight are written by Eileen Shanahan, who, in her daily articles on the House and Senate hearings, along with her occasional columns in the Sunday Week in Review, provides a detailed picture of the range of viewpoints proffered in the hearings. She also manages to convey, through the wide-ranging scope of her reporting, the more general discussion about the possible meanings of *equality* and *women's rights* in American society at the end of the 1960s. As a result, Shanahan presents the ERA as a complicated piece of legislation with potentially far-ranging ramifications for society and the status of women.

An example of Shanahan's prescient reporting can be found in one of her Week in Review columns titled "Equal Rights: Who Is against It and Why." In the column, Shanahan manages to suggest not only the biased process of the congressional hearings themselves but also the complicated nature of the debates over what it would mean for American society to have such an amendment. She points out the "stacked" nature of the hearings by revealing that the acting head of the Judiciary Committee, Senator Sam Ervin of North Carolina, had only picked witnesses who were against the ERA amendment. She goes on to gently mock Senator Ervin for his "oratorical flights" about the "'good Lord's plan' that men and women be different."[47] Her critique of the congressional hearings, along with her mocking of Senator Ervin, asserts the worthiness of the ERA as a topic for serious consideration and also conveys, through the revelation of the prejudicial behavior of Senator Ervin (and his Judiciary Committee), the very inequality the ERA was intended to negate.

Shanahan then goes on to discuss the testimony of Myra K. Wolfgang, a national and local officer for the Hotel and Restaurant Employees and Bartenders Union, who, like Senator Ervin, opposed the amendment. Yet, as Shanahan makes clear, Wolfgang's objections were not based on an idea of a retiring and fragile domestic femininity—Wolfgang, according to Shanahan, was "no 'pussycat' embracing the idea that domination by males is her natural and happy fate"—nor were her objections based on an idea of the "good Lord's plan," but they were based on what amounted to a class divide between women. Shanahan reports that, in Wolfgang's view, the negation of laws protecting women from having to work overtime would amount to real hardship for the thousands of working mothers who had to go home after work and take care of their households. Shanahan describes Wolfgang's testimony at length, suggesting in the process the class antagonisms between women: "With a jerk of her head toward the college-educated women who were filling most of the seats in the hearing room, [Wolfgang] went on to say that 10-hour days might be all right for 'lady lawyers,' and other women in the professional and managerial fields whose jobs are not physically exhausting, who can pay for *household help* whose husbands are more disposed to lend a hand at home and whose children, if any, are probably grown."[48] But for the women in the Hotel and Restaurant Employees and Bartenders Union, Wolfgang argued, laws protecting them from the demands of their employers were both necessary and particular to their roles as mothers and housewives as well as workers. As for the "lady lawyers," who, as Shanahan reports, believed women had to take the risk of hardship in relation to family life for the ultimate benefit of being regarded as equal, Wolfgang asserted that "such women [did] not know what real hardship [was]."[49]

In her reporting of Wolfgang's testimony, Shanahan resists any temptation to stack the deck of representation. Rather than letting one perspective or idea of women's lives dominate her report, Shanahan covers the range of arguments. Wolfgang's concerns are given equal space by Shanahan to those of the ERA's advocates, many of whom were active in the women's movement and included representatives from NOW. For many women's rights activists, like Friedan, who had helped form NOW in response to the inertia of the Equal Employment Opportunity Commission (EEOC) and in the face of widespread discrimination against women seeking employment in the early 1960s, the ERA would effectively legislate the end of "sex-segregated" work. The representatives of NOW included union members as well as "lady lawyers," and the organization's political platform asserted the need for state-sponsored child care and pregnancy leave, as well as the end of discriminatory hiring practices.[50] By including the multiple perspectives heard during the hearings, Shanahan is able to present the ERA discussion as a debate with no clear answers and no simple right or wrong position. Similarly, Shanahan does not reduce the arguments over the ERA to competing ideological beliefs about the innate natures of men and women, but instead situates them within the context of a national discussion about the place of work, the family, and women in society. In Shanahan's reports the ERA hearings become an opportunity to discuss questions of social organization and power, and women appear as political actors and agents rather than imagistic symbols for popular notions of social life.

The debates over the ERA as reported by Shanahan revealed not only the multiplicity of viewpoints among women, as much as between men and women, but also the complex sociality of American women in the postwar years. Contrary to the domestic ideology of the Cold War years, which promoted a privatized femininity defined by motherhood and a domesticated sexuality defined by marriage and life in the suburbs, the 1950s were a much more complex and contested time for American women.[51] The number of working women, often in low-paying administrative and service jobs, increased markedly in the postwar years with more women in the labor force in 1955 than during the Second World War.[52] The 1950s had also seen the politicization of women in the civil rights movement and in the nascent homophile organizations of middle-class gay men and lesbians, as well as their continued participation in unions and antinuclear organizations. By the late 1960s, following the emergence of the New Left and anti–Vietnam War movements and in conjunction with the rise of Black Power and the radicalization of the civil rights movement, the national public sphere had other political actors on the scene—actors made newly visible through the TV screen. The images of African American women on the frontline of civil rights protests in the south, and of white women screaming obscenities at young children as they walked to school, for example, disturbed the cultural imaginary of American national belonging. Out of the home and on the streets, American women—of multiple race and class backgrounds—were seen in ways that unsettled the taxonomies of America's imagined community.

This unsettledness was evident in the range of news stories that appeared in the *New York Times* in relation to, or inspired by, the phenomenon of women's liberation in 1970. Shanahan's reportage was a prime example of news stories that appeared in the paper suggesting the complexity of an American social domain riven by conflict in the late 1960s. Other stories —on the bias of the courts in sentencing women, on the gender inequality of Wall Street, and on the discriminatory hiring policies of educational institutions—also appeared in 1970 and acted as supplementary commentary for the paper's extensive coverage of the ERA debates.[53] Just by the mere fact that these stories appeared as *news* stories rather than articles in the Food, Fashions, Family, Furnishing section, which usually housed stories of "interest to women," was evidence of a marked, if gradual, shift in the perception of "women's issues" and their place in society. Yet it is the ambivalence of the paper's attitude to "women's rights" that remains the overwhelming legacy of its coverage in 1970. While Eileen Shanahan's articles (and, as we shall see later, Marilyn Bender's feature articles for the paper) framed the "fight for equality" as a social and political phenomenon that spoke to various publics and constituencies of women, the paper undermined that appeal with a competing tendency to reduce the women's liberation movement to spectacle.

An example of the spectacle-ization of the women's liberation movement can be found in Robert Sherrill's news-feature article on September 20 for the Sunday magazine. A photograph of two women holding up a large placard declaring "Male Chauvinism Beware" dominates the cover of the magazine, while the headline for the article reads, "That Equal-Rights Amendment—What, Exactly, Does It Mean?" The contrast between image and headline—the women, hidden by the large and unwieldy placards they hold, seem to be cowering behind the boldness of their message, as if they are incapable of controlling the furies unleashed by their own demands, while the headline, in contrast, holds the promise of a reasoned analysis of the amendment's implications—continues throughout the article. What, on the level of reportage, purports to be a discussion of the possible effects of the amendment's passage becomes, on the level of cultural symbolization, an attempt to portray women as constitutionally incapable of assuming the equality they strive for.

Hovering between the lines of Sherrill's article is a portrait of women as either quaint and naïve grandmothers, who politely espouse equal rights without really knowing what they are asking for, or shrill and fanatical "militant feminists," who will stop at nothing, least of all reason, in their quest for rights. Thus, for example, Sherrill describes Marjorie Longwell, the chairwoman of the National Woman's Party, as a "cheerful, grandmotherly Californian," who, when asked whether she thought women should be subject to military conscription if the ERA was passed, responds with, "why certainly. . . . If I were between the ages of 18 and 26 I'd be ashamed if I weren't willing to fight for my country against the communists," only to later state, when asked if women should fight on the front lines, "I don't think any lady would want to shoot another lady's son."[54] In contrast to the description of Longwell, women's liberationists are portrayed as urban "guerrilla fighters" who wouldn't have any problem shooting another woman's son: "In the last couple of years the legislators had become vaguely aware of guerrilla fighting in more barbarous parts of the nation, like New York City, where amid the smoke of burning brassieres and shrill cries for free abortions, the clash of armies was heard by night."[55] The confused ramblings of elderly bluestockings are placed in comparison with an image of radical feminists drawn through contrast and ridicule—the exaggeration of "armies" and "guerrilla fighting" exacerbated by the reduction of their protest to "shrill" cries for abortion and the smoke of "burning brassieres." These images draw upon recent memories of American cities burning as the result of race riots and antiwar demonstrations, images that punctuated the 1960s and were afforded a dramatic place in the public imaginary thanks, in part, to the representational gravitas of writers and observers like Norman Mailer. Here, the specters of these recent clashes are at once evoked and made ridiculous—their social significance de-realized through the invocation of an analogy with women's rights.

The image of the women fighting for the ERA as ignorant and innocent "ladies," who have only the shakiest understanding of what it is they are fighting for, continues in Sherrill's description of the ERA's journey through Congress. Representative Martha Griffiths of Michigan, the chief proponent of the amendment in Congress, is portrayed as befuddled and not in control of her historical facts—despite the fact she had masterminded the amendment's successful passage through the House. The garbled quote accompanying her photograph—"This amendment . . . will mean you cannot go backward. . . . We could go backward—Germany did, you know. . . . Didn't Hitler say, 'Every woman into the kitchen'?"—lies in contrast with the elegance of the quotes accompanying the photographs of Senator Ervin and Representative Celler, the chief opponents to the amendment. While Representative Griffiths and other female advocates of the amendment come across as confused and vague, Senator Ervin and Representative Celler are presented as reasonable and astute politicians, despite the obvious irrationality of their anti-ERA arguments (Representative Celler is quoted as saying, "there is more difference between a male and a female than between a horse chestnut and a chestnut horse").[56] Indeed, the views of congressmen are given credibility precisely through Sherrill's characterization of the pro-amendment activists as "ladies." When a congressman confides, anonymously, that the success of the amendment is due to "some women with time on their hands and nothing can be more dangerous than an idle woman," his opinion is validated by Sherrill's own critique of the women activists as "professional elitists, women who can afford the luxury of crusades."[57] Lionel Tiger will deploy a similar class critique in December in *Time*'s "Women's Lib: A Second Look." Sherrill's portrait of the pro-amendment activists as charming, middle-aged, middle-class ladies, who, having found a *crusade*—a word that conjures memories of organizations like the Women's Christian Temperance Union and of women in the public sphere as Christian do-gooders and meddlers—take it upon themselves to "henpeck" Congress into passing the amendment, provides one of the first examples of what will turn out to be a common criticism of the women's liberation movement by both the mainstream media and a good many feminists looking back at the movement.[58]

Differences in perspective on the possible effects of the ERA are displaced in the article by an emphasis on portraiture drawn through metaphor. Lady protestors and women's liberationists become figures who evoke specific histories of protest and the feelings of contempt, ridicule, and fear through which collective memories of those histories circulate in the present. In his study of collective memory, Maurice Halbwachs argues that "it is language, and the whole system of social conventions attached to it, that allows us at every moment to reconstruct our past." Language itself works as a kind of archive, and it is through the conjuring power of words that past worlds, images, and notions are evoked in the present. Halbwachs continues, "society cannot think except in regard to given facts, persons, and events, there are no ideas without images."[59] For Halbwachs, the continuity of collective memory as social thought is enacted, at least in part, through specific types of people that are reproduced through the circulation of particular metaphors and images. It is through these images and metaphors that the world of the past is conjured in the present and given meaning. It is through images and metaphors that meaning is produced as impression or "atmosphere," to use Virginia Woolf's necessarily vague term for the affective apprehension of gender (or sex in her terms), rather than as concept or argument.

Sherrill's portrait of the pro-amendment activists as middle-aged, middle-class white ladies draws upon precisely this kind of collective cultural memory and can be attributed to the public space in which the ERA fight was conducted (the rooms and corridors of institutional power), as well as the relative historical visibility of white, middle-class women as political activists. His characterization of ERA advocates as housewives with time on their hands also drew upon the domestic ideology of the postwar years, which depicted women as domestic goddesses who fortified the nation against communism by running their homes with technologically inspired efficiency.[60] Here, then, the image of the lady protestor is a comfortingly familiar one in that it suggests a continuity of women's rights protesting that will not, as history has already proven, dramatically transform the social domain and threaten the norm of middle-class family life. Moreover, echoes of the domestic goddess of middle-class suburbia enabled Sherrill to depict the pro-ERA activists as a crowd of one. Rather than the "armies" of militant feminism, the bored housewife, even in her millions, suggested the isolated figure of a woman alone.

Although the lady protestor was a comforting counterimage to the militants, the inadequacy of the respectable, middle-class white lady as a representative figure for the women's movement is evident in Sherrill's need to situate the lady protestor in relation to the "guerrilla fighters" of radical feminism. It was these feminists, and not the lady protestors, who were, by September, dominating the news with their increasingly outlandish demonstrations and opinions. For Sherrill, the harmlessness of the lady protestor is accentuated by the activities of her alter ego, the militant feminist, but his comparison between the two risks further disturbing normative constructions of femininity, a predicament Sherrill doesn't seem able to escape, precisely because those norms had become much less stable by the end of the 1960s. While the lady protestor evoked images of the nineteenth- and early twentieth-century Christian do-gooder, the guerrilla fighter evoked much more contemporary images of radicalism, including that of Angela Davis, whose notoriety as a fugitive and symbol of black militancy in 1970 eclipsed Kate Millett's moment of fame.

The portrayals of Davis in the *New York Times* in 1970 act as the negative imprint to Sherrill's article and, indeed, the paper's coverage of women's liberation as a whole. In contrast to the paper's increasing use of ridicule and contempt in its coverage of women's liberation, Davis is depicted as a "real radical," and her apparent transformation from middle-class university professor to violent revolutionary is narrated as a warning to white America of the dangers of black militancy.[61] The difference between Davis as a real radical and the pseudo-radicals of women's liberation is invoked through the disarticulation of race from gender: Davis's militancy is signified by her race, and her gender is rendered invisible by her blackness. Women's liberationists, in contrast, are identified through their gender— an identification that renders their claim to militancy either pretentious or ridiculous. Although Sherrill is quick to dismiss the women's liberation militants as pseudo-radicals (burning a bra is not, after all, the same as being on the FBI's Ten Most Wanted list or engaging in a street battle with police), the use of the term *guerrilla fighters* risks associating women's liberation with the contemporary revolutionary movements of the U.S. urban ghetto and Global South, suggesting, as a result, a much more troubling phantasmatic image of feminism as a border-crossing transcultural and transnational rebellion.

In fact, the alignment of feminism with national liberation movements was intended by the women's liberationists themselves—the use of *women's liberation* rather than *feminism* a testament to that intention—precisely because they wanted to resist the historical conjunction of women's rights with the bourgeois preoccupations of lady protestors as well as assert a political and conceptual affinity between feminism and anticolonial liberation struggles.[62] Sherrill's dismissive reference to "shrill" bra burners demanding free abortions ridicules the notion that feminists could be thought of as liberation fighters; yet his deployment of "guerrilla" to describe women's liberationists also emphasizes, rather than diminishes, the movement's own claims of a political relation between feminism and the liberation struggles of people of color and the poor at home and abroad. What begins as a mocking portrayal of lady protestors, in an attempt to reduce and contain the political and social implications of the ERA fight, becomes, by the end of the article, a wildly oscillating portrait of feminism that conjures, through the exaggerations of contrast and ridicule, a vivid and evocative fantasy image of radical feminism. Instead of containing feminism in narrowly defined representational figures, Sherrill's article works to encourage a proliferation of fantasies of just who feminists are and what they want. "Normal" femininity, in contrast, becomes increasingly unimaginable as Sherrill's article veers from one fantasy figure to the other.

The evocativeness of Sherrill's fantasy image, I would suggest, is produced through the aliveness of terms like *guerrilla* in the late 1960s. Throughout that decade *guerrilla* was a word that reverberated across different political and social landscapes; it had an affective currency that incited the imaginations of those involved in the movement as well as those on the outside looking on suspiciously. For those in the movement, the guerrilla was the figure of liberation; he (and sometimes she) conjured up images of the urban revolutionary but also of the oppressed and disenfranchised rising up and opposing state and imperial power. In 1967 Che Guevara, a revolutionary guerrilla fighter in Latin America throughout the 1950s and 1960s, was murdered in Bolivia and became an iconic figure for leftist groups and movements in the West. Conversely, the guerrilla was a particularly apt figure for expressing the paranoia and suspicion of postwar public political discourse. Guerrillas operate subterraneously; they subvert from within using the tactics of stealth and surprise and by drawing upon inside knowledge of social relations and spaces. The witch hunts of the McCarthy era had provoked a widespread cultural distrust of appearances and a commonly held belief that "subversives" were deceitful pretenders of normality. The internal threats of the Communist and the pervert in the 1950s become, in the 1960s, the threat of the Black Panthers, the Young Lords Party, and, by the end of 1969, the Weathermen and other revolutionary and anarchist splinter groups of the disintegrating New Left. A distrust of the visible and the discomforting sense that we cannot really know people by the way they look structured the response by the authorities to the radical movements of the 1960s (the FBI's infiltration of various groups and organizations and official belief that many of the student and civil rights groups were run by Moscow are examples of paranoid state thinking). This distrust of appearances also radically undercut the epistemological certainties of gender, sexual, and racial norms. By suggesting a link between internal enemies of the nation (like the Communist, pervert, or black militant) and women's liberation, Sherrill's use of the trope of the feminist as revolutionary guerrilla fighter provokes the idea that women's liberation was both subversive and dangerous—a menace from within—and also that the heretofore readable images and representations of American womanhood were not to be trusted; that white, middle-class women were not necessarily what they seemed to be.

Guerrilla was also a word that echoed beyond the borders of the United States, connecting the social upheaval and conflict of the 1960s to other moments and places of civil unrest. While the mythmaking events of the American Revolution and Civil War operate in the national imaginary as metaphors of belonging, which work to bind the nation together through the exclusion of undesirable others and the overcoming of conflict, a word like *guerrilla* could invoke, in the present tense of the late 1960s, the unadmitted trauma of those events—the social breakdown and dissolution of state power that threatened the American colonies and then nation in the 1770s and 1860s. (For example, Carl Davidson, an SDS leader, wrote that the riots in Newark and Detroit in the summer of 1967 "marked the beginning of the second American Revolution," thereby making an explicit connection between the urban revolt of the Black Power movement and the revolutionary war against Britain.)[63] As a word that could conjure "multidirectional" collective memories of social conflict and associate them with the national liberation movements of the sixties, *guerrilla* incited fears of social breakdown as the implosion of boundaries between races, classes, and nations.[64] In addition, subversion from within connotes the invisible, subterranean mixing of different people wrought by the weakening of state power and the forging of alliances between different peoples and classes. In contrast to the lady protestor, then, the guerrilla fighter as an image of women's liberation also evokes, in the cultural imaginary of America's imagined community, the fear of what has been, and still needs to be, excluded from the domain of American citizenship. It is a term that does not simply suggest a particularly extreme form of feminist protest against the social constraints experienced by women but what the breakdown of those constraints might bring—the mixing of different peoples and the dissolution of white, male power.

Fears of civil unrest and social and sexual chaos are also linked, through the deployment of *guerrilla fighters*, to the new forms of political protest on display in the postwar years. While Senator Ervin and Sherrill can jocularly condescend to the "charming ladies" who visit Ervin's office insisting they want to be drafted into the Army, the civil rights, Black Power, and New Left activists of the 1950s and 1960s had already changed the political landscape, producing, in turn, a different kind of political protestor. Rather than the hallowed corridors of institutionalized power, it was the streets, parks, neighborhoods, bars, cafeterias, and private homes that were the new politicized spaces in which contests for social transformation and recognition were being fought. The activists of the newly emergent women's movement were more likely to be seen conducting impromptu street theater and holding consciousness-raising sessions in members' homes than knocking on the doors of contemptuous senators. The dated feel of Sherrill's "lady protestor," as well as, perhaps, Shanahan's respectable citizen activist, would have to give way to the more prescient and troubling portrayal of the women's liberationist, a figure who would come to embody a whole swath of cultural and social anxieties concerning race, class, women, and the social and sexual "freedoms" of late twentieth-century America.

The inability of either the lady protestor figure or the respectable citizen activist to signify the disruptive force of women's liberation by 1970 is encapsulated by the editorial on the ERA fight in Congress titled "The Henpecked House," published on August 12. The editorial called for the Senate to regard the amendment with careful consideration because the "constitution and the rights of women are too important for any further playing to the ladies gallery."[65] The discomforting disjuncture between a mocking representation of women as "the ladies gallery" and the seeming recognition of the importance of their rights echoes the contrasting treatment of the ERA fight by Shanahan and Sherrill. While Shanahan attempts to bring into view the complicated constituency of women who may, or may not, agree on the potential ramifications of the ERA, Sherrill is intent on reducing the ERA fight to a spectacle of femininity, which is, in turn, constituted through the projection of particular classed and raced figures. What "The Henpecked House" reveals is that the spectacle of femininity through which a national domesticity was visualized in the postwar years (the white, middle-class housewife of Cold War home security) was becoming increasingly illegible as a signifier of nationness by the late 1960s— even to the *New York Times*. The cultural forms through which white femininity was maintained as a site for the production of national belonging were breaking down and would have to be remade.

URBAN GUERRILLAS

On August 26, 1970, an array of women's liberation groups, in cooperation with NOW, organized the nationwide Women's Strike for Equality. Called for in commemoration of the fiftieth anniversary of the ratification of the Nineteenth Amendment to the U.S. Constitution, which was the culmination of the women's suffrage movement, the strike was envisioned by one of its principal organizers, Betty Friedan, as a day when American women would refuse to go to work—whether that meant the work they did in the home or in wage-paying employment. On the day itself, women across the country went onto the streets and held rallies in public squares and parks. As Ruth Rosen writes, "in cities and towns across the country, women marched, picketed, protested, held teach-ins and rallies, and produced skits and plays."[66] Approximately thirty thousand women of different ages, classes, and races marched down Fifth Avenue in New York City, some carrying posters with irreverent messages—"Don't Cook Dinner—Starve a Rat Today" and "Don't Iron while the Strike Is Hot"—while others pushed strollers or escorted their grandmothers.[67] The strike made the front page of the *New York Times* and was generally regarded as a success by the organizers, with membership in NOW increasing by 50 percent in the months following the protest.[68]

The day after the strike the *New York Times* issued an editorial that, despite offering a similar argument, was markedly different in tone and content from "The Henpecked House" editorial of just two weeks before.

"The Liberated Woman" editorial projected a portrait of women's liberation that was dismissive and negative while also agreeing with many of the
movement's political goals. Curling its lip with disdain, the editorial criticized the women's liberationists as "publicity seeking" exhibitionists. Following this dismissal is a self-satisfied claim that the New York Times has
long advocated the three main platforms of the women's movement: liber-
alized abortion laws, affordable daycare, and greater access to the professions for women. Acknowledging a "revolution" in the "status of women" in
the twentieth century, the editorial draws on arguments made by feminists,
including Betty Friedan and Shulamith Firestone, stating that the benefits
of scientific and technological advances had created the condition of practical equality for men and women. No longer a prisoner of her physical and
biological disadvantages, thanks to developments in mechanical and reproductive technology, the American woman could and should enjoy the benefits of educational and professional opportunities in the same way as her
male counterpart. Yet, the editorial goes on to assure its readers, "many
values will remain unaltered"—especially those that place the family at the
center of American social life. For it is the "enduring" fulfillment of motherhood, according to the New York Times, that will continue to draw many
women back to the home, despite the pull of economic and social independence offered by modern society.[69] The difference in tone in this editorial
is marked by a shift in the emotional work of the lady protestor. While in
"The Henpecked House" the activist housewife is the object of derision,
in "The Liberated Woman" she is associated not with the meddling do-
gooder of the early twentieth-century social purity campaigns but with the
Cold War mother figure of the privatized space of domesticity. Rather than
contempt, the emotion generated by this editorial's plea for the enduring
fulfillment of family life is nostalgia. The lady protestor, no longer the
object of derision, becomes a reassuring symbol of a way of life and an idea
of woman that evokes an ahistorical national social continuity and stability.

Although "The Liberated Woman" voices support for the legislative
goals of the women's liberation movement, it also asserts that such changes
will not fundamentally transform society. Those women "who have no
taste for marriage or childbearing" will, according to the editorial, remain a
distinct minority in society despite feeling "less constrained," while the
"publicity-seeking exhibitionism" of the women's liberation movement will
remain a fringe consequence of the need for the movement to be heard.[70]
The acknowledgment of the "revolution" in the status of women is wed-

ded to an even more insistent need to assert that women will not change as a result of that revolution—a paradox that can only make sense through displacement and concealment. Here, then, the hypervisibility of the "attention-getting" liberationist, who has "no taste for marriage or child-bearing," acts as a depository and container for the unarticulated fear that women are indeed changing as a result of the revolution in their status. And that fear gets articulated through the use of the term *exhibitionism*, invoking sexual perversion or, more to the point, echoing the very old trick of equating women's entry into the public sphere with her sexual exposure.

The accusations of exhibitionism directed at women's liberation by the *New York Times*'s editorial page also work to contain notions of a national femininity within the boundaries of respectable middle-classness. Through the absent presence of collective cultural memories of other public female figures, like the prostitute or lesbian—figures that, from the nineteenth century, have been the boundary figures marking the distinction between healthy bourgeois selves and racial and class degeneracy—the "attention getting" women's liberationist acts as a reminder of women who, in their spectacularized nonconformativity, have, historically, occupied a space outside the domain of middle-class heteronormativity. And it is these conjured figures from the past who infuse the women's liberationist with meaning in the present. Sexual outsiderism and social abjection, fates of otherness that are always already racially coded in the modern nation-state, become the implicit, invoked threat posed to those women who would join women's liberation. Through the conjuring of ghostly figures of feminine abjection, the editorial page of the *New York Times* actively participates in the remaking of sexual and gender norms, a process of differentiation that relies upon the social grammar of race and class that constitutes the domain of national belonging.

Spectacularizing the women's liberationist as an exhibitionist also puts the incoherency of normal femininity out of view and encourages the reader to turn away from the possibility of feeling differently offered by women's liberation's refusal of respectability. Yet, in relation to the movement's explicit refusal of respectability as a claim to political empowerment, spectacularizing the liberationist as an exhibitionist also provides an image of a wrong or embarrassing femininity that can incite other kinds of investments, ones located in the transformative promise of feminism. It is in this instability of meaning that the women's liberationist becomes a strange and ambivalent figure in the paper's coverage of the movement: she figures the phantasmatic possibilities—possibilities rooted in the histories of feminine abjection—of women's liberation, as well as the limits placed on its becoming.

As a boundary figure that both contains and expresses the repressed fear that women have and will continue to change as a result of the "revolution" in their social and cultural possibilities, the women's liberationist appears throughout the *New York Times*'s coverage of movement protests in 1970. The first women's liberation demonstration to grab the headlines was the sit-in at the *Ladies' Home Journal* offices in March. Organized by various women's liberation groups, including the radical feminist groups the Redstockings and the Media Women, the sit-in lasted more than eleven hours and ended with the editorial staff of the magazine agreeing to let the movement write a women's liberation supplement for the forthcoming issue of the magazine. The *New York Times* journalist assigned to cover the demonstration, Grace Lichtenstein, adopts a tone that is both amused and, at the same time, uncommitted to a particular frame or story line. Although Lichtenstein dismisses the demonstrators by calling them "girls," she also pokes fun at the magazine. Her aim is to portray the entire event as somewhat absurd: while she quotes Lenore Hershey, the female managing editor at the magazine, as saying "any group that can come in here and behave like this is not competent to put out a magazine," she also archly notes that Hershey was wearing a "sisterhood is powerful" button "given to her by one of the demonstrators."[71]

Despite her noncommittal tone, Lichtenstein deploys the same representative strategy as Sherrill, distinguishing between the political claims and arguments of the movement and the liberationists themselves. While some of the magazine's employees are quoted as dismissing the demonstrators as "ridiculous," Lichtenstein reports that others agreed with many of their arguments. The criticisms raised by the demonstrators, including gender inequality in the *Ladies' Home Journal*'s employment and promotion practices, are either implicitly or explicitly accepted in Lichtenstein's report. But the demonstrators themselves are portrayed in generally disparaging terms. Some of the "girls" (most notoriously, Shulamith Firestone) are described as "lunging" at John Mack Carter, the editor-in-chief of the magazine, while others are depicted helping themselves to Carter's cigars and smoking them. The barely concealed sexual innuendo of the demonstrators as obsessed with men and sex (and cigars!) is further suggested by Lichtenstein's listing of the articles the demonstrators wish to write: "Can Marriage Survive Women's Liberation?" and "How to Have an

Orgasm." The portrait of the protestors as sex obsessed and penis envious is used not so much to dismiss their claims but to express anxiety about the implications of their demands. The difficult question of how to achieve equality in employment and representation in the media is avoided in favor of the uneasy equations of Lenore Hershey as a powerful woman in a man's world and women's liberationists as women who want to be men.

The article also demonstrates that the media was one of the primary sites for women's liberation protests. The Miss America protest in Atlantic City in 1968, at which demonstrators crowned a sheep Miss America and placed a Freedom Trash Can on the boardwalk for women to throw, but not burn, their bras into and other paraphernalia of femininity,[72] was the first nationally recognized demonstration by the women's liberation movement, and it revealed that the activists understood that their fight had to be fought in the domain of cultural representation as much as in Congress. Even Betty Friedan, who as president of NOW campaigned vociferously for more emphasis to be placed on legislative gains and economic issues rather than media representations, sex, and bodies, explained in an interview with Diedre Carmody of the *New York Times* that the Women's Strike for Equality was needed to show "the visible power of women at city hall." As Carmody goes on to write, "the majority of women in the liberation movement object to the general attitudes of society that picture women as inferior to men."[73] How women are represented—"pictured"—becomes a primary factor in the style, if not always the content, of movement protests in 1970.[74]

The ambivalence in the rendering of women's liberationists as exhibitionists is on display in the *New York Times*'s coverage of the Women's Strike for Equality (fig. 1.2). The newspaper's large front-page photograph depicting a mass of women marching down Fifth Avenue can be understood as a moment of apprehension in all senses of the word. The photograph "seized upon" and arrested the movement in one image, while simultaneously "laying hold of the senses" of the readers.[75] The double effect of this image, which seems to grasp the movement in its entirety while also conjuring a perceptual feeling of and for the movement, enabled women's liberation to be present in the public sphere but at the cost of making the movement of its emergence—its becomingness and indeterminateness—invisible. At the same time, the image of tens of thousands of women marching in New York City also suggested political power. What is also apprehended here, then, is the future—an apprehension that is about anticipation and fear of what is unknown and yet to come.

The ambivalent effect of the New York Times's attempt to seize hold of the women's liberation movement, while also denying its future anterior possibilities, is further emphasized within the body of the paper's coverage of the strike. The apprehension of political power suggested by the image of the march is undermined by the paper's narrative containment of the demonstration. One article on the Women's Strike for Equality leads with the headline "Leading Feminist Puts Hairdo Before Strike" and is concerned with describing Friedan's "emergency appointment with her hairdresser" in preparation for the strike, the dress she was wearing on the day, "a raspberry colored shift," and her concern that people will think "Women's Lib girls don't care about how they look."[76] And while Linda Charlton covers the day under the headline "10,000 in Parade Flood the Street," and lists events happening around the country, the article by Grace Lichtenstein, on the same page, asserts that "for the vast majority of women, yesterday was a day simply to go about one's business—whether that meant going to a job, attending a Broadway matinee, having one's hair done, or washing the baby's diapers."[77] Insistence on the quotidian ordinariness of women's lives (hairdressers, diapers, worrying over their appearances) de-

FIG. 1.2. *Strike for Equality*, by William Sauro, *New York Times*, August 27, 1970, 1. Courtesy of Redux Pictures.

flects attention away from the abnormality of women refusing to work and demonstrating in public, and the possibility of women behaving, looking, and speaking differently is refuted, despite the presence of images that suggest precisely that possibility. It is in this disjuncture—between representative frames that situate women within the scripts of bourgeois femininity and domesticity and the images of public demonstrations that picture women as a multiple and diverse public—that the ambivalence of the movement is most vividly on display in the media coverage of women's liberation in 1970.

The reduction of the mass of women marching down Fifth Avenue to an image of women worrying about their appearance or "washing the baby's diapers" attempts to depoliticize and domesticate the event. Rather than depicting the marchers as cigar-smoking extremists, the paper reverts to the image that would bring the most comfort to those anxious about a possible revolution in gender relations: the white, middle-class housewife. As a result, any presence or voice from women who do not fit that comforting image becomes a divisive depiction of marginality. It is in this vein that the NOW member and strike supporter Eleanor Holmes Norton is quoted without any mention of her being black, while another speaker—her name, tellingly, not provided—from the Third World Women's Alliance is immediately identified as black, presumably because she "expressed skepticism" about the strike and called for "revolution."[78]

The Women's Strike for Equality coverage, while extensive, reduced the "massed bodies" of women's liberation to a familiar and uniform image of women that excluded any notion of the movement as a more indeterminate phenomenon with various potential and actual constituencies. Even in the more considered analysis of the strike, which appeared in the weekend edition of the *New York Times*, the emphasis was on separating the "crazies" from the majority. Judy Klemesrud's generally positive review of the strike in the Week in Review section of the Sunday paper also included the observation that "every kind of woman you ever see in New York was there: limping octogenarians, bra-less teenagers, Black Panther women, telephone operators, . . . Puerto Rican factory workers, nurses in uniform." Yet even her acknowledgment of the variety of women at the Fifth Avenue march was used to dismiss the "stereotype" of the women's movement as a "lesbian plot." Klemesrud goes on to assert the inaccuracy of the "lesbian plot" theory by revealing that the "Radical Lesbians" at the march were generally ignored by the other marchers and left to cope as best they could with police harassment.[79] She ends her article with a return to the sane majority of the women's movement, those women who "ignore" the "crazies" and concentrate on the "gut" issues, such as equal pay for equal work. Here, the marginal figure is the radical lesbian, and she is used to mark off the domain of normal femininity busily being constructed in the *New York Times*'s coverage of the march. In terms of the coverage of the march as a whole, the lesbian becomes associated with the black militant—the two figures deployed by the paper to contain the virtual possibilities of women's liberation—and the absence of any clear articulation of a relation between the two offers the necessary interpretive space for conjuring an affective reaction to both.

The acknowledgment of class, race, and ethnic differences within the ranks of the strike's supporters is, again, subverted by the need to reassure the reader that members of the women's movement are the familiar women of middle-class suburbia. This time, however, the threatening specter of "the lesbian plot" is also raised—suggesting that the apprehension of massed bodies as political power brought with it the fear of possible and actual alliances between women across race, class, and ethnic lines. The figure of the lesbian, whose "alliances" with other women are her raison d'être, becomes a displacement and a signifier of that fear as well as a threat posed to women who would assert the primacy of their relationships with other women over their relationships with men.

In its coverage of smaller protests and specific group affiliations, the *New York Times* did tend to suggest the multiple constituencies of the women's movement. Articles on the relationship between feminism and communism appeared in 1970,[80] as did articles on black and white feminist involvement in Black Panther protests,[81] and participation in multimovement conferences that brought women's liberation, the Black Panthers, the Young Lords Party, gay liberation, and New Left groups together.[82] Charlayne Hunter, in her article on black women and feminism for the *New York Times* in November 1970, reported that many black women "discussed" feminism, even though they were usually suspicious of predominantly white organizations like NOW and groups like the Redstockings. As Hunter reports, black women were "doing" feminism as much as, if not more than, white women but in their own groups and with a different set of goals.[83] Although Helen H. King's article "The Black Woman and Women's Lib," penned for *Ebony* in March 1971, essentially dismissed the women's liberation movement as white and irrelevant to black women, the responses to the article in the Letters section of *Ebony*'s April issue revealed not only the range of opinion on the women's movement within the readership of the magazine but also its status as a "hot" topic.[84] For the *New York Times*, as for the national media as a whole, black feminism was left off stage, its presence occasionally glimpsed in articles like Hunter's but mostly ignored —its invisibility a threatening spectrality that provided the necessary shadow for the media's organizing of the meanings of women's liberation in relation to white, middle-class femininity.

THE LESBIAN PLOT

The bewildering variety of movement manifestations, cohorts, protests, and connections with other movements and causes meant that the picture of the women's movement in 1970 was confusing but omnipresent. As Linda Charlton wrote in her analysis of the Women's Strike for Equality for the *New York Times*, "they have marched down Fifth Avenue, they have, at other times, burned bras and written books and pressured Congressmen and made speeches. They are the Women's Liberation Movement, and whatever that is, almost everyone's heard of it."[85] The need to shape that confusing omnipresence, however, became more decisive in the media's coverage of the movement as the year went on, and the dependence upon the familiar figure of the middle-class housewife with time on her hands would give way to an image that would be more condemnatory of the movement and, at the same time, more revealing of the social anxieties the movement provoked. In the *New York Times*, the pages of the Food, Fashions, Family, Furnishings section, along with the Sunday magazine Features pages, became the primary sites for working out the meaning of the women's movement. It is in these "human interest" articles, along with those in popular news magazines like *Newsweek*, *Time*, and *Life*, that the media constructed an image of the women's movement that would speak both to the anxiety the movement created and the need to contain its threat.

Articles that sought to explain the movement to the uninitiated appeared in the mainstream press all through 1970. Feature articles by female journalists, who often expressed a sense of conversion to the cause, appeared in the news and women's magazines,[86] as well as in the *New York Times Magazine* and the paper's Food, Fashions, Family, Furnishings page. Articles like Marilyn Bender's "The Women Who'd Trade in Their Pedestal for Equality" and Susan Brownmiller's feature article for the *New York Times Magazine*, "Sisterhood Is Powerful: A Member of Women's Liberation Explains What It's All About," attempted to explain the movement from its genesis to descriptions of particular groups and their relationships with each other.[87] Articles for the Food, Fashions, Family, Furnishings page attempted to give the historical background of the movement, situating it in relation to the women's rights and suffragist movements of the mid-nineteenth and early twentieth centuries,[88] while others gave the dissenting view its hearing.[89] The overall effect of these articles was to not only record the presence of a feminist movement in American society and history but also to depict its overwhelming and disparate heterogeneity in the present.

The women's movement as reported in 1970 is not the one remembered today. Instead of the coherent portrait of the "overly aggressive, man-hating, ball-busting, selfish, hairy, extremist,"[90] of our contemporary cultural imaginary, the *New York Times*'s features articles often presented a movement that overwhelmed any simple representation of women and what they stood for. Yet such dizzying heterogeneity was accompanied by a palpable uneasiness evident in the use of words like *epidemic* in articles on the movement's growth and resulted, as 1970 progressed, in the repeated invocation of lesbianism as symptom and sign of that unease.

Marilyn Bender's article, which appeared in February 1970, detailed the movement's range of positions and goals and drew upon a disparate array of spokeswomen, including the not yet famous Kate Millett. The result is an effective representation of what Bender calls "an eclectic" and "amoebalike" movement.[91] Yet in the last part of the article, Bender's contorted presentation of the movement's position on marriage suggests that the call for economic independence and social autonomy, so apparent in the movement's other goals, could not be forthrightly demanded in relation to women's intimate relations with men. Bender places calls for the overthrow of the "archaic traditions of marriage" side by side with reassurances that not only are those calling for the overthrow of marriage themselves married but also that marriage between two people who are "in love" should be encouraged. The one mention of homosexuality in relation to marriage—"homosexuality may be one viable alternative"—is left hanging alone in its own one sentence paragraph with no commentary or discussion, as if a consequence of the breakdown of marriage has been glimpsed but cannot be acknowledged or incorporated within the narrative of feminism's emergence as a political movement.[92] Lesbianism appears, literally, as an interruption in Bender's confident and sympathetic appraisal of the movement, an interruption that is also a moment of revelation: women's liberation was indeed disruptive of the social institutions of marriage and family and the intimate sexual and emotional relations between men and women.

Susan Brownmiller's feature article for the *New York Times Magazine*, "Sisterhood Is Powerful," like Bender's, also offers a detailed presentation of the movement. Yet Brownmiller's view is that of an insider, her role as journalist explicitly put in the service of the women's liberation movement, and as such, she is keen to clear up any misunderstandings and to solve any apparent contradictions. Her appeal is to the "reasonable" woman (the one presumed to read the *New York Times*), and so her advocacy for the movement is given in the name of common sense. While she describes some of the more radical groups within women's liberation, she is always careful to suggest that their positions, such as the Feminists' statement that marriage is slavery, are minority opinions. Moreover, she gestures throughout the article toward an expansive common ground between the women of women's liberation and the readers of the *New York Times*, which is an assumed rather than expressed common ground of heterosexuality.

The accusation by male observers that the movement was nothing but a "lesbian plot" should be dismissed, according to Brownmiller, not in the name of solidarity with lesbians but in the knowledge that the "few militant lesbians" in the movement offered no threat to its basic heterosexuality. The lesbian issue, the reader is assured, is a "lavender herring" rather than a "lavender menace." The reassurance that heterosexuality is the common ground that unites women within the movement is then solidified with a quote from Anne Koedt at the end of the article: "When our movement gets strong, when men are forced to see us as a conscious issue, what are they going to do? . . . I don't know, but I think there's a part of men that really wants a human relationship, and that's going to be the saving grace for all of us."[93] Koedt's hope for a future in which women will be able to participate in heterosexual unions that are more "human," as a result of women's liberation forcing men to be more "conscious" of women, becomes the promise of women's liberation. Brownmiller reassures not only her male readers that women want to be with them but also her female readers that feminism will enable not just more heterosexuality but better heterosexuality. Women's liberation is transformed from a political movement that criticizes the economic, social, and cultural status of marriage to a movement that not only offers the hope of new and better heterosexual relations but will enable its continuity. But in order to assure the continuity of heterosexuality, homosexuality has to be invoked—as a name and as a possibility—as something to be disavowed or rejected. Brownmiller's refutation of lesbianism as a "lavender herring," like Bender's strangely muted utterance that "homosexuality may be one viable alternative" to marriage, depends upon its continued conjuration and only adds to the sense that lesbianism was a haunting presence within the movement—something that appeared between the lines and images of a respectable feminism in the making.

Coexisting with the informative articles offered by the Food, Fashions, Family, Furnishings page were profiles of movement "leaders." Through the writing of crude psychobiographies, journalists sought to explain the psychological and private contexts that would provoke women into becoming feminists. These profiles, along with articles about traditional female roles and those written by "authorities" on sex and gender, became, in relation to the figures of the lady protestor and urban guerrilla fighter, a commentary on the challenge made by the movement to traditional conceptions of femininity. It is out of this discourse on femininity, with heterosexuality as its organizing paradigm, that the figure of the feminist-as-lesbian starts to emerge within the context of popular representations of the women's movement.

By far the most expansive profile was by Paul Wilkes on Betty Friedan, which appeared in the *New York Times Magazine* at the end of November 1970.[94] Structured as a biography, the article looks back to Friedan's childhood and her past experiences in order to explain her current status as public feminist. Wilkes tries to fit Friedan into a well-worn narrative, that of the ugly girl who can't get a man. Quotes from Friedan are used to bolster the story: "I was that girl with all A's and I wanted boys worse than anything." Her reason for turning down a graduate fellowship in psychology is presented in terms of her fear that she would become "the old maid college teacher." The portrait of Friedan as a young woman becomes one of loneliness, and neediness, focusing on her status as an outsider (her Jewishness, like her supposed ugliness, given as a reason for her lack of friends and boys) and resulting in her discontent and restlessness. Yet the logic of the story breaks down when Friedan meets her future husband, Carl Friedan. In this part of the story, Friedan gets the man and the life of a respectable, working, middle-class woman—everything she had feared she wouldn't get. What ultimately becomes the source of her discontent, then, is not a lack of men or sexual fulfillment but her inability to be what she thought she wanted to be. Friedan finds that she doesn't fit into the role of the wife who cooks, nurtures, and stays alluring for her husband, all while also having her own career. This realization does not come from a simple refusal of that life but from an attempt to occupy it and her failure to do so. Wilkes ends his article with Friedan's plaintive, "I don't want to go to bed alone until the revolution is over," reassuring his readers that Friedan still wants "boys." The reassurance of Friedan's heterosexuality is undercut by the discomforting conclusion that middle-class femininity is a set of social practices and "cultural competencies" that can leave women feeling dissatisfied and unfulfilled.[95] Even if Friedan were to get a boy, the point of her story, her book, and her politics was to state that it wouldn't be enough. In this story, feminism does not come from the outside, as a challenge to the precepts and privileges of middle-class life, but from within. Friedan's feminism is an effect, not simply a critique, of bourgeois heteronormativity.

The problematization of femininity as a set of culturally inscribed social practices, which secured the privileged domain of middle-class hetero-respectability as national norm, was also apparent in antifeminist views—evidence of a more general discursive shift on gender and sexuality in the late 1960s.[96] In the feature article "She Takes a Stand against Liberation," Joan Cook profiles Mrs. Helen B. Andelin, author of *Fascinating Womanhood*, a book that instructs women on how to become "domestic goddesses." Femininity as role-playing is discussed quite freely, and Andelin essentially presents a set of techniques for becoming the ideal wife and mother. As in the profile of Betty Friedan, the idea that femininity is a practice and not an innate state is assumed. Moreover, the idea that women can "do" femininity more or less effectively produces the reciprocal idea that they can "do" masculinity more or less effectively. Andelin warns her readers against wearing "tweeds or tailored clothes" and dismisses equal rights legislation by declaring that women "would have to take on masculine traits" in order to do a "man's job" and should, therefore, stay at home. There is no suggestion that it is impossible for women to assume masculine traits, just a warning about the dangers of doing so. In her rejection of women's liberation, Andelin doesn't so much project the norm of middle-class femininity as reveal its precariousness.

Thus, while it is an uncontroversial assumption in both articles that femininity is a set of practices and techniques, there is a pervasive anxiety concerning the willingness of white, middle-class women to reproduce it. Wilkes had to remind his readers that Friedan was still in need of men despite her feminism, and Andelin felt the need to warn women against exhibiting so-called masculine traits. The perception that gender can be done more or less well, and that it can operate dissonantly within the terms of a heterosexual duality, produced the attendant anxiety that women were not the sum of their roles and that they could, and did, transgress the gender divide. Women's liberation, in its questioning of the desirability of marriage and the inevitability of motherhood and its vociferous debunking of "normal" sexuality, only accentuated the sense that femininity as a social norm was under attack. As a consequence, reasserting gender distinctions through the reproduction of idealized bodies, and accusing feminists who refuted or resisted those distinctions of being lesbians, became a dominant tactic of the mainstream media in the latter half of 1970.

Recourse to scientific authority and the recuperation of a biologized notion of sexual difference became another way of reasserting gender distinctions. The featured article for the *New York Times Magazine* on October 25, "Male Dominance? Yes, Alas. A Sexist Plot? No," by the Rutgers anthropologist Lionel Tiger, was the most conspicuous example. Adopting an apologetic and dispassionate tone, Tiger (one of the posse of critics *Time* used in its "Women's Lib: A Second Look" attack on Kate Millett) asserts that patriarchy came about not out of any malevolent intent of men but through a "biological heritage" that is "millions of years old."[97] Conceding that advances in modern technology had created virtual equality between men and women in many areas of life, he nevertheless asserts that biology still determines the behavior of each sex: women will always be more passive and nurturing, and men will be more aggressive. In Tiger's biologizing view, the duality between men and women is fixed and absolute with no possibility of ambiguity or variation. Any attempt to overturn "biological heritage," he warns, would have grave consequences—for the women who advocate it and for their children too. While Tiger's performance of a dispassionate tone casts his arguments in terms of "facts" rather than politics, the effect of his argument is to insinuate the unnaturalness of feminists who would question the biological basis of heterosexual relations. By going against millions of years of biological history, an essentially static history in Tiger's view, feminists were turning against their own nature and risking the happiness of their children as a result.

If Tiger insinuates a portrayal of women liberationists as unnatural, Morton Hunt's article in *Playboy* fleshes it out.[98] *Playboy*'s preoccupation with, and marketing of, male-orientated heterosexuality made it a fitting venue for a particularly revealing article on the anxieties surrounding the threat posed to the heterosexual order by women's liberation. With admirable historical detail, Hunt explains the context for the movement's emergence and some of the valid reasons for its existence. Yet, despite his apparent magnanimity toward the goals of women's liberation, Hunt's ultimate objective is, like Tiger's, to draw the line between social conceptions of gender difference and biological ones. While it may be understandable that women should want to fight for equal pay and equal access to professional jobs, and that distinctions between female and male intelligence are spurious, it nevertheless remains true, according to Hunt, that women's essential nature is different from that of men. It is the "complementarity" of "heterosexual love," in which male and female "serve and complete each other" in a bond that is "so necessary and fulfilling," that women are at their most content. It is "productive of well-being," according to Hunt (and his attendant flock of "experts," including Dr. Spock), for "man and woman to look different, smell different, act somewhat different."[99]

Hunt's sentimental and lyrical defense of the heterosexual union, which he sees as a practice that leads to self-fulfillment for both men and women, is voiced in relation to his intemperate condemnation of women's liberationists, who, in their extremism, threaten to spoil the fun for everyone. The article begins with Hunt's description of the "muscularly named" Cell 16 group from Boston, who, wearing "tight pants, polo shirts and heavy custom-made mountain boots," looked like "pre-adolescent tomboys spoiling for a fight."[100] These women, Hunt warns his male readers, are the "kookie . . . advance scouts" of the "vast, slow moving army of females" that make up the women's movement.[101] Women like Roxanne Dunbar, "with her monkish haircut, karate postures and vicious rhetoric," and "Abby Rockefeller, with her bare calloused feet and battered forehead" (thanks to her insistence on smashing bricks in half with her head), become the exemplars of antifemininity (they "may not be *your* kind of girls") and serve as Hunt's portrait of liberationists made ugly by their refusal to be girls. His repeated warnings that liberationists are not simply lesbians and frigid neurotics tends to cement the association, and the reader is left with an uncompromising portrait of ugly, humorless, karate-chopping, man-hating neurotics. The fear that the liberationists might be, in fact, a bunch of lesbians whose frigidity is more a refusal of men than a symptom of sexual incapacity, becomes evident in the fact that they are also described as fierce and uncompromising zealots out to destroy the happy union of heterosexual love. They may be ugly and masculine, but they are also "strident . . . fiery evangelists and raging nihilists" (i.e., political activists as well as sexual perverts) who want to wipe out "*all* role differences" and who are after the "bigger game—the withering away of heterosexual desire and heterosexual intercourse."[102]

Hunt's castration-anxiety portrait of women liberationists as pathological fundamentalists is found in fragments and innuendoes elsewhere in the media coverage of the movement. In letters to the editor and op-ed pieces in the *New York Times*, negative responses to the movement, primarily from women, are couched in terms of sexual and psychological dysfunction. Rather than objecting to the material goals of women's liberation (which are generally accepted as valid), most commentators and letter writers direct their displeasure at the liberationists, who become figures or embodiments of a shameful and embarrassing kind of womanhood. Thus, for example, Susan L. Peck in her letter to the editor describes liberationists as suffering from "personal maladjustment covering a large spectrum of ills from sexual problems to ego-image."[103] Similarly, in her op-ed piece for the *New York Times*, Jean Stafford writes of the "belligerents" whose "hollering" and "jokelessness" only "obfuscate[s] a good many justified grievances," and whose "most hysterical" and "most puritanical" of "scolds seem to elide" the fact that there is "a difference between men and women."[104]

By December 1970 and *Time*'s "Women's Lib: A Second Look" at the women's movement, the association between humorless zealotry, sexual and emotional maladjustment, and women's liberation had been repeatedly circulating in the mainstream media. Any sense of the movement's heterogeneity and "amoebalike" form, evident in the *New York Times*'s coverage of movement protests and the ERA fight earlier in the year, had given way to a repeated and insistent portrayal of women liberationists as dysfunctional and pathological figures associated with the spectral images of urban guerrilla fighters and the even more threatening figures of the black militant and Third World revolutionary. The recuperation of a biologizing discourse of gender in relation to the circulation of these figures worked to evoke collective memories of sexual and racial degeneracy, which had first defined white, middle-class femininity as national norm in the nineteenth century. The lesbian, as a boundary figure between white respectability and class and racial otherness, became the means through which a feminism that could be reincorporated into the domain of white femininity as national norm was negotiated.

Indeed, the issue that came to dominate coverage of the movement in the last month of 1970 (and for the next few years) was lesbianism. Judy Klemesrud's article for the *New York Times*, which was about the press conference called by "leaders" of the movement after *Time*'s attack, captured the melodramatic tone of the moment: "The lesbian issue, which has been hidden away like a demented child ever since the women's liberation movement came into being in 1968, was brought out of the closet yesterday."[105] The lesbian as the "demented child" of the movement suggests not only the notions of degeneracy, immaturity, and unreasonableness already associated with lesbianism in the postwar years but the notion that she haunted not just women's liberation but the nation—its monstrous offspring hidden away but now fighting to get out.

The ambivalence intrinsic to the lesbian's effectiveness as a symbolic figure for women's liberation was also a product of the shift in the discursive production of lesbianism in the postwar era. By the early 1960s, the sexuality and lifestyle of the lesbian were publicized and discussed in a variety of public domains—including mass-mediated pulp novels, popular psychology, and journalistic exposés.[106] In contrast to the insinuations and allusions through which notions of lesbianism circulated in the early twentieth century, by the late 1960s lesbianism was identified as a pressing social problem needing legal and medical intervention. Lesbians were creatures of publicity and seen as members of a group or "sexual underworld," rather than as isolated and sick individuals. Instead of lonely outsiders who could occasionally provoke a voyeuristic and diagnostic curiosity on the part of politicians and doctors, they were seen as threats to the social fabric of American society because they created a different "way of life," one that challenged the dominion of the heterosexual, middle-class home. And as a social problem, the postwar lesbian was a very public symbol of a rampant and predatory female sexuality. Sensationalistic media exposés of gay and lesbian underworlds, along with equally sensationalistic studies by popular psychologists of the "hidden disease" of female homosexuality, were part of a postwar cultural context that sought to express as well as contain changing conceptions of female sexuality, which were also part of a changing society.[107] As a highly potent and contorted figure of social change, then, the lesbian symbolized not only the disciplinary power of medical, social, and cultural authorities but also the emergent subcultures and counterpublics they were attempting to control.[108]

Postwar reconfigurations of the lesbian were part of a radical reorganization of the discourses of sexuality in the 1950s and 1960s. The studies of male and female sexuality by Alfred Kinsey in the late 1940s and early 1950s, and Masters and Johnson's study of the physiognomy of sexual behavior in the 1960s, were dominant cultural reference points for a conception of sexuality that had become unmoored from the moralizing discourses of Cold War domestic ideology and its central animating figure: the married couple. Sex and marriage, as Kinsey's studies made emphatically clear, were far from coextensive. The sexual appetites of men and women were directed at a variety of objects and satisfied by a variety of methods. Kinsey's studies, especially *Sexual Behavior in the Human Male*, which was published with great fanfare in 1948 and enjoyed multiple reprintings, declared that homosexual behaviors were far more widespread in American society than had previously been thought, a claim which he supported through data presented as scientific evidence and exhaustive personal testimonies of "ordinary" Americans. Through their documentation of the diversity of practitioners and practices, the studies also made it worryingly clear that there were no physiological or social markers that would make "a homosexual" obviously different from their straight counterparts. Homosexuality was perceived as a widespread phenomenon in American society at the same time that it became less about a distinct type of person and more about practices that exceeded identity. In tandem with Kinsey's studies, Masters and Johnson's concentration on the biophysicality of sexual practices further removed the discourses of sexuality from that of morality and specific—stigmatized—bodies. Through their carefully calibrated scientific observations of the female body during intercourse, they debunked the myth that a woman's sexual pleasure and satisfaction was to be found vaginally and, by extension, in her reproductive role. Thanks to Masters and Johnson, the clitoral orgasm gained the stamp of scientific proof, and female sexuality too became the locus of an anxiety-laden epistemic uncertainty. Rather than part of the holistic idea of romantic love and marriage, sex was about human "behavior" and practices on and between bodies. If you could have sex and do it well, then you were a healthy and fulfilled human being. In this context, the lesbian was just one, although the most threatening, configuration of a "single" female sexuality in the 1960s. Others included, as Hilary Radner points out, the single girl of Helen Gurley Brown's *Sex and the Single Girl* (1962) and popular cultural icons like the Bond girls. What these conceptions of female sexuality represented, as Radner makes clear, is the decoupling of sexuality and the location of fulfilled selfhood in the consumer driven practice of a "healthy" sex life, a life that desired—and needed—a variety of objects.[109]

The difference between Brown's single girl and the feminist-as-lesbian, of course, lies in the connection between the lesbian's "single" female sexuality and the feminist's political activism. The swinging single girl of the 1960s might, like the feminist, believe that "each woman has the right to fulfillment defined in her own terms," but unlike the feminist, she did not question the social institutions of American heteronormativity or their capitalist underpinnings.[110] While one could argue, therefore, as Radner does, that the construction of new sexualities based on individual "fulfillment" rather than reproduction were endemic to the culture as a whole in the 1960s,[111] it was the women's and gay liberation movements that politicized the discourses of sexuality and made their relation to the public worlds of American business and governance explicit. The irony today, of course, is that the feminist-as-lesbian as an image memory of women's liberation tends to signify the perceived essentialism of women's liberation, when, in actuality, she emerged as a symptom and effect of the movement's radical questioning of essentializing notions of sexual difference.

Paradoxically, perhaps, the feminist-as-lesbian was also symptomatic of the "apprehension of massed bodies" of women whose primary association was with other women. The sensationalistic exposés of gay and lesbian underworlds, which appeared in the postwar decades, suggested an "epidemic" of homosexuality overtaking American cities. Jess Stearn, in *The Grapevine* from 1964, writes of a "hidden populace" of lesbians who were part of a "vast, sprawling grapevine" who met in secret and "*crowded* the publishing, theatrical, and modeling fields, and studied the arts and sciences."[112] While in the 1950s, the popular psychologist Frank Caprio writes, citing another "expert" in the field, that "homosexual attachments among women are far more prevalent than the public suspects," and that "lesbianism is becoming an increasingly important problem."[113] The perceptions of Caprio and Stearn, that gays and lesbians had formed their own subterranean worlds and posed an increasing threat to the world of middle-class respectability, formed part of the general cultural paranoia of Cold War American society.

At the same time, both Stearn and Caprio, like other social commentators in the postwar era, pointed to the social freedoms experienced by men and women during the Second World War and a widespread feminist sensibility throughout the twentieth century as reasons for the "increasing" incidence of lesbianism in American life. Caprio writes that the feminist movement of the early twentieth century had "given women 'Freedom from Man'" and an opportunity to express their "masculine component," of which smoking cigarettes was one such expression.[114] A sense of proliferating freedoms for women were, along with a pathological sexuality, part of the portrait of lesbianism in the postwar era. The lesbian was no longer just a lonely discontented woman who wanted to be a man, she was one of thousands, part of an "epidemic" of women who were forming their own communities and "grapevines" and living lives of relative "Freedom from Man."

And, as Madeline Davis and Elizabeth Kennedy show in their oral history of a working-class butch-femme community in midcentury Buffalo, *Boots of Leather, Slippers of Gold*, protopolitical communities of lesbians were able, from the 1940s onward, to form social worlds that were, if only tenuously, distinct from heterosexual, middle-class society. Similarly, John D'Emilio's history of the homophile movement in the 1950s and 1960s reveals that the postwar decades saw the emergence not only of quasi-organized communities of gays and lesbians but also of political groups like the Mattachine Society and the Daughters of Bilitis, who were intent on gaining social visibility and legitimacy for lesbians and gays.[115] The growth of lesbian communities with distinct cultures and forms of social organization, as well as an increasingly politicized demand for social visibility, were also part of the context from which the lesbian became such a potent figure for women's liberation. That the virtual possibilities of lesbian publics and social worlds was often found in the melodramatic sexiness of pulp novels, in working-class butch-femme communities, and in the racial mix of urban ghettos and underworlds, only added to the sense of "apprehension" of women's liberation's massed bodies.[116]

CONCLUSION

As an image memory of women's liberation, the feminist-as-lesbian figure, drawn in the press first through allusion and insinuation and then direct accusation, is an effect and a remainder of the mainstream media's attempt to fashion a representational frame for its coverage of women's liberation. Rather than the movement's dizzying heterogeneity, which journalists and commentators struggled to define or account for, the feminist-as-lesbian figure was a cohering and limiting portrait that depicted the women's liberationist as a fanatical and irrational pervert—a portrait that worked to reproduce and redefine the parameters of a normal, respectable femininity that could also incorporate a feminism that would not threaten its comforting constraints. Conversely, the figure was also a symptom of the social anxieties of the postwar era—anxieties that formed the impetus and the context for the emergence of women's liberation as a social movement. Women's liberation's publicly articulated association (at least initially) with Third World national liberation struggles, the Black Panthers, and other domestic liberation movements, in conjunction with its strong critique of marriage and bourgeois norms more generally, challenged some of the most sacrosanct parts of Cold War domestic ideology and explicitly and viscerally brought to the foreground of the national political sphere the diverse constituencies of politically active and brazenly unfeminine women in America.

By the end of the 1960s and with the escalation of violence against the nationalist and new social movements of the era, white femininity was being seen—on television and in the print media—out of context. As a locus for the production of national belonging, white femininity could not function as a stable site for securing the pure space of American citizenship; instead the spectacle of white, middle-class women as urban guerrillas, rather than lady protestors, suggested a nation that had become strange to itself. With the emergence of women's liberation onto the national scene by 1970, the lesbian became part of an affective economy, along with the black militant and urban guerrilla, that associated gender transgression with sexual pathology, political radicalism, and racial otherness. The circulation of these figures, and the histories of social exclusions they evoked, reinvested white femininity with the comforting aura of bourgeois hetero-respectability and homeliness. For women's liberation, the struggle over the meaning of lesbianism it was now engaged in would not, simply, be a struggle over the inclusion of sexual minorities into the larger body of the movement. Rather, it would be a struggle over the relationship of feminism to the whiteness and bourgeois values that marked the privileged domain of national belonging.

Which brings me back to Kate Millett: "the lesbian" of Time's expose in December 1970. By framing the question of Millett's sexuality, and by inference the sexuality of all women's liberationists, in terms of her being a non-woman, Time, like Irving Howe and the rest of the critics in the magazine's "Women's Lib: A Second Look," risked exposing the incoherency out of which ideological constructions of a race and class-based femininity were constructed as national norm. Ironically, it is this kind of unwelcome ambiguity concerning who American women were in 1970 that the drawing of the prototypical women's liberationist sitting at the center of the "Women's Lib: A Second Look" article so viscerally captures. In Flying, her autobiographical account of her participation in the early years of women's liberation, Millett also captures this ambiguity when she writes of the moment at a movement meeting when she was asked to call herself a lesbian:

Five hundred people looking at me. Are you a lesbian? Everything pauses, faces look up in terrible silence. I hear them not breathe. That word in public, the word I waited half a lifetime to hear. Finally I am accused. "Say it! Say you are a Lesbian." Yes I said. Yes because I know what she means. The line goes, inflexible as a fascist edict, that bisexuality is a cop-out. Yes I said yes I am a Lesbian. It was the last strength I had.[117]

Millett's hesitancy in naming herself, even though she had waited "half a lifetime" to hear the word *lesbian* said publicly, is due, in the most immediate sense, to the fact that she was married at the time to the sculptor Fumio Yoshimura. Yet Millett's hesitancy is also an admission of the failure of any word or interpretation to capture or define someone's political or sexual possibilities. The moment when feminism and lesbianism became explosively conjoined, then, was a moment of acute ambiguity and ambivalence that has, like Millett's moment of misleading clarity, been covered over by an image memory that seems, at first glance, to be obvious in its meaning. Millett's sexuality, despite *Time*'s attempts to show otherwise, was not something that could easily be explained or defined. Indeed, her inability to "come out" in a way that would suggest the full complexity of her sexual relationships and practices is a premonition, perhaps, of what some of the costs of asserting sexual identities in the name of women's and gay liberation would be. Likewise, women's liberation was, in 1970, a movement in the making and in the midst of challenging social institutions and norms. What those challenges would bring was unclear and would depend upon the outcome of a cultural struggle and social war being fought in the cultural domains and class- and race-riven streets of American society. Race, gender, and sexuality were categories of experience and political mobilization brought into question by women's liberation and other feminist movements in 1970 rather than certainties from which political demands could be made.

It is out of this ambiguity and ambivalence that the figure of the feminist-as-lesbian became not simply a representative figure produced by the mainstream media but the site of a struggle over the meanings of women's liberation and the possibilities of its political horizons. The second-wave movement in 1970 was not a settled, uniform organization with a clear set of goals. Rather it was a gloriously undisciplined phenomenon characterized by a disorienting array of differently aligned cohorts and a radical questioning of the social order that often brought the most sanctified of common-sense beliefs under review. The configuration of the feminist-as-lesbian, as drawn in the press and popular discourse, was an attempt to efface the tumultuousness of the movement's presence in American society and to resettle the internal borders of a nation that imagined itself as white, middle-class, and monogamously heterosexual. Yet, as an effect of these subjugating forces, the figure is also a remainder of the upset that the movement caused in its challenging of the institutions of heteronormativity, bourgeois respectability, and the cultural imaginings those institutions and values incited.

2

"GOODBYE TO ALL THAT"

Killing Daddy's Girls and the
Revolt against Proper Femininity

Unhampered by propriety, niceness, discretion, public opinion, "morals," the respect of assholes, always funky, dirty, low-down SCUM [Society for Cutting Up
Men] gets around . . . and around and around . . . they've seen the whole show—
every bit of it—the fucking scene, the dyke scene—they've covered the whole
waterfront, been under every dock and pier—the peter pier, the pussy pier . . .
you've got to go through a lot of sex to get to anti-sex, and SCUM's been through it
all, and they're now ready for a new show.—VALERIE SOLANAS, SCUM Manifesto

They were admired, envied, pitied, theorized over until they were sick of it, offered
drastic solutions or silly choices that no one could take seriously. They got all kinds
of advice from the growing armies of marriage and child-guidance counselors, psy-
chotherapists, and armchair psychologists, on how to adjust to their role as housewives. No other road to fulfillment was offered to American women in the middle
of the twentieth century.—BETTY FRIEDAN, The Feminine Mystique

On May 1, 1970, on the opening night of the nationally organized Second
Congress to Unite Women in New York, a group of women who would
later call themselves the Radicalesbians dimmed the lights in the audito-
rium, stripped off their coats and shirts revealing T-shirts with *Lavender
Menace* emblazoned on them, and took the stage, accusing the women's
movement of "sexism" and of "discriminating" against lesbians within their
own ranks.[1] The group also distributed copies of their position paper, "The
Woman Identified Woman," in which they not only made an explicit connection between lesbianism and women's liberation but, in their description of the lesbian as "the rage of all women condensed to the point of
explosion," also suggested that the lesbian was the symbol—the embodiment even—of women's liberation.[2] For two hours, congress participants—

including the not yet infamous Kate Millett—enthusiastically accepted the Lavender Menace's invitation to come up to the stage to discuss the difficulties lesbians faced living in a "heterosexist" society. Although the congress as a whole was a tumultuous affair, with conflicts over movement "stars" and class leading some women, as Alice Echols notes, to rename the meeting "The Congress to Divide Women," the zap action by the Lavender Menace was deemed a great success by the congress participants, many of whom enjoyed what Ann Snitow described as the action's "wit and vaudevillian charm."[3] In the final meeting the resolutions proposed by the Lavender Menace were adopted by the congress, including: "1. Women's Liberation is a lesbian plot. 2. Whenever the label lesbian is used against the movement collectively or against women individually, it is to be affirmed, not denied."[4] Meanwhile, the Lavender Menace's position paper "Woman Identified Woman" soon "swept through the nation's women's liberation groups," becoming one of the most influential, and controversial, papers of the women's liberation movement.[5]

It was Sidney Abbott and Barbara Love in *Sappho Was a Right-On Woman*, published in 1972, who first employed a narrative of crisis for the events of 1970—including the expulsion, by the National Organization for Women (NOW), of lesbians from the New York chapter of NOW, the Lavender Menace zap action at the Second Congress to Unite Women, and *Time's* "Women's Lib: A Second Look" article on Millett and the movement in December of that year. Understanding a crisis event in sociological terms as a "social drama" with the potential for a creative or recuperative transformation of social relations, Abbott and Love describe the events of 1970 as necessary upheavals in the movement's quest for a "new equilibrium": because of the crisis over lesbianism women's liberation could now imagine its constituency differently and conceive of its feminist project in less heterosexist ways.[6] Abbott and Love's narrativization of these events echoes through the few historical studies and memoirs of women's liberation, nearly all of which consistently interpret the eruption of the lesbian issue in 1970 as a major turning point in the trajectory of the movement. Although unlike Abbott and Love, these later accounts tend to interpret these events less as necessary upheavals in the progressive development of the movement and more as inaugurating the fragmentation of the second wave into discrete identity-based movements.[7]

The significance of the zap action by the Lavender Menace in historical accounts of the women's liberation movement stands in contradistinction to the number of people it involved and the range of contentious issues that were being discussed at the Second Congress to Unite Women as well as within the women's liberation movement more generally at that time. The Lavender Menace zap action was just one of many unscheduled events at the congress. Other groups had effectively charged the conference partici- pants and the wider women's liberation movement of being classist and racist, and the workshops that followed the zap action included ones on class and race as well as lesbianism.[8] Furthermore, the events Abbott and Love describe all took place in New York and involved the same small cast of characters, while most of the initial upheaval over lesbianism in NOW was felt largely within the confines of the organization's New York chapter rather than nationwide.[9] Elsewhere—in terms of constituency and geogra- phy—the "lesbian issue" had either been broached without uproar or ap- parent division or was not a matter of primary concern. As Abbott and Love acknowledge, in other parts of the country women's liberation groups had managed to think and write about lesbianism and the women's move- ment in a much more "gradual and natural" way than had happened in New York in 1970.[10] The West Coast Regional Membership of NOW, for example, had passed a resolution in April 1970 demanding NOW's full ac- ceptance of lesbians and lesbianism as a feminist issue. And the *Berkeley Tribe*, a West Coast underground newspaper, carried articles in November 1970 on gay and lesbian themes that clearly and matter-of-factly made the connections between the women's and gay liberation movements.[11]

Conversely, much of the positioning of women's liberation groups in 1970 had little, or nothing, to do with lesbianism. As Wini Breines notes in her study of the early years of the women's liberation movement, many groups, including Boston's Bread and Roses, identified as socialist femi- nists and offered anticapitalist and anti-imperialist positions that high- lighted issues like racist state population controls and sexist admissions policies to schools and universities.[12] Groups like the radical feminist Red- stockings and the socialist feminist Chicago Women's Liberation Union (CWLU) concerned themselves, on the one hand, with establishing that the oppression of women by men was the primary contradiction in society and, on the other, with situating sexism within a general system of political and economic inequity. Neither group included in its initial manifesto acknowledgment of lesbianism as an issue relevant to their political plat- form. While the CWLU drew upon the abstract political language of uto- pian Marxism in order to write about women's "social situation" and the political and economic "institutions" that shaped it, the Redstockings utilized the counterculture rhetoric of righteous anger and outrage to argue for the overthrow of a male-dominated society. According to the Redstockings, the "domination" suffered by women was that perpetuated by "male supremacy" rather than institutions.[13] The CWLU avoided discussing the sexual politics of heterosexuality altogether in its inaugural manifesto. And although the Redstockings located the heterosexual couple as the foundation for all socially exploitative relations, it did not result in the group moving toward the political possibilities of lesbianism for radical feminism. Instead, as Karla Jay notes of her brief membership in Redstockings, it mostly resulted in an obsessive preoccupation with men: "Many Redstockings talked about men all the time the way dieters obsess about food. There were times when some of us, including a few of the heterosexuals, felt it would be more productive to focus on ways in which women could interact with each other positively."[14]

Other feminist constituencies like those in the more formal and centrally organized NOW, as well as the feminist groups and organizations emerging out of the black and Chicano nationalist movements, focused, in different ways, on economic and social justice issues. NOW's political platform in 1970 included abortion rights, free daycare for women workers, and the passing of the Equal Rights Amendment (ERA). Chicana groups like Hijas de Cuauhtemoc, which emerged out of the Chicano student movement in California in 1970, and black feminist organizations like the Third World Women's Alliance, which had formed in 1969 out of the Student Nonviolent Coordinating Committee's (SNCC) Black Women's Liberation Caucus, articulated an anti-imperialist critique of the racist underpinnings of Western capitalism. The cultural struggle over representations of femininity for these groups took place within the context of the freedom movements from which they emerged and tended to focus on the social and psychic effects of racist stereotypes. Although sexuality as a field of experience was included in the discussions these groups participated in, both in their consciousness-raising efforts and the "print cultures" they engendered, the focus—at least in 1970—was on reproductive rights and the contesting of machismo in personal and political relationships within the community rather than an explicit critique of heterosexism more generally.[15] In Toni Cade's mass-marketed black feminist anthology *The Black Woman*, published in 1970, none of the contributors thought it necessary to mention lesbianism or argue for its relevance to their feminist positions. Of much more concern was finding an effective way for black men and women to work together within the Black Power movement. While a few contributors did discuss sexuality, this was done solely in terms of male-female relationships, and a more expansive discussion of black female sexuality was avoided.[16]

The question I pursue in this and the next chapter is not so much why "the lesbian issue" came to shape subsequent narratives of the emergence of women's liberation' as a distinct political movement but how it did so. In chapter 1 I examined the ways in which the media's coverage of the movement contributed to the configuration of the women's liberationist as the white, angry, sick, and demented feminist-as-lesbian exhibited in *Time*'s "Women's Lib: A Second Look" exposé of Kate Millett in December 1970. Here I approach the figure from the opposite direction. By tracking the way particular terms, figures, and phrases become charged with meaning as a result of their circulation in the public statements, position papers, and polemics of the movement, I examine the way in which the lesbian became not just the figure through which the media increasingly organized its interpretation and representation of women's liberation as a rebellion from the privileged domain of bourgeois femininity but also the figure through which women's liberation took shape as a movement of feminist revolt. Part of my intention, then, is to demonstrate the way in which the rhetorical terms of the movement's feminist revolt inevitably implicate it in a mass-mediated domain of proper femininity even if, and perhaps especially when, it also takes up an abjected figure of that domain as its primary figure of revolt. But if the movement reveals the grounds of its feminist rebellion to be the domain of a mass-mediated femininity, then its figuring of that rebellion through the lesbian also enacts a process of alienation from that domain—making strange the norms and aspirational values of a femininity that, in Lauren Berlant's terms, "magnetizes" women to the promise of a good and better life.[17] Ultimately, the women's liberation movement's endorsement of the lesbian as a figure of feminist revolt vividly illuminates this uneasy ambivalence between an attachment to and estrangement from proper femininity.

I begin with the movement's press conference in support of Kate Millett following the *Time* attack in December 1970, and then I track back and out to Robin Morgan's widely circulated clarion call for the separation of women's liberation from the New Left, "Goodbye to All That," to Valerie Solanas's scum *Manifesto*, published in 1968, and finally to Betty Friedan's 1963 classic, *The Feminine Mystique*. I read these texts as participating in the enactment of women's liberation becoming a distinct feminist movement rather than as taxonomical descriptions of its social and political arrival onto the scene of American history. By being attentive to the metaphors, phrases, figures, and deployments of slang or colloquial speech in these texts, I want to examine the work they do: how they produced alignments between particular subjects, objects, and collectivities and not others and how, as a consequence, they could incite feelings of belonging and identification for some women and not for others.[18] In particular, I focus on the dynamic force of anger as an emotion of *againstness* that, to follow Sara Ahmed's argument, gives a movement like women's liberation its particular shape: its constituency, its style of presentation and address, and the objects through which its protest is enacted.[19] The above texts express their anger as a discomfort with and rebellion against the heteronormative demands of both the mainstream and counterculture public spheres. They all consistently turn to the lesbian as the figure that could animate and illustrate that anger or, in the case of Friedan, figure the fear of its repercussions, and as such, they participate in the enactment of women's liberation as a movement that is shaped by what it is against.

In chapter 1 I read along the grain of the mainstream media's coverage of the movement's emergence as a major news story and event in 1970 in order to dispel the illusion of coherency in the media's representations of the movement. Returning to the range of the mainstream media's coverage of the movement revealed not only how the lesbian was neither an inevitable nor natural figure of representation for the movement but also how the media's struggle to represent the movement simultaneously exposed the cultural and political stakes of the movement's protest—not simply *for* women's emancipation but *against* the heteronormative claims of white privilege as a national norm. In this chapter I read along the grain of the women's liberation archive in order to counter subsequent critiques leveled by feminist historians and theorists that the women's liberation movement was a white, middle-class movement overly preoccupied with bourgeois problems. For these critics, the movement was too quick in assuming a commonality of experience for all women (a criticism of course that echoes one made at the time by men in the New Left and Black Power movements as well as African American women in the black feminist movement). This is a critique most often made in relation to figures like Friedan and Morgan, but it is also one directed at lesbian feminism of the

1970s, which has been accused of calling for a separatist feminist politics on the basis of an implicitly racist and explicitly essentialist notion of women's innate difference from men. I question such critiques because they tend toward the tautological—the women's liberation movement was a white, middle-class women's movement because the women in it were predominantly white and middle class—and because such accusations leave unexamined the way in which the white middle-classness of women's liberation was a historical effect of its moment of invention. Indeed, instead of simply confirming this critique by revealing the ideological assumptions at work in texts like *The Feminine Mystique*, my reading of this archive is an attempt to track the ways in which it produced women's liberation as a particular form of (white) feminism that emerges in relation to but distinct from proper femininity. By enacting their rebellion from the claims of normative femininity through the figure of the lesbian, the texts of women's liberation do not simply reproduce white, middle-class femininity. Instead, they do something to it, and in the case of Valerie Solanas and even Betty Friedan, they come close to exploding it as a fantasy worth investing in.

"WOMEN'S LIBERATION"

On December 17, 1970, in New York City, Kate Millett, surrounded by supportive fellow participants in the women's liberation movement, including Ti-Grace Atkinson, Florynce Kennedy, and Gloria Steinem, read the following statement to a group of national and local journalists:

> As members of Women's Liberation we are concerned with all forms of human oppression, including the oppression of homosexuals. Therefore, we deplore *Time* magazine's malicious attack on the movement, operating from the premise that it could malign or invalidate us by associating us with Lesbianism. Far from being vulnerable to this clear appeal to prejudice, we take this occasion to express our solidarity with the struggle of homosexuals to attain their liberation in a sexist society which oppresses them legally through the penal code, denies them economic security in employment, and subjects them to every manner of social and psychological harassment.
>
> Women's Liberation and Homosexual Liberation are both struggling toward a common goal: a society free from defining and categorizing people by virtue of gender and/or sexual preference. "Les-

bian" is a label used as a psychic weapon to keep women locked into their male-defined "feminine role." The essence of that role is that a woman is defined in terms of her relationship to men. A woman is called a Lesbian when she functions autonomously. Women's autonomy is what Women's Liberation is all about.[20]

The press conference was organized as a direct response to *Time*'s "Women's Lib: A Second Look" and stands as one of the more public attempts by feminists to counter the discourse on lesbianism circulating in the national media in 1970. The press conference was organized by a variety of women from different groups and organizations who chose, as the first sentence of the statement indicates, to speak as members of "Women's Liberation," rather than as individual representatives of particular groups. While the decision to speak as "Women's Liberation," according to Abbott and Love, was taken to counteract the impression that the statement was representative of any particular group's position, the effect was an even more emphatic, if unintentional, suggestion that all feminists were in agreement with the positions articulated in the statement.[21] This show of a misleading unity and homogeneity, in conjunction with the national press coverage of the conference, combined to produce an imprint event, part of what we might call, in Foucauldian terms, an "emergent" moment in the women's liberation movement's entry into history, whereby history is understood, to paraphrase Drucilla Cornell, as not just there but there as it is known.[22]

Emergence, according to Foucault, is a "moment of arising," when the eruption of forces from "the wings to center stage" produces an apparition: a new stage in the struggle for social presence and knowledge that becomes decisive, not as "the final term" in a historical development but as an "episode" in a "series of subjugations."[23] Although Foucault tends to work on a larger historical canvas than I am doing here, his concept of emergence is still helpful for understanding more localized historical "eruptions," when particular fields of experience become problematic and, as if in a flash, highly contested. To think of the "crisis" over lesbianism in 1970 as an eruption of forces that augments a shift in how lesbianism, feminism, sexuality, and femininity are known in the mid-twentieth century in the United States is to locate that shift not in the designed intent of movement activists, nor in the nefarious practices of the media, but in the "interstices" of their confrontation with each other. The association of lesbianism with feminism, which had haunted feminism through inference and indirect suggestion since the first decades of the twentieth century, suddenly becomes, in the conjunction of the media coverage of the movement (and in particular the *Time* article) with the movement press conference, explosively and explicitly conjoined. This moment is apparitional, I would suggest, because its effects exceed the intentions of both the movement and the media. The confrontation between the increasingly malicious and vitriolic attacks on the movement in the press and the responses of the movement to those attacks produces a moment when what is known and knowable about femininity, lesbianism, and feminism becomes uncertain. Lesbianism becomes the scene of a struggle—to define and set the limits of what is possible for, and knowable about, women's liberation. The apparitional effect of historical emergence is, for Foucault, where the truth of history lies, not in the totalizing narratives of teleological progress or dialectical transformation but in the "exteriority of accidents." History is propelled, Foucault asserts, not by "destiny or regulative mechanisms" but by "haphazard conflicts."[24]

Reading the crisis over lesbianism in 1970 as a moment of emergence, as an effect of a haphazard conflict, reminds us that it is merely one episode in a "series of subjugations" that forms the history of women's liberation and of feminism more generally. The conflict over lesbianism in 1970, in all its haphazardness, is part of the struggle of American feminism over the terms through which it presents itself as a political project of social transformation—a struggle that takes place in social and cultural conditions not of feminism's choosing or invention. But it also reminds us that as an episode in that struggle, the crisis over lesbianism produced apparitional effects that exceeded the immediate context of its emergence. Through the accusations of the media and the internal homophobia of the movement, lesbianism became an upsetting problem for women's liberation in 1970. It was upsetting in terms of the emotions it engendered within and outside women's liberation and also in terms of the significant shift it caused in the place and meaning of lesbianism in American society and culture. Lesbianism was something that had, as if in a flash, become difficult, something that could no longer be assumed as already known or, for women's liberation, viewed as an "issue" outside of feminist concerns. Instead, "the practical horizon of intelligibility" of lesbianism and its relation to feminism was no longer apparent or settled, and as a consequence, it demanded thought—an active thinking and working through of its meaningfulness and knowability for feminism.[25]

We can read the press conference statement, then, as an imprint event in the history of women's liberation in the United States that is also, in its responsiveness to the media, an active thinking through of the meaning of lesbianism for feminism. And it is through the irruptive force of lesbianism as a problem for feminism that the apparitional effects of this moment can be traced. Through a series of associations enacted in the statement, *women's liberation* becomes an animated term that doesn't simply resist but actively participates in the affective economy through which the media was attempting to fashion a perceptual image of women's liberation in the national public sphere. In my reading of the press-conference statement I suggest that what animates the term *women's liberation* is the statement's resignification of the word *lesbian* on the one hand as a "psychic weapon" used against women and on the other as a term that denotes a woman who "functions autonomously." It is in the two uses to which the term *lesbian* is put that we can locate both the affective power of the press conference statement's recircuiting of the meanings of lesbianism for the movement and also its effectivity as a performative of women's liberation.

What is striking—surprising even—about the press conference statement, and what tends to get lost in narrative accounts of the women's liberation movement, which assume a certain inevitability concerning the "crisis" over lesbianism, is how hard it has to work to make the connections between women's liberation and lesbianism. There is no suggestion of an obvious or inevitable homology between the two. Instead the statement offers an explanation as to why homosexual liberation and women's liberation are related social movements. In order to offer that explanation the statement mobilizes what Eve Sedgwick defines as the two contradictory modes of "homo/heterosexual definition"—the universalizing view and the minoritizing view.[26] The first paragraph begins by defining women's liberation as a universalizing rather than minoritizing protest movement: "As members of Women's Liberation we are concerned with all forms of human oppression, including the oppression of homosexuals." Rather than claim women's liberation as one identity-based movement among others, this sentence seeks to disperse the specificity of the category "women" into all forms of "human oppression." The emphasis, in this sentence, is on the "forms" of oppression rather than the persons oppressed. Implicit in this universalizing move is the potential of women's liberation to be a social movement that attends to the discursive formations and structural relations that constitute race, class, sexual, and gender oppression. And, in-

deed, many if not all of the early women's liberation groups were as concerned with questions of race and class as they were with questions of
gender—as the inaugural manifestos of the CWLU and Bread and Roses, to
name but two, testify.[27]

The universalizing move in the first paragraph of the statement also
allows for an association to be made between women's liberationists and
homosexuals: each are battling against oppression and, as a result, each
have in common the goal of striving for their liberation and freedom. Yet,
in making the connection between sexism and homophobia as related
forms of oppression, a distinction between different *types* of people is enacted. The statement expresses its "solidarity" with "the struggle of homosexuals," and as a result homosexuals become a different species from
women, their struggle equivalent to but different from the struggle of
women. Here, women's liberation is now constructed as a minoritizing
movement, defined precisely by the singularity of its focus on women and
their struggles. The tension between the claim to be a collective, universalizing social movement and the political imperative to "organize around
your own oppression" is evident and reveals not only the contradictions
embedded within the politics and shape of all the new social movements of
the 1960s and 1970s but also the limits of intelligibility concerning the
objects—the issues or problems—that shaped their protest.[28] The terms
available to women's liberation are unable to articulate the relationship
between structural and embodied oppression in a way that makes both
apparent at the same time. This limitation was not just linguistic but also
political: how women's liberation (and other movements of the era) imagined its public and shaped its goals emerged out of a discursive incoherence that circumscribed its imaginary domain and conceptual apparatus.

The incoherency of moving from a universalizing to a minoritizing view
of the women's liberation movement generates a compelling fusion of feminism and lesbianism in the statement, which simultaneously covers over
its inherent contradictions. In the first paragraph the more established
conception of the relationship between feminism and homosexuality—as
distinct but related civil rights issues—is maintained. Yet, in attributing the
cause of the homosexual's oppression to a "sexist society," the statement
also sets the ground for a more fundamental connection between women
and homosexuals. If it is sexism that causes the homosexual's status as an
oppressed minority, then homosexuality must have something to do with
gender inequality. In the case of lesbians, this gender inequality must have

something to do with them being women.[29] So, although the first paragraph of the statement seems to be maintaining the more usual conception of the relationship between feminism and homosexuality as separate but related civil rights issues, the paragraph also, simultaneously, suggests, through its depiction of sexism as the source of oppression for homosexuals, that women and homosexuals are one and the same: they are both oppressed because of sexism. What this covers over, of course, is the differences between male and female homosexuality as distinct social and sexual fields of experience, as well as the complex and potentially contradictory proliferation of possible gender alignments and identifications between different groups of people.[30] In the desire to refute the idea that the media could "malign" and "invalidate" women's liberation by associating it with lesbianism, the press conference statement works to make the relationship between the two even more, not less, binding. The effect of this reversal is the collapsing of the feminist into the homosexual: they become figures that mirror each other through a shared oppression. The oppressions faced by homosexuals listed in the first paragraph—legal, economic, psychic, and social—come to stand implicitly as the oppressions also faced by women.

Indeed, in the second paragraph the homology between lesbianism and feminism is articulated more forcefully, and the accusation of association becomes a claim of identification. If *lesbian* is a "label" used as a threat to keep women "locked into their male-defined feminine role," then it must be indicative of a different—nonfeminine—way of being for women. The negative characteristics associated with lesbianism in the *Time* exposé of Millett in December 1970—gender inverted, psychologically flawed, and sexually incapacitated—are transformed into positive attributes. The lesbian's inability to be a "proper" woman and her sexual frigidity (with men) are invoked as a refusal to be locked into the "male-defined feminine role." Rather than the failed or "non-woman" used to keep other women in line, the lesbian is now cast as an ideal for feminism in that, unlike the heterosexual woman, she is free of being defined by the desires and needs of men. The term used to represent this ideal is *autonomy*: women's liberation is fighting for the attainment of a self for every woman that is independent of men and free of the imposition of restricting gender and sexual roles. As a figure for this ideal, the lesbian becomes not only the "real" woman in our midst but the "real" women's liberationist—the woman who actively resists the social and psychic oppressions of a sexist society.

As an ideal type for feminism, the lesbian also figures in the statement as a signifier of the future promise of women's liberation. If the achievement of an autonomous individuality for every woman (her independence from her "male-defined feminine role") is a—possibly *the*—goal of women's liberation, so too, the statement asserts, is the attainment of a "society free from defining and categorizing people by virtue of gender and/or sexual preference." Here, the lesbian also figures as the promise of a future lack of sexual or gendered identity. Unlike gay liberation, in which the call to "come out!" and be visible was the act of liberation—don't hide, just be and you shall be free—here the goal is not for women to reveal themselves (the assumption is we already know who they are) but to transform themselves. Claiming the label *lesbian* is less about revealing the authenticity of your gayness, the "truth" of your being, and more a declaration of intent and an incitement to action. In this formula, the figure of the lesbian becomes the "magical sign" of a different future for women, and lesbianism as a practice becomes the means (acting autonomously) to achieve it.[31]

The redeployment of the lesbian as a signifier of women's liberation and its promise of a feminist future is enacted less through a coherent argument than through a recircuiting of the emotions that infused the figure with meaning (for women's liberation) in the first place. The writers of the statement are not unaware that the media's accusations against the movement operate primarily through emotion rather than reason; the *Time's* article is "deplored" not for its inaccuracy but for its maliciousness and its attempt to "malign" the movement. In rejecting the attacks of the media, the statement invokes women's liberation as a body that has been hurt and that has suffered as a consequence. Although the statement rejects the idea that women's liberation is "vulnerable" to the attacks of the media, the feeling of vulnerability is nevertheless present through its displacement onto the homosexual. It is the homosexual who suffers "every manner of social and psychological harassment" and who comes to stand as the representative figure for the social and psychological hurts suffered by women too. Instead of the fear and disgust invoked and put into circulation through the media's lesbian-baiting of the movement, the press conference statement invokes the pain and suffering of women and homosexuals and transforms the figure of the lesbian from one of shame to one of defiance. The "psychic weapon" of labeling a woman a lesbian becomes the stigmata of a defiant and courageous woman—a woman who "functions autonomously."

Lesbianism is not defended in the press conference statement as just one feminist issue among others. Nor is it, ultimately, defended as a related but distinct civil rights issue. Nor would it be quite accurate to say that lesbianism is asserted in the statement as a political identity for women's liberation. Forged in the confrontation between the media and the movement over how women's liberation was to be known and represented, the lesbian emerges in the press conference statement as a shorthand notation through which the protest and claims of women's liberation are evoked. The lesbian becomes both a signifier of the women's movement's political project—"women's autonomy"—and the figure through which a perceptual image of the movement, as full of women acting autonomously by defiantly refusing their "male-defined 'feminine role,'" is brought vividly to life.

In the two or three years following the press conference statement, women's liberation became, in Alice Echols's words, "convulsed" by the gay-straight split.[32] Ruth Rosen writes that the "urge to separate not only from men, but also from the nonlesbian women's movement, sometimes seemed irresistible" to many previously straight feminists at this time.[33] The feminist paper *off our backs* became the venue for a heated debate between those liberationists who argued for a separatist feminist politics and those who accused lesbians of trying to "take over" the movement and of practicing "sexual fascist politics."[34] In February of 1971 one of the first recognized lesbian separatist collectives, Amazing Grace, set up house in Washington, D.C., at the same time that another, the Furies, began meeting in their own consciousness-raising group. While Amazing Grace lasted exactly one week, the Furies was more successful, managing to be a collective for nearly a year and writing what became some of the most influential essays on the theory and practice of lesbian feminism.[35] The acrimony between increasingly self-identified lesbian feminists and those feminists who were either straight and/or suspicious of the absolutist politics of groups like the Furies has been read, in hindsight, as an inevitable outcome of the events of 1970. The factionalism and hardening of political positions during the gay-straight split are interpreted as a testament to the limitations of an identity-based political movement that, in its focus on the sexual and psychological oppression of women, led to an essentialist, or "gynocentric," view of women's difference from men, which also prevented the predominantly white women's liberation movement from addressing the differences between women.[36]

While these accounts of the effects of the gay-straight split are not without explanatory power, they too quickly foreclose the interpretive possibilities of reading the press conference, and the events of 1970 that propelled its enunciation, as doing something other than offering one of the first arguments for lesbian feminism as a distinct feminist identity politics. After all, many of the feminists who wrote and supported the statement neither identified as lesbians nor went on to espouse lesbian feminism. That is, to read the statement retroactively as part of the movement's progress toward lesbian feminism is to miss the accidental and contingent nature of its taking up of the lesbian as a figure that could illuminate the scene of women's liberation's revolt and symbolize its political claims. Forged in the crucible of widespread anger within the movement at the overt hostility of both the media and movement men, the lesbian becomes a figure that animates that anger but in a way that binds her to the accusations directed at women's liberation by the press and New Left men (among others). That the statement reads the lesbian as signifying both political defiance and social autonomy reveals her to be a product of the liberal Marxist, humanist rhetoric of the 1960s social movements more generally, and in this sense, the statement participates in enacting women's liberation as a feminist political project imagined within the terms of a Western democratic political tradition, which understands liberation in terms of the autonomy of subjects and locates the ground of political action in claims for social justice and change. But at the same time, the taking up of the lesbian as a figure of feminist rebellion cannot be contained by the immediate context of its utterance. As a figure for women's liberation, the lesbian associates social autonomy and liberation with social and sexual abjection: it does not, therefore, simply confirm women's liberation as a bourgeois humanist, feminist political project; it also simultaneously suggests the limits of that project. Instead of reading the lesbian conjured in the press conference statement as a symbol of the movement's bourgeois preoccupations, then, I approach her as an access point to the contingencies of the movement's struggle to enact itself as an emancipatory feminist political project—she provides us with an opening to encounter the rhetorical and political conditions of women's liberation's possibility as a movement. By following the figure of the lesbian conjured by the press conference statement, as it moves toward other imagined scenes and figures of rebellion in the women's liberation archive, it is possible to track the repercussions of those contingent conditions for how feminist historians and theorists have since come to interpret the events of 1970 and the place of the gay-straight split in the history of second-wave feminism.

The conflict, therefore, is not between females and males, but between
SCUM—dominant, secure, self-confident, nasty, violent, selfish, independent, proud,
thrill-seeking, free-wheeling, arrogant females, who consider themselves fit to rule the
universe, who have free-wheeled to the limits of this "society" and are ready to wheel on
to something far beyond what it has to offer—and nice, passive, accepting "cultivated,"
polite, dignified, subdued, dependent, scared, mindless, insecure, approval-seeking
Daddy's Girls, who can't cope with the unknown, who want to hang back with the apes,
who feel secure only with Big Daddy standing by, with a big strong man . . . who have
reduced their minds, thoughts and sights to the male level, who, lacking
sense, imagination and wit can have value only in a male "society."
—Valerie Solanas, SCUM Manifesto

The women's liberation movement's embrace of anger as a radicalizing emotion that could shake women free of their attachments to the myths and illusions of political machismo, normative femininity, and the heterosexual contract, did not begin, of course, with the press conference statement in December 1970. The early polemics and position papers of the movement are full of irreverent and spiky denunciations of everything from housework, gynecological exams, schools, the military, and "phallic imperialism." The use of slang and colloquialism in these texts enabled an exaggeration of feeling that became the dominant form of communication for the movement. The rhetorical deployment of emotion was the means by which women's liberation interpellated its public and incited women not yet in the movement to join. One of the most widely distributed polemics of the early years of the movement, and one that announced women's liberation's defiant independence as a political movement, was "Goodbye to All That," Robin Morgan's scathing condemnation of the New Left. The essay was first published in February 1970 in *Rat*, an underground newspaper of the 1960s that Morgan and other women in the movement took over in protest because of its demeaning representation of women. The take over of *Rat* by women's liberationists can be read as an act of insurgency in which the right to speak was simultaneously claimed as the right to speak out of turn, a speaking out that used anger to literally interrupt what Avital Ronell calls the "hetero-rhetoricism" of the New Left countercultural public sphere.[37] Through its eruptive use of anger, "Goodbye to All That" does not so much present an argument for women's liberation as blast through the phallic coolness of New Left colloquial speech and reveal its negative underside: nonnormative, noncompliant femaleness.[38]

Drawing upon movement slang and repeating it in an incantatory style, Morgan deploys a mocking, sarcastic tone designed to expose the hypocrisies and contradictions between the New Left's stated political aim of liberation for all people and its rhetorical and symbolic (mis)use of women. The men of the New Left are, Morgan writes, "the good guys who think they know what 'Women's lib,' as they so chummily call it, is all about—and who then proceed to degrade and destroy women by almost everything they say and do: The cover on the last issue of *Rat* (front *and* back). The token 'pussy power' or 'clit militancy' articles. The snide descriptions of women staffers on the masthead. The little jokes, the personal ads, the smile, the snarl."[39] Morgan's repetition of the metaphorical descriptions of feminism used jokingly in *Rat*—"pussy power," "clit militancy"—within the context of her repudiation of them as degrading and destructive (rather than funny), acts as a displacement that disrupts the relationship between subject and object through which they emit meaning. In Morgan's essay (the quotation marks highlighting their importation) these metaphors come to stand for the attitudes of movement men toward women rather than as portraits of feminist women in the movement. Now, the metaphors are meant to incite anger rather than humor, outrage rather than contempt. Women, Morgan declares, are the objects of a "sexist hate and fear" usually covered over by the "liberal co-optive masks" worn by "the real nice guys" in the movement.

In recircuiting the emotional force of the sexist phrases and metaphors used by the New Left, "Goodbye to All That" enacts a rejection of the hetero-rhetorics of the New Left. At the same time, this recircuiting situates "women's liberation" as the rejection or negation of a heterosexism that sees women as sexual objects and domestic helpers. The production of women's liberation as anti-heterosexist is made possible precisely through the expression of anger. As an emotion that is an effect of a subject or group being "against" something, in this case the sexist attitudes and practices of New Left men, anger is also "for something," as Sara Ahmed points out in her analysis of the uses of anger for feminism.[40] To react in anger pulls you toward the object of your anger but in a way that is also simultaneously a rejection, a turning away from it. We see this simultaneous pulling toward and turning away from the object of anger in Morgan's essay: in saying "goodbye to all that" (movement men, the New Left, the editorial board of *Rat*, sexist hatred, and fear of women) Morgan names individual men, including well-known figures like Paul Krassner and Jerry Rubin, and describes their sexist actions and attitudes in detail.[41] Yet, as Ahmed also asserts, the turning away enacted by anger is "shaped" by what made you angry in the first place, and that shaping depends upon your interpretation —the reading you have—of what made you angry.[42] Here, then, is the productive or performative part of Morgan's anger. In her reading of the sexism of New Left men, Morgan also, inevitably, generates a particular view of feminism and of women's liberationists—a view that is bound to, but not determined by, what it is she is rejecting.

The relationship between the object of Morgan's anger and the production of women's liberation as anti-heterosexist is revealed in a passage in which the insults directed at women by movement men are revealed to be, and claimed as, the characteristics of women's liberation: "Let it all hang out. Let it seem bitchy, catty, dykey, frustrated, crazy, Solanisesque, nutty, frigid, ridiculous, bitter, embarrassing, man-hating, libelous, pure, unfair, envious, intuitive, low-down, stupid, petty, liberating. WE ARE THE WOMEN THAT MEN HAVE WARNED US ABOUT."[43] To let it all hang out is not an injunction to refute an enemy or accusation by asserting an oppositional position or identity. On the contrary, it calls for a revelation or uncovering of what women have been accused of being. To let it all hang out is to exceed the boundaries of the narrowly defined femininity projected onto movement women to keep them in their place; it is to expose what has made men so fearful and hateful in the first place. To let it all hang out is also a call for women to let go of the fears and inhibitions that have kept them bound to normative practices and notions of femininity. By exceeding the boundaries of an acceptable femininity, and refusing to be afraid of the consequences, women become "the women that men have warned us about"— they reveal themselves to be the "bitchy, catty, dykey, frustrated" women that movement men have accused them of being. Women's liberation, Morgan warns the New Left, is a movement full of just the kind of crazy, embarrassing, man-hating women they fear.

But in becoming the women that men have warned against, in letting it all hang out, movement women don't simply become the embodiment of men's fears, they also become strange—to themselves and to men. Here, Morgan's essay also shows us what Daniel Gross calls the "irreducibly social" nature of emotions like anger.[44] Made possible by, and as an effect of, the social differences between white men and women in the New Left, the anger expressed by Morgan can *only* be articulated in relation to what it is against, and as a consequence, her anger is inevitably contained by the social worlds in which she is acting. To put it simply: Morgan can only be a (New Left, white, middle-class) woman angry at how she has been belittled and dismissed as a sexual plaything and movement domestic and never an angry brown or black man or woman, and this has consequences for how that anger is read and what it is capable of enacting politically. And yet, although Morgan's vision of women's liberation in this essay can only be articulated in relation to the accusations of New Left men, this articulation also opens up a space of representational uncertainty and possibility. "Women are Something Else," Morgan goes on to write, when they act out and against the attitudes of men and the norms through which they have been known.[45] To name women as "something else" is to invoke an unrepresentability—we do not yet know what women can be. This unknowingness is prefaced by the qualifier used in the passage above: "*let it seem bitchy, catty.*" To seem to be something is to not actually be it, a negation that signals the emptiness of being "something else"—the unknowable (future) effects of women acting out and letting go. To let it all hang out and to *seem* to be bitchy, catty, dykey, then, does not inevitably end up confirming the already established configurations of "woman" as the figure of proper femininity or, indeed, of "women's liberationist" as the figure of feminism. Rather, it makes those configurations and symbolizations unstable and disturbing, revealing the lack of a coherent and natural femininity or feminism that they simultaneously cover over and reproduce. As a social emotion, anger both binds and disturbs: it is an emotion predicated on ambivalence rather than conviction.

The figure that animates Morgan's articulation of women's liberation as the women that men have warned us about is Valerie Solanas, the troubled writer who had achieved her own notorious publicity when she shot the artist Andy Warhol in the spring of 1968 out of a paranoid fear that he had stolen the manuscript of her play *Up Your Ass*. Solanas's shooting of Warhol, in conjunction with the publication of her underground polemic SCUM *Manifesto*, erupted onto the scene of the emergence of women's liberation in the national public sphere and provided a moment of intensification for the movement's revolt. Taken up by radical feminists in New York as a cause célèbre for women's liberation, Solanas became a kind of limit figure for the movement, paradoxically expressing the inexpressable of their protest against heterosexism. From her dismissal of "the male rebel as farce" to her depiction of SCUM as "dominant, secure, self-confident, nasty, violent, selfish, independent, proud, thrill-seeking, free-wheeling, arrogant females," Solanas's inversion of the masculine as a universal category, and her contemptuous denunciation of bourgeois respectability in the name of a radical rejection of America's "money-work system," echoes throughout Morgan's essay.[46] In "Goodbye to All That" Solanas and her polemic are invoked as the enigmatic presentiments of a women's liberation imagined through the figure of the angry street dyke and produced through a politics of destruction and repudiation rather than progress, persuasion, and inclusion.

Living on the fringes of the intersecting domains of the New York avant-garde art scene and countercultural Left, Solanas's social and psychological precariousness, and willingness to use violence, created a context of delegitimization for SCUM that also, paradoxically, provided a discursive space for it to be heard. Dismissed as the deranged rantings of a lunatic lesbian, SCUM Manifesto was a public utterance of the unsayable for the women's movement. Scattered with incendiary statements calling for men to commit suicide and women to become killers, as well as vitriolic attacks on a whole host of targets—radical men, the president, daddy, daddy's girls, hippies, and couples—SCUM Manifesto punctured through the decorum of acceptable political speech, revealing an irrational, furious, and outraged underside to feminism's rational calls for social justice and political equality. Solanas wasn't an honorable dissident or hero of the revolution. Rather, she was, as Avital Ronell writes in her deconstructive rumination on Solanas's manifesto, "psycho. Butch-dykey angry, poor, and fucked-up."[47] She was an abject figure—a crazy woman—through which Morgan, for one, could imagine and invoke a feminism that was not about pleading, persuading, or even simply demanding change but about saying a huge "Fuck You!"—to New Left men but also to the coercive, manipulative, ineffable "atmosphere" of a normalizing, sexist, disciplinary society. Through her outrageous actions and public statements, Solanas provided an opening for a grappling with, and a refusal of, the respectable and the normal, and as such she "profanely illuminated" the scene of the battle in which Morgan and women's liberation were engaged.[48]

That battle, as Solanas makes clear, was not between "males and females" but between SCUM and daddy's girls. In an uncanny echo of Virginia Woolf's assertion that for a woman to be creative she had to murder "The Angel in the House," Solanas locates the scene of a feminist revolution in the war between women "unhampered by propriety, niceness, discretion, public opinion, morals," women who are "always funky, dirty, low-down," and those women who "have reduced their minds, thoughts and sights to the male level," women who are "nice, 'privileged, educated,' middle-class ladies."[49] In other words, the battle to be waged will be over the practices and discourses that produce white, middle-class femininity as national norm, practices and discourses productive of class and racial privilege and organized through a heteronormativity that locates women's social presence firmly within bourgeois domesticity. In contrast to the middle-class ladies of American heteronormativity, Solanas's SCUM women will operate outdoors—on the streets and in the anonymous public spaces of the urban metropolis. By being street-wise, funky, dirty, and low-down, the women of SCUM would enact a feminist revolution by disturbing the ordering coherence, exclusivity, and legitimating decorousness of white, middle-class femininity.

The women of SCUM are imagined by Solanas as antisocial insurgents and street guerrillas working from "the gutter" and through "furtive, sneaky, underhanded" means.[50] Their goal, if they have one, is to "unwork" the system by looting instead of shopping, obtaining a job only to refuse to work at it, and by destroying property and equipment. The places of SCUM's subversive actions are the streets and public spaces of the city rather than the suburban home or traditional political institutions. The women of SCUM are, as Solanas writes, "too childish for the grown-up worlds of suburbs, mortgages, mops and baby shit, too selfish to raise kids and husbands, too uncivilized to give a shit for anyone's opinion of them, too arrogant to respect Daddy."[51] Instead of a submissive adherence to the scripts of normative femininity and the future-directed politics of national reproduction, the women of SCUM act on "their own animal, gutter instincts" and go "prowling for emotional thrills and excitement" rather than husbands and houses.[52] Theirs is a politics of negation and transgression imagined through a radical disidentification with the symbolic spaces and figures of national womanhood. And as a politics of negation and transgression, SCUM acts against the law. To be a criminal is, for Solanas, to disrespect the laws, both codified and symbolic, that have defined and constrained the lives of women. The women of SCUM are "individuals" in Solanas's terms, not because they pursue the liberal ideal of legal and economic autonomy but because they reject being a part of the "mob"—the group organized under the category, "woman," the name through which women are reduced to "daddy's girls." SCUM are "cool and selfish" because they reject the name woman, the laws, and the "Law of Daddy": "If SCUM ever marches, it will be over the President's stupid, sickening face; if SCUM ever strikes, it will be in the dark with a six-inch blade."[53] Repeating the phrase "if SCUM ever," Solanas deploys a conditional grammar of threat that dismisses marching and striking as empty political gestures, as playing by daddy's rules.

Solanas's refusal of the law and the norms of bourgeois respectability is expressed through the metaphors and figures of racial otherness and psychological regression. The antisocial practices of SCUM are the actions of women "too childish" and too "uncivilized" to accept the burdens of social and sexual reproduction. The childishness and selfishness of SCUM invokes both the wildness of an anterior social space of human "backwardness," most often imagined through the racist discourses of nineteenth-century colonial eugenics and national segregation, and also a pre-Oedipal polymorphous sexuality that refuses the stringent demands of a mature heterosexuality. Solanas's outlaw women are subversive because they operate from "the gutter"—the spaces of social abjection and exclusion in which figures like the street hustler and dyke come to symbolize the breakdown of the internal frontiers of the nation-state—the borders that are meant to contain the middle class within a domain of hetero-respectability and racial orderliness. Solanas's SCUM revolution won't happen through marches and movements—through a protest that is also an appeal to the laws of daddy's bourgeois society—but through the mayhem wrought by refusing to acknowledge the legitimacy of those laws. The "couple-busting" of SCUM, like the destruction of property and the killing of daddy, are actions designed to blast open a social space for the proliferation of experiences and social relations beyond the heteronormative domains of the bourgeois, capitalist nation. In Solanas's manifesto, it is the marginalized social spaces of racial and sexual otherness that are the sites of feminist revolution, for these are the places of exile and anger—the places in which women most conspicuously, and often violently, fail to be daddy's girls.

Solanas's vengeful and disrespectful fantasies of female revolt provide Morgan with an imaginary landscape through which she can express her feelings of anger and frustration at New Left men and the pervasive sexist atmosphere of the movement. The women of SCUM, brought most vividly to life in the figure of Solanas herself, become both the affective repositories for Morgan's feelings and a vehicle for their transmission. Yet, by invoking Solanas and the SCUM Manifesto in her criticisms of New Left men, Morgan also opens up a new vista of feminist protest, one quite distinct from the predominantly middle-class social milieu of the New Left. By drawing upon the rage of Solanas, Morgan infuses her production of women's liberation with the images and feelings of social marginalization and sexual outsiderdom. Here, the angry dyke as a figure for women's liberation does not simply represent a rejection of heterosexism, or hatred of men, but a refusal of the prescriptive interpellations of a proper femininity organized through the classist and racist exclusions of a national public sphere imagined as white and middle class. The possibility opened up for women's liberation by Morgan's invocation of Solanas's SCUM Manifesto is this: to become the "women that men have warned us about"—to become women free of the constraints and claims of the feminine role—will require the death of daddy's girls.

Solanas and her SCUM Manifesto tend to flicker in and out of contemporary studies of the second-wave era. Her paranoia and psychosis are discomforting reminders of a long tradition of dismissing unconventional, socially marginal, and sexually suspect women as mad. And indeed feminist scholars looking back at the era of the second wave have tended to respond to Solanas with a wary suspicion that her notoriety has been used to dismiss—de-realize—the everyday struggle and material achievements of the numerous women's movements of the era.[54] Other feminist critics, like Avital Ronell and Dana Heller, have attempted to recuperate Solanas as a lost figure of radical feminism. For Ronell and Heller, Solanas is a reminder of "feminism's unacknowledged debt to the margins of the representable and the representative."[55] Her incendiary statements and vitriolic attacks are unsettling, rather than just silly or uninteresting, according to Ronell, because they are fueled by "a spark in the real."[56] That is, Solanas's irrational, angry utterances speak to the unrepresentability of the complex mix of feeling, thought, and action through which women experience their social worlds as hurtful and oppressive and through which feminism necessarily seeks to act in the world. The tension between these two feminist responses to Solanas, responses that are, in a sense, both right, reveals the problem of trying to account for the eventfulness of women's liberation through narratives that try to rationalize its achievements and failures or categorize its politics and processes of identification. That Solanas can be both a distraction from the material achievements of feminisms in the 1970s and a figure that illuminates the potentiality of women's liberation's rebellion returns us to the eventfulness of the movement's "moment of invention"—its spontaneous inventiveness and simultaneous boundedness to the context of its emergence. Rather than attempt to recuperate Solanas as a lost radical figure of women's liberation or, alternatively, condemn her to the darkness of a wrong or embarrassing feminism, it would serve us better to think of her as a figure through which women's liberation imagined the possibilities of its disidentification from the norms and values of proper femininity. She operates, in the present, as an access point to the entangled feelings of attachment to and repudiation of proper femininity put into circulation by the emergence of women's liberation. Those feelings, in turn, are the trace effects of the complex histories of sexual and social subjugation that produced not only the possibility and the desire for a movement like women's liberation to emerge but also the taking up of the lesbian as a figure of feminist rebellion.

DEATH TO DADDY'S GIRL: A POSTSCRIPT

There was another figure stalking the city streets of a feminist imaginary in 1970. This figure also carried a weapon, though hers was a "small razor cupped in her fingers," and the face she slashed was not daddy's but that of her "street brother."[57] If Valerie Solanas and her SCUM women are the figures that animate the anger expressed in "Goodbye to All That," thereby organizing the emotional force of Morgan's production of "women's liberation" as a rallying cry to kill daddy's girls and become the women that men have warned us about, then Haden, Middleton, and Robinson's "A Historical and Critical Essay for Black Women" conjures up another figure of feminist anger and protest. Like Solanas's street hustling SCUM women, the poor, urban black women of Haden, Middleton, and Robinson's essay also feel rage, but theirs is the rage of self-hatred and betrayal, of being caught up in the "white male jive," which would either bind them to a pathetic mimicry of white, bourgeois femininity or condemn them to the social abjection of a racial otherness marked by the stereotypes of the jezebel and sapphire. The angry, self-destructive black women of America's urban wastelands become the people through which Haden, Middleton, and Robinson both confront and refuse the false choices of American racism, "this big white world of male supremacy, this way-out white capitalism" (318). As "smashers of myths and the destroyers of illusion," the women of Haden, Middleton, and Robinson's urban imaginary will shatter the habit of "deep thoughts and everyday attitudes"—the habit of an American dream that is white and male and about "money, machines, and property"—by confronting their own histories of defeat and submission and creating a self-identified domain of black womanhood. And unlike Solanas's street guerrillas who are consumed by a paranoid self-absorption, the black, female revolutionaries conjured by Haden, Middleton, and Robinson are not alone. Associated with "a whole bunch of brown and yellow poor folks out there in the world," including the National Liberation Front (NLF) fighters in South Vietnam, these revolutionaries operate on a much larger battlefield than Solanas's SCUM women (324; 323). The object of their anger is both more complex and dispersed, not simply middle-class femininity but "America" as a transnational, colonizing enforcer of global capitalism.

I bring up Haden, Middleton, and Robinson's essay because of the affinities between their imaginary landscape of female revolt and Solanas's and its reverberation in Morgan's essay. But I also bring up their essay in order to remember the differences between those landscapes. While both Morgan's essay and Haden, Middleton, and Robinson's work circulated in the same movement networks, and were published at the same time and in the same anthologies, the objects of their anger were distinct from one another. The at once subtle but vast difference between Morgan's anger at New Left men and Haden, Middleton, and Robinson's anger at "the big white world of male supremacy" produced different feminist solutions and different images of women's liberation. Those different solutions and images are a testament to the complex historicities of sexual, gendered, and racial subjugation that situate women of color and white women in contrasting, often mutually antagonistic, social roles. And yet, the affinity between Solanas's knife-wielding street hustler invoked in Morgan's essay and Haden, Middleton, and Robinson's poor, urban black woman with a razor cupped in her hand offers us, in the present, a glimpse of something not effectively realized during the moment of women's liberation's arising: the possibility of an alignment between black and white women based on corresponding if not equivalent social exclusions. The angry dyke figure invoked by Morgan could not possibly signify the complexity of black women's anger and their demands for social justice, but it does evoke a connection between the urban domains of economic and racial marginalization and those of sexual outsiderdom as a rebellion against the domestic and sexual dependencies of white, middle-class women. It is this immanent connection that illuminates in the present the contested terrain of women's liberation's protest in 1970 and the possibilities of its revolt.

Who knows what women can be when they are finally free to become themselves? Who knows what women's intelligence will contribute when it can be nourished
without denying love? Who knows of the possibilities of love when men and women share
not only children, home, and garden, not only the fulfillment of their biological roles, but
the responsibilities and passions of the work that creates the human future and the full
human knowledge of who they are? It has barely begun, the search of women for themselves. But the time is at hand when the voices of the feminine mystique can no longer drown out the inner voice that is driving women on to become complete.

—Betty Friedan, *The Feminine Mystique*

I want to turn back to an earlier, scene-setting, image for women's liberation's rebellion that was still circulating at the time Solanas was writing her
scum *Manifesto*—an earlier, we might even say depressive, incarnation of
daddy's girl. Betty Friedan begins *The Feminine Mystique* with a problem
that, as she quickly makes clear, evades any attempt at clear definition. The
"problem that has no name" was "a strange stirring, a sense of dissatisfaction, a yearning" felt by the suburban wife and mother; it was a "strange
feeling of desperation" that contradicted the material comfort and ease of
her life.[58] For Friedan, "the problem" was hard to define precisely because
it manifested itself through feelings rather than measurable "data." Despite
the outward appearances of social success, many of the middle-class white
women Friedan interviewed for her book are gripped by an emotional
malaise they cannot easily account for or explain. If Robin Morgan's anger
at New Left men and the sexual and domestic dependencies they assumed
for (white) women was animated by Solanas's dyke rage against the du-
plicitous daddy's girls of bourgeois America, then *The Feminine Mystique* is
animated both by the mass-mediated disaffection of those very same daddy's girls, as well as the specters of social dis-ease and corruption that their
disaffection produced in the cultural imaginary. Through the metaphor of
the feminine mystique, Friedan provided a shorthand notation for the
uneasy and seemingly unnamable unhappiness of many postwar American
women, which, in turn, incited feminist imaginings far in excess of the
modest proposals Friedan offered as solutions to "the problem with no
name." By reading Friedan's hugely influential conception of the feminine
mystique *against* Morgan's invocation of the angry dyke of Solanas's scum
Manifesto, I want to consider how they operated as figures of and for the
emergent women's liberation movement that were at once "contrary" but

also "close to" or "drawing toward" each other, as the multiple meanings of *against* suggest.[59] It is through these figures, and their relation to each other, I want to suggest, that we can access the "private," which is to say, the publicly mediated and represented terrain of sexual and domestic dysfunction of the emergent women's liberation movement's rebellion against proper femininity.

Friedan's preoccupation with the sexual and psychic dissatisfactions of middle-class suburban housewives was not particularly original in the early 1960s, nor were her findings. As Daniel Horowitz notes in his biography of Friedan, *The Feminine Mystique* was one of a number of mass-marketed books devoted to mapping out the social, economic, and psychological parameters of middle-class femininity (and its antithesis, as the relative explosion of "pulp sexology" books concerning gay and lesbian subcultures in the 1960s also testify).[60] Helen Gurley Brown's *Sex and the Single Girl*, F. Ivan Nye and Lois W. Hoffman's *The Employed Mother in America*, and Morton Hunt's *Her Infinite Variety: The American Woman as Lover, Mate, and Rival*, all came out within a year of *The Feminine Mystique*.[61] And as Joanne Meyerowitz argues in her essay on the impact of *The Feminine Mystique* on the historiography of postwar American culture and feminism, Friedan's findings of discontent among suburban housewives feeling trapped in domesticity were often-repeated laments in the media by the early 1960s, while her solutions—that women should have creative or professional life goals supplementary to their domestic duties—were borrowed from the human potential psychologists already administering to the psychic pain of postwar middle-class Americans.[62]

What accounted for the success of *The Feminine Mystique* had less to do with its findings or Friedan's analysis, much of which was as contradictory as the problem the book was attempting to explain, and more to do with its vivid evocation of the fantasies and anxieties of postwar American culture. As Meyerowitz writes, the book's enormous and instantaneous popularity was due, in part, to Friedan's "compelling elaboration" of the "familiar themes" of mass culture, rather than to an effective countering of those themes.[63] Friedan's reliance on interviews and short stories from women's magazines as her primary sources meant that *The Feminine Mystique* acted more as an amplifier of cultural fantasies and fears. It is in Friedan's overreliance on magazine fiction and personal stories that Meyerowitz finds fault with *The Feminine Mystique*; by rehearsing the cultural narratives she sets out to explain, Friedan overlooks the more contradictory messages of postwar popular culture—precisely the kinds of messages that would allow cultural critics and historians to get at the more contested and diverse terrain of postwar American women's lives.[64] And yet, although I am in sympathy with Meyerowitz's desire to counter Friedan's overly influential rendition of postwar domestic ideology, I want to bring our attention back to the story, or stories, Friedan tells in her book. It is through these stories that Friedan offers a "compelling elaboration" on the theme of the discontented housewife, and it is in these elaborations that Friedan ends up telling us other stories—of the suburban nymphomaniac, the lesbian professional, and the sissy son—that expose, rather than solve, the intrinsically incoherent and troubling cultural notions of a class- and race-bound femininity. The feminine mystique worked as a cathectic metaphor for postwar American society, it seems to me, precisely because it had the connotative capacity to invoke this incoherence and give expression to the feelings of discontent it provoked.

Most of the criticism aimed at Friedan from feminist critics has centered on the solution she offers to the feminine mystique rather than on her rendition of it. But like Meyerowitz, these critics tend to overlook the connotative power of Friedan's metaphor, as well as what might be understood as the *productive* lack of correspondence between her explanation of the problems middle-class women faced in midcentury America and her solution to them. The story Friedan offers as the necessary counter to that of the discontented housewife—the story that would clear the mists of the feminine mystique and allow women to see their possibilities anew—was that of individual "self-actualization." The rhetoric and terms Friedan used to articulate this story of liberatory autonomy were rooted in the existential-inflected work of midcentury American psychology, particularly the work of human potential psychologists like A. H. Maslow and Erik Erikson.[65] The goal of self-actualization was based on the idea that life was an adventure and that people lived through a cycle of development. The potential to change and to achieve an "authentic" self not only propelled people through their life adventure but was "actualized" through the creative work they undertook.[66] The "will" to achieve this self-actualization was something intrinsic to every human "organism" and was nothing less than "having the courage to be an individual."[67] Rather than simply adapting to society, Friedan told her women readers, they should strive toward a future completion. The feminine mystique, in contrast, had coerced American women into following the cultural guidelines of their society—to conform to the

image or ideal of a domesticated femininity petrified into a state of perpetual passivity—at the expense of realizing their full human potential. By
appropriating the ideas and rhetoric of human potential psychology, a
scientized rewriting of nineteenth-century liberal humanism, Friedan
called on women to forgo their efforts to "adjust" to society's image of an
ideal femininity and to have the courage to be individuals—to "put forth"
the effort "to become all that they have it in them to become."[68]

In contrast to Solanas's understanding of SCUM as selfish, thrill-seeking
individuals, Friedan's notion of a healthy individuality is derived in large
part from the universal subject of the bourgeois imagination, and it is
through the conflation of personal happiness with the satisfactions of a
creative career that we witness Friedan's attempt to suture the goals of her
feminist appeal for social and economic equality to the affective genres of a
mass-mediated normative femininity, if not always their narrative representations. A future completion for women, which would include sexual satisfaction with a loving husband, would come from work—creative work that
"contributed to the human community." Work governed by the punch card
and organized into endless repetition would only subject people to a static,
stunted sense of self. Rather than the technologically enhanced, consumer-
driven drudgery of housework, the professions and the arts would offer
women the space to create and to contribute something other than consumer goods and domestic neatness to society. A woman's "private" happiness, in other words, would come from her active participation in the
public sphere. Friedan offers detailed statistics in order to demonstrate
that women with college degrees and a career are more likely to live in
happy and contented marriages and to have satisfying sexual relationships.
And in her last chapter, "A New Life Plan for Women," Friedan calls on
women to construct a life plan that includes education and a career that
would carry them through and beyond their child-rearing years. By continuing in education and pursuing a career, Friedan asserts, women not
only will make themselves happier and more contented—as wives and
mothers as well as creative individuals—but will also inspire other women:
"Every girl who manages to stick it out through law school or medical
school, who finishes her MA or PhD and goes on to use it, helps others
move on."[69]

Friedan's assertion of self-actualization, as social, psychic, and sexual
liberation for women, is framed by the stories she tells to illustrate the
enigmatically destructive force of the feminine mystique. These stories

draw directly upon the sensationalist rhetoric of popular cultural narratives of the fallen or dysfunctional woman and, as a result, are far more vivid and compelling than the rather abstract homilies deployed in her feminist adaptation of human potential psychology. In the world of the feminine mystique, which is the fantastic world of mass-mediated fears of women's sexual and social ambition, sex becomes the easy solace of women who don't, or can't, grow up. In fact, Friedan's attempt to draw a contrast between a woman's "authentic" identity, achieved through creative work, and one derived entirely from her sexuality is undone precisely through her overuse of sensationalistic media stories. The reader of *The Feminist Mystique* is left with an overwhelming sense of women "immersed at the sickly level of sexual phantasy."[70] And while Friedan offers a rather muted attempt to link the saturation of sexual fantasy in the public sphere to the expansion of consumer capitalism into the "private" sphere, her fidelity to human potential psychology as an explanatory framework for the malaise of middle-class women leads her to locate the source of their sickness, and future liberation, in their actions and desires. The overall effect of Friedan's use of mass culture and popular psychology is to emphasize, rather than diminish, the sexualization of middle-class women in midcentury American culture.

Whether parasitic mothers feasting on the burgeoning sexuality of their sons, nymphomaniac young wives using sex to "erase their lack of identity," or vampiric lesbian professionals eschewing the humanizing comforts of heterosexual coupledom, the suburban landscape of Friedan's America is littered with the generic figures of midcentury sexual wantonness and depravity. Intricately intertwined with Friedan's portrayal of female sexuality as a ravenous sickness are her warnings against the equally rapacious spread of homosexuality: "sex without self," Friedan writes, fosters not only the sickly fantasy of an Oedipal family drama but also the "murky smog" of homosexuality enveloping America as ominously as the feminine mystique. Drawing upon the same sexological discourses that construct the lesbian as a psychologically flawed and sexually incapacitated "non-woman," Friedan equates an identity defined through sexuality with immaturity and an undeveloped sense of self. Rather than being concerned with the larger problems of the world—the threat of communism, the nuclear bomb—women trapped in the web of the feminine mystique or the murky smog of homosexuality are reduced to "naval gazing" and sordid sexual dramas that inhibit their self-actualization, as well as that of their children and husband.[71]

Friedan's salacious depiction of suburban life leaves the reader with a portrait of the middle-class American family as the site of overwhelming psychic and sexual dysfunction.[72] Her solution of sexually fulfilling marriages based on complementary careers in the public sphere remains unpersuasive not only because, as a model of female emancipation, it depends on the invisible labor of working-class women but also because it remains, within the context of Friedan's elaboration of the feminine mystique, a vague promise rather than a compelling story or image in its own right. The future perfect marriage cannot viscerally counter the stories and images offered as present sexual dysfunction. Here, the power of the feminine mystique as a connotative metaphor escapes Friedan's attempts to limit its suggestiveness. Rather than simply a metaphor for the housewife trap, the feminine mystique also conjures up the problem of middle-class femininity as hetero-domesticity. The "sickly" fantasies of the Oedipal drama become the destructive magic of the private sphere—the sexual desires and family feelings that trap women as much, if not more, than housework.

As feminist critics have noted, Friedan's formulation of both the "problem" women faced in midcentury America and its possible solution were formed through a class-specific set of values and norms that did not, ultimately, question the place of the bourgeois nuclear family in American social life or the need for gendered roles in society. And yet, in her attempt to separate a woman's "authentic identity" from a sexual one, Friedan reanimated the paradox of femininity for feminism. In addition, although Friedan's imagined community of American women was highly problematic, both in how she conceived of community and defined individuality, she nevertheless presented her readers—and the emergent women's liberation movement—with a capacious metaphor that, in its use of mass-cultural fantasies of women's desires and fears, could invoke their feelings of dissatisfaction and frustration with the expectations and demands of the social world, if not the material realities of most American women's lives. The feminine mystique suggested a complex constellation of frustration, dissatisfaction, and a "strange feeling of desperation" that captured the attention of postwar American society precisely because it identified a "problem with no name." That is, it identified a nebulous atmosphere of sexual, social, and psychic subjugation that, in its inability to be contained and expressed by a single narrative or image, went beyond any one class or group of women and escaped any neat categorization or comforting account of origins. The amoeba-like malleability of Friedan's metaphor incited postwar feminist imaginings, not only because it "legitimated open protest" against "the 'housewife trap'" and "affirmed the undeniable anger many middle-class women felt as they increasingly tried to pursue both domestic and non-domestic ideals,"[73] but also because it captured and disseminated a "sensate knowledge" of hetero-domesticity as an often alienating and dissatisfying social practice for many American women.[74] Read against Solanas's SCUM *Manifesto*, Friedan's "problem with no name" conjured the unhappiness of daddy's girls—an unhappiness made manifest in the spectacularization of the middle-class suburban home as the space of a strange and perverse dysfunction.

When read as part of a progressive narrative of U.S. feminist history, *The Feminine Mystique*—and "the problem with no name" it attempts to illustrate—becomes an exemplary text of liberal feminism and a totemic remainder of the second-wave movement's bourgeois preoccupations and assumptions. But placed in circulation with other texts and phrases from the emergent moment of women's liberation—like Valerie Solanas's SCUM *Manifesto* and Robin Morgan's "Goodbye to All That"—Friedan's book can be seen to be doing something else. In her explorations of the psychic pain and sexual dysfunction of martini-slurping housewives, Friedan maps out a fantastical landscape of feminist contention that is at once familiar and strange. The scenes of heterosexual domesticity in which the middle-class white woman is supposed to find her raison d'être become, instead, the scene of her estrangement from the ideal she is supposed to embody and represent. Rather than white, middle-class women per se, it is the consumerist fantasy of national belonging located in the privatized domains of bourgeois family life that is revealed to be as "sickly" and sick inducing in Friedan's exposé of "the problem with no name." The whiteness and middle-classness of the women Friedan interviews and writes for are not so much emblematic of their normality but more the signs of their perversity—their inability to be happy, sexually satisfied, and fulfilled mothers and wives.

The imagined terrain of women's liberation's revolt conjured through texts like the press conference in support of Kate Millett in December 1970, "Goodbye to All That," SCUM *Manifesto*, and *The Feminine Mystique* was one in which the scripts and scenarios of white, middle-class femininity were the source of discomfort, anxiety, and depression, as well as the targets of an angry denunciation. And it was in relation to these scenarios of respectable femininity that the lesbian was first used by the mass media as a "psychic weapon" to "keep women locked" in their "feminine role" and then taken up by the women's liberation movement as its figure of revolt. It is not surprising, therefore, that for many, if not all, of the young, white women, who joined the women's liberation movement in the late 1960s and early 1970s, the objects against which they fashioned themselves as radical feminists, and as lesbian feminists, would be housework, the vaginal orgasm, and marriage, for example, rather than the larger, more nebulous and abstract capitalism, sexism, and racism. And yet to read this revolt as a continuation of feminism's white middle-classness across the breach of women's liberation's angry confrontation with the coercive constraints and appeal of the feminine role is to miss the way in which that confrontation necessarily made proper femininity something less than an aspirational norm for women or, indeed, the uncontestable ground of modern feminism. Read in relation to each other, the widely circulated texts and often repeated phrases of the early women's liberation movement map out a terrain of feminist contention that brings into question, and upsets, the constellation of norms through which white, middle-class femininity mobilized a national heteronormativity in 1970. And if women's liberation ultimately failed to free itself from its attachment to those norms, the movement's troubling relation to them nevertheless opened up a space for a feminist politics of refusal and negation—figured through the lesbian— even if it did not always enact it. In 1970 women's liberation did not kill off all the daddy's girls, but it did, fleetingly, open up a space of rebellion that we might even now call Solanasesque.

3

BECOMING WOMAN IDENTIFIED WOMAN

Sexuality, Family Feelings, and
Imagining Women's Liberation

It may be that a second wave of the sexual revolution might at last accomplish its aim of freeing half the race from its immemorial subordination—and in the process bring us all a great deal closer to humanity. It may be that we shall even be able to retire sex from the harsh realities of politics, but not until we have created a world we can bear out of the desert we inhabit.—KATE MILLETT, *Sexual Politics*

Lesbianism is to feminism what the Communist Party was to the trade union movement. Tactically, any feminist should fight to the death for lesbianism because of its strategic importance.—TI-GRACE ATKINSON, *Amazon Odyssey*

With the publication of *Sexual Politics* in the summer of 1970, women's liberation produced one of its most widely read and polemically ambitious texts. Echoing in intention the broad historical sweep and universalizing arguments of Simone de Beauvoir's *The Second Sex*, Kate Millett's book set out to "formulate a systematic overview of patriarchy as a political institution" by attributing its historical and social constancy to the "political aspect" of sex.[1] In the first part of the book Millett offers a theory of sexual politics as a "social constant" running "through all other political, social, and economic forms,"[2] while in the second she offers a historical overview of patriarchy as a social system, which could ebb and flow with the fluctuations of the modern sexual revolution and counterrevolution. She concludes the book with the work of four male writers—Norman Mailer, Henry Miller, D. H. Lawrence, and Jean Genet—which she reads as offering exemplary instances of sexual politics in literature or, in the case of Genet, as offering insight into the arbitrariness of its ideological apparatus. Though the book began life as a doctoral dissertation, it was published by a mainstream publisher and marketed to a general audience. At the same time, parts of Millett's "Theory of Sexual Politics" circulated in the alternative media networks of the New Left and women's liberation movements prior to the book's publication, with an essay of the same name appearing in Robin Morgan's mass-marketed anthology *Sisterhood Is Powerful*, published in 1970. With its near simultaneous appearance in movement media networks and the national public sphere, the book was received with great fanfare and not a small amount of controversy in both the women's liberation movement and the mainstream media.[3]

As Cora Kaplan notes in her short essay on *Sexual Politics*, one of the book's most lasting contributions to feminist theory and literary criticism is its reading of literature as both a venue and source for the production of sexual norms and values. In the aftermath of Millett's passionate, if overly positivistic, critiques of high literary depictions of sex, it is now almost impossible to read the representation of sex in literature and film without addressing it as an ideological issue.[4] And read within the context of the newly emergent gay and women's liberation movements, Millett's insistence on criticizing the sexual explicitness and presumed radicalism of writers such as Norman Mailer and Henry Miller, as being both homophobic and misogynistic, opened up the possibilities for a wide-ranging critique of heterosex in both movements. Indeed, the explosive appeal of *Sexual Politics* in 1970 can be attributed to the way in which it participated in a mainstream and countercultural fascination with the emancipatory possibilities of sex. From Hugh Hefner to Herbert Marcuse, sex as play and desire rather than reproductive hetero-coupledom was thought of as a potential practice of freedom from the instrumentalization of modern capitalist society or, in Hefner's case, the disciplinary and financial burdens (for men) of middle-class family life. Millett's intervention in this widespread fascination with the liberatory possibilities of sex, of course, significantly shifted the terms of the discussion by inserting a strong feminist critique of the inherent masculinist bias in the institutions and representations of sexual practice. And yet, she too located the future emancipation of women in a new sexual revolution, one that would not only free women from their feminine role but would also free sex itself "from the harsh realities of politics."

In locating the source of women's subjugation in sex as well as their potential emancipation, Millett's thesis can be read as doing what Michel Foucault famously accuses the gay and women's liberation movements more generally of doing: finding the truth of one's being in sex and, therefore, of extending rather than challenging the racist biopolitics of the modern nation-state.[5] Nevertheless, it is in Millett's, albeit theoretically fuzzy and unevenly developed, notion of "sexual politics" that we find one of the more enduring and suggestive conceptual remainders of second-wave feminism. The term conjoins her definition of the political as "power-structured relationships, arrangements whereby one group of persons is controlled by another" through "techniques of control," with her equally succinct identification of "coitus" as a "charged microcosm" of psychological feelings, social relations, and cultural values.[6] In her suggestion that sexual relations operate as a locus for the production of social power, Millett's notion of sex echoes, rather than contradicts, Foucault's near contemporaneous definition of sexuality as a "dense transfer point for relations of power."[7]

To think of Millett's understanding of sexual politics as an echo of Foucault's definition of sexuality is not to make it the same or to think of it as an immediate precursor to Foucault's perhaps more sophisticated theoretical elaboration. Rather it is to think of it in Benjaminian terms as a "blazing up" from the past and from a different theoretical archive (radical feminism as distinct from poststructuralism) that allows us to see, in a flash, a connection between the two. What we glimpse in early second-wave attempts to map the relationship between the sexual and the political is a struggle to understand the subjugation of women through social institutions, ideologies (like the family and heterosexuality), and through what Pierre Bourdieu would later call "family feelings." Foucault's decentering and spatializing of power allowed him to conceive of sexuality as a field of power that shifted the focus of analysis away from the individual as the source of desire and/or feeling and toward an emphasis on practices, relations, and discourses. Bourdieu would later take up Foucault's understanding of power in his conception of the family as a "field of forces" and "struggles" that constructs social reality through the reproduction of social space and relations. In Bourdieu's terms, the family is enacted as an "instrument" in the construction of reality through the two-way relationship between the "objective structures" of the social and the "subjective mental structures" of each family member (i.e., all members of society)—structures that are themselves socially constructed.[8] Family feelings, then, are the "obliged affections and affective obligations" that form what we recognize collectively to be conjugal, maternal, paternal, and filial love. Our disposition to feel or love in these recognized ways comes from what Bourdieu calls "the practical and symbolic work that transforms the obligation to love into a loving disposition."[9] Millett, along with radical feminist contemporaries like Shulamith Firestone, Anne Koedt, and Ti-Grace Atkinson, attempted, like feminists before them, to expand the doing of politics into an understanding of the family as an "instrument" of social reproduction, and they, along with other gay and women's liberationist thinkers like Laura X, Martha Shelley, Allen Young, and Craig Rodman, also identified sex as a source and conduit of power.[10] It is this effective dispersal of the political into the realm of social relations, conceived at the same time as sexual and "psychic," that forms one of the key interventions of early women's and gay liberation problematizations of the "personal" in relation to the idea and practice of politics.

In this chapter, my reading of the archive of women's liberation shifts from texts that conjured the terrain of women's liberation's revolt against the scenarios and narratives of proper femininity to those that elaborated its political goals and claims. The emphasis is on the "rhetorical possibilities" of the movement's calls for women's freedom and claims to a feminist collectivity rather than, as in the last chapter, on the scenes and figures of its rebellion. Attention to the rhetoric of women's liberation enables the tracking of its communicative power, its "liveliness" and "vivacity," to borrow again from Daniel Gross's study of seventeenth-century political rhetoric.[11] Analyzing the rhetoric of women's liberation, in other words, makes it possible to trace the conditions of the movement's political visibility, and viability, for different constituencies of women. In this chapter, then, I focus on how the feminist-as-lesbian emerged as a shorthand notation for the movement's political aspirations and imagined constituency. Again, the questions are not why did papers like the Radicalesbian's "The Woman Identified Woman" or phrases like "the personal is political" become so influential as foundational claims or statements for women's liberation, but how did these position papers and phrases participate in the circulation of particular images and ideas through which "women's liberation" became a counterpublic with its own symbolic lexicon and political constituency.

What kinds of emancipatory claims were invoked and made meaningful through the figure of the lesbian in these texts, and what kinds of freedoms for women, and in the name of women, were being imagined as a consequence?

As in the last chapter, my reading along the grain of the archive of women's liberation tracks the production of a feminism that came to be marked by its whiteness and middle-classness, despite the movement's often explicitly antiracist and anticapitalist political platform. But in this chapter, I shift my attention from examining the way in which the movement took shape as a predominantly white woman's movement to examining the way in which the movement's claiming of a political collectivity, in the name of women, produced ideas of free or independent women, which were implicitly, and inevitably, marked by race and class exclusions. Sexuality was the primary site of women's liberation's claims to a political collectivity—women's freedom was increasingly imagined by the movement through their emancipation from the affective and social obligations of family life and the coercive demands of heterosexuality. But as Kate Millett's utopian linking of women's freedom with the freeing of sex from politics at the end of *Sexual Politics* also suggests, sexuality was simultaneously idealized as a field of human experience that could potentially liberate women from social and cultural constraints—including those of race and class. What I am most interested in tracking, then, is the way in which the early movement's theoretical and polemical texts produced an unsettled and contradictory understanding of sexuality that can be read as revealing the densely problematic relationship of the personal to the political and of feminist claims to a political collectivity through the politicization of sexuality, at that time. Rather than collapsing the political into the sexual, as many queer and poststructural feminist critics of the second wave and of lesbian feminism in particular would have it, these texts tend to pose the question of their relation rather than explain or solve it—in much the same way in fact as Foucault's enigmatic and under-theorized call for "bodies and pleasures" rather than "sex-desire" at the end of *The History of Sexuality, Volume One*.[12]

The feminist-as-lesbian, once again, becomes the figure that provides an entryway into the eventfulness of women's liberation; in this case, the struggles of women's liberation to imagine a collectivity in the name of women and to enact political claims on its behalf. She, along with phrases like "the personal is political" and "the lavender menace," becomes an access point to women's liberation's contingent, that is to say, compromised and contained, emergence as a movement with a distinct political culture. While chapter 2 was concerned with countering feminist historical narratives that seek to explain women's liberation's "failure" as a feminist movement in terms of its preoccupation with the private and the domestic (read, white middle-class problems), in this chapter the concern is with reading against the grain of the related accusation by queer theorists and sex-positive feminists of the movement's adoption of a political lesbianism, which, in its essentialism, was exclusive not only of other kinds of nonnormative lesbian or queer sex but also of other kinds of feminist protest and collectivity. By approaching the feminist-as-lesbian as an access point to the tumultuous beginnings of women's liberation, and by reading along the grain of the movement's archive, I want to open up the complexity of women's liberation's rejection of normative heterosexuality and its attendant production of a politicized lesbianism. I do so in order to trace, rather than condemn, the productive force of the movement's claims to a political collectivity, even if it will also lead, as it surely must, to a confrontation with some of the unintended effects of those claims.

THE PERSONAL IS POLITICAL

Although, as recent sociological studies of the various feminist movements of the second wave make clear, particular constituencies of women faced different contingencies in their coming to feminism, a focus on personal experience was common across the diversity of feminisms produced at this time.[13] For black and Chicana feminists, as for white feminists in women's liberation, personal experience was the beginning point for their critical resistance to the masculinist ideologies and practices of their "parent" movements—Black Power, the Chicano movement, and the New Left—as well as to the dominant discourses of gender, class, race, and sexual privilege operating in the national public sphere.[14] As Kimberly Springer argues in her analysis of black feminist organizations in the second-wave era, for many black women involved in the civil rights and black nationalist movements, their coming to feminism was forged in the "fissures created by contradictions in rhetoric and action—rhetoric of freedom juxtaposed with concrete sexist behaviors black women witnessed and sometimes experienced" in organizations like the Congress on Racial Equality (CORE) and the Student Nonviolent Coordinating Committee (SNCC).[15] Concrete "sexist behavior" was practiced across the social, racial, and geographic borders that separated the different movements from each other, and it included such things as exclusively male strategy meetings, demands that women cook and look after the children, and coerced sexual relations. In conjunction with the repressions and effacements of a Cold War domestic ideology that sought to contain women in a classed and raced ideal of consumer driven family life, the everyday intimacies of the sexist practices of movement men became the catalyst for the eruption of feminisms across race and class difference in the late 1960s—Robin Morgan's "Goodbye to All That," discussed in chapter 2, is but one example of such an eruption.

In addition, multiple feminist analyses of cultural, sexual, and psychological oppression in the postwar era took place within the context of the failure of politics to offer either an explanation or a set of actions that could address the new domestic and international realities of the Cold War period. A loss of confidence in the grand narratives of revolution and progress, engendered in the most immediate sense by the crimes committed by both the Allies and the Nazis in the Second World War, provoked what Wendy Brown has diagnosed as "an era of profound political disorientation" in the postwar years.[16] While neither Marxism nor liberalism were superseded or replaced as grand political theories, the erosion of their constitutive premises created a fragmentation of the notion of what counted as political action and a multiplication of interpretations of what politics was.[17] Different constituencies (nationalist, indigenous, civil rights movements, students, women, gays) began to conceive of different ways of doing the political and, as Foucault writes of the era, "to ask politics a whole series of questions that were not traditionally a part of its statutory domain."[18] Women's liberation, like other second-wave feminisms, rather than being anterior to or simply an agent of this political disorientation, was formed by it. The incoherencies of its mixture of liberal ideals and Marxist analysis and its confusion of revolution with the personal and intimate lives of women were symptoms of the breaking down of the foundations of modernist political narratives. The politics of women's liberation was a strange and incoherent mixture because politics—what it was and how to do it—was, in the late 1960s, open to debate.

The incoherence of what politics was, and how to do it, manifested itself in phrases like "the personal is political," which, by 1970, had become a powerfully enigmatic statement of and for women's liberation. That "the personal is political" now tends to operate as a kind of motto, or better still, an epitaph on the tombstone of a feminism now remembered by many as inadequate or lacking in some way, speaks to its unmooring from the historical context in which it emerged. "The personal is political" has become an empty phrase—empty, that is, of the complex historical moment that engendered it. Indeed, we are now more likely to hear it as the birthing cry of that most infamous of second-wave crimes: essentialism. As a performance of essentialist thinking, "the personal is political" is read as literally equating personal experience with the political. Women's experience becomes, as Joan Scott has argued in a different context, the foundational site from which a feminist politics is fashioned, and as a result, some women's experiences—those of the feminists who write and theorize about them, namely, white, middle-class women—become the authentic, defining ground for who "women" are and what feminism is.[19] In this reading, "the personal is political" signals a naïve collapsing of "women" into "experience" and "politics," which has resulted in the privileging of white, middle-class women as the site and source of (second-wave) feminism. But what if the meaning of the phrase was never so singular and fixed? What if we read its elegant simplicity as an enigmatic trace from the past of women's liberation and, therefore, as potentially productive of multiple interpretations? Rather than understand "the personal is political" as a statement that (belatedly) describes a settled theoretical position, then, I want to approach it here as a phrase that had the capacity to conjure multiple, even contradictory, feminist claims to a political collectivity at the time of women's liberation's emergence. "The personal is political" became a magical phrase for women's liberation, not least because it could accommodate a diverse array of investments in a projected commonality of women's experience. But more than this, "the personal is political," like the metaphor of the feminine mystique discussed in chapter 2, simultaneously invoked and made strange a domain of experience not typically subject to political inquiry—not simply "the family" or heterosexuality but the "affective obligations" and messy desires of a female sexuality they engendered and organized.[20]

The phrase "the personal is political" is usually attributed to Carol Hanisch, who published a position paper under that title in New York Radical Women's "Notes from the Second Year: Women's Liberation" in 1970. Although, as numerous contributors to the Women's Studies Listserv (WMST-1) note, the phrase, or set of ideas that produced it, can be traced back through the theories of the New Left and civil rights movements to the postwar sociologist of American corporate culture C. Wright Mills and beyond.[21] And according to Carol Hanisch in an essay reflecting on the significance of her paper published in 1970, it was in fact Kathie Sarachild and Shulamith Firestone, as editors of "Notes from the Second Year," who gave her paper its title.[22] This qualification by Hanisch reveals the improvisational way in which the ideas and concepts of women's liberation were formed. It also reminds us that the thought of women's liberation was formed out of political contestation and epistemological uncertainty rather than coherent political agendas and theories. As Hanisch writes, it "is important to realize that the paper came out of struggle—not just my struggle in SCEF [Southern Conference Educational Fund] but the struggle of the independent WLM [women's liberation movement] against those who were trying to stop it or to push it into directions they found less threatening."[23]

Hanisch initially wrote her paper in 1969 as a response to another SCEF member's contention that consciousness raising was just "therapy."[24] Arguments over the utility of consciousness raising were taking place across the movement in the late 1960s as the New Left and civil rights movements sought to come to terms with the explosion of women's liberation groups across the country. The suspicion, even antipathy, expressed in the civil rights and New Left movements toward women's liberation was due, at least initially, to the inherent critique of the organized Left posed by the rise of women's liberation groups as distinct and often entirely separate entities. While many of the newly formed women's liberation groups expressed their difference from the Left in terms of a desire to address the specificity of their "own oppression," the New Left and civil rights movements tended to view the rise of women's liberation as a turning away from politics on the part of the women involved and, more pointedly, as a turn toward a bourgeois preoccupation with "personal problems." This story of women's liberation's rise as a separate movement is, as I discuss in chapter 2, a familiar one; yet the agonistic framing of the narrative tends to cover over a much more profound challenge to dominant ideas of the political posed by women's liberation's emergence—a challenge that began in the New Left and civil rights movements and of which women's liberation was as much an effect as a cause.[25]

Another "living document" of the 1960s, one positioned by its authors as "open to change with our times and experiences," was the Port Huron Statement, written during the Students for a Democratic Society (SDS) national conference in Michigan in 1962.[26] A hugely influential manifesto, the Port Huron Statement was the most detailed expression of a significant reorientation of the political in the United States in the postwar years.[27] In Marianne DeKoven's view this reorientation can best be understood in terms of the "pivot" the statement "enacts" from "modern democracy to postmodern populism," a shift linked, according to DeKoven, to the statement's focus on developing a "politics of the self."[28] This shift is most evident in the statement's preoccupation with constructing a new kind of citizen activist, and in her reading of the statement, DeKoven tracks the structure of feeling that augments the appearance of this new citizen activist. Like a phoenix rising out of the ashes of an American society sick with "apathy" and "complacency," the students identified by the statement as the vanguard of their generation, acting initially out of a sense of indignant frustration with their contemporary moment, will "give form to the feelings of helplessness and indifference," permeating their generation and "transform[ing] 'modern complexity' into 'issues that can be understood and felt close up by every human being.'"[29] For DeKoven, this construction of the student as citizen activist situated in time and place often sits uneasily with the statement's utopian passion for total social transformation—an uneasiness that signals the statement's confused mix of modern and postmodern impulses. And for DeKoven it is precisely this confusion that marks the statement's significance for postwar reorientations of the political. It is in the linkage between a preoccupation with changing the habits and "inner life" of a particular group of Americans and acting for the total transformation of American society—the seemingly "unattainable" and "unimaginable" utopia of achieving an actually existing participatory democracy—that we witness in the statement a move away from the universalizing politics of orthodox Marxism and liberal humanism and toward the situated, fragmented, and provisional politics of the postmodern present.[30]

DeKoven's historicizing analysis of the Port Huron Statement sets the ground for understanding the link—articulated most forcefully if also enigmatically through the phrase "the personal is political"—between the New Left and women's liberation movements. The statement's focus on self-transformation, and its call for a politics that could be "felt up close," created the space for women in the movement to interrogate their own feelings of alienation and helplessness. And it is this space that Hanisch identifies for women's liberation as the space of consciousness raising: "I continue to go to these meetings because I have gotten a political understanding which all my reading, all my 'political discussions,' all my 'political action,' all my four-odd years in the movement never gave me. I've been forced to take off the rose colored glasses and face the awful truth about how grim my life really is as a woman. I am getting a gut understanding of everything as opposed to the esoteric, intellectual understandings and no-blesse oblige feelings I had in 'other people's' struggles."[31] For Hanisch as for the Port Huron Statement, a politics that can be "felt close up," that offers a "gut understanding" of the world, enables self-knowledge and self-authenticity as well as the opportunity to "participate" in political action. But there is a qualitative shift here in how Hanisch articulates the relationship between the personal and the political and how the Port Huron Statement articulates that relationship. In the statement the emphasis is firmly on the benefits of (localized and informal) political action for self-transformation: "Politics has the function of bringing people out of isolation and into community, thus being a necessary, though not sufficient, means of finding meaning in personal life; ... the political order should ... provide outlets for the expression of personal grievance and aspiration ... channels should be commonly available to relate men to knowledge and to power so that private problems—from bad recreation facilities to personal alienation—are formulated as general issues."[32] Here, the personal isn't so much political as translated into something else through political action and discourse: "private problems" are to be reformulated as "general issues." The personal, in other words, is a problem to be solved in the striving toward a participatory democracy of authentic, autonomous, free-thinking selves. In Hanisch's articulation, in contrast, the personal becomes the site of interrogation and the focus of political action rather than simply its beneficiary. For Hanisch, "experiences and feelings" are the things that need analysis and action precisely because they affect political action and organizations in ways politics remains unknowing about: "Women have left the movement in droves. The obvious reasons are that we are tired of being sex slaves and doing shitwork for men whose hypocrisy is so blatant in their political stance of liberation for everybody (else). But there is really a lot more to it than that. I can't quite articulate it yet."[33] What that something more is, and remains, is the often unrepresentable yet highly contested affective and emotional grounds of women's liberation's claims to a collective political identity.

The struggle to find a language that could give form to the problem of the personal as a problem that politics could address and change is evident in much of the early theorizing of the second wave. In fact, many of the now classic texts of the emergent women's liberation movement were preoccupied with locating the source of women's oppression in feelings of sexual exploitation and dissatisfaction, and by 1970 the critique of psychosexual relations between men and women dominated the theoretical and polemical output of radical feminism.[34] Essays like Marge Piercy's "The Grand Coolie Damn" and position papers like Laura X's "On Our Sexual Liberation" argued for a radical feminist politics, not just in terms of an exposure of gender hierarchies in the social and political domains but also in terms of the sexual practices and emotions between men and women. While Laura X's paper is an angry denunciation of the so-called sexual liberation of the 1960s, in which she portrays the pill as just one more form of male control over women, Marge Piercy, in an echo of Robin Morgan's "Goodbye to All That," takes the New Left to task by portraying it as a movement full of "machers" using sex to manipulate and exploit their female comrades. Sex, according to both Piercy and Laura X, as well as for lesbian feminists like Sue Katz, who wrote the equally polemical "Smash Phallic Imperialism," was the current through which power operated in the relationship between men and women.[35] Similarly, Millett's criticisms of the family as the historical generator of (hetero)sexual politics had much in common with Shulamith Firestone's rewriting of historical materialism in *The Dialectic of Sex*, which was also published in 1970 but was largely eclipsed at the time by the magnetizing power of *Sexual Politics*. Firestone's historical dialectic essentially reverses Marx's privileging of the public sphere of work over and against the private sphere of reproduction. She argues, in contrast, that the real dynamic of human history is "psychosexual," not economic. For Firestone, the "basic reproductive unit" of the biological family instituted a psychic as well as material relation of "dominance-submission," which then organized all other forms of social organization. In this dialectic it was love and sexual desire in the form of heterosexual reproductive relations, not capital, that had to be destroyed.[36]

Women's liberation is imagined in these texts as freedom from the sexual dependencies and exploitation of heterosexual coupledom and family life. The personal that needs to be exposed to the demystifications of political analysis and critique is both the quotidian world of hetero-domesticity and also the intangible atmosphere of love and desire that maintains and reproduces it. Conversely, nonexploitative sexual and emotional relationships with others are either implied or invoked—increasingly in the form of lesbianism—as a route out of the subjugations of heterosexual family relations and toward social and sexual freedom. It is these imaginings, and the claims to a commonality of women's experiences they enact, that also make "the personal" the scene of an intense disidentification with women's liberation by many black women and women of color during the early years of the second-wave movement.

Indeed, as Sara Evans writes in her influential account of the "roots" of women's liberation in the civil rights movement and New Left, there was, by the late 1960s, a profound "lack of trust and solidarity" between white and black women in the civil rights movement.[37] Kimberly Springer largely agrees with Sara Evans's analysis, although she also notes that the lack of trust between black and white women was exacerbated by the failure—of both black and white women—to confront the particularity of their situatedness as women *in relation* to each other. As Springer writes, for white women in the movement, "black women's race *erased* them as women with some degree of power in the organization," while black women "deemphasized their gender because they prioritized their racial identity in the struggle for black self-determination."[38] Evans notes that while many black women in SNCC were, by the mid-1960s, project leaders and field organizers, white women were feeling increasingly marginalized in a movement that was turning toward Black Power and away from "the beloved community" idea of interracial activism. In addition, the "freedom summer" of 1964 had exacerbated what Evans delicately calls the "intricate maze of tensions and struggles" around the issue of sex between white women and black men in the civil rights movement.[39] If a significant number of white women in the movement felt they were being reduced to sexual and domestic helpmates, black women felt they were being increasingly relied upon to take on the burden of organizing and planning actions while being ignored as potential partners by men in the movement. The ambiguous honor of being regarded as "one of the boys" left many black women feeling, if not deeply resentful, at the very least ambivalent toward white women and their hypersexualized status within the movement.[40]

In the sense that it continues to be remembered as a significant, even foundational text of women's liberation, the most notable response to the "intricate maze of tensions and struggles" between black and white women in the movement is Casey Hayden and Mary King's "Sex and Caste: A Kind of Memo." Hayden and King wrote their paper in the fall of 1965 and addressed it to "a number of other women in the peace and freedom movements," many of whom were black. There has been much feminist commentary on the limitations of Hayden and King's conception of the sex caste system as analogous to racism, and I'm not interested in rehearsing it again here. However, I am interested in reading the paper against the grain of its status, albeit contested, as a foundational text for women's liberation's emergence as a movement with its own political claims and domain of struggle. I am interested, in other words, in tracking how the paper's assumption of "the personal" as intimate heterosexual relations necessarily results in its failure to do what it sets out to do: namely to "open up a dialogue" with other women so that "we can start to talk to each other more openly than in the past and create a community of support for each other."[41] Through a symptomatic reading of "Sex and Caste: A Kind of Memo" I want to demonstrate how, during the emergent moments of women's liberation, black and white women came into incommensurate contact with each other through what, in the abstract terms of formal categories, they had in common: heterosexuality, sexism, and motherhood.

The hesitant, even timid tone of "Sex and Caste: A Kind of Memo"—signaled from the start by its subtitle—can be attributed in one sense to the difficulty of defining its object. As the authors note, to write or speak of a "common-law caste system" is "complicated" by the fact that it operates "subtly," that is, beyond and in excess of recognized institutional or structural formations such as the family, the law, or work.[42] Instead, the sex-caste system seems to be at its most pervasive and effective, according to Hayden and King, when it operates through intangibles like "perspectives" and feelings. It is the "caste-system perspective" that assigns women the role of cleaner, secretary, or jealous love rival in the movement "freedom house," and it is the "deeply learned fears, needs, and self-perceptions" of the women themselves that keep them in these roles. Here, the site of "the sex-caste system" is figured as the movement "freedom house," which is revealed, as if by a cruel joke, to be the all too familiar home of women's subjugation. For Hayden and King, the "problem" of the sex-caste system is felt most acutely in the intimate scenes of a domesticated space of heterosexual relations—a space that cuts across the divide between private and public and between radical politics and conservative social forms. It is "women and [their] personal relations with men," implicitly imagined as a universal organizing principle of human society, that Hayden and King locate as the site of the "struggle" against the sex-caste system and the feelings and perspectives it engenders.

Another related reason for the hesitant tone of "Sex and Caste: A Kind of Memo" can be attributed to the authors' keen awareness that "the problems" they are rather uneasily attempting to name incite intense emotions. Acknowledging that many men in the movement feel exposed by discussions concerning women's roles and feelings and resort to dismissive laughter, Hayden and King are also quick to note that women in turn often "feel silly" and "learn not to trust our inner feelings" when faced with men's derision. And perhaps their awareness that the memo could provoke powerful emotions leads Hayden and King to resort to generalities and vague words rather than the specificity of example and illustration. As it is, the sex-caste system remains a general problem for Hayden and King, and they leave the particularities of the "struggles" women face in their personal relations with men to the imaginations of their readers. And while the vagueness of "Sex and Caste: A Kind of Memo" might, on the one hand, be attributable to understandable fears of opening up a pandora's box of female resentments and anger and men's equally robust contempt, it can also be attributable to a series of assumptions about precisely what is of most concern or difficulty for women in their daily lives. While Hayden and King address their memo to women in the movement in order to "open up a dialogue," "the community of discussion" they envision is not one of internal critique and self-reflection among and between women, but one of mutual "support" that will help individual women "deal with ourselves and others" as they go out into the world and, as the essay implicitly assumes, have sexual and domestic relations with men. The assumption is that women share common problems and that those problems are not simply generated by the same thing—personal relations with men—but that they are felt and experienced the same way by all women.

The black women addressed by "Sex and Caste: A Kind of Memo" are interpellated as being just like the authors, and the problems they experience in the movement are presumed to be the same as those experienced by white women. But more than this, the space for dialogue, and the idea of community for women, is predicated on the practices, feelings, and perspectives the memo wishes to bring into question—what we might now call heteronormativity, which is at the same time a class and raced ideal. In its attempt to open up the sex-caste system as a problem to be discussed, the memo encodes the personal as a set of practical and affective relations between men and women, and it is this presumed domain of experience that then becomes the locus for a feminist critique of social norms. The unintended effect of this encoding is that the object of feminist critique also becomes the ground for that critique, and the norms that secure the domain of privatized hetero-experiences as prepolitical are secured rather than brought into question.

The position of women in SNCC was raised as an issue as early as the summer of 1964, when a group of women staff members, led by Ruby Doris Smith Robinson, attempted to confront the swirling atmosphere of sexual transgression, experimentation, exploitation, tension, resentment, and abuse that characterized "the freedom summer" for many of the women—black and white—in the movement. According to Sara Evans this was the first, and last, attempt by black and white women in SNCC to come together and address the sexual politics of the movement. As Cynthia Washington writes in a retrospective essay on her time in the civil rights movement, Casey Hayden's complaints in the fall of 1964 about the limited roles for women in the movement "didn't make any particular sense" to her because she was running her own voter registration project in Mississippi. Washington remembers "thinking how crazy [white women] were. I couldn't understand what they wanted."[43] For Washington, as for other black women in SNCC, the burdens of responsibility for the projects and actions they organized and the people they supervised, with few resources and little assistance, outweighed any simple enjoyment of "independence" or authority, and their "relative autonomy" as project directors and field workers distinguished them, in their view, from the women Stokely Carmichael had in mind when he made his infamous joke that the only position for women in SNCC was "prone."

The struggles Cynthia Washington and other black women faced (like those of Barbara Smith who, after her own experience at a predominantly white women's liberation conference, also thought "those women were *crazy . . . perfectly crazy*")[44] were ones that would be addressed in the consciousness-raising groups of black feminist organizations rather than in "the community" Hayden and King envisioned. As Springer writes, the goals of the Black Women's Alliance (BWA), which grew out of SNCC's Black Women's Liberation Caucus in 1969 (and later became the Third World Women's Alliance), were to "dispel the myth of the black matriarchy[,] . . . to re-evaluate the oppression of black women in slavery," and to "redefine the role of the black woman in revolutionary struggle," specifically by countering the "sexism of black nationalist rhetoric."[45] That is, the problems for black women in SNCC, while perhaps covered by general categories like "sexism" or even "the sex-caste system," were the effects of a distinct if related historical trajectory from that of white women—one that produced very different affects, experiences, and practical knowledge. It is for this reason, perhaps, that the only reference made by Hayden and King in their memo to the relationship between black and white women in the movement appears, as if from nowhere, at the end of a paragraph detailing the restrictive domestic roles of women in the movement: "There are problems with relationships between white women and black women." With this last, enigmatic statement, Hayden and King invoke the incommensurability of the historical experiences of black and white women—both in the movement and beyond—and open up the possibility that the locus of the personal as a problem for feminism was not, in fact, "personal relations" between men and women but the practices, scripts, feelings, and histories that make up the social field of femininity—precisely the contested field of experience that held black and white women in relation to each other.[46]

Today, "the personal is political," in the context of women's liberation, tends to operate more as a screen memory than as a conjuration of the varied, and unsettling, challenges made to the workings of social power in the second-wave era. As an explanation for the rise of women's liberation, Black Power, and gay liberation, "organizing around your own oppression" does not begin to suggest the highly charged and densely complex set of events that saw the emergence of these so-called identity movements out of the dissolution of the New Left and civil rights movements. The dispersal of the political into multiple localities, and the attendant opening up of the personal as a domain for political action and thought, incited diverse, often conflicting, but sometimes corresponding responses by different constituencies of women. "The personal," in other words, became a problem for feminism during the emergence of the second wave rather than simply the site of the movement's becoming or future solution. The desire to find a politics that could be "felt close up," that touched individual women in ways that gave them "a gut understanding" of their social worlds, necessarily meant that individual women apprehended their lives differently. What counted as the personal, then, became a highly charged area of contention for feminism during the second-wave era precisely because it both drew upon and laid claim to—in the form of consciousness raising— the sensate knowledge of women whose experiences were the product of distinct historical trajectories.

When the Radicalesbians stood up at the Second Congress to Unite Women in 1970 revealing T-shirts with the words *Lavender Menace* blazoned across them, they were responding to an insult that was also, at the same time, a strangely apt premonition of what would happen to cultural configurations of lesbianism as they came into contact with women's liberation. If "the personal is political" figured the ground of women's liberation's political claims as the psychic and affective world of hetero-femininity—a figuring that invoked the fault lines of class and race, and which threatened the nominal fantasy of a unified women's movement—lesbianism became the scenario through which those claims were most acutely and explosively dramatized. It was Betty Friedan who, according to Susan Brownmiller, first "groused" about lesbians in women's liberation as "a lavender menace" threatening to "warp the image" and the goals of the larger women's movement.[47] The term, while an obvious identification of the Radicalesbians with gay liberation and homosexuality in general, was also an echo of the late nineteenth- and early twentieth-century figure of "the lady in lavender"—that supposedly passionless but nevertheless sexually suspect spinster who devoted her life to woman's rights—and was perhaps conjured up by Friedan as a way to call forth memories of that earlier historical moment as a presentiment of the lonely future women's liberation's distracting preoccupation with "bedroom issues" was threatening to engineer for American women.[48] Whatever Friedan's actual intentions, the invocation of the lady in lavender generated the specter of a bourgeois feminism incapable of fusing political demands for greater social freedom with the more "personal" demands of sexual liberation and autonomy for women. And certainly the formation of lesbian feminism during the early 1970s can be read, and has been read, as failing to maintain in productive tension sex as a plenitude of acts and pleasures with politicizations of sexuality as a force field of experience.

By the time the Furies published a series of highly influential papers on lesbianism as a practice of political separatism in 1972,[49] and certainly during the "sex wars" of the late 1970s, which culminated in the painful public confrontations between antipornography and sex radical, pro-pleasure feminists at the Barnard Conference in 1982, lesbian feminism had come to be known by many feminist, gay, and queer activists as an essentialist and often oppressively dogmatic form of feminism, which reduced "good" sex and "good" feminism to the necessarily vague ideal of loving relationships between women-identified women.[50] In the space of a decade, the Lavender Menace had been transformed from the scourge of a liberal, equal rights–orientated feminism into bourgeois imperialists threatening the discursive and sexual diversity of a counterpublic feminist sphere. And today, of course, collective cultural memories of lesbian feminism abound within U.S. academic feminism and beyond as a thoroughly unsexy and implicitly racist and classist form of identity politics.

But it didn't have to be this way. In this section I move from a discussion of "the personal is political" as a phrase that conjured the imagined commonality of women's experience from which women's liberation made claims to a political collectivity, to an exploration of the specificity of those claims. The focus of my analysis is on tracking how the lesbian became a figure that provided a form for thinking women's liberation as the freeing of women from the obliged affections and affective obligations of the "sex-caste system." In order to emphasize the projective and creative force of women's liberation's configurations of lesbianism, I return to the moment just before "lesbian feminism" became an identifiable—and knowable—form of feminism. That is, instead of approaching lesbian feminism as a coherent political project to be excavated, and critiqued, in retrospect, I want to pay attention to how a description of lesbians as "a lavender menace" worked as a "fantasy echo" of feminist political projection in the early years of the women's liberation movement. *Fantasy echo* is Joan Scott's term for conceptualizing the process of identification that makes it possible for specific groups or individuals, at "particular and discrete moments in time," to fashion themselves as social and political actors.[51] For Scott, the term invokes the complex interplay of imagination, repetition, and condensation at work in any attempt to identify and mobilize a collectivity: "Fantasy is at play in the articulation of both individual and collective identity; it extracts coherence from confusion, reduces multiplicity to singularity, and reconciles illicit desire with the law. It enables individuals and groups to give themselves histories."[52] All identities are imagined, and all identities are imagined through recollection—of past political or social scenarios that serve as resources for, and as symptomatic echoes of, the fantasies at work in the attempt or desire to fashion a new identity in the present. However, in her use of the word *echo*, Scott reminds us that identification does not work through a simple mimicry of past ways of identifying (as a woman, a feminist, a lesbian) but through "a delayed return" or inexact invocation that, in its incompleteness, creates "gaps of meaning and intelligibility" between one invention of identity and another. It is these gaps that form the historical difference between one act of feminist identification and another; they are also the point from which we can interrogate the conflicts and contradictions the fantasy of an identity both reproduces and masks.

Scott's conception of the fantasy echo is useful here, I think, because it locates the problem of identity for a political movement in the tension between the historical embededdness of any claim to a political or social identity (the fashioning of something new out of the old that is the process of identification) and the necessary play of fantasy that reverberates across time and space, enabling the kinds of collective association demanded by social movements like women's liberation. As an analytic term, *fantasy echo* requires us to locate the affective force and emotional appeal of "a lavender menace" in the contingencies of its particular moment in time. As an echo of the lady in lavender figure of the late nineteenth and early twentieth centuries, and as a fantasy scenario of lesbian revolt against feminist, and antifeminist, homophobia in the present tense of the early women's liberation movement, the term *lavender menace* evoked sexual outsiderdom as a claim to social and sexual freedom, but it did so in a way that tended to contain its upsetting and destabilizing possibilities within the paradigm of a bourgeois femininity. It is precisely this conflict between social and sexual outsiderism as a practice of freedom *and* political mobilization, and the failure of women's liberation to solve it, that the term *lavender menace*, as an incitement to imagine a new feminist collectivity in 1970, both reproduces and covers over.

As a symbolic figure of the nineteenth-century women's rights movement, the lady in lavender suggested the liminality of the New Woman's social position within a rapidly changing American public sphere. Carroll Smith-Rosenberg, in her analysis of the emergence of the New Woman in the late nineteenth century, argues that middle- and upper-class women's attempts to fashion a public space and identity for themselves at the turn of the century were shaped by a generational conflict that erupted along the faultline of a gendered public and private social order.[53] The first generation of New Women, born in the 1850s and 1860s, tended to claim a public voice and social power through an appeal to civic duty and moral responsibility, which was, in effect, an attempt to expand the influence of the private sphere and to provide women an easier passage from the private to the public sphere of work and politics. They represented themselves as selfless "warriors for social justice"; their participation in the public sphere was justified in the name of their moral superiority over men rather than in terms of a positive claim for sexual, political, and social independence.[54] In contrast, as Smith-Rosenberg argues, the later generation, born in the 1880s and 1890s, actively asserted a distinct sexuality as part of their claims to the public sphere. In an attempt to become visible as social beings with their own sexuality, a younger generation of women drew upon consumer cultures and mass-mediated forms of publicity to fashion sexual and social identities for themselves that extended the legibility of middle-class femininity beyond domestic, heterosexual coupledom. For women who desired other women, the claim to an autonomous sexuality also led to an appropriation of the medico-scientific discourse of sexology in order to publicize their desires and styles of personhood. The "mannish lesbian" of the early twentieth century, while emerging out of a sexological discourse intent on taxonomic distinctions between pathological and normal sexuality, was, as Esther Newton has argued, one of the few identities available to women who wanted to publicly assert their desire for other women.[55]

In the shift from one generation to another the lady in lavender gives way to the mannish lesbian, and while that shift is complex, incomplete, and mutlifaceted, it is also a shift that signals a transition, for feminism, from one public sphere to another: from the political public sphere of civic life to the mass-mediated public sphere of cultural struggle. The later generation's assertion of social and sexual independence was made through an identification with masculinity and a disidentification with the "passionless" virtue of the earlier generation—a disidentification that also enacted the shift from one public sphere to another. And so, while sexologists such as Krafft-Ebing and Havelock Ellis made the connection between lesbianism and feminism explicit in their theories of sexual pathology—indeed, their taxonomic work was at least in part an attempt to wrest some sort of "expert" control over the expansive claims of an increasingly assertive bourgeois women's rights movement—the taking up of their theories by middle-class women in the 1910s and 1920s tended to lead in the opposite direction: to a disjuncture of the political and the sexual. Although a sexual strangeness and uncertainty was certainly inferred and suggested in portrayals of feminists during the first decades of the twentieth century, any direct accusation of sexual perversity was impossible within a middle-class-dominated media in which, for the sake of propriety, newspaper editors and journalists could not utter those accusations out loud, even if they knew enough to think them.[56] Similarly, although women who lived with and loved other women formed a significant part of the feminist movement during this time, lesbianism, unlike "free love" or the idealization of "companionate marriage," was never a part of the movement's political platform.[57] During the emergence of the modern feminist movement, then, conceptions of a mannish lesbianism and feminism circled around each other, informing the legibility of each but never becoming explicitly and publicly conjoined: the political and social activism of the feminist came at the expense of a perception of women as diverse and expressive sexual beings, and the sexuality of the mannish lesbian came at the expense of an apprehension of her (potential or actual) political and social association with other women.[58]

If we turn now to the era of the so-called second wave, it might be said that Anne Koedt, in her highly influential essay "The Myth of the Vaginal Orgasm," presented an argument for women's liberation that, in contradistinction to the earlier feminist moment, successfully combined the conflicting political and sexual aspirations of the two generations of New Women mapped out by Smith-Rosenberg and Newton. First presented as a paper at the inaugural national women's liberation conference in Chicago in 1968 and then published in *Notes from the Second Year* in 1970, "The Myth of the Vaginal Orgasm" became one of the most widely circulated and published papers of the women's liberation movement.[59] Drawing on the popular behavioral and physiological studies of Alfred Kinsey and Masters and Johnson, Koedt located the social and psychological oppression of women in a medico-scientific mythology of female sexuality and declared that women needed to redefine not only their sexuality but also their social freedom in terms of what gave them orgasmic pleasure: the clitoris. The clitoris is claimed by Koedt, not only as the physical source of the female orgasm but also as a synecdoche for women's potential autonomy from men and, indeed, the entire sexual order of the heterosexual contract. With Koedt's essay we witness what the phrase "the personal is political" could only suggest and what the first generation of feminists could not quite imagine: the location of an emancipatory feminist political practice in an exploration of the potentiality of female sexuality. In "The Myth of the Vaginal Orgasm," the female body as an agent of pleasure is also the site of a future social liberation for women. Following in the footsteps of her main scientific sources, Koedt locates the possibilities of sexual fulfillment in bodies and practices rather than psyches and social norms, but unlike Kinsey and Masters and Johnson, Koedt explicitly connects sexual fulfillment for women to social emancipation—an emancipation imagined by Koedt as the opening up and proliferation of diverse human relationships for women.

In my reading of "The Myth of the Vaginal Orgasm" I track the tensions inherent in Koedt's linking of women's liberation as a political project to women's ability to experience and explore different kinds of sexual pleasure. Koedt's call for the "redefinition of female sexuality" as a political project for women's liberation echoes the claims made by the second generation of early twentieth-century New Women for sexual autonomy and political power. But unlike the earlier generation of New Women, whose fantasy of a public female collectivity could not easily incorporate the self-fashioning of mannish lesbians, Koedt's focus on the body, and on the clitoris in particular, situates the basis for a collective feminist identity in the possibilities of female sexual autonomy, possibilities imagined by Koedt at the end of her essay through the figure of the lesbian. What in the earlier feminist moment remained contradictory trajectories—the claims to a sexual autonomy imagined through a "female masculinity," and the claims to a female collectivity imagined through idealized notions of a normative femininity—are, in Koedt's essay, condensed into one. Yet, as we follow the links Koedt makes between the clitoris, female sexual autonomy, lesbianism, and women's liberation to other movement position papers and documents in 1970, it becomes clear that Koedt's condensations do not so much solve the problem of the contradictory aims evident in the earlier feminist moment as reorganize their affective, sexual, and political implications.

Koedt's focus on the physiology of bodies and sexual practices is a direct challenge to the midcentury medico-psychoanalytic "experts" who had determined, through copious case studies and ethnographic research, that marital sexual dysfunction was often the result of female frigidity. Through a literalization of Freud's theories of female sexuality, these "experts" had defined female sexuality as a coming of age story in which a young girl, on reaching puberty, would "transfer the center of orgasm to the vagina" in order to facilitate mutual reproductive sexual pleasure with a male partner (199). In the narrative constructed by American psychoanalysts, the vaginal orgasm became both the achievement and destination of a successful and mature femininity, while frigidity was the fate of women who failed, or refused, to follow the script. To counter the narrative thrust of these accounts, Koedt drew upon scientific studies to argue that the vaginal orgasm was a myth based on "false assumptions about female anatomy" (198). The vagina, Koedt asserts, is physically incapable of producing an orgasm as it has few "end organs of touch" and is "not in fact a highly sensitive area."[60] The clitoris, in contrast, has the "same structure and function" as the "head of the penis," and it is through clitoral stimulation that women physically achieve climax whether or not that climax was psychically or, indeed, vaginally inspired (202).

Koedt's turn to physiology and away from narrative allows her to open up the possibilities of female sexuality by literally interrupting the story of femininity with the "facts" of a woman's body. With "no other function than that of sexual pleasure" (202), the clitoris becomes, for Koedt, the physical evidence of a female sexuality independent of social and reproductive imperatives. What this sexual independence might mean for women is left up in the air—her call for women to redefine their sexuality oscillating between finding "mutual enjoyment" with men (199), through the adoption of "new techniques," and suggesting that women "might equally seek other women as lovers" (206). While this oscillation in Koedt's essay between heterosexual and homosexual satisfaction can be read as indicative of a general—homophobic—uneasiness about the political and social implications of a female sexuality organized around the clitoris, it can also be read as indicative of the potentially liberating uncoupling of sexual desire from object choice implicit in Koedt's focus on bodies and practices. I say *might* because homophobia and female sexual autonomy are immanent in their relation to each other. It is the potential multiplicity of meaning inherent to the notion of an independent female sexuality and the unresolveability of that potential into a clear conclusion one way or the other that produces the affective force of Koedt's essay—an affective force mobilized by the symbolic appeal of the clitoris.

The ambiguity of the clitoris as a symbol of women's sexual and social autonomy is enacted rather than solved in Koedt's essay. Locating female sexuality in clitoral stimulation can lead to the exploration of different kinds of sex acts with different partners and in different social and sexual scenarios, but it can also be used to suggest the sameness of women as a protopolitical collectivity. In linking anatomy to the emancipatory project of women's liberation, Koedt's essay invokes both possibilities while leaving the question of their relation to each other unresolved. We see the animating force of this ambiguity in Koedt's discussion of the reasons why men maintain the myth of the vaginal orgasm. Echoing Beauvoir's analysis of the asymmetrical duality between masculinity and femininity, Koedt argues that the vaginal orgasm is an effect of men, operating as the standard and the norm, defining women in terms of what "benefited" them. The refusal of men to recognize women as "total, separate human beings" and their fear of being "expendable" if the locus of female sexuality switches from the vagina to the clitoris, all contribute to the pervasiveness of the myth as well as the violence of men's attempts to control women (204–5).[61] Through her listing of men's fears, Koedt simultaneously voices the goals of women's sexual liberation: if women switched the locus of their sexuality to the clitoris, they will become "total, separate human beings," and their sexual and social dependence on men will be broken. But as the site and sign of this future autonomy for women, the clitoris also signals a process of emancipation for women that is not, or not only, temporal but spatial. As the "cardinal vestige of [women's] masculinity," the clitoris suggests sexual transgressiveness rather than transcendence—a move from a female sexuality predicated on vaginal passivity to a masculine sexuality predicated on desire and pleasure. Here, then, women's sexual and social liberation is prefigured by the invocation of female masculinity—an invocation that is conjured through collective memories of the lesbian rather than normative notions of femininity.

And in the final paragraph of "The Myth of the Vaginal Orgasm" the lesbian does, indeed, make her appearance: "Aside from the strictly anatomical reasons why women might equally seek other women as lovers, there is a fear on men's part that women will seek the company of other women on a full, human basis. The recognition of clitoral orgasm as fact would threaten the heterosexual institution. For it would indicate that sexual pleasure was obtainable from either men or women, thus making heterosexuality not an absolute, but an option. It would thus open up the whole question of human sexual relationships beyond the confines of the present male-female role system" (206). Although Koedt writes that the recognition of clitoral orgasms makes heterosexuality an "option" rather than an "absolute" for women, her linking of women's sexual freedom with their ability to be "fully human" undercuts her sense of a benign plurality. A woman's ability to feel sexual pleasure independently of men leaves open the possibility that she may not only seek other women out as sexual partners but also on "a full human basis." This is, as Koedt recognizes, the threat of lesbianism to men. The utopian part of Koedt's argument, however, comes at the end of her ruminations on what the future of a clitorally organized female sexuality would look like: "recognition of the clitoral orgasm" would not only present an alternative to heterosexuality, it would also "open up" human sexuality beyond "the present male-female role system" (206). For Koedt, lesbianism becomes the scenario through which the project of sexual liberation as women's liberation is imagined as a future escape from gender roles. Yet what makes it possible to imagine lesbianism in this way—the symbolic and signifying capacity of the clitoris —folds back into the imagined future of a feminist collectivity the troubling specter of female masculinity.

This uneasy conjuration of a female masculinity in the midst of a utopian vision of genderless human beings resonated throughout the women's liberation movement's theoretical explorations of lesbianism in 1970. Anne Koedt herself published a number of articles on the relationship of lesbianism to feminism in 1970 and 1971, including "Loving Another Woman," in which Koedt interviewed a feminist who had recently embarked on a sexual relationship with another woman.[62] Reading this interview in relation to two essays by Ti-Grace Atkinson and the Radicalesbians' position paper "The Woman Identified Woman," distributed at the Second Congress to Unite Women, reveals the process of elision through transformation by which the lesbian, and lesbianism, were refashioned by the women's liberation movement as a political identity and practice. The fantasies at play in this refashioning reveal not only the contradictory investments in "women" as a category of belonging and political collectivity for women's liberation but also the disavowals of marginalized sexual subcultures and publics inherent to those investments. The point, however, is not to condemn this process of creating new political identities and collectivities through the rejection and exclusion of marginalized subcultures and alternative political identities—that would be too easy and would, in any case, only enact another elision: for all political identities and collectivities are fashioned out of a process of exclusion and omission. Rather, the point is to follow the process of creation through exclusion and omission that is the work of a fantasy in the making. By doing so we can open up the question of what was being wished for in the lesbian fantasies of women's liberation.

Koedt's "Loving Another Woman" was first published in 1971 in *Notes from the Third Year* and reprinted in the women's liberation anthology *Radical Feminism* in 1973. Written as a series of questions and answers, the interview operates pedagogically, the trajectory of Koedt's questions leading the interviewee from a description of her becoming conscious of her attraction to another woman to the relationship of women's liberation to the gay and lesbian movement. While Koedt's questions are designed to map a relationship between the personal and the political that would transform the meaning and possibilities of female sexuality for women's liberation, they also reveal an anxiety about what would change, or be left behind, as a consequence of those transformations. The questions Koedt asks shape the answers offered by the interviewee, and it is in the dialogue between Koedt and her interviewee that the fantasy—and fear—of a feminist future for women's liberation is revealed.

The anxiety about the transformational potentiality of lesbianism for women's liberation is most tellingly revealed in the questions Koedt asks concerning the comparative satisfactions of heterosexuality and homosexuality—a concern that belies her own emphatic assertion of a general *lack* of sexual satisfaction in heterosexual relations for women in "The Myth of the Vaginal Orgasm." By asking the question, "Is the physical aspect of loving women *really* as satisfying as sex with a man?," Koedt betrays a disbelief in homosexuality that simultaneously reveals her investment in heterosexuality.[63] This investment later leads her to ask the interviewee if she could "'go back' to men" if her relationship with her lover ended. In using the phrase, "go back," albeit in quotation marks, Koedt suggests that men are being left behind as feminists look to each other as sexual, as well as political, partners—a suggestion that also evokes the fear that familiar notions of femininity, those notions made meaningful through the institutional and cultural reproduction of heterosexuality, are also being left behind. Koedt's anxiety that men (and by implication, femininity) are being left behind by feminism is responded to by the interviewee through an idealization of androgyny as a feminist future that could include men: "At a certain point, I think, you realize that the final qualification is not being male or female, but whether they've joined the middle. That is—whether they have started from the male or the female side—they've gone toward the center where they are working toward combining the healthy aspects of so-called male and female characteristics. That's where I want to go and that's what I'm beginning to realize I respond to in other people" (92).

As a fantasy of the feminist future, androgyny seems to solve the problem of leaving men behind by incorporating them into a happy, healthy middle ground, where people will love each other and be attracted to each other because of their particularity rather than the genericness of their gender. The interviewee "didn't fall in love with 'a woman,'" she tells Koedt, she "fell in love with Jen" (90). Here, the politics of women's liberation is reduced to "raising consciousness" about "sexual roles" in order to remove them from the scene of sexual desire. In this version of the feminist project, lesbianism becomes an option for women and a means to some other (androgynous) end. Lesbianism is reimagined in the liberal terms of a progressive march toward choice and equality in which a prepolitical, pre-sexual sexuality will flourish once the obstacles of gender roles that prevent "men" and "women" from relating to each other as human beings are re-moved. What underwrites the collectivity of women in this feminist imagi-nary is neither their political association, nor the physiological marker of their sameness (the clitoris), but a prepolitical, universal humanity that is offered as an escape from gender.

In order for this fantasy of a genderless future for women and sexual desire to emerge, other kinds of gendered sexual practices have to be dis-avowed. These disavowals not only enact the production of androgyny as a (liberal) ideal for the feminist future, but they also reinscribe the political as a distinct domain of human activity from sexuality. What is really being hoped for, then, I would argue, in the dialogue between Koedt and her interviewee, is a future in which politics will be removed from the scenes of sexual desire—that desire will, once again, be innocent of the corrupting influences of a social world stratified by gender, class, and race hierarchies, a liberal and bourgeois dream if ever there was one. This hope for sexual and social innocence—in the midst of feminist politicizations of "the per-sonal"—emerges as the counterimage to what gets disavowed in the inter-view: lesbians "who play the male seduction game" and participate in the "sex role system." Interestingly, it is these lesbians who are seen by the interviewee as acting politically: "This confusing of sexual *partners* with sexual *roles* has also led to a really bizarre situation where some lesbians insist that you aren't really a radical feminist if you are not in bed with a woman. Which is wrong politically and outrageous personally" (93). The women who confuse partners with roles are the political absolutists, the lesbians who intimidate women into becoming "real" radical feminists by bullying them sexually. The invocation of butch-femme sexuality in the condensation of gendered sex with political absolutism elides the politici-zation of androgyny as a feminist ideal in the interview. It also works to displace the fear, implicit in the dialogue between Koedt and her inter-viewee, that politicizations of sexuality will not only force an estrangement between women and the femininity that keeps them bound to men but will also force women to confront the sociality of their own desires. In the feminist future being imagined, the figures of the bullying butch and her passive femme victim become the affective repositories for a fear of what a feminist revolution might bring: female sexuality unleashed from heterosexuality. This fear is the underside of a longing for escape from the messy, power-infested social world and its corrupting sexual desires.

In 1970 Ti-Grace Atkinson, too, wanted a future without the corrupting sexual desires of a social world organized through heterosexuality. But unlike Koedt and her interviewee, who imagined that future through a "return" to a prepolitical and genderless sexual innocence, Atkinson saw the feminist future in a politics that would allow women to escape from sexuality altogether. Much beloved in the press in 1970 for the "extremism" of her views and haughty Southern belle looks, Ti-Grace Atkinson was a former NOW protégé of Betty Friedan and the enigmatic intellectual founder of the radical feminist group the Feminists, one of the first feminist groups to call for the abolition of marriage as an exploitative and oppressive institution of male supremacy.[64] In Atkinson's New York speech to the Daughters of Bilitis in February 1970, and in her rejected *New York Times* op-ed column in response to *Time*'s outing of Kate Millett in December of that year, we witness one of the first presentations of political lesbianism as a practice of freedom for women's liberation.[65] Although neither Atkinson's speech nor her op-ed were published immediately (both ultimately appeared in her *Amazon Odyssey*, published in 1974),[66] they circulated informally through hearsay in movement networks and by reference in other feminist publications and papers, and by the end of 1970 they had become some of the most notorious and polemical statements of lesbian feminism in the early women's liberation movement.[67]

In her speech on February 21, 1970, to the Daughters of Bilitis, the lesbian organization founded by Del Martin and Phyllis Lyon in 1955, Atkinson summed up her comparative analysis of lesbianism and feminism with these words: "The raison d'être for feminism is the class disparity between men and women. The raison d'être of lesbianism is sex, which is an apparent evasion of class disparity."[68] In setting up an opposition between politics and sex, with feminism on the side of politics and lesbianism on the side of sex, Atkinson's initial analysis of the relationship between lesbianism and feminism suggests not simply a distinction but a mutually antagonistic relation between the two. For Atkinson, sex, which she sometimes does and sometimes does not collapse into sexual intercourse, is "the premise of male oppression" (85). Not only does intercourse place women in a secondary, receptive role in the act of having sex, it also provides "the link between the wife and mother roles" (86). In order for feminism to be revolutionary, Atkinson's argument continues, it has to reject men and the "premise" of their oppression of women, that is, sex. In contrast, lesbians, who exist only as a "counterclass" to men, are by definition "totally dependent, as a concept as well as an activity, on male supremacy" (85). Although, in rejecting a male partner the lesbian may suggest resistance to the institution of male supremacy, she doesn't free herself from the heterosexual dyad, according to Atkinson, she merely switches sides: "Because lesbianism involves role-playing and, more important, because it is based on the primary assumption of male oppression, that is, sex, lesbianism reinforces the sex class system" (86). In this initial analysis of the relationship between feminism and lesbianism, the lesbian remains a "reactionary" figure for Atkinson, her little space of freedom from marriage and motherhood gained at the expense of her capitulation to sexual role-playing and the sex class system.

Yet by December of 1970, as a direct response to the *Time* exposé of Kate Millett, Atkinson's understanding of lesbianism's relationship to feminism had undergone a radical reversal: "Lesbianism is to feminism what the Communist Party was to the trade union movement. Tactically, any feminist should fight to the death for lesbianism because of its strategic importance" (134). Rather than place lesbianism in a dichotomous relationship with feminism—one sexual, the other political—Atkinson now positions lesbianism as the vanguard of the women's movement. The lesbian's sudden appropriateness for the role of vanguard comes from Atkinson's now more expansive understanding of her as the "criminal element" within the class of people called women. Invoking Solanas's SCUM *Manifesto* and translating its fantasy of female revolt against bourgeois coupledom and daddy's girls into an explicitly political project, Atkinson situates lesbians in the "buffer zone" between the oppressor, men, and the rest of the oppressed class, women. In their flouting of their assigned (feminine) role, lesbians exhibit the threat of women to the "oppressor" and, like the Communists in relation to the trade union movement, they become the scapegoats for their less flagrantly oppositional sisters. Atkinson's analogy, equating the Communist Party's relationship to the trade union movement with the relationship of lesbians to other women, now positions the lesbian as the movement's true radical and lesbianism as its most subversive political practice.

Atkinson's rearticulation of the relationship between feminism and lesbianism is made in terms of a Marxist political imaginary full of the metaphors of civil war. For Atkinson, the threat of women actively choosing to become lesbians lies less in the promise of sexual autonomy or a future androgyny and more in the enactment of political association: "It is this commitment, by choice, full-time, of one woman to others of her class that is called lesbianism. . . . There are women in the movement who engage in sexual relations with other women, but who are married to men. These women are not lesbians in the political sense. These women claim the right to "private" lives. They are collaborators. There are other women who have never had sexual relations with other women, but who have made and live, a total commitment to this movement. These women are lesbians in the political sense" (132). Atkinson's insistence that lesbianism be understood *politically*, by which she means within the context of a theory of class oppression and revolution and not, therefore, in sociological or psychological terms, allows her to define lesbianism as a political practice of liberation rather than as an ontological reality for particular women. In this version, lesbianism is reconfigured as a means of working toward revolution; it is not understood as an identity that reveals the true desires of anyone or offered as an alternative way of life. Women who choose to become lesbians within the context of the women's movement are now women who most clearly and visibly choose to define themselves politically as a body of people separate from men. The practice of lesbianism becomes a revolutionary act and identifying as a lesbian becomes a way of organizing and enacting class solidarity.

While Atkinson's transformation of the lesbian into a figure of revolution rather than sexuality or pathology can be read as a refreshingly blunt call for women to cut the ties that bind them to the scenes and conventions of their oppression, the wish it reveals for women as political actors, to completely separate themselves from the messiness of emotional dependency and sexual desire, also negates the world from which feminism emerges as a political practice. In Atkinson's vision of revolutionary feminism, politics is posited not as a practice of acting in and on this world but as a rejection of it. The scenario of feminist activism being imagined here figures lesbianism as a kind of great leap forward and over the messy ground of women's social and emotional relationships with others. And while that leap forward might imbue the figure of the lesbian with an appealing sense of social freedom and emotional and sexual unattachment, it also negates what made the lesbian suitable for the role of the feminist vanguard in the first place: her life as "the criminal element"—the subcultural, class-marginal worlds of role-playing sexual and social nonconformity.

In the desire to remake the lesbian into a figure for feminism—a desire compelled, at least in part, by the identification of feminists as lesbians by nonfeminists—both Koedt and Atkinson invest her with a futurity that is also, at the same time, an attempt to free her from her own historicity. It is in this attempt to disarticulate the lesbian's feminist future from her mannish and "role-playing" past that we see the fantasy echoes of feminist identification at play in the re-remaking of the lesbian as a figure for women's liberation. The contradictory impulses of a feminism, which seeks to open up sexual and social possibilities for women while also wanting representation in the public sphere with an identity that names its constituency, are here subsumed into a progress narrative of liberation as transcendence and/or escape from the psychosociological contexts of feminine subjugation. For both Koedt and Atkinson, lesbianism sets the scene for the story of women's liberation they want to tell. It also organizes the feelings through which they incite other women into becoming women's liberationists. By presenting the politics of women's liberation as a transcendent return to a presocial innocence, or as a liberatory escape from the social, they have to retell the story of what it is women need to transcend or escape, and in so doing they reinscribe women's liberation's attachment to the class- and race-inscribed sociopsychological worlds of feminine subjection. It is in this oscillation between escape and transcendence and a return to the scenes of social and sexual subjugation that women's liberation enacts its confrontation with the invisible—psychological and normative—lines of oppression in a sexist, homophobic, classist, and racist society. And it is through this oscillation that lesbianism becomes both a figure of and a difficulty for the movement: it provides ready-made scenes of liberation from alienation and subjugation, but it also returns women's liberation to the problem of a sometimes intimate estrangement between and among women.

The Lavender Menace's (later Radicalesbians) "The Woman Identified Woman," more than any other early position paper, enacts the contradictory impulses inherent to the affective force of the lesbian as a figure for women's liberation.[69] In the paper's transformation of the lesbian into a metaphor for the movement, we witness both an appropriation of and an attachment to the scenes of emotional and social alienation that lesbianism offers the movement as resources for political mobilization. We also witness an attempt to transform that alienation into a somewhat hazy uplifted future of "maximum autonomy" for all women. The vivid and melodramatic terms with which the paper presents its biography of the lesbian stands in stark contrast to the poetic vagueness of its depiction of a "woman identified" future. This shift in emotional register between past and future places the weight of feeling firmly in the past—an emotional undertow that tends to undermine the paper's narrative trajectory toward the disarticulation of a future, woman identified feminism from older more seemingly defeated ways of being women (and lesbians). It is in this riptide effect that we can witness how lesbianism was not simply dismissed or transformed by women's liberation but was a difficulty—a problem that was also, at the same time, the appropriated venue for the movement's claims to a political collectivity and freedom for women.

"The Woman Identified Woman" begins with what is, in effect, a portrayal of a particular type of person—one with a history and a psychology: "What is a Lesbian? A Lesbian is the rage of all women condensed to the point of explosion. She is the woman who, often beginning at an extremely early age, acts in accordance with her inner compulsion to be a more complete and freer human being than her society—perhaps then, but certainly later—cares to allow her." Invoking the diagnosis of the lesbian offered by midcentury clinical psychoanalysis and pulp sexology, the portrayal goes on to describe the "tortuous journey through a night that may have been decades long" of a woman at odds with society and its expectations of her. Yet, unlike the expert diagnosis that sees the lesbian's inability to inhabit her femininity as a sign of her failure to be true to her nature, the paper's portrait is of a heroic, willful being struggling to be true to her "inner compulsion." As the lesbian weaves her lonely way through life, she takes on the stigmata of social judgment—a branding that forces her to "evolve her own life pattern" and to "question and analyze what the rest of her society more or less accepts." It is in this forced exile from the normal that lesbianism also becomes the negative space of a potential freedom for all women: as the lesbian finds herself "on the other side" of her "tortuous journey through [the] night" of social ostracization and alienation, she gains "the liberation of self, the inner peace, the real love of self and of all women." In this retelling, the familiar story of the lesbian's "well of loneliness," of her psychic pain and social abjection, does not end in death and defeat but in the opening up of a future to "be shared with all women" (240).

Here, then, the familiar story of lesbian loneliness and social abjection is transformed into a metaphor for the social and psychic suffering of all women: "A lesbian is the rage of all women condensed to the point of explosion." But in this act of appropriation something other than simple co-optation is at work. The fantastical image of a figure "condensed to the point of explosion" with the stored-up rage of centuries of female suffering, echoes Walter Benjamin's description of the surrealist's bringing "to the point of explosion . . . the immense forces of 'atmosphere' concealed" in everyday things. As Avery Gordon notes, the point of the surrealists' work for Benjamin was its capacity to "shatter habit." By making everyday objects and social routines strange, the surrealists attempted to disrupt conventional ways of seeing and habitual ways of relating to the world, and in so doing they were, in Benjamin's terms, attempting to "win the energies of intoxication for the revolution."[70] If we return to the original context of "The Woman Identified Woman"—the Lavender Menace's zap action at the Second Congress to Unite Women—then it seems to me that the desire to intoxicate through a disruption of the conventional and the habitual was precisely the intention of the Lavender Menace's deployment of a fantastical image of the lesbian. Like the surrealists, the Lavender Menace was attempting to shatter habit—in this case, the habit of homophobia, of thinking, feeling, knowing what was called at the time the sex-caste system, what we might now call heteronormativity.

But as much as the metaphorization of the lesbian for women's liberation was an attempt to blast through the conventions of heteronormativity and win "the energies of intoxication" for the feminist revolution, it was also an attempt to create a more capacious and less threatening idea of lesbianism for women's liberation. As Alice Echols writes in *Daring to Be Bad*, the paper, and in particular its title, was designed by the Lavender Menace "to assuage heterosexual feminists' fears about lesbianism."[71] And so while the paper begins with a portrait of the lesbian as a person with an "inner compulsion" to be free, it also, in the very next paragraph, simultaneously dismisses lesbianism as a "category of behavior" symptomatic of a "sexist" society (241). The term *lesbian*, the paper goes on to assert, does not identify a type of person with a distinct sexuality, but it is a "label" used by men to keep women who try to "assert the primacy of [their] own needs" (241). In the wish to solicit the identification of straight women with the feeling of lesbian alienation rather than its sexual and social practice, lesbian is not claimed as the—authentic—feminist identity women in the movement should aspire to or adopt. In fact precisely the opposite is claimed: lesbian is an "inauthentic" identity because it is a "by-product" of a sexist society. Rather than an attempt to persuade straight women to become "political lesbians," then, the paper is more concerned with making the word *lesbian* less "sticky," to use Sara Ahmed's adjective for signs that accumulate affect, and reorientating its affective power toward a more general (which is to say, less full of the accretions of historical and social context) expression of women's psychic and social independence from men.

The turn to *woman identified* and away from *lesbian* in the paper pivots on the rejection of femininity as the condition of women's dependency on men. Drawing on Beauvoir's *The Second Sex*, the paper defines femininity as men's "image of us"; it is only by rejecting this image—an action that requires looking into the "void" of women's "real situation"—that women will be able to become "whole" persons. But in an act of displacement that is designed to mitigate the risks of this move—especially for those women who have attained a measure of social and cultural privilege through their ability to perform femininity more or less successfully—this look into the void of difference simultaneously becomes a confrontation with "one's self." The turn to *woman identified* and away from *lesbian* is also, then, a turn away from confronting the implications of what it might mean for women to reject femininity. Instead of the specters of masculine women and other nonconforming and marginal female figures—precisely the specters conjured up at the beginning of the paper to incite feelings of alienation and defiance—"the woman identified woman" offers the comforting illusion of a familiar femininity continuing over and across the social ruptures of a feminist revolution.

This comforting familiarity is the promise of woman-identified feminism offered—as a realization of the future—at the end of the paper:

> Together we must find, reinforce and validate our authentic selves. As we do this, we confirm in each other that struggling incipient sense of pride and strength, the divisive barriers begin to melt, we feel this growing solidarity with our sisters. We see ourselves as prime, find our centers inside of ourselves. We find receding the sense of alienation, of being cut off, of being behind a locked window, of being unable to get out what we know is inside. We feel a realness, feel at last we are coinciding with ourselves. With that real self, with

that consciousness, we begin a revolution to end the imposition of all coercive identifications, and to achieve maximum autonomy in human expression. (245)

The dream envisions each woman's autonomy coming from her ability to act with and for other women. Although the commonality between women is expressed in terms of "a struggling incipient sense of pride and strength" —that is, in terms of a political will—rather than through experience or anatomy, the imagery of the dream undercuts the notion of political alliance, revealing instead an investment in the idea of "realness." As barriers "begin to melt" and "locked windows" open, women do not travel across the no-man's-land of sexual difference: they find "their centers" and "coincide" with themselves. The emphasis here is on a falling away of the obstacles that have prevented women from getting their "authentic selves" out into the open. In this dream, the revolution will not force women to confront their differences with other women, nor will it transform women into something unrecognizable in the present. Rather, it will enable them to come out into the open and transcend the pain of self-hatred and mutual distrust.

But at the same time, the dream offered by "The Woman Identified Woman," in its struggle to relate the affective power of the lesbian as a general feeling of collectivity for all women, also inadvertently reveals the risks involved for women working toward a feminist revolution: the risk of association with other women, the separation from men that it would entail, and the risk of becoming something else, of no longer conforming to the terms and conditions of the socially and culturally constructed norms of femininity. The lesbian becomes a meaningful figure in "The Woman Identified Woman," not as the embodiment of the right way to live or the true way of being a feminist, but as an incitement to imagine women's liberation—an incitement that simultaneously reveals the limitations as well as some of the possibilities of that imagining.

For most feminist and queer theorists looking back at women's liberation, "The Woman Identified Woman" does not represent a contradictory attempt to imagine the possibilities of women's liberation through the figure of lesbianism. On the contrary, it is usually read as one of the first and most influential statements of lesbian separatism. Linda Nicholson, in her anthology of second-wave feminist theory, calls the paper one of "the most powerful early statements" of "gynocentric" feminism. In the developmental narrative that underwrites her taxonomy of Anglo-American feminist theory, "The Woman Identified Woman" is an example of early second-wave essentialism, its assumption of "a fundamental difference" between men and women leading to its call for separatism as a way for women to learn to love themselves and each other.[72] Ruth Rosen, in her historical account of the transformative effect of the second-wave women's movement on postwar American society, characterizes the paper as a provocation directed at straight women in the movement still attached romantically to men, and she defines it as an early statement of "lesbianism as a political choice."[73] And for Rosalind Baxandall and Linda Gordon writing in *Dear Sisters*, their published archive of documents from the women's liberation movement, "The Woman Identified Woman" was a notorious early statement of lesbian feminism in the movement, not only because it theorized "lesbianism as a political choice and equat[ed] it with feminist anger" but also because in doing so it "omitted sexuality" from its definition of lesbianism and suggested that "one's sexuality is completely changeable at will."[74]

Similarly, Judith Halberstam's discussion of lesbian feminism in *Female Masculinity* exemplifies the criticisms directed toward this form of feminism by queer and gay activists and scholars. Halberstam notes the prescriptive tendencies of lesbian feminism's assertion of a "pure feminist desire" and argues persuasively that the emphasis on sameness and equality in lesbian feminist notions of sexuality "de-eroticizes" sex and encourages a sense of "sexual defeat" rather than adventure and exploration. Halberstam offers a very amusing reading of a particularly unsexy rendition of "woman identified woman" sex, and she is right to point out the political righteousness and prescriptive dogma of lesbian feminism's overt hostility to butch-femme sexuality and the butch figure in particular. However, her lack of interest in figuring out why lesbian feminism was imagined and fashioned the way it was at the time it was means, ultimately, that lesbian feminism remains, despite her protests to the contrary, a "convenient bogey" against which the more complex and historically varied practices of female masculinity can be illuminated. The problem here is twofold: first, lesbian feminism is not afforded any historical complexity of its own, and so the much more entrenched and conservative "cultural feminism" of the 1980s is allowed to stand as emblematic of lesbian feminism as a whole; second, the whiteness and middle-classness of many self-identified lesbian feminists is allowed to stand as both the source and explanation for its limitations as a political and sexual practice, and as a result white, middle-class femaleness is assumed as an ahistorical constant that lesbian feminism simply reproduces in its practices and ideas rather than contests or changes.[75]

Common to all these commentaries, despite the diversity of emphasis and disciplinary context in which they attempt to interpret the political and cultural effects of lesbian feminism, is a desire to flatten out the contradictions and incoherencies of its emergence as a distinct form of feminism. In the need to clarify, situate, and categorize, "The Woman Identified Woman" is transformed into a declarative statement of lesbian feminism, or lesbian separatism, that then gets to stand as evidence of a coherent theoretical position that has since been superseded. Missing from these returns to the early textual productions of what we now call lesbian feminism, I would argue, is a reckoning with the movement's varied and contradictory attempts to produce an idea of the personal as the location for a feminist politics of sexual and social emancipation. By following the movement's preoccupations with heterosexual relations, women's sexual pleasure, and the "obliged affections" of family life, a return to the past of women's liberation becomes less a project of epistemological clarification, whereby the political claims of the movement can be judged as either right or wrong, and more a project of elucidation, whereby the figures and phrases it created and deployed to think the feminist project anew can be recovered as historically contingent inventions of the movement's moment of emergence. By tracking the productive detail of the movement's political thinking, the fault lines between what could and could not be imagined by women's liberation can be exposed to a different kind of accountability in the present, one that is open to the contingencies of the movement's beginnings. If the lesbian was transformed by women's liberation into a political figure that elided the heterogeneity of her sexual and social past, then that transformation was more ambiguous, unstable, and fraught with feeling than our retroactive portrayals of it have tended to suggest.

The Lesbian is one of the least known members of our culture. Less is known about her—and less accurately—than about the Newfoundland dog. In the 1960s, two books on the Lesbian appeared. Both were written by men, and both were liberal attempts to deal with the worst stereotype about Lesbians—which says they are men trapped in women's bodies. Both failed to destroy the stereotype, since they only described behavior and since the authors were largely unable or unwilling to deal with the Lesbian's emotional life. Neither book was the product of any social scientific discipline. There may still not be a first-rate psychological or socio-psychological study on lesbians.

—Sidney Abbott and Barbara Love, *Sappho Was a Right-On Woman*

The profile of the lesbian comes from *Sappho Was a Right-On Woman*, published two years after "The Woman Identified Woman" and written by two women closely involved in writing the earlier essay.[76] The quotation, and indeed the entirety of *Sappho Was a Right-On Woman*, speaks to the difficulty feminists in the early years of women's liberation faced in their attempts to articulate a relationship between politics and sexuality. Here, the lesbian has returned as a person with a history and a psychology. Like the Newfoundland dog, she is a type, a species, someone with a particular pedigree. Although the lesbian's true character or pedigree, unlike that of the Newfoundland dog, remains a mystery, this doesn't invalidate past "expert" investigations of her so much as validate the need for further investigation—as the authors' lament for a "first-rate" sociopsychological study testifies. And although the book is structured as a story in two parts —from abjection to liberation or from "What It Was Like" to "Living the Future"—the story the authors tell of the lesbian's emancipation depends upon her prior existence as a social and sexual outcast. In *Sappho Was a Right-On Woman* the lesbian is returned to the medico-psychological discourses feminists like Atkinson, and indeed the Lavender Menace, sought to free her from, and as a consequence the radical project of women's liberation "returns" to the familiar contexts of a liberal, rights-based feminism—one that demands social recognition and institutional access rather than revolution or refusal.

The reasons for this return to familiar notions of the lesbian and to a rights-based feminism, as I have attempted to demonstrate in this chapter, are to be found in the contradictory impulses of the women's liberation movement's political imaginary. The movement's professed liberatory politics of transcendent escape from the social scenes of female subjugation lay in uneasy relation to the movement's simultaneous enactment of a politics of resistance and revolt. The angry denunciations of New Left sexism in Robin Morgan's "Goodbye to All That," for example—and the invocation of Solanas's politics of negation that animated that anger—work against the futuritial longing for escape from the private scenes of sexual dependency and humiliation expressed in Anne Koedt's and Ti-Grace Atkinson's essays. While one demands a confrontation with, and puncturing of, the nebulous "atmosphere" of heterosexism, the other demands an overcoming of it—as if it were always already clear exactly what it was feminism was "against." This internal dissonance between confrontation and transcendence set the scene for women's liberation's cultural struggle over the terms of women's social presence in American society. It also provided the figures through which the movement thought its political project. Through these varied and multiple shorthand notations—"the personal is political," "the lavender menace," and "woman identified woman"—I have tried to demonstrate how thinking about women's liberation as enacted through contradiction and ambivalence might unsettle the ways in which sex-positive feminists and queer theorists have tended to narrate the political and cultural limitations of second-wave lesbian feminism.

Like other protest movements of the 1960s and 1970s, women's liberation was not a particularly ideological movement. Its confusing mix of Marxist rhetoric, liberal Enlightenment ideals, and what we might call, following Fredric Jameson and Marianne DeKoven, an emergent postmodern skepticism directed toward the transformative possibilities of institutional and centrally organized politics, suggest the movement's lack of investment in the truth-telling promises of political ideology.[77] Rather than ideology, women's liberation engaged in a politics of emotion: it attempted to incite revolt against the ineffable atmosphere of heterosexism as much as it tried to present cogent arguments for legislative change. In any case, the arguments the movement presented for affordable daycare, equal employment opportunities, and reproductive rights were not the source of the movement's upsetting presence in the national public sphere in 1970. We have to look elsewhere for the upset—in the conjuncture of media and movement configurations of radical feminism, in the objects against which women's liberation fashioned its political and cultural imaginary, and in the disjuncture between the counterpublic sphere of women's liberation and the national public sphere of American political orthodoxy. It is in these domains of cultural struggle that we witness the movement's troubling of the distinctions between politics and sexuality, between public actions for social change and the intimate practices and affects of sex. If, as we tend to assume today, the women's liberation movement was a predominantly white, middle-class women's movement, then what does that mean? How did that whiteness and middle-classness manifest itself in the objects against which the movement articulated its protest, or in the production of particular figures and metaphors that shaped the movement's political imaginary? Perhaps the bourgeois values of the movement are most tellingly present in its idealization of transcendence as a political goal. It is certainly in the desire to overcome or escape the social messiness of sexual subjugation and desire that women's liberation enacts its political appeal as an appropriation of the scenarios of sexual, class, and racial otherness. But while this may be so, to leave the story there is to miss the way in which the lesbian, in figuring women's liberation's rejection of the claims of heterosexuality and the family obligations it generated, did not simply become yet another—essentializing—example of "woman" as the subject position from which to make political claims, but instead became the animating figure of the movement's struggle to articulate its political project as something more than a fight for rights and social justice, as something more and less tangible than the terms with which women's liberation necessarily represented itself. If the gay-straight split is to be understood as a defining event in the trajectory of women's liberation as a feminist movement, then it is not because it augmented the fracturing of an already heterogeneous movement, nor because it announced the birth of lesbian feminism as a coherent and essentializing identity politics, but because it contributed to the disassembly of the modern category of women as a foundational category of feminism and to the dispersal of feminism into multiple sites of political contestation and struggle.

4

FEAR OF *FLYING*

Kate Millett, the Difficulty of the New,
and the Unmaking of the Feminist-as-Lesbian

If Kate Millett had been my friend, I hope I would have told her this: Keep your notebook for yourself, but publish another book—or none at all just now. The cure for being exhibited is not to exhibit oneself. The remedy for exploitation is not self-exploitation. Kate: Not all confessions end in absolution. I think the Confession is a cocoon, and the inhabitant of this one is not yet flying, despite her claims. I wish for her book a speedy oblivion, and for herself, other and better books.—ELINOR LANGER, "Confessing," *Ms.*, December 1974

There is something about this book that provokes. It tells too much, reveals too much.—KATE MILLETT, "The Shame Is Over," *Ms.*, December 1975

At the beginning of *Flying*, her autobiographical account of the early years of the women's liberation movement, Kate Millett laments: "I can't be Kate Millett anymore. It's an object, a thing. A joke at cocktail parties. It's no one. I'm only the fear in my gut."[1] Millett's sense of loss comes from the realization that, by the winter of 1970, she had been "slammed with an identity" that made her "mute with responsibility" (23). Being outed by *Time* magazine as bisexual and then simultaneously forced to identify herself as a lesbian by some in the movement—"Say it! Say you are a lesbian!" (15)—left Millett caught in the headlights of identificatory pressures that demanded of her a representativeness. She had to be one thing or another: lesbian icon of the movement or its bisexual betrayer. As resistance to those pressures, *Flying* was to be a "quietly desperate search for self" (83) in which Millett not only sought to evade the claims of "that monster created in my name" (25)—the "notorious. Sick, done for creature" (7) portrayed in the media—but to become someone new: "and now I will be who I am becoming" (240).

Millett began writing *Flying* in the immediate aftermath of the crisis enveloping the women's liberation movement in 1970 over lesbian visibility and straight respectability.[2] Written as a documentary of the year and a half following the publication of *Sexual Politics* in the summer of 1970, *Flying* offers the reader a more complicated life than the one-dimensional identifications demanded by "movement fanatics" and, more especially, the media. At nearly six hundred pages, *Flying* is an assemblage of present-tense impressions of immediate experiences, memories, free-association thought riffs, and anxious or boasting asides to the reader. Millett describes in detail relationships with friends, girlfriends, and her husband; she documents her participation in women's liberation events, gay liberation marches, and her efforts to finish a film (*Three Lives*), as well as her travels to and from England; and she uses flashback to describe childhood experiences and memories, including an experience of childhood molestation and the divorce of her parents. Following no single narrative theme or structure, *Flying* reads like a dazzling and disorientating explosion of life in which time speeds up and slows down and in which present day experiences are infused with fantastic projections and memories of other, earlier experiences.

Flying was first published in 1974 to reviews in the mainstream press that were, as Millett notes in her response to the criticism, "curiously infuriated [and] curiously unanimous" in their objections.[3] For the reviewers, feminist and otherwise, the apparent lack of order and careful crafting of self meant the book was a failure.[4] Read against the "disengaged, self-critical, self-distanced, and self-scrutinizing brand" the reviewers posited as the ideal of autobiographical writing, *Flying* was judged to be "self indulgent" and full of an "ingrown confusion."[5] The "unconventional loves," anxious preoccupations, and moments of paranoid self-doubt documented by Millett were, for many of the critics, "shabby" and "indecent" revelations best left in "private journals."[6] Indeed, the lack of a conventionally crafted self and detailed descriptions of (pretty tame) lesbian sex became, in the minds of at least two of the critics, part of the same problem: Millett's inclusion of her lesbian relationships in *Flying* was evidence of her inability to differentiate between what was important and what was not in the writing of an autobiography. Millett's crime was her inability, or refusal, to make distinctions between the "trivial" and the "important," the private and the public, in her portrayal of self.[7] Rather than the recognizable genre of autobiographical writing, with its detailed descriptions of career or political accomplishments followed by reserved descriptions of family life and relationships, Millett's autobiography was not only an unreserved spectacle of the private and unconventional but in its formal indifference to the conventions of autobiographical writing it was also an undoing of the distinctions between private and public that ordered the respectable world of American literary review.

The response of the mainstream reviewers in 1974 all but assured that *Flying* would succumb to the "speedy oblivion" Elinor Langer had wished for it in her review of the book in *Ms.* Although republished by Simon and Schuster in 1990 and again by the University of Illinois Press in 2000 (along with *Sexual Politics* and *Sita*—a memoir of a doomed love affair), *Flying* has, like most of Millett's books, spent long periods of time out of print. And like the rest of Millett's oeuvre, *Flying* has received little scholarly attention—Annette Kolodny's "The Lady's Not for Spurning: Kate Millett and the Critics" is one of few exceptions.[8] That *Flying* is largely forgotten today—lost to oblivion—is an example of the way in which so much of the remembering of women's liberation happens in tandem with forgetting—a forgetting that is, as Marita Sturken writes of the politics of memory making in general, "highly organized and strategic."[9] Millett has become an abject feminist figure, the eccentricity of her experimental life and political ideas as recorded and enacted in *Flying* seemingly unintelligible in the feminist present. Yet, as a document born of the furor surrounding the emergent women's liberation movement and the infamy of Millett's own public exposure as lesbian icon of the movement, *Flying* can also be read as a remainder of the events that first produced the feminist-as-lesbian as a figure around which social contest and change occurred during the early years of women's liberation. By writing an autobiographical text in the immediate aftermath of being outed by *Time*, Millett destabilizes the coherence of the feminist-as-lesbian as an image memory of the movement by making her, in effect, come alive.

My intentions in this book have been to render problematic accounts of women's liberation that pay little or no attention to its eventfulness. These accounts narrate the history of the movement as a story of either political failure or fulfillment and call for a disidentfication from, or nostalgia for, the movement in the present. My attention now turns to the question of how we might produce different accounts of the movement, ones that would refrain from the ordering mechanism of a developmental narrative and offer instead *accountability* to the movement's multiplicity and un-knowability as an event that is not over. As in the previous chapters, I turn to the figure of the feminist-as-lesbian, but now I follow her as a spectral remainder of the movement's complex beginnings rather than as a generative figure for its political revolt and claims.

I read *Flying* as a remnant from the past of women's liberation that provides a route back to the historical context of the feminist-as-lesbian's emergence as a figure of and for women's liberation. My reading of *Flying* resists the perspective of a queer and feminist present that, with the benefit of hindsight, already "knows" its limitations as a text of feminist and queer self-fashioning. Millett, like many of the women drawn to women's liberation, is a well-educated, white, middle-class woman whose turn to feminism was due, at least in part, to a visceral sense of being excluded from a social world that was supposedly hers: the white world of economic and social privilege.[10] The feelings of depression, betrayal, and anger that propelled women's liberation into motion as a predominantly white woman's movement were also, simultaneously, the feelings that revealed the movement's attachment to the cultural and social domains of proper femininity. Rather than simply judge *Flying* as a textual remainder of women's liberation's whiteness—as evidence of the movement's exclusionary politics or, indeed, as a relic of a desire for the movement in the present—I attempt to read it in its "moment of invention," to use Tani Barlow's phrase for the future-anterior present tense of a past political event.[11] Reading *Flying* as a text that both participates in and witnesses the invention of women's liberation returns us to the productivity of the movement's political claims and practices—their creativity and contingency—and as such it allows us to think about the whiteness of women's liberation as something the movement produced, but within an unsettled and unsettling political context that rendered its social and cultural coordinates less fixed and less taken for granted.

Indeed, as a project of self and world making that was also an attempt to document the immediate whirl of a life lived as the newly anointed lesbian icon of women's liberation, *Flying* is an active, aesthetic, and formal working on and struggling with the social, cultural, and emotional context of women's liberation's emergence as a distinct feminist movement. And as a documentary of the present tense of women's liberation, rather than a memoir of its pastness, *Flying* is a text written in between the past and future of women's liberation and of American feminism in general. That in-betweenness is the inchoate, heterogeneous time of the present, where the performativity, or sayingness, of an emergent time exists entangled with the saidness of history and of what is already known and familiar.[12] In periods of significant social upset and political instability, as in the time of the late 1960s and early 1970s, the incipient unsettledness of the present can also be disquieting, provoking social anxieties and fears that exacerbate and dramatize the uncertainties of meaning and comprehension that mark the movement of time. *Flying* was written at a time of social disquiet and political flux when the meanings of women's liberation's revolt and the objects that shaped its political challenges were unsettled and unsettling. The disturbing, inchoate early years of women's liberation—a period too often straightjacketed into narratives of political fulfillment or failure and then summarily forgotten in the present tense of feminist concerns—was the context for Millett's struggle to fashion a self and world in resistance to a public sphere that had already named her as bisexual and as the lesbian betrayer of women's liberation. Part of my intention in this chapter, then, is to emphasize the difficulty, for women's liberation and by implication all political movements, of creating something new. More particularly, read-ing *Flying* allows us to return to the contingencies of self and social change in the present tense of a moment in which people do not fully know what it is they are doing nor where it will lead. By reading *Flying* in its moment of invention, and being attentive to its mediation of the historical in relation to the subjective, I want to keep the moment—1970—open and bring "its ghosts and specters . . . flaring into the present."[13]

THE MAKING OF A FEMINIST GROTESQUE

The women's liberation movement was still an insurgent movement in 1970. The movement's political claims and styles of protest were not yet part of the fabric of everyday life; it was still strange and risky to be a feminist or, more particularly, a "women's libber." As part of the explosion of media interest in the movement in 1970, many mainstream magazines and newspapers, as I discuss in chapter 1, offered their readers detailed profiles of movement luminaries, those women designated by the media as its leaders, in order to portray and explain the "typical" women's liberation-ist. The articles on Kate Millett following the publication of *Sexual Politics* were part of this concerted media effort at portraying and displaying women's liberation as specific bodies and social types. Yet the success of *Sexual Politics*, both in terms of sales figures and reviews, meant Millett's status as movement "star" by the late summer of 1970 was unsurpassed. The radical challenge of Millett's thesis in *Sexual Politics*—that patriarchy was a political institution governing all Western societies and a "sexual revolution" was necessary in order to free women and men from the oppressiveness of gender roles—meant that Millett was not only the most famous women's liberationist of the latter half of 1970 but, within the context of the mainstream media, one of the most controversial. Millett's national notoriety in the summer and fall of 1970 also meant that she was regarded with suspicion within the ranks of women's liberation—the success of her book and subsequent media exposure seen as evidence of personal ambition rather than commitment to the movement. By the end of 1970 Millett was, for some in the movement at least, a "sell out" to the media kings of capitalist America.[14]

The controversy swirling around Millett in the summer and fall of 1970 only increased when the unconventionality of her private life became public knowledge.[15] Unlike Friedan's careful presentation of herself as an activist housewife,[16] Millett was more open and less reserved with the press about her bohemian, "downtown" life. As a sculptor, former academic, as well as movement activist, Millett lived her life in conscious contradistinction to the norms of middle-class suburban life. Married to the Japanese sculptor Fumio Yoshimura, but only in order to avoid an immigration deadline that would have meant Yoshimura's deportation, and openly supportive of gay liberation (she writes in *Flying* of having "chattered Gay Lib politics with Barbara Love the whole day *Life* interviewed" her), Millett's life in 1970 was presented in both the mainstream press and in her own writing as brazenly unconventional (15). Although Millett's difference from the norm of respectable, middle-class femininity echoed that of the thousands, if not millions, of women who were active in or aligned themselves with the various protest movements of the 1960s, the success of *Sexual Politics* catapulted Millett's unconventionality into the public spotlight—it became a visible sign of her political beliefs as well as evidence of women's liberation's difference from the normal. Who Millett was, how she lived her life, and the relations she had with others became almost as influential as her book in shaping an image of women's liberation in the public sphere.

On August 31, 1970, one month after the publication of *Sexual Politics*,

Kate Millett was the front-cover poster girl for *Time* magazine's overview of the women's liberation movement. In a photograph of a painting by Alice Neel, which was in turn made from a photograph (Millett refused, she states in *Flying*, to pose for the magazine because she did not want to be a figurehead for the movement),[17] Millett's face dominates the cover (fig. 4.1). As with the drawing of a women's liberationist in the magazine's "Women's Lib: A Second Look," Millett's eyes look at no one. Leaning toward the reader, she has the grim and vacant look of the fanatic, the crudely effective simplicity of Neel's brushstrokes effacing any sense of the particularity of Millett's personality. Long, unkempt black hair frames a face full of sharp angles, flat planes, and stark shadow, while the too big, masculine white shirt she is wearing dominates the lower half of the cover. The black-and-white contrast between hair and shirt and the grim angularity of the face invoke a primordial strength, especially when seen against the backdrop of luscious green foliage. In this portrait Millett is a terribly angry and masculine Eve come back to haunt Adam.

Neel's portrait of Millett as a fanatical, Eve-like figure sets the tone for the magazine's overview of the movement in which Millett is accorded the status of movement "ideologue." The article asks "Who's Come a Long Way Baby?" and sets up the reasons for the movement's rise in terms of a "battle of the sexes" sweeping the nation: "Everywhere, women's liberation organizations are urging women at home or in the office 'to confront your own unfinished business of equality.'" That unfinished business, the article asserts, includes not only "equal pay for equal work," abortion reform, state-supported childcare, and job opportunities but also, for "the most radical feminists," the "toppling" of the entire "patriarchal system." According to *Time*, Millett is the soothsayer or "Mao Tse-tung" of the radical feminists, "a sometime sculptor and longtime brilliant misfit in a man's world." It is Millett's "remarkable" book that has provided the women's liberation movement with the coherent theory and radical reasoning necessary for its "assault" on the "patriarchal" system of American society.[18]

The article goes into admirable detail about the positions, groups, and historical context of the movement, presenting facts and figures that lend legitimacy to the movement's claims that women are second-class citizens in terms of access to the professions, graduate education, lack of daycare support, and legal safeguards against violent assault. Quoting a variety of activists on the movement's political beliefs, including Robin Morgan and the "extremist" Ti-Grace Atkinson, the article also sets out the variety of

FIG. 4.1. *Kate Millett*, by Alice Neel, *Time*, August 31, 1970, cover image.

philosophical and political positions in the movement. Yet it is the arguments of Kate Millett, running as a commentary throughout the article, that become, for *Time*, the voice of the movement. Her call for a "cultural revolution" and her description of the family as "patriarchy's chief institution" are presented as the radical "truth" of the women's liberation movement's political ambitions.[19] As the angry Eve or Mao Tse-tung of the movement, *Time* presents Millett as the revolutionary with brains, her voice the true voice of the "most radical" wing of the women's liberation movement.

In contrast to the rather intimidating intellectual figure of the overview, the accompanying profile of Millett offers a more ambiguous picture. Here, the crude contrasts of Neel's painting are undone by details of a personal life that escapes any kind of dichotomous ordering. In noting Millett's work as a sculptor and her academic achievements at Oxford and Columbia University, the profile reveals a woman who has traveled far from the tenuous middle-class respectability of her Midwest origins. Millett's distance from the conventional is also suggested by her marriage to Fumio Yoshimura, his foreignness destabilizing the cultural inscriptions of heterosexuality as social norm that their marriage is meant to reproduce. Their stated decision not to have children because the "family system" would cause them to feel "possessive" of each other only adds to the seeming eccentricity of their marriage.[20] And with its revelations of Millett's difficulty in obtaining a teaching job on her return from Oxford (she eventually would teach at Barnard while enrolled in the PhD program in English at Columbia), her parents' unhappy marriage and divorce, and the violence and eventual desertion of her father, the profile shows Millett's life to be more adventurous, and difficult, than the conventional narrative of middle-class womanhood would admit.

Although the profile offers details from Millett's life that belie any simple representation of her, its tone simultaneously works to familiarize Millett, producing, as a consequence, a portrait that is incoherent rather than illuminating. The interviewer constantly refers to Millett as "Kate," suggesting a friendliness and familiarity that works against the Mao Tse-tung image of the overview. Millett, the reader is now encouraged to assume, is just like "us"—the readers of *Time*. Similarly, the quotes from Yoshimura—"she was a very ordinary American liberal when I met her"—and her mother—"Kate's missing the boat if she appears on the Mike Douglas Show without her hair washed"—return Millett to the domesticated attachments of marriage and family, diminishing her political ideas and positions by making them the personal, somewhat endearing, somewhat ridiculous opinions of a somewhat wayward wife and daughter. The revelation of the complexity and very real difficulties of Millett's life is undercut by the simultaneous attempt to present Millett as just another American woman, albeit one with her eccentricities.

The details of Millett's life exceeded and disrupted the conventional narrative of a "good middle-class white girl" who becomes a "happily married lady" and is now "content and happy." These details also undercut the stridency and fanaticism of the "movement ideologue" fashioned by the overview article, as do Millett's self-deprecating humor, humility, and voice, which "barely" gets above a "murmur," as described in the profile.[21] The contrast between the angry Eve of the Neel painting and the photograph of Millett accompanying the profile, in which a more rounded, hippie-ish Millett with comical thick round glasses is laughing and looking far from earnest, further exemplifies the incoherency of the magazine's portrayal of Millett. Who Millett is and what she represents are questions raised rather than answered in *Time*'s review of the women's liberation movement. Rather than the overdetermined symbolic figure—the "Mao Tse-tung of women's lib"—Millett emerges as a more complicated, less readable person, her unknowability demonstrated by the magazine's inability to fit her into any one role or image of who women are or, indeed, who feminists are.

Four days after the *Time* article, Marie-Claude Wrenn of *Life* magazine offered her own profile of Millett (fig. 4.2).[22] With the rather incongruous title "The Furious Young Philosopher Who Got It Down on Paper," and accompanied by five photographs in which Millett is laughing in three, kissing Yoshimura in one, and generally looking far from furious in another, the profile exhibits some of the same incoherency evident in *Time*. While in *Time* Millett's shape-shifting emerges out of the disjunctures between the two uses to which she is put (movement ideologue and the "real" woman behind the book), in *Life* the portrayal of Millett's strangeness is much more deliberate. In Wrenn's account, Millett's unconventionality becomes explicit evidence of a wayward or "wrong" femininity.

The article begins with what was, by then, a standard analogy: "Kate Millett is 35, very angry and the author of a scholarly polemic which is to Women's Lib roughly what *Das Kapital* was to Marxism."[23] The movement and its designated representative are transformed in this sentence into ahistorical typicality. They become part of the media event unfolding in

1970 in which past political theories and movements are collapsed into a present that is producing strikingly different ideas of political collectivity and social change. In contrast, Marx and Millett exist on a plane of representative interchangeability, their respective theories and lives reduced to a sameness that eviscerates the heterogeneity of time and space and the historical memories of past political movements, battles, and struggles that make each political event unique. While the analogy draws upon the red-baiting typical of the moment (all leftist protest movements in the 1960s were subject to the accusation that they were full of Communists, an accusation that simultaneously implies foreignness, both literally and figuratively) in relation to the women's liberation movement, it also implies the topsy-turvy world of gender inversion. By equating Millett with Karl Marx the article suggests that she is "strange" (non-American), not only in terms of a radical politics but also in terms of her (and the entire women's liberation movement) thinking that she is the equal of men, in this case the big man of the Left himself, Karl Marx. The association of Kate Millett with Karl Marx—an association accentuated by the alliterative echo of their initials—is deployed not only to diminish the history and range of radical political movements and theories but also to suggest the absurdity of a political woman who was also an intellectual: she can only be a poor imitation of the real thing.

The inference that Millett is a poor imitation, or pathetic mimic, of men structures the entire profile. At the end of the opening paragraph, after a quick listing of Millett's "dismissals" of such "great American novelists" as Norman Mailer and Henry Miller, Wrenn concludes that "for Millett, the only author who comes close to a true understanding of the feminine role in society is Jean Genet, a homosexual."[24] The conjoining of Millett and Genet in sympathetic agreement invokes the intertwining of homosexuality and femininity as a foreign and strange combination, especially when put into contrast with the very heterosexual, very American Mailer and Miller. The unstated conclusion that Millett is misguided in thinking that a homosexual rather than a heterosexual man would know more about women produces, through the correlative relationship of homophobia with misogyny, the association of the homosexual with women, the one invoking and confirming the illegitimacy of the other. Here, Millett's mimicry of men is reflected through a further alienation: her championing of Jean Genet over Miller and Mailer, emphasizing her distance from "real" men and, indeed, "real" women.

The furious young philosopher who got it

"I wanted to make men sensitive," says Kate Millett. Her book has gone through five printings in two months.

Kate Millett is 35, very angry and the author of a scholarly polemic which is to Women's Lib roughly what *Das Kapital* was to Marxism. With scholarly barbs, hundreds of footnotes, a 300-item bibliography, a selective perusal of history and literature, *Sexual Politics* sets out to prove that the male-dominated superstructure has put down women for centuries; that temperament is less a matter of biological heredity than a brainwashing by parents, peers and society at large; that the relationship between the sexes is more sinister and explosive than that between classes and races. It dismisses Norman Mailer as a "prisoner of the virility cult," D. H. Lawrence's books as "the very personification of phallic divinity," and declares that Henry Miller's "ideal woman is a whore." For Millett, the only author who comes close to true understanding of the feminine role in society is Jean Genet, a homosexual.

A bristling, assertive book, *Sexual Politics* somehow resembles its author even though, as she says, "All it is is my goddamn Ph.D. thesis." She won't write that way again—"My style is more run-of-the-mouth Americanese like Henry Miller. I use lots of four-letter words." As a thesis, however, it secured her a degree—granted with distinction—from the department of English literature of Columbia University. Her impetus for writing it came when Barnard fired her

as an instructor two years ago. "I was too much of a middle-class threat. I wore sunglasses to faculty meetings and took the student side during the strikes." After a three-day cry she cooled her Irish temper and settled down to work, furiously.

"I wrote it bang, bang, bang," comments Millett. "Like wow! A triple orgasm. Christ. I was so defensive. I had to overstate my case and find the most brutal episodes. I hope I pointed out to men how truly inhuman it is for them to think of women the way they do, to treat them that way, to act that way toward them. All I was

An artist before she entered the movement and turned to writing, she shows off her sculpture of a double bed.

trying to say was, look brother, I'm human."

Kate Millett is married and a sometime artist who once had a story in LIFE (June 9, 1967) on her whimsical sculpture. She shares a two-story Bowery loft in New York City with her Japanese sculptor husband, Fumio Yoshimura. Her book is even dedicated to him for the moral support he provided during the writing. They met in Japan in 1961, lived together in the U.S. and were married five years ago after he received a deportation notice giving him 20 days to clear out.

The writing of *Sexual Politics* was motivated at least partly by the author's private hurts. She grew up, the middle of three daughters, in a stormy Irish Catholic home in St. Paul, Minn. "We were constantly reminded that we weren't sons," says Millett, "that we were mistakes." The

father abandoned the family when she was 14 and left the mother to scrape together a living for her three offspring.

A brilliant student, she had collected a Phi Beta Kappa key, a B.A. *magna cum laude* from the University of Minnesota and a first-class honors degree from Oxford before trying to find a job in New York. "Everywhere it was the same question," she remembers. "Can you type?" Finally she landed a job as a file clerk in a New York bank. "That's all America thought I was worth," says Millett resentfully. "God, by that time I would have gotten a plumbing license just to earn a living."

Kate Millett is more of a theorist than an activist in the movement although she belongs to a number of women's liberation groups, including ("though I'm not into that") a radical lesbian organization. She can easily stay up all night working on a feature-length women's liberation documentary movie, then rush off the next morning to a NOW demonstration. She'll refuse to ask an "authoritarian male" for directions, ends up driving her Ford convertible the wrong way up a one-way street and through a red light while a policeman yells "Wake UP!" as the car skims by. "Safety first," says Kate unperturbed. "But we didn't make up the rules. So I figure we can do whatever the ●●●● we want." Her own confidence is supported and affirmed by equally angry women she has met in the movement. "Women feel so insecure because they have so little self," she says. "But you go around feeling neurotic and then, Christ, you find out that you're not alone."

MARIE-CLAUDE WRENN

In pseudo-karate garb, she harangues a mixed audience during a showing of a Women's Lib documentary film

FIG. 4.2. Kate Millett kissing Fumio Yoshimura and Kate Millett smiling, "The Furious Young Philosopher Who Got It Down on Paper," by Claude Marie Wrenn, *Life*, September 4, 1970, 22–23.

down on paper

Holding her head from fatigue, Millett answers a midnight phone call. Below, she kisses her husband, a Japanese sculptor, goodby before leaving for a radio interview. They have been wed five years. "The exploitation of women rests on everything," says Kate. "It's all through our culture."

By portraying Millett's intellectual and political ambitions as queer mimicry, the article is able to insinuate that Millett may also mimic men in other ways. *Sexual Politics* is described as a "bristling, assertive book," which "somehow resembles its author." And Millett herself is quoted as saying her style "is more run-of-the-mouth Americanese like Henry Miller. I use lots of four-letter words." Her "bristling assertiveness" and colorful language suggests a pretension to masculinity characteristic of postwar notions of the lesbian, a possibility uttered in the article through denial: "She belongs to a number of women's liberation groups, including ('though I'm not into that') a radical lesbian organization."[25] While the insinuation of lesbianism sits uneasily within the article's acknowledgment of Millett's marriage to Yoshimura, it is in that ambiguousness—her being neither one thing nor another—that the construction of Millett as a feminist grotesque is most vividly drawn.[26]

The article ends with an anecdotal story presumably told to Wrenn by Millett about getting lost in her car. Wrenn uses the story to characterize Millett and, by association, the movement as a whole as misguided and absurd, as women "in error."[27] Having got lost, Wrenn writes, Millett refuses help from an "authoritarian male," which results in her going "through a red light" in the wrong direction on a one way street and having a policeman scream at her through the window, "Wake UP!"[28] The policeman's scream is also the article's scream: this woman is truly lost; she thinks a homosexual man knows more about women than heterosexual men; she thinks she's the equal of men; and she might be a lesbian. What was, in *Time*, an inability to portray Millett in the full complexity of her life, becomes, in *Life*, a determined portrayal of Millett as a marginal, misguided, and eccentric figure: a woman in error.

When *Time* published "Women's Lib: A Second Look" on December 14, 1970, the magazine's previous position of indulgent, if bemused, onlooker has now become one of contemptuous authority. Millett's designated role as movement ideologue transformed into that of bisexual betrayer of the movement. Her "disclosure" that she was a lesbian at a Gay Liberation Front meeting at Columbia University became the reason to discredit both her and the entire women's liberation movement as a "bunch of lesbians." The suggestion and innuendo of the *Life* article are now no longer enough. Accused of bisexuality, Millett is transformed into an explicitly abject figure in the reconstitution of the boundaries that separate the domain of respectable femininity and its constellation of raced, classed, and sexual others. Yet it is in the article's slide from an accusation of bisexuality to one of lesbianism, again the fact of Millett's marriage spoiling any attempt to invoke a simple split between straightness and homosexuality, that the portrayal of Millett as grotesque reveals the inherent, disquieting instability of the internal frontiers between respectable femininity and its others. In the inability to fix Millett into place—to have her be one thing or another—*Time*'s outing of Millett, as well as the profiles offered by *Time* and *Life* in the summer, reveal something of what was at stake in the movement's fight for what many in the movement called a woman's right to be regarded as human. Neither lesbian nor straight, married yet not, a bohemian, an artist, a scholar, and a feminist theorist, Millett became a public spectacle of the risk-taking inventiveness and active changeability of many of the women in the early years of women's liberation. And as a designated representative figure for the movement, Millett disturbed the intelligibility of white, middle-class femininity as national norm, making it seem strange and incoherent. The contradictoriness of her (various and shifting) identities signaled a transgression of gender and sexual identities in twentieth-century America and threatened—if only viscerally—the domain of American national belonging as white and middle class.

"RESPECTABILITY IS DEATH, MOTHER"

By 1974 the political and social tumultuousness of the late 1960s had given way to a ruthless regime of state and police repression of the radical Left and Black Power movements.[29] The kidnapping of Patty Hearst by the Symbionese Liberation Army in February of that year was represented in the media as a bizarre, if compelling, leftover from the radicalism of the late 1960s. The FBI's infiltration and surveillance of the antiwar and Black Power movements, along with the internal political disputes and ideological disagreements that had preoccupied both movements since the late 1960s, resulted in the effective dismantling of an organized Left by 1974. Meanwhile the Watergate scandal would unfold in all its gripping detail throughout the first half of the year, culminating in the resignation of Richard Nixon on August 8. Though Nixon's fall from power was precipitous and dramatic, his presidency helped establish a decisive conservative turn in American politics and society. The so-called Southern strategy, which brought Nixon electoral success in 1968, incited and exploited racial divisions in order to secure the South for the Republican Party and contributed to the fracturing of the Left into discrete identity-based groups.[30] In conjunction, the implementation of neoliberal economic policies and the oil embargo crisis created a political and social context in which those on the margins of society once again disappeared from national view. By 1974 both Black Power activists and radical feminists were in retreat from the national public sphere. Black Power activists focused their attentions on local politics and community work when not harassed by the authorities or incarcerated, while many women's liberationists moved into single-issue organizations, joined professional lobbying groups, participated in self-help cultures, or simply stopped participating in any kind of organized political activity.

Millett had also drifted out of the public spotlight by 1974. Although still a participant in various political causes and invited to give lectures on college campuses, she was no longer the subject of media attention. Short-term teaching stints in California and an increasingly convoluted love life had put her marriage to Yoshimura under strain, and in July 1973, when visiting her family in Minnesota, she was forcibly institutionalized with suspected manic depression. Although both her lawyer and an attending psychiatrist successfully testified that she was neither a danger to herself nor others and did not, therefore, need to be institutionalized, the event was symptomatic of an increasingly erratic and eccentric lifestyle.[31] In relation to Millett, and other women active in the various protest movements of the 1960s, mental illness would become a placeholder for, and an explanation of, their political ideas and practices. The reduction of feminism to the personal lives and psyches of individual women's liberationists was not simply becoming a cruel historical irony by 1974, it was also an effect of the increasing privatization of the American public sphere by the mid-1970s.[32]

An increasingly privatized national public sphere contributed to the unease and dismissiveness with which *Flying* was greeted by mainstream reviewers in 1974. The public spectacle of Millett's experimental and unconventional life in 1970 had become, by 1974, an unseemly display of personal dysfunction and literary ineptitude. The politics of women's liberation were absented from the field of interpretation; instead, the criticisms of the book are made through the reassertion of a distinction between politics and the personal. In this interpretation, *Flying* fails as a feminist memoir because it indulges in personal self-revelation rather than disciplined political analysis. Although the reassertion of the distinction between a private life and the public sphere is made, at least by some of the book's critics, in order to question the collapse of the personal into the political evident in some feminist practices and theories, it also tended to reassert politics as the domain of experts and professionals and the personal as a domain anterior to political struggle. This reassertion of the distinction between a personal life and politics in the reviews of *Flying* works to make the relation between the two once again invisible to critical analysis. And so instead of reading *Flying* as a public practice of feminist self-fashioning (it was, after all, published by a mainstream press), the critics tended to read it as a private failure of autobiographical writing. Millett is judged as a type, a particular sort of feminist with the kind of personal failures that exemplified the errors of women's liberation.

In her review for the *New York Times*, Jane Wilson writes that *Flying* is an autobiographical work of "dazzling exhibitionism" and of such "ingrown confusion" that it leaves the reader "lagging" and "disorientated."[33] She charges Millett not only with manipulating her friends and readers in her "driven . . . need" to "order and control, to present at last her chosen image of herself," but at having failed to do so, as though a much "sadder, more complex and less innocent figure" signals a failure of autobiographical writing. Millett's documentary style, Wilson asserts, leads to a "warts and boredom" all-inclusive portrayal of life that fails to differentiate between what is important to record and what is not, resulting in an unseemly exhibition of self rather than the carefully crafted portrayal of a successful autobiography.[34]

For Wilson, as for many of the reviewers in 1974, Millett's apparent exhibitionism and supposed lack of judgment is most evident in her inclusion of detailed descriptions of her love affairs with women. Indeed, Wilson judges *Flying* a failure by implying a determining connection between established norms of literary style and heteronormative sexuality. She praises *Sexual Politics* for its "oblique approach" to its subject matter; it made for a "cooler and somewhat more productive discussion," in contrast to the "cry of pain" of *Flying*. She feels Millett has good reason to believe that the "trashy Times Square" lesbian novels she burnt in a fit of shame have left an indelible mark on her writing style. In fact, according to Wilson, there is altogether too much lesbian sex in *Flying*; it tends to serve as some kind of "erotic propaganda." She praises Vita (a friend and lover of Millett's and, therefore, a character in *Flying*) for her "restraining" comment, "you've got to stop saying I kissed the soft of her neck twice in ten pages." For Wilson, a cool articulation and restraint in tone and content are all markers of good autobiography. In contrast, lesbian sexuality, in its excessiveness and trashiness, seems to disrupt Millett's field of vision: Wilson complains that, in contrast to the overheated passages on lesbian sex, Millett "writes of heterosexuality as of a relaxing creature comfort in the same category as a warm bath or a mug of hot chocolate."[35] In other words, heterosexuality—the true subject of sexuality—is reduced to an amusing sideshow while the real sideshow—homosexuality—is given center stage with its endless trashy lines and sex scenes. Not only does lesbianism become the cause of bad writing for Wilson, it distracts Millett from seeing the world clearly, from differentiating between what is important, the "real" world of heterosexuality, and what is not, the bizarre and tacky world of homosexuality.

Wilson objects to *Flying* because it refuses to offer up the expected. Millett's articulation of self traverses the established demarcations between men and women, heterosexuality and homosexuality. The world she depicts is a topsy-turvy one with the established hierarchy between public and private, gay and straight, often reversed. Rather than presenting a carefully crafted version of self, Millett exposes herself, revealing personal flaws—vanity, narcissism—as well as the private shame of lesbianism, which, for Wilson, become evidence of her lack of judgment and writerly "focus." But I would argue that Millett's self-revelation in *Flying* is always more than just personal; she also exposes the fragility and artificiality of the borders that separate gay from straight, public from private. By writing across these borders, and exposing their constitutive relatedness, Millett exhibits not simply herself but a lack of investment in the ordering categories of sexuality and gender that produce the middle-class self as social norm, which is what Wilson uses to identify the ideal of autobiographical writing. It is for this exposure, I would suggest, as much as for the revelation of lesbian sexuality, that Wilson condemns *Flying* as "exhibitionism."

Like Wilson, Elinor Langer, in her review of *Flying* for *Ms.* magazine in December 1974, views Millett's portrayal of sexuality as one of the most problematic aspects of *Flying*, describing the book as "heavily pornographic." Langer also refers to *Time*'s outing of Millett as "the premature and hideously public declaration of her sexuality." The idea that *Flying* is pornographic, and that the *Time* article accusing Millett of lesbianism was "hideously public" (rather than, say, hideously wrong), is directly related to Langer's more general argument that *Flying* is not "disciplined autobiography" but rather a confessional outpouring of personal grief and grievances, which, in its pure subjectivism, reveals itself to be "pointless." Langer's objections to *Flying* form part of an argument that, by 1974, is directed toward the women's movement as a whole. For Langer, the movement's "lack of a genuinely critical tradition," its propensity for being self-congratulatory and for indulging in self-revelation rather than analysis, only inhibits feminism's political and social aims. The movement's "exploration" and "elevation of the personal" reduces feminism and feminists to spectacles—a tendency *Flying* exemplifies, according to Langer, rather than problematizes.[36]

Langer's criticisms of *Flying* are made in terms of a call, directed at the women's movement in general, for high standards. While self-revelation and subjectivity are "useful as instruments of insight in small groups and writing classes," they "can look shabby" and even "indecent" when made public. What should be revealed in an autobiography and what should remain in private diaries becomes, for Langer, the difference between having "standards" and "doing something badly."[37] Millett's inclusion in *Flying* of detailed descriptions of her sexual experiences with women become, therefore, evidence of her doing autobiography "badly." Yet, considering that *Flying* is nearly six hundred pages long, the passages detailing sexual experiences—both heterosexual and homosexual—are relatively few, certainly not comparable to "a Mailer short story," as Langer suggests. The incongruity between Langer's preoccupation with sex and the relative lack of it in *Flying* leads one to conclude that it is not the fact of sex, nor even the quantity, but the type that Langer objects to. Millett's autobiography is, for Langer, a spectacle of confessional outpouring, not because she refuses to analyze the world around her but because she admits to, and writes of, experiences that are usually hidden away in private journals or sensationalized in (trashy) Times Square novels.

While Langer's questioning of the focus on the personal at the expense of a more historical and structural analysis of the social condition(s) of women's lives was an important argument to make in 1974, her refusal to read *Flying* outside of the canon of "disciplined autobiography," and her equation of descriptions of lesbian sex with the "heavily pornographic," reveals her investment in the literary values and social judgments of a hegemonic bourgeois culture, which had defined the distinctions between public and private in gendered terms in the first place.[38] Rather than read *Flying* on its own terms as something that, as Kate Millett wrote in her response to Langer, "refuses and eludes any literary category,"[39] seeking to

contest the marginalization of lesbian sexuality from the publicness of heterosexuality, Langer chooses to read it through the literary and sexual standards that work to maintain those distinctions. The Millett that Langer
sees in *Flying* is the "tangled," "pitiful," and "pornographic" figure first
drawn in the *Time* exposé of 1970—a woman who betrays and confesses to
her inability to fit into the conventions of normal womanhood. Here, then,
the failure of *Flying* is to be found in Millett's inability to uphold the ideal of
American womanhood—an ideal that depended on, and generated, a set of
cultural values and social norms that secured rather than brought into
question the gendered and raced terms of an American national imaginary.

The feminist-as-lesbian, as I have argued, emerged in part out of the
profiles of Kate Millett in 1970 as a way of containing the threat of women's
liberation in a figure that suggested political eccentricity and social insub-
stantiality. The reviews of *Flying* by Wilson and Langer draw upon and
reanimate those profiles and organize how these reviewers read the book.
Flying is read through the screen figure of the feminist-as-lesbian, who, in
turn, operates as a shorthand notation for the errors and failures of women's
liberation. And as shorthand notation, the figure effectively incorporates
the book into an affective economy of shame and contempt through which
the feelings that render women's liberation meaningful in the national
public sphere circulate. Wilson's and Langer's inability, or refusal, to read
Flying outside the spectacle of the feminist-as-lesbian figure prevents them
from attending to the possibilities in the experimentation of Millett's written self. To let people see the unfinished product—a self made out of fear
and fantasy as much as sociological and historical fact and whose body and
thoughts move outside the frames of conventional femininity—is to risk
becoming unrecognizable. In the danger of not being recognized lies the
potential for women to become something beyond the idea of "woman"
and the fantasies of national and gendered belonging it enacts. For Millett,
as we will see, *Flying* was an attempt to move toward that unrecognizability
—which was also at the same time herself reflected back to her—and into a
new self, one that would get beyond the strictures of conventional, generic
depictions of women. That Millett's attempt to do so was regarded in 1974
as a confessional outpouring of pornographic explicitness and then largely
forgotten is less a testament to the perspicacity of the reviewers and more a
testament to the way the figure of the feminist-as-lesbian already worked by
the mid-1970s as a screen memory of the movement, effectively covering

over and burying its unknowability, experimentalism, and upsetting presence in American society.

While the reviewers of *Flying* criticized Millett for its "confessional outpouring," and for making a spectacle of herself, one of the first questions to ask, it seems to me, is why would Millett choose to write an autobiography and risk further public exposure after the humiliations of the *Time* attack. Are we to conclude that Millett was, despite her protestations to the contrary, actually rather fond of the limelight? Perhaps she took a perverse, even masochistic, pleasure in being outed as queer. Or perhaps, as Wilson and Langer argue, she was simply embarrassingly misguided in thinking that self-revelation was an effective response to her predicament. To pose the "problem" of Millett's decision to write an autobiography through questions like these presumes that Millett's decision can best be understood in terms of the vagaries of an individual psyche or alternatively that women, never mind feminists, have control over the terms of their representation and how those representations are taken up and read by others. While reviewers in the feminist and gay press were much more open to the political project of *Flying*—indeed, many of the reviewers in the alternative press lauded the book for being courageous in revealing the psychic and social pain of being both feminist and queer—they also read the book as a coming out narrative, a reading that tends to secure, rather than bring into question, the sexual ordering of American social life.[40] In these reviews, Millett becomes a brave gay woman rather than failed feminist, and the unsettledness of her historical moment, along with the ambiguity of her sexuality, gets lost in the effort to fix and locate her representativeness.

In *Between You and Me: Queer Disclosures in the New York Art World, 1948–1963*, Gavin Butt explores how gossip about artists in the United States in the 1950s and 1960s enacted a "refashioning of aesthetic practice" and a decisive shift in the discursive intelligibility of male sexuality in the postwar era.[41] His richly suggestive readings of the careers of artists like Larry Rivers and Andy Warhol reveal how both men manipulated gossip about their lives in order to fashion distinctive public personas—personas crafted in the glare of epistemological uncertainty about their sexuality. The crucial point, for Butt, is that both artists managed to enact a public staging of themselves as artists through a refusal to stabilize the sexual and gendered meanings of their lives. Although neither man, as Butt is careful to point out, controlled how their performances of self as an artist were received in the public spheres of the art world and mainstream media, their skill at presenting themselves as the subjects of gossip incited an expansive discourse about their work and their stature as artists. In other words, they generated a sense of their cultural and artistic importance that others, critics and audiences alike, took up and elaborated upon. I bring up Butt's study here in order to pose Millett's public staging of self as a counterexample to the postwar male artists he studies. Although Millett also refused to stabilize the sexual and gendered meanings of her life, her aesthetic technique of self making—writing an autobiography—in conjunction with the explicit politicization of her self-fashioning and social identity as a woman, all work to close down rather than open up discursive spaces for "interpretive play."[42] There is a refusal to see and to speculate about Millett's indeterminate sexuality and uncertain feminism in the reception of *Flying*, which speaks to the limited and overdetermined terms through which women are seen as subjects worthy of being spoken about or, for that matter, public figures worth gossiping about.

A scene from *Flying* might stand as a metaphorical staging of this lack of curiosity about women's self-fashionings. In this scene Millett describes being accosted by a man at a party in the early 1960s. The man asks her why her nails are so short: "My mouth is preparing to say because of the plaster I work in plaster I told you I was a sculptor, always so proud to say it waiting my chance to say I am an artist when I meet people. 'But of course they are short because you are a lesbian'" (154). Even though Millett is at a party full of artists, her eagerness to tell the man she is a sculptor, and her pride at the thought of doing so, reveals that it is an identity she has to assert rather than one she can just assume. The contradiction of being both a woman and an artist is then made brutally clear through the man's declaration that her fingernails are short because she is a lesbian. The man's position as rich patron to the artists at the party adds to his aura of authority; it is an economic and social relation that allows him to assume that he knows who and what Millett is. Millett does not get to speak her own identity; on the contrary, the social space for her self-fashioning as an artist is ruthlessly shut down by the man's insistence that he shall be the one to define her and give her presence at the party meaning. In this short interaction, Millett is reduced to an object for the man rather than a subject for herself. Her social presence as an artist is de-realized by being named a lesbian, a naming that, rather than opening up the interpretive possibilities of her life, eviscerates Millett's subjectivity from the social scene of the party.

While rumors of homosexuality add to the epistemological uncertainties circulating around figures like Warhol and Rivers in the 1960s, and contribute to their artistic auras, in this scene from *Flying* lesbianism is used as an accusation in order to make Millett a less interesting and less complex figure. Through a process of subtraction rather than addition, *lesbian* becomes a name, or label, that takes the place of *artist* as an identity through which we can know something about Millett. Butt suggests that rumor and gossip defer any finality of meaning; they "are discursive ways of perpetuating phantasmatic realms of collective life, of expressing the fears and desires entertained by particular communities." By keeping the discursive spaces of interpretation open, a community can "relieve the tensions of uncertainty" by explaining things through speculation and rationalization.[43] Although gossip or rumor might work to contain what has been identified as the cause of anxiety to a community (as was the case with rumors of homosexuals in the State Department in the McCarthy witch hunts of the 1950s, for example), they can also generate social presence and cultural visibility for those who are its subjects and betray a curiosity and interest in the people and things gossiped about. In naming Millett a lesbian, the man at the party, like the reviewers of *Flying*, betrays no such curiosity. Rather, he reveals a desire to fix Millett's identity in place and shut down its interpretive possibilities. The scene Millett relates displays not only the limited social space for women to fashion selves outside the conventions of normative femininity but also the relative lack of a social world, a public, that would witness— be curious about—such inventiveness.

The call for a social world that could witness the inventiveness of Millett's self-fashionings, and those of women's liberation in general, is evident in Millett's own answer to the question, why write an autobiography? Making a clear distinction between confession as the admittance of sin and Rousseau's notion of confessions as confidences or the "sharing of experience," Millett argues in her response to Langer that in *Flying* she is writing "against [the] shame" of her public exposure as queer.[44] Her use of the word *against* invokes an intimacy, or closeness, as well as an antagonism or resistance to something. It is in this uneasy ambiguity between a closeness to and a movement away from the shame of public exposure that Millett demonstrates the lack of a subject position from which to speak as herself, that is, as a self not already spoken of and through the terms of American heteronormative culture. Neither simply self-revelation nor evidence of (an unadmitted) fondness for being publicly queer, Millett's decision to write an autobiographical documentary of the year and a half following her transformation into a public figure might be more productively understood as an attempt to invent herself—and a world—out of the shaming experience of her public exposure. Millett says as much in her response to Langer: *Flying*, she writes, forms part of the "next stage" of the women's movement in which, rather than "arguing for [their] humanity," women are "expressing" their humanity, "living it and creating it."[45] Rather than read *Flying* as an admittance of sin, as the revelation of something "shabby" and "indecent" that should be disavowed in the name of a proper or appropriate feminism, Millett invites her feminist interlocutors to read it as a sharing of experience and as an expression of a life that is in the process of being created. What is crucial to remember here is that, for Millett, the invention of a new self, and a new way of life, can only be fashioned out of something shabby and indecent—out of a public sphere that had already named her as both bisexual and the lesbian betrayer of a movement. There is no outside from which Millett can form a self resistant to the norms through which she was already known and made intelligible—to herself as well as to others. Nor is there a respectable position from which Millett can take up the claims of feminism, as Wilson and Langer assume in their criticisms of *Flying*. Rather, what deserves to be remembered here is Millett's exposure, not simply of herself but of the lack of subject positions in 1974 from which to speak as a feminist and queer woman, and the lack of a social world that would be curious about her subjectivity in the making.

The world-making intentions of women's liberation are also evident in Millett's decision to write an autobiographical response to the notorious figure created by the national press. Millett's self-exposure took place in the context of a women's movement that regarded *experience* as a central term in its political theories as well as the beginning point for its political and cultural practices. As Ellen Willis, the journalist and former member of New York Radical Women (NYRW), writes, women's liberation "focused on the immediate facts of daily life" rather than legal reform or grand political theory. By being attentive to the practices of everyday life—the details of housework, childcare, and sex, for example—and the feelings they incited, women's liberation was interested in confronting gender relations on the level of how they were enacted and felt rather than on the abstract level of policy.[46] Widely distributed essays like Patricia Mainardi's "The Politics of Housework" from 1969 and Koedt's "The Myth of the Vaginal Orgasm" from 1968 focused on the micropolitics of vacuuming and sexual intercourse as sites for feminist resistance. The guiding assumption in essays like these was that gender oppression was not instigated from on high but reproduced through the emotional coercions and the habituated social conditioning of family life. Contrary to the criticisms of *Flying* by Wilson and Langer, Millett was practicing the politics of women's liberation by focusing on the quotidian and the ineffable. Her "warts and boredom" approach was a political as well as an aesthetic decision that meant, by virtue of the fact that the life under view was a nominally unnotable life (her brief moment of fame notwithstanding), documenting experiences that were usually judged unimportant and uninteresting.

The centrality of experience for women's liberation came out of the practice of consciousness raising, the principal form of organization in the movement.[47] *Consciousness raising* was a term coined by Kathie Sarachild, one of the founding members of NYRW, to describe the process of developing "class consciousness" among women through a collective speaking out about their experiences.[48] Speaking out would take place in small groups, which were then expected to analyze and "evaluate" the testimony of each member and "arrive" at an "understanding of oppression wherever it exists in our lives—our oppression as black people, workers, tenants, consumers, children . . . as well as our oppression as women."[49] The use of consciousness raising in women's liberation was inspired by "tell it like it is" meetings in the civil rights movement and by the campaigns to politicize peasants and indigenous peoples in the revolutionary struggles of Latin America and China. Common to all these practices of raising consciousness was the belief that the subjugated knowledges of the disenfranchised and marginalized would be the source of their liberation. The people were the experts when it came to their own lives and their own oppression, and it would be their experiences that would provide the tools for emancipation.

The taking up of consciousness raising in women's liberation was similarly meant to assert that women were the "real experts" on women, and the source of their eventual liberation lay in their becoming conscious of their experiences as an oppressed class of peoples. While consciousness raising became a widespread practice in the early 1970s (to the extent that it was even practiced by groups of women who had very little sympathy for, or connection to, women's liberation), it was also, from the very beginning, a highly contested practice. Many feminists, especially those who regarded themselves as socialists and who were still active in the civil rights, anti–Vietnam War, and New Left movements, regarded consciousness raising as self-indulgent "therapy" and argued that it detracted from action. For others, especially women of color, poor women, and lesbians, the demand that women find "the common root" of their oppression often induced a silence regarding their differences from white, middle-class, heterosexual women —the women who dominated women's liberation. The tendency in consciousness raising to assume that experience was the authentic ground for producing knowledge about women's lives signaled a naïveté about the relationship between personal experience and a political solution in women's liberation. To locate the expert knowledge of a group of women in the everydayness of their experiences effectively occluded other forms of experience and foreclosed critical scrutiny of the historical constitutiveness of the experiences they were analyzing. The result, for many feminists, both within and outside of women's liberation, was that the experiences of white, middle-class women became both the unproblematized ground for second-wave feminist concerns and the source of the movement's political theories.

These criticisms of consciousness raising are not unfamiliar to contemporary feminist perspectives on women's liberation. Indeed, the story I narrate is a familiar one, perhaps too familiar. I want to suggest here that the familiarity of the story and the general acceptance of its meaning within contemporary American feminism enacts a forgetting. The contested politics of consciousness raising, as well as its capacity to produce unexpected and surprising testimony by its participants, tends to get lost in the— understandable—eagerness to point out the limitations of its promises. As much as consciousness raising ended up reproducing white, middle-class heterosexuality as the sociocultural norm of American society, it also contributed to its destabilization by making the ideal categories of bourgeois American life seem strange and unsatisfying—even to those women who might be most interested and most able to uphold them. There was a strong utopian impulse for self- and collective transformation intrinsic to consciousness raising, which generated a willingness on the part of many of its practitioners to reveal what were felt to be personal failings and shameful secrets. Karla Jay notes in *Tales of the Lavender Menace*, her memoir of the women's and gay liberation movements: "C-R totally altered my vision of who I was and where I was going." Even for skeptical participants like Jay, who felt marginalized by a presumed heterosexuality and frustrated with the silences around poverty and race, consciousness raising provoked "private epiphanies" and provided an intellectual tool kit that enabled her to "dissect," with a certain "objectivity and precision," her own experiences.[50] Speaking of their experiences within the context of consciousness raising did not so much tell women the truth of who they "really were" as it enabled many to question the truths by which they had come to understand themselves, creating as a consequence virtual possibilities of a different way of being and doing. At its best, consciousness raising "posed skeptical questions" about the present tense of American heteronormative bourgeois society.[51] And it is the sense of anticipation intrinsic to this questioning in consciousness raising that the reviewers miss in their readings of *Flying* and that has largely been forgotten in collective memories and historical accounts of the movement.

For Kate Millett, who participated in consciousness-raising groups in women's liberation both before and after her moment of fame, the sharing of experience in *Flying* might better be understood as a utopian desire for self- and collective transformation. Millett too had mixed reactions to consciousness raising: it "smacks of an evangelism faintly embarrassing to a lapsed Catholic and art snob," but it was also a practice that engendered "fear and joy" in its participants (90). For Millett, consciousness raising was the "democratic guts" of the movement (90). If consciousness raising provided a space, if not always a "safe space," for women to explore their experiences in relation to those of other women, then writing an autobiographical text allowed for the exploration of a self in relation to itself and to those others it anticipated as its (feminist and queer) public. Millett was branded a betrayer of the women's liberation movement by *Time* for her sexual nonconformity and accused of betrayal by some in the movement for allowing herself to be portrayed in the press as a happily married woman despite her affairs with women, and *Flying* would counter those accusations by "detailing the truth in print" and presenting Millett in all of her complexity (70). She would no longer be a feminist icon or lesbian betrayer; she would be an artist, an activist, a writer, a friend and lover of Fumio Yoshimura, and a friend and lover of women. Instead of being the "sick and silly" woman in the national press, she would be a new kind of woman, one who has experienced "all the possible pleasures of freedom" (123). In this sense, *Flying* was also about testing the limits of established forms of self-presentation for women, not only those that stigmatized Millett in 1970 but those that circumscribed and limited the possibilities for feminist and queer collective invention. Rather than confession, Millett asserts, she was "writing to find out [who she was]" (81), which can be understood as a form of action rather than representation: "And now I will be who I am becoming" (240).

"I CAN'T BE KATE MILLETT ANYMORE"

Flying begins with an account of the "fugue state" (the title of the first chapter) Millett found herself in following the *Time* exposé.[52] Through what Annette Kolodny, in her insightful essay on *Flying*, calls a series of "almost tiny film clips of association and reference,"[53] the reader learns that Millett has just arrived back in New York after a trip to London, that she is trying to complete a film, that she feels alienated from all the "normal" people and constantly on the verge of a breakdown, and that she is also trying to write another book. The explosion of information and confusing array of times, places, and people in the first five pages presents a fractured and disassembled self. Millett is all over the place—literally and figuratively at a loss. Through this proliferation of association and reference, Millett sets out what will be the governing style of her autobiography. Rather than a coherent, progressive, narrative, *Flying* offers a collage of experience, memory, and feeling that constructs an experience of self that is multiple, fractured, and produced through shame.

The fugue state opens with a scene in which Millett is sitting on top of a double-decker bus in London on her way to the airport. While being on the top deck gives Millett a sense of freedom—she can smoke and survey the city as the bus travels along its streets—it also leaves her feeling on view and vulnerable to the world around her: someone on the bus "threatens her," beer advertisements—"Take Courage"—mock her, and the cover of her book—*Sexual Politics*—stares out from bookshop windows like an "enemy" accusing her (3). The sense that she has been exposed to the gaze of the world with the publication of *Sexual Politics* causes Millett to feel as if a "partition" was "installed that separated [her] from the someone who felt and existed" and who now sees everything "through dirty plexiglass" (26): "London Airport. Whole bunch of Americans with southern accents. All the normal people. Everyone looks all right. Man takes a picture of his bride. People sit on the plastic chairs. They do not show that they see. If they see. But all this year I have seen it, the strangeness. Looking right through the terror in it. City after city. As if I saw too much. Discovered the trap in things. I cannot tell you what it is" (6). If the bus figures Millett's sense of being on display, of being exposed to the gaze of the world while also being able to see and travel through it, the airport figures as a transitional space, not simply from one place to another but from the lived world of "ordinary" people to the public world of iconic or symbolic representativeness. The transformation from private person to public figure enacts a separation from the known world that is also felt as a burden rather than as a liberating escape: it causes Millett to see "too much." What Millett sees can be interpreted from the above passage as the "trap" of normality—the familiar arrangements of objects and people in space, the scenarios of everyday life (sitting on plastic chairs, waiting at airports or train stations, getting married) that, in their repetitiveness, promise the familiarity of social continuity. Millett's alienation from this world is felt as a loss, which, in turn, reveals her sense of having once belonged to it. What is interesting to note here is that Millett's detachment from the world is not presented as an accomplishment, as the desired outcome of her feminist protest, but as the acutely discomfiting result of her public exposure as a lesbian.

In her analysis of shame as an emotion that reproduces social relations and national identities, Sara Ahmed writes that shame brings about "an intensification" of the subject's relation to itself. In shame, "the badness of an action is transferred to me."[54] You feel ashamed of what you are rather than what you did, a feeling generated through the exposure of yourself before another. You feel yourself as wrong or bad most acutely in relation to another—the one who has witnessed you doing something wrong. At the same time, shame is also an emotion that can spur a creative reconstitution of identity. In the moment of feeling shame a person becomes both painfully aware of their isolation from others but also, simultaneously, aware of their relation to those others: it is your perception of the other's judgment of you that makes you feel exposed as different or wrong. As Eve Sedgwick has argued, it is in this "double movement . . . toward painful individuation, toward uncontrollable relationality" that shame offers creative possibilities for queer self-making.[55] The restorative potential of shame is, however, ambivalent in its effects. Shame can work to reconfirm the ideal the subject is exposed as having failed to live up to or embody, but in revealing the subject's failure to inhabit or approach an ideal, shame can also provoke a different orientation of the self to others and the world. Shame is neither a liberatory nor a conservative emotion—as if an emotion can be inherently either thing. Rather, emotions, like subjects, are irreducibly social and, therefore, historically contingent in their effects.

Millett's response to being famous in the above passage is structured through shame. In becoming a public figure Millett suffers the painful individuation of being revealed as wrong, as "sick." Her identity—as movement leader or its lesbian betrayer—has come not from her own subcultural self-fashionings but from the claims and judgments of the public sphere. The accusations by *Time* and by movement "fanatics" are felt as an exposure—she is now seen by the world, and in being seen Millett feels, paradoxically, not seen but negated: she is an "object," a "joke" at parties, a "creature of publicity, offensive, dirtied, notorious" (7). In the moment of fame Millett sees herself reflected in the judgments of others, which is a kind of birth. She is forced to see herself as someone apart from herself and from the world around her. It is a moment of estrangement that is also, at first, a form of submission rather than resistance: her identification with the "sick and silly" woman of the *Time* exposé is absolute; she is "sick. Done for."

Immediately following Millett's account of her feelings of exposure and alienation after her public outing, she recounts a memory from childhood. In what we might now read as a convention of queer autobiography, Millett's retrospective connection between childhood shame and her more recent public shame bears witness to the feelings of loss and failure out of which her becoming lesbian in *Flying* is fashioned. Walking home from school on a cold winter's day, the young Millett gets into a stranger's car thinking that the man is acting out of kindness—there is a blizzard—and that he must be a friend of her father's. At the beginning of the ride, Millett is sure of her world: "We turn toward the river, history test, comfort of warmth, security, convenience. Sense of protection so familiar. I am a girl. People take care of me" (8). As the ride continues, however, the social coordinates of her world begin to break down and fear replaces the feeling of familiarity and belongingness. The man doesn't seem to know where she lives, then he starts to touch her while exposing himself, and the world around her is at once unfamiliar: "Great purple flesh in his lap long huge horrible. Is that what one looks like? This is real now. It's danger" (9). Later, after running away, she realizes with horror that she has lost her "turtle," the orthodontic retainer to keep her teeth straight: "Pink plastic in the new white powder almost dark outside the car among the trees. . . . I cannot go back and find it. At dinner a fever till they find out it is lost. It is my fault" (9).

The "turtle" and the "great purple flesh" become the objects that signal Millett's transition from one way of being a girl in the world to another. The pinkness of the retainer in conjunction with the white snow suggests a loss of innocence but, more specifically, a loss of girlishness as innocence. In contrast, the purple of the penis suggests the redness of sexual danger (and desire) but also a pink that has "gone wrong"—an innocence that has become disgusting in its transformation into something huge and horrible. By being exposed to the purple flesh, Millett takes on its horribleness as her own; she now sees herself through the perspective of the other, the man with the purple flesh, and she too becomes disgusting: "Telling on him is telling on me" (9). Up until this point, Millett has understood her place in the world: she is a girl who gets taken to school and is cared for by adults. The stranger destroys Millett's known world through physical action and the exposure of his penis, the violence of his act forcing a separation between the young Millett and the world she knew. She is no longer, simply, a nice young girl who is taken care of but someone who has, through the actions of others, become something else—something disgusting—a sexual object and repository for the desires and fantasies of others. The memory of childhood molestation becomes an event through which Millett comes to know something about herself, not through her own actions but through those of others.

Millett associates this memory with a cluster of others from her childhood: she becomes ill with pneumonia, her father leaves home, and her mother goes out to work. Linking these memories together is an overwhelming feeling of guilt. The loss of her retainer is connected with wanting her father back and desiring to live with her Aunt Christina. As she lies in bed the young Millett remembers the man in the car, her head getting "hot," wishing sometimes for him to return (10). Driving in her mother's "little Ford" she sees her father's "Merc" and wishes she were her Aunt Christina's daughter, "her house beckoning me like a lover down Virginia Avenue as we pass the corner. Why can't I be her daughter, live with her, no husband now no kids of her own, all that money" (10). The ambivalence of Millett's shame in these memories is revealed in the oscillation between an identification with her mother and her desire for what the man in the car introduced her to—not just the possibilities of sex but, in association, the grandeur and freedom of her father's and aunt's world.

Millett's more public humiliation after the publication of *Sexual Politics* is situated in *Flying* as a present echo of her childhood estrangement from the known world. The private intimacies of her relationships with women are transformed into simplistic emblems of her status as lesbian outsider and betrayer of an entire movement. Like the episode with the man in the car, the moment of fame is one when Millett sees herself through the eyes of others, realizing, in the process, that she is always already there for someone else's needs and desires. To be publicly exposed as a lesbian by the national press is to be seen by America for America. If she was once a young girl who became aware of herself as a sexual being through the actions of a stranger, Millett is now a woman whose identity as a lesbian is forged through being named as such by others. Through her shame, Millett exposes not only her own feelings of subjection to the desires and wants of others but also the process by which a sense of self comes from an awareness of the world's use of you. And rather than offer a recovery from shame through the projection of an ideal alternative self, Millett makes the scenarios of shameful self-exposure the situation from which her becoming feminist, queer, and lesbian is made. In her shame, then, Millett reveals the dispossession intrinsic to the production of subjectivity. But at the same time, in the negation of self that shame produces, Millett bears witness to the process of her painful detachment from the gendered and raced norms of American social life.

Writing "against shame"—becoming shameless—structures Millett's creative, world-making response to the events of 1970. To write against the shame of one's public exposure as lesbian icon is, simultaneously, to write for a life lived beyond the supposedly recognizable categories of straight and queer. Flying, Millett tells us, is about "creating myth out of a handful of Lesbians in New York City and a few other friends" (288); it is about the "cult of friendship" (266), where lovers are friends and vice versa: "What I want is outrageous: all the possible pleasures of freedom. I want to get beyond the old system of possession, the notion of person as thing owned. . . . I'm experimenting with life, trying to get it right, to do it better, . . . trying to create a new kind of social existence" (123). Conversely, and as recent critiques of gay shame as an extension of white normativity make clear, by writing against the shame of her public outing as lesbian, Millett reveals her attachment to a world that could make her feel shame in the first place. When shamed, as Ahmed reminds us, you feel yourself exposed as having failed by seeing yourself through the eyes of an ideal other. That ideal other, for Kate Millett and women's liberation (insofar as it was a movement that imagined itself within the terms of a national public sphere), is the white, middle-class woman who signifies the heteronormativity of femininity in American culture and who organizes the class and family romances of Millett's desires and fantasies.

But if shame organizes Millett's relations to the world in *Flying*, it does so in ways that do not tend to take up its promise of recovery—despite her experiments with a new life. Instead of transforming her shame into pride, as a convention of gay liberation would have it, Millett stays masochistically enthralled with the feelings of humiliation, suffering, and abjection it elicits. It is Millett's attachment to shame, I contend, that reveals the ambivalent nature of her attachment to the normative world and her attempt to free herself from it. Moreover, Millett's shame, a shame that was both personal and public, illuminates the process by which the fantasies of escape and transcendence of women's liberation were fashioned out of the scripts and scenarios of proper femininity, and this suggests that in order for white, middle-class women like Millett to be free of the claims and seductions of proper femininity, they would have to engage in a process of estrangement from its appeal rather than, as the liberatory politics of the movement promised, declare a simple refusal or transcendence of it. For Millett to fly away from the demands of (white, middle-class) femininity does not mean an escape from or an outright rejection of them but an at times humiliating exposure of herself as a white woman. To become a women's liberationist, the Millett of *Flying* suggests, if not always knowingly, is to become off-white—strangely, exaggeratedly, awkwardly, excrutiatingly, monstrously a white woman.

"THIS NETHER WORLD"

So far, my reading of *Flying* has concentrated on demonstrating how shame, as the structuring emotion of self-fashioning and world making, provides us with an opportunity for thinking through the problem of feminist resistance to normative femininity for the predominantly white, middle-class women's liberation movement.[56] Rather than craft a refusal of, or complaint against, normative femininity, Millett's shame is revealing of her own failure to be the "good woman"—a failure that, in turn, enacts her becoming feminist and/or a lesbian. I now want to shift my attention to the way in which shame structures the ambivalent relationship between past and present through which the temporality of social change is produced in *Flying*. This ambivalence is enacted both in the scene of writing and on the level of narrative. Millett juxtaposes writing as a becoming and as a movement away from moments of injury with a constant return to, and recounting of, painful memories. Two scenes from *Flying* capture this uneasy relation between recounting and escape and illustrate the productive capacity of shame as an emotion that enacts the aspirational idea of women's liberation, and gay liberation for that matter, through collective memories of social and psychic loss, which literally write women's (and gay) liberation into being as a political protest and movement with a particular history and imagined collectivity.

In the first scene, Millett, having just returned to her consciousness-raising group for the first time since being anointed a movement leader by the media, decides to go with Claire, her new friend from the group, to a gay bar for a drink. They end up in a bar down the street that Claire identifies as the Inferno but which Millett realizes used to be called Paolo's. She is surprised by its location—"Odd how I always forget the location"— but simultaneously informs the reader that she has been here many times before, having "often driv[en] around for hours searching [for the bar] through the labyrinth of repression" (96). The simultaneity of forgetfulness and remembering illustrates Millett's relationship to her own queerness and to the public spaces of queerness:

> Place of shame. One goes here to remember. In case the new life lets you forget. It takes but a second to locate each figure arrested in the same gesture as ten years before, the entire tableau frozen just as I dreaded it. Feeling safe, I fancy I look good hitting the door, with someone, swimming fast through the mob at the bar. But still nervous at being sized up, still not many inches away from the wallflower nights in years-ago bars clinging in desperation to a fifty-cent beer.
>
> All the last romantics crowded into one room. And do we look awful. The whole charm of the place lies in the fact that it shouldn't exist. Every thrill the forbidden has to offer. And I love them all. This shame is ours, our rebate, our ghetto of the heart. How logical of gay politics to put a priority on finding new places of assembly, weaning us from this tinseled fleur de mal. But something in me never wants to relinquish what took so many years hunting down. This emptiness I discovered: all I would ever receive in exchange. (96–97)

Echoing Stephen Gordon's descent into the miasma of ruined lives that was the queer underworld of Paris in the 1920s in Radclyffe Hall's *The Well of Loneliness*, as well as David's similar journey to the gay bar of his own sordid desires in James Baldwin's *Giovanni's Room*, Millett writes of her entrance into the bar as a journey of descent into the past, which is also the anterior "nether world" of social abjection. It is a world, Millett declares, that she has now escaped: "After eight years in the straight world, some clothes, a dash of self-respect, I'm damned if I'll ever again disfigure myself to fulfill some twisted notion of how a 'pervert' should look" (97). Millett's simultaneous invocation and dismissal of postwar butch-femme subcultures, and the medical model of sexual perversion through which they were interpreted, is presented as a step toward a different, more liberated—self-respecting and straight-like—future. By "swimming fast" through the "mob," Millett "fancies" she can escape being a part of the tableau. Unlike the figures around her, "arrested in the same gesture as ten years before," she has moved on; she is "with someone" who makes her "look good" (97). Being with someone younger, someone who looks good, is presented as evidence of Millett's escape from the nether world, her desire and identity neither stuck in the timelessness of sexual anteriority nor in repeating the same gestures of sexual longing and identification, which the figures still stuck in the bar are condemned to do.

Yet, Millett's disarticulation of her presence in a gay bar from her memory of gay bars is undone by her movement through it, which returns her to a scenario of queerness that is instantly recognizable and familiar: she is "still not many inches away" from her "wallflower nights" in the same bar years ago. Millett's initial disidentification from the scene she surveys turns to identification as she enters into it: "And do we look awful." The figures arrested in time are a memory of her own coming to queerness: they are incorporated into her sense of herself as a lesbian and as queer. She "love[s] them all" because they are witnesses to her queerness—its thrill and forbiddenness, as well as its shame. These figures and the scene they enact make it possible for Millett to be queer. This "ghetto of the heart" is not simply hers but the movement's too. While "gay politics" has founded new meeting places and new ways of being gay, Millett warns against forgetting and relinquishing these hard fought for places. It is the gay bar and its "tinseled fleur de mal" atmosphere that has provided queers with the possibilities, and the feelings, for a distinctly queer way of life. Here, then, Millett articulates the pastness of the gay bar with its "sick subcultures" (97) to the future of gay and women's liberation. The uneasy movement from the present tense of a gay bar, still teeming with a "mob" of patrons, to the gay bar tableau frozen in time reveals the ambivalence of the relationship between the queer "ghetto" and a liberated gay future. For Millett, this ambivalence is her secret shame, as well as the difficulty of a past that feminists and queers must, somehow, hold onto as they move toward a different future: "We queers keep everyone straight as whores keep matrons virtuous. I have borne this label so long it is a victory to embrace it, a way of life accepted. For the kids and the converts this nostalgia over a sick subculture is merely gratuitous. Yet there are times I am angry they do not know the past, are free to forget what should never be forgotten" (97). Millett's mixed feelings about the gay bar, her "love and hate" of such places, refuses the defiant comforts of nostalgia for lost or marginalized subcultures as well as the future promises of sexual utopianism—the same promises she declared herself a believer of in *Sexual Politics*. Instead, Millett stays stuck in her ambivalent attachment to queer forms of social life, exposing her investment in the classed and raced idealizations of heterosexual privilege and also the difficulty of making a new life for queers and feminists, one in which neither celebration nor disavowal of the past will do.

In the second scene, Millett narrates her reasons for writing a memoir by staging a dialogue between herself and Doris Lessing. The scene takes place in a section appropriately titled "Blick: The English Notebook," a title that echoes and pays homage to Lessing's *The Golden Notebook*. In this section, the third part of the book, Millett has traveled to England, a journey that gives her distance and perspective on the "new life" (the title and subject of the second part of the book) she is attempting to live in New York—the life of sexual and social experimentation. While in England, Millett, the now infamous author of *Sexual Politics*, visits Doris Lessing for lunch and asks her a question: "Do you worry you will lose writing?" Lessing's reply, "No, I know now that I can do it. . . . My problem is wondering why I should," and the matter-of-factness with which she says it "astounds" Millett, "she says it simply. Just that command is what a lifetime has given" (357).[57] Millett's astoundedness comes with her assumption that writing, and specifically the writing of literature, can open up new worlds and new possibilities of self-expression for women. Evoking the poet raconteurs of her father's family, Millett views art and literature as domains for self- and collective reinvention. At the same time, that world of invention is also the world of the "humid rhetoric of academia," the stultified language of her "poor damned thesis," *Sexual Politics* (357). If writing can invent new selves and new worlds, it can also oppress and elide through the representation of others and their worlds. Part three of *Sexual Politics* rages against the sexual objectification of women in Anglo-American literature. Taken within the context of Lessing's increasingly experimental writing and corresponding disillusionment with organized politics by the early 1970s, her ambivalence about writing can be read here as a crisis about form and its relation to action: writing realist novels, like joining formal political parties, were acts of participation in the world as it is rather than effective challenges to it.

Millett's response to Lessing's mixed feelings about writing and its capacity to enact different ways of seeing and acting in the world comes in her admiration of *The Golden Notebook*: "Let me tell you what it meant to me. . . . It's the moment your heroine shall we say . . . finds herself in a toilet at the outset of her period. . . . And the blood is running down her legs while she struggles with toilet paper. . . . In a book! Happens every month of adult life to half the population of the globe and no one had ever mentioned it in a book" (357). Millett's admiration of *The Golden Notebook* in this passage is deployed as a framing device for her readers. She wants us to read *Flying* in the same way that she read *The Golden Notebook*: as an inventive, if not fictive, documentation of experiences without traditions, with "no language. No history of agreed values" (358). And like Lessing's novel, *Flying* experiments with form as well as language in order to better apprehend and share those experiences. What is interesting about Millett's response to Lessing is her choice of scene, which suggests both the political value Millett places on the exposure of the intimate details of a woman's "private life" as well as her commitment to the idea of a commonality among women such exposure promises. Here, then, we see again Millett's investment in the cathartic force of shame as a political act of self-exposure, which is also an investment in a future where "half the globe" will recognize their similarity to each other. What makes Millett's sharing of experience with no language or history of agreed values more complicated in relation to this promise of commonality, however, is that it will also include her sexual relationships with women.

Millett's sharing of her experiences of childhood molestation, the loss of her father, and the desire to live with her Aunt Christina are all offered as memories that produce, in part, her queerness in the present. Yet these memories of loss and desire are never exact in their production of sexual self-knowing. They are, instead, displacements for feelings of sexual excitement and longing that have no ready-made narratives or scenarios for expression. When Millett writes of a childhood love affair with her friend Nancy, the shame she felt was produced in retrospect, after the outside world had passed judgment, implying that the two girls initially experienced their love affair without shame: "'Cause people act funny about us when we say we're in love. Before Thanksgiving vacation we told the seniors and they laughed, kind of scary, like when you've made a mistake" (11). That something more than or before shame remains inexpressible and can only be present through the failure of conventional narratives of love and desire to explain it. Millett provokes a disjuncture between representations of normative female sexuality and what has yet to find a form of expression—not lesbian sexuality or love exactly but feminist and queer worlds of sexual pleasure and friendship.

Indeed, rather than a revelation of commonality, Millett's attempts to write against the established narratives of love and desire by documenting her various love affairs tend to become dramatizations of her being neither one thing nor another—neither lesbian nor straight. Her marriage to Fumio Yoshimura and her affairs with women are not presented as part of a developmental narrative of sexual awakening and liberation, instead they are an expression of boundless love—her only problem being how to get "right the balance" (288). The idea of choosing one or the other, gay or straight, is rejected in favor of being both, of living in and across both worlds in the utopian hope of making them one. Traveling from an early evening dinner with her married friends Lila and Reno to a late night lesbian dance on the eve of the gay liberation march in 1971, Millett becomes the wandering sexual subject, linking both worlds together and simultaneously undoing their inner coherence: "Watching the two of them, one on each hand, man and woman in their world, knowing that in an hour I enter a cavern of Lesbians in a loft on an obscure downtown street. Watching them with loving eyes and feeling all the tension of two worlds, two cultures sealed away from each other, two entire societies separated so often it seems permanently, the crevasses between tearing me apart like a mulatto who passes. When do things come together?" (197). The self-aggrandizement of Millett's metaphorical (mis)use of the mulatto figure transforms her in the above passage into a suffering sexual hero who risks being torn apart by the thrills and threat of escape and possible capture. Here, Millett's experimentation with life is presented through the exaggerations of melodrama: the social precariousness and painful individuation of her being neither one thing nor another, neither straight or gay, transformed, through the appropriation of a sentimentalized figure of racial suffering, into something both risky and brave. Although she wishes for a resolution—when do things come together?—the affective power of the scene is concentrated in her invocation of the mulatto as a figure that signals the promise and threat of categorical evasion as well as the sentimental charge of being wronged. What matters in this scene, in other words, is not the professed desire for a world where "things come together" but the melodramatic terms of Millett's self-fashioning: she presents herself as a sexual adventurer who suffers, in a pleasurable kind of way, from her ability to cross the border between being gay and straight. Melodrama, like shame, provides Millett with the necessary feelings of social exposure and hurt that allow her to dramatize her separation and alienation from the so-called normal world as a loss that is also revealing of her attachments to the scenarios of love and desire the world has offered her and through which she understands herself as a sexual and social being. The thrill and possibility of women's and gay liberation comes not from an outright rejection or negation of the gay and straight past but out of a rerouting of its affective and imaginative possibilities.

"THE NEW LIFE"

Divided into five parts—"Vertigo," "The New Life," "Blick: The English Notebook," "Trajectory," and "Landfall"—*Flying* presents a life lived both as escape and as a perpetual taking off.[58] The flights of escape are the attempts by Millett to free herself from the entrapments of her moment of fame and from the "patterns" of her childhood (545). The second sense of flying suggests the journeys Millett is attempting to make: into new experiences, new ways of "apprehending" things, and new ways of living (360). Although both senses of flying occur and recur throughout the text, the flights they chart do follow a certain trajectory. By "Landfall," the fifth and final part of the book, the swirling collage of documentary and flashback with which Millett presents her life gives way to a narrative focused almost exclusively on the present. In this section, the flights Millett has taken do not end so much as become the form through which she understands her life: she has not reached a conclusion; she is not in heaven (though she does end the book in Provincetown); rather, she has come to realize that her life is "about change" (403). The "desperate search for self" with which Millett began the book does not end, finally, in the attainment of a new and better Kate Millett but in the realization that the process of discovery and change *is* her life.

What is interesting about Millett's conclusion is not what we might now recognize as its rather naïve investment in the liberatory potential of "change" but what the traveling she documents and the accumulation of details she presents reveal about the impossibility of escaping the world that made you. Millett's "quietly desperate search for self" does not come through a disidentification from the "monster" created in her name or from a sense of the limitless possibilities to be anything she wants to be. Rather, it comes from living with, and writing against, the shame of her public self. *Flying*, then, also becomes a metaphor for the heady emotional charge of risking so-called normal life and of exposing oneself to the eyes of the world. The result of this risk taking is not, finally, the production of a new feminist self but a destabilization of the cultural conventions and social coordinates that would make Millett recognizable as a particular kind of woman. Rather than the recovery of (a new and better) self, shame opens up a disjuncture in *Flying* between Millett and the identities and subject positions she is called upon to occupy. It is through this disjuncture and Millett's inability to be properly one thing or another that we find evidence of the difficulty, as well as the possibility, of changing the way one inhabits the world.

Throughout the first four sections of *Flying*, Millett turns repeatedly to memories of her parents and their painful marriage. Her parents become the figures through which she orientates herself as a desiring subject, her parent's marriage a family romance that provides the impetus, and model of comparison, for all others. By moving toward her parent's marriage and writing against its heterosexual plot, Millett disrupts the coherence of sexual difference, offering, as a consequence, an account of her lesbianism that is close to, even implicated in, its gendered narratives of desire. In a description of the difference between her father and mother, class and gender are revealingly combined by Millett in relation to her newly acquired, ageing Ford convertible car: "Millett and Feely, money and fear. . . . Mother's peasant finds this car a crime. The aristocratic Millett in me argues beguilingly for the glamour of its ride. Most men love a car like this. They look at it and see their own youth. Mine too. Discovering in one horrified moment that I cling to it because it's Celia. . . . Because it means last summer" (72). Sex and sensuality—Celia and the summer—are metonymically linked through the car to men, to her father, and the Milletts. The various descriptions of her father leave a trail of associations that invoke masculinity as freedom (to roam independently of familial ties and responsibilities), wealth, and danger but also as signifying pleasure and sexual adventure. Her father is a scary but also exhilarating alien force—he's a bully, the "man I should hate," but he could also "Sing. Tell stories" (230)—his absence, both physical and emotional, offering the necessary distance for Millett's projected fantasies. Associated with her father is her Aunt Christina who rode about town in "open cars . . . wearing bearskin coats, drinking booze" (72). Infused with the power and freedoms of her class, Aunt Christina becomes the embodiment of a powerful womanhood free from the anxiety and defeat of Millett's mother. In contrast to the grandeur of the Milletts, her mother's family, the Feelys, are "peasants," descendants of the "sniveling" Irish, who are "thoroughly unpleasant in their poverty" (72). Imagined through the "terrible powerless tears," fragile respectability, and determined celibacy of her mother, femininity becomes the domain of inhibition, poverty, asexuality, timidity, and being "wronged" (230).

Millett's account of the breakdown in her relationship with Vita, her friend, lover, and secretary, is written in relation to, and against, her parent's marriage. Her decision to take Vita as a lover was part of her experimentation with a new life. Rather than have friends and lovers, Millett wants, she tells the reader, to break down the distinction and create a "cult of friendship" in which possessiveness and monogamy were things of the past (123). But the new life she is trying to cultivate cannot overcome the class and gender dynamics through which she feels her desire. Millett portrays Vita in terms of the class relations that their roles as employer and secretary invoke. Despite her actual upper-middle-class background, Vita is the "indominatable proletarian woman, utterly righteous, her heavy inexorable steps approaching without mercy, a fanatic armed with exact orthodoxy, one hundred percent pure" (198). Intertwined with the particular physical characteristics of Vita (she is described in other passages as awkward and self-conscious, never moving or dressing right) are the ideological constructs of the working class as ugly, clumsy, and, in their one-dimensionality, fanatical. Millett's sense of Vita as "proletarian" in her affect and physicality invokes memories of her mother, and both are directly associated with the other: "Mother would always let me drive, her foot frantically pedaling the floor but finding nothing since the brake is on my side. . . . Strangling just before the head-on collision, the little gurgling noises in her throat every time she spots a car. I was my father, her tormentor, always untrue. A deceiver. And now Vita" (199). The "gurgling noises" her mother makes are a correlative of her "crying like an animal" during dinnertime arguments (10). Similarly, Millett describes Vita as an outraged child who screams and has loud violent tantrums (164). It is the bodiliness of their outrage that provokes distaste. And it is the visibility, the disgraceful physicality of the poor that Millett inscribes onto Vita and her mother, while Millett becomes her father, the deceiver. Millett's identification with her father here is an uncomfortable one: his masculinity is neither idealized nor rejected but is felt, rather, like the crown of thorns she imagines wearing as symbol of her taking on the sins of her father, as both burden and possibility. Through the memories of her parents, and the emotions that animate them, Millett makes femininity and masculinity morally and historically burdensome, and as such, they are presented in *Flying* not simply as material for sexual experimentation but also as inhibiting constraints on Millett's attempts to invent a new life.

In contrast to the painful sense of repetition that the failed experiment of her relationship with Vita invokes, Millett's intense, romantic relationship with Celia in the summer of 1970 is remembered as the new life realized, albeit briefly: "The three of us in love with friendship, living in an old house, a commune with a bunch of college kids, youngsters who were Fumio's apprentices. The great dinners and the music afterwards, wild flowers on the table. We slept like three children in a row. Celia in her bed beside us" (73). Millett's memories are of "the three of us," not just herself and Celia but also Fumio, her husband. The relationship represents the new life because it was about living in a "commune," among a group of people and within the context of "friendship," rather than within the exclusivity of a marriage. Grace, beauty, enigma, and wit are all characteristics Millett associates with Celia and the life she covets. It is almost the world of the Milletts and her father, Celia's white, Anglo-Saxon credentials adding necessary distance from the familial home, the "home" of her mother: "Celia gave me the Milletts again, myself recovered" (243).

But as with her relationship with Vita, Millett's love affair with Celia is fraught with conflict. Early in their relationship, Celia tells a story of the time when the local Catholic school, which both she and the children of her family's Irish workforce attended, refused to allow her to go to confession. In response, Millett tells of being forced to go to confession and compelled by her mother, and by guilt, to go to church. This mutual revelation of difference is told in an atmosphere of humor: "We both laughed, sun in the six big windows, those early June days, thinking we had solved the class problem with our love" (72). Desire and sex are at first seen as transformative, as a way to resolve difference. But Celia is desired rather than identified with. Millett likes Celia's story because it tells of Celia's difference from herself: to be excluded from confession was, in fact, a sign of Celia's privilege. It is this conflict, one that echoes and repeats the class disparities through which Millett comprehends her parents' marriage, that is, finally, unresolvable in Millett's relationship with Celia: "Wasn't I Irish gentry after all, a Millett, with their looks, their arrogance? Then trips to New Haven with the door locked on me, I turned out to be not a Millett, but Mother—the one who gets hurt. Hearing Mother's voice—'you are always for the underdog'—as if it were a reproach. But it was what she made me, her lesson" (72).

Millett can identify herself as the oppressed—the Irish, the working class, her mother—but only if she is also a desiring subject looking for something more. Alternatively, she can desire all that the privileged have but only if she remains separate and therefore justified in her sense of injustice and pain. Celia is "the Milletts remembered" not only because she offers the promise of the new life—of summers full of friendship, laughter, wit, and beauty—but because she is like her father and his sisters with their "looks, their arrogance," while Millett is like her mother, the underdog. Millett comes to interpret her relationship with Celia as a trap laid for her by the "magic or the terror" of her desire, a desire instituted by the family romance of her parents' marriage (538). The documenting of her love affairs with Vita and Celia become a placeholder for the virtual, not yet articulable "new life." Although her affair with Celia was, like her relationship with Vita, ultimately a repetition of the patterns Millett wished to free herself from, the moment when she looked into Celia's eyes and thought she "could beat the system" (538) becomes the image of the promise of a different future, one where possession and power, the norms of heterosexual marriage, will give way to a "commune" of love.

By part four of *Flying*, Millett's attempts to free herself of the roles of heterosexual love and the patterns of her parents' marriage become a life lived in constant motion. There is no alternative world of lesbian love for Millett to find. Instead, she records her constant journeying from place to place, person to person. Rather than the situatedness of marriage, home, and children, Millett travels from one snatched moment to another, from her loft in New York City to her farm in upstate New York, to New England, to England, and to Provincetown. Her old Ford convertible becomes both the sign and the vehicle for her roaming desire: from Fumio at the farm to memories of Celia while driving to Vita in New York, to the summer in Provincetown with Claire.

This frenetic motion—made possible by her participation in the new-ness of the gay and women's liberation movements and her transformation into a public figure—destabilizes the established patterns of life and the Oedipal narratives through which Millett understands them. Happiness comes in brief, transient moments: lying on the floor of a boat looking up into Claire's hair or sitting across from Fumio at the farmhouse table under the blue tulip lamp. The transience of each moment also threatens to extinguish them: each moment suddenly lost as Millett moves to another, the fragility of her connections to other people provoking anxiety at the thought of their possible loss. Fumio's voice lonely on the telephone and Claire disappearing from the room are signs of their distance from her, even as she asserts "but I am here" (492). Like Icarus flying too close to the sun, the risk of freedom in Millett's constant to-and-fros threatens to break everything apart, including her relationships with others. But this constant movement, as an effect of a desire produced through the politics of gay and women's liberation, also causes a proliferation of sexual and social experi-ences, and it is through this proliferation, this excess, that Millett writes a new life into being. While Millett's desire for Celia comes through fantasies of class privilege, itself an echo of her childhood desire for the world of her Millett aunts, her relationships with others—with Claire, Fumio, and Vita —ruptures any sense of inevitability or fixity in the Oedipal narrative of class envy. After the eruptive force of women's and gay liberation, there is no one story, no single scenario, that could capture Millett's "real" sexual self or enable her, in Lauren Berlant's terms, to stay attached to the prom-ises of normative femininity. Similarly, it is through the proliferation of documented experience that Millett is able to write against the public persona of her lesbianism. Rather than the static figure of the "sick and silly" lesbian comes the movement of sex with various people, male and female. The movement toward others and the proliferation of relationships in *Flying* is both a witnessing and an enactment of the politics of women's liberation. As a disorganized, grassroots social movement, women's libera-tion was less an organization with a platform than a disruptive, disturbing, and upsetting force in postwar America. Millett's experimentation with life formed part of the *movement*—the disruptive, destabilizing activity—of women's liberation: rather than the transformation or rejection of white, middle-class femininity, the promise of women's liberation, here, lies in Millett taking the risk of becoming someone other than what she thought she was.

The metaphors of movement in *Flying*, the traveling toward others, toward new experiences, and away from established forms of knowing and doing life, do not extend toward any transformative contact with women of color.[59] Indeed, the few scenes depicting black-white relationships mostly concern Millett's relations with black men and tend to draw upon mass-cultural fantasies of black men as either Uncle Tom figures or dangerous rapists. It is instructive to note the contrast in Millett's imaginative interpretations of race and homosexuality: while lesbian desire is presented throughout the book as a disruptive force—as a potential means of provoking a disjuncture in family and class hierarchies and the public fantasies of sexual desire and romantic love they animate—her relationships with black people, as she records them in *Flying*, tend to reassert the distinctions between black and white as a form of sexual exoticism and threat in the case of black men and as pure absence in the case of Millett's few interactions with black women. Black women are "far away" in *Flying* (129), literally in the case of Millett's friend Milly, who lives in Germany, but also socially and politically. Millett's failure to make contact, to move toward black women, is symptomatic of the failure of her feminist imaginary, as well as the failure of her interpretative devices—the family romance, the drama of class—to confront not simply her own privileged position as a white, middle-class woman but also the radical possibilities of her experimentations with a new life. And yet Millett's willingness to expose the failure of her imagination by including—without metaphorical embellishment or ideological explanation—her fantasies and reactions to the few black friends and people she encounters during the course of writing *Flying* makes for an uncomfortable and revealing exposure of that failure.

Millett dedicates *Flying* to her friend Zell, an artist who died while Millett was writing the book. In her description of his funeral, and subsequent reflections on their friendship, Zell emerges as a benevolent father figure, full of wisdom and self-sacrifice and just a little too good to be true: "His black face under the white hair glowing with Faulkner, with Marlowe. . . . He'd dig me out from under a pile of freshman themes written badly and reluctantly by middle-class kids who merely endured their education, to remind me what a student really is" (77). Through a series of contrasts—of Zell's white hair and black face and the comparison of his innate goodness, evident in his desire to learn, with the sense of the entitlement and complacency of white students—Millett projects Zell through the screen of the Uncle Tom figure. Though the whiteness of his hair is a visible signal of Zell's goodness, his black face is a reminder that, though he is white-like, he can never be white. Millett's sentimental portrait of Zell works through the way the intelligibility of the Uncle Tom figure secures her privileged position as white while also screening her from having to confront that privilege: he was a good man and her friend.

Millett also deploys mass-mediated narratives of race in her memories of another black male friend, Jack Thomas, and like her portrayal of Zell, her memories of Thomas serve to reinscribe the difference between white and black that reconstitute the inviolability of (her) whiteness. The screen figure through which Thomas is viewed is the black rapist. Her memory is of Thomas raping her ex-lover and friend Zooey; but it is also of her own sexual encounter with Thomas, an encounter that derives its eroticism and pleasure for Millett through her association of it with the rape of her friend. Millett's memories of the rape are imagined—she wasn't there—but she nevertheless offers them to the reader as if she were: "Wanted both of us and she wouldn't, so he forced her, huge body of a football player pinning her to the bed, bruising, beating her" (66). Immediately following this imagined scene, the narrative switches to a trip Millett takes with Thomas to Coney Island: "People staring at us on the train, nigger and white chick. Staring right back. . . . When we got back to his place, thinking as he entered me there goes the sound barrier—hoping I had not said it out loud 'you're black'—a whole piece of America breaking in me, free" (67). The explicit danger and violence of the rape scene frames the eroticism of the later scene: the breaking of a sexual taboo, the open defiance of the couple on the train, is eroticized through the cultural memory of Reconstruction era sex and race panics over the supposed black male covetousness of white women. The exclamation "you're black" marks the sexual transgression (you're not white like me) but also simultaneously reaffirms the boundaries between white and black (your blackness makes me white).

The pleasure and danger of Millett's encounter with Thomas echoes her encounters with white women, especially Celia. The transgressiveness of interracial heterosexuality, like the transgressiveness of homosexuality, comes from the "virtual possibilities" it opens up, as Foucault puts it, in the social fabric.[60] Yet, while Millett's relations with white women are indeed risky—they bring into question her sense of self by disturbing the comforting illusions of the interpretive devices through which she understands herself as a desiring subject—her relations with black men as presented in *Flying* are, in the end, neither risky nor transformative. There are no feelings of shame or stigma attached to Millett's relations with black men. Instead they are presented in *Flying* as a way to stare right back at America. The moment of penetration does not provoke a disassembling of self but a breaking free (of America). The silent moan of pleasure—"you're black"—announces the orgasmic moment as one of separation and difference rather than a breaking down of borders between self and other.

If Millett's relations with black men are presented through the screen figures of the Uncle Tom and the black rapist, her relations with black women conjure no such fantasies—not the mass-cultural clichés of a sentimentalized relationship between black and white women nor, for that matter, the promise of a beloved community glimpsed, if not always realized, in the alliances between black and white women in the civil rights movement. Milly, her one, identified, black female friend, lives in Germany, and her geographical distance becomes a metaphor for her emotional and political remoteness, a remoteness that is associated with her blackness: "Sit in the sun and listen to Milly's voice far away black exile in Deutschland" (129). That "black exile" is understood by Millett as a need for distance from white people: "If I wouldn't come to her place she wouldn't come to mine. . . . And once Fumio and I ran over to the storefront on Third Street wanting to invite her for a big Sunday dinner . . . 'Uh uh. Not eating with no more white folks ever again.' Just like that. No explanation, though we knew she'd quarreled with Nickelman the Sunday before" (130). Millett calls this incident Milly's "surly black girl number" (129). Implicit in this description is the assumption that blackness is a put on Milly performs to artificially alienate herself from others. Black is neither an embodied quality (Milly can put "it" on or not) nor is it a process of social differentiation and marginalization (blackness has something to do with Milly, it's her "number"). Rather, race becomes a mask, a performance of otherness that hides what would otherwise be, presumably, a self like Millett's. The "exile" of Milly, then, can be read as a resistance to the demand, made by Millett in this passage, that she be like white people and, specifically, that she be like Millett. Milly's refusal to visit Millett—"if [Millett] wouldn't come to her place she wouldn't come to [Millett's]"—becomes a rebuke of Millett's refusal to "visit" her, to move toward her difference (from Millett).

The lost possibilities inherent in Millett's rendering of her failure to move toward Milly are eerily suggested by the similarity between the two names and become apparent when we learn that, like Millett, Milly is both an artist and a lesbian. Although Milly sublets Millett's art studio, and her home in Germany is a studio, there is no explicit identification by Millett of Milly as a fellow artist. And while Millett imagines Milly with "a beau over there, some racist Kraut," she finds out that she lives with another woman, a fact about which Millett makes no comment (129). That lack of comment —the failure to make a connection—as if Milly's lesbianism and identity as an artist bear no relation to Millett's, speaks to the lack of cultural memories of transformative encounters between black and white women in American history. It also speaks to a lack of cultural forms and scenarios that would express a desire for connection, for alliance, between black and white women. But it also speaks to the failure of Millett and other white women at the time of women's liberation to confront that loss as a loss. Although, as Wini Breines makes clear in her study of the early women's liberation movement, many predominantly white women's liberation groups were in fact preoccupied with questions of race and class and articulated an antiracist and anticlassist politics, it was their failure to form lasting political alliances with black feminists that remains part of the "puzzle," as Breines puts it, of the complex and contested phenomenon that is the women's liberation movement. Indeed, Breines's desire to "re/remember second wave socialist feminism" is an attempt to confront the loss of those potential alliances and to account for the conundrum of a largely white feminist movement that was often explicitly antiracist in its politics.[61] Part of the failure of women's liberation to forge cross-race alliances, despite its political commitment to a transformation of race relations, I would suggest, lies precisely in the lack of collective memories, and fantasies, of transformative encounters between black and white women and in the inability of many white women's liberationists to move toward the difference of black women, something Breines herself acknowledges in her documenting of the starkly different responses of black and white feminists to the history of women's liberation.[62] But instead of condemning Millett's failure of imagination and the inability of her interpretative devices both to confront the privilege of her whiteness and also to apprehend the transformative possibilities of contact (personal and political) between white women and women of color, we might better read it as an opportunity to account for the lost possibilities of women's liberation's attempts to enact an antiracist politics. Those lost possibilities are what haunt U.S. feminism in the present, but they are also the "something to be done" in the present tense of American feminism.[63] They are reminders and remainders of the failures that are the starting point for thinking again—about women's liberation, about race, and about feminism.

"FOR I HAVE SPILT MYSELF IN THIS BOOK"

In the fifth and final part of *Flying*, Millett's frenetic movement from place to place comes to an end. Millett travels to Provincetown—another magical place in the making of a particular image and idea of postwar gay America—in order to spend the summer with Claire, her new young love.[64] Written of as a kind of resting place, a place for final reflections on the "flights" she has taken, Provincetown also becomes, for Millett, an idyllic context for the expression of a love that has, she insists, finally broken free of the patterns of her childhood. Claire's youth and beauty, as well as her "strangeness"—her interest in mysticism and metaphysics contrasting sharply with Millett's avant-garde artistic and political milieu—suggest a separateness, a mutual autonomy that Millett now finds constructive rather than threatening. Watching Claire "walking alone in her heroic mood," Millett sees her "alone, herself" and "separate at a distance and respected" (345), while she looks on also alone but nevertheless able to see and be with her. It is in this communion of separation and difference that Millett asserts that she has "overwhelmed her childhood. Free of its patterns finally" (546).

Millett also ends *Flying* with Fumio. He is her "sane adult," the one she calls while in Provincetown, "idiotically sobbing in Japanese that [she] love[s] him, adore[s] him," that she has "ended that awful book" (*Flying*), and will "come up to the farm and just live quietly with you and write it" (542). All through Millett's experiments with the new life, her trials and tribulations with Vita, with Celia, and through her burgeoning relationship with Claire, Fumio remains a constant, uninterpreted presence in the book. She cannot fit her relationships into one pattern nor give an account of her lesbianism that would make sense. At the beginning of *Flying* Millett asks herself: "Who would understand my loving him [Fumio] while loving others?" (24). It is a question that she cannot, finally, answer—the last image in *Flying* suggesting that it is in that lack, in the failure to make things whole and logical, that Millett finds both the truth of her experimentations with life and hope for the future: "Gulls, so many of them I try to count them but they split and break I cannot place and order them in the sky. Flying in a haze of wings noises cries. Chaos and serenity together" (546).

Millett's reading of her experiences through shame and the interpretive devices—the family romance, the drama of class—with which she understood her parents' marriage reveal her commitment to a self-exposure that, rather than creating an alternative fantasy and/or subcultural world of sexual experimentation, demanded a sometimes discomforting, sometimes self-aggrandizing, revelation of inadequacy and desire. If her resistance to her sick and notorious lesbian self is imagined through the gendered and raced idealizations of a class, it is the undoing of her constant movement, as well as the conflict between her desire for women who remind her of her upper-middle-class aunts and her identification with the "powerless tears" of her mother, that points to the impossibility, "the trap," of normality. In *Flying*, Millett does not write against *Time*'s effigy by posing a more accurate alternative but by undoing its impossible coherence. It is the excessiveness of a life uncovered and lived as a becoming with no guarantees and no final revelation that the critics of *Flying* objected to. Instead of the projected ideal of a carefully constructed self, Millett spills herself, hoping that this, her self-exposure, would produce a different Kate Millett, one who emerges from her participation in the enactment of a new, feminist and queer, world.

In approaching *Flying* as a remnant of the immediate context out of which the feminist-as-lesbian was fashioned as a figure for women's liberation, I have tried to be accountable to the contingencies of its moment of invention. And by following Millett's experiments in self and world making in the aftermath of her public outing as lesbian icon of the movement, I have attempted to track the productivity of Millett's inability to free herself from the fantasies of class and race privilege that organize her self-understanding in the text. Indeed, Millett's spilling of self is instructive in what it reveals about how shame as a social emotion can incite feminists and queers to reproduce the ideals that keep them attached to the very things they are attempting to be free of. And at a time when the gay and women's liberation movements were actively attempting to refashion sexual possibilities outside the model of gender inversion, which, as a consequence, too often demonized the subcultural worlds of butch-femme sexuality, and when neither lesbian feminism nor queerness could yet provide a politico-cultural context for her experimentations with a new life, Millett's excessive unassimilability lays bare the limitations of her self-fashioning. But Millett's experimentation is also revealing, in the present, of the difficulty of trying to change the way one feels, and inhabits, the world. The politics of women's liberation was a project of radical collective and self-transformation—that the women who participated in its promise failed to transform the terms through which they were socially and culturally legible as women does not negate the possibilities inherent in their attempt. To fly, as Millett's use of the Icarus myth suggests, is to risk detaching oneself from the ground of the normal—in Millett's case, the ground of white privilege as imagined and ordered through the habitus and genres of a proper femininity. The relative formlessness of *Flying*—its catchall accumulation of quotidian detail, memory, and sexual fantasy easily overwhelming Millett's rather cursory attempts to shape the book into a narrative of rebirth—signals Millett's attempt to break free of social and aesthetic convention, while simultaneously revealing her attachment to their promises of a better, happier world for women. But if Millett's ultimately self-aggrandizing attempt to fly free of social constraint and the pull of history did not leave her liberated from the normative claims of her world, her masochistic return to the scenes of her failure to be a good daughter, wife, lover, and feminist make her, and the movement she was a part of, much less readable today as "normal" women.

5

LOOKING FOR THE GHOSTS

Remembering Women's Liberation

So many women I know now standing up new and huge with beginnings then falling over the next moment. Want to go far then relapse back into the little woman,
the past jiggles underfoot and we capsize continuously.—KATE MILLETT, *Flying*

At least in the United States, considerable effort has been put into reassurances that
feminists are "normal women" and that our political aspirations are "mainstream."
With the best of intentions (which include prominently the wish to be maximally
inclusive) this normalizing strategy cannot conceal its class basis and attachment
to "upward mobility" which depends upon leaving others behind. Furthermore, it
concedes much to the misogyny which permeates the fear of "losing one's femininity," "making a spectacle of oneself," "alienating men" (meaning powerful men) or
otherwise making "errors." Most importantly it leaves uninterrogated the very
terms and processes of normalcy.—MARY RUSSO, *The Female Grotesque*

In the third and final segment of the HBO film *If These Walls Could Talk 2*,
released in 2000, a rather prosperous and unrelentingly happy lesbian couple, Kal and Fran, played by Ellen DeGeneres and Sharon Stone, sit down
in their interior designer nest of appropriately arranged beige and cream
furniture to have a conversation with a gay male couple about becoming
sperm donors for their longed for child. As they clutch each other's hands
and bob their blonde heads in dismay while the men try to argue for
parental access to the future child, the likeness of the two women exudes a
comforting image of togetherness and sameness. Although the soft butch
look of DeGeneres offsets Sharon Stone's California girl femme-ness, these
two women are not a study in contrast: they go together like beige and
cream furniture rather than "boots of leather and slippers of gold."[1] The

rest of the segment, cloyingly titled "Miss Conception," follows the women through their adventures with reproductive technology—their visit to the sperm bank, picking through the profiles of anonymous donors, and humorous attempts to impregnate Fran (even the expense becomes a source of humor)—until, with the pregnancy test finally showing them the good news, they giggle and dance to Natalie Cole's "This Will Be." As Kal and Fran celebrate the coming of their child—a child who will, thanks to their careful choice of donor, look just like them—the failures of the lesbian past shown in the first two segments of the film, specifically the inability of closeted lesbians in the pre-Stonewall period to participate in the reproduction of the social world and the conflicts between women, gay and straight, wrought by politicizations of sexuality during the women's liberation movement, are overcome. Thanks to increasing access to technology, money, and the commodity pleasures of American bourgeois life, lesbians, the film assures us, echoing another of its appropriated songs, this time from Aretha Franklin, are now doing it for themselves.

Dana Heller, in her essay on popular memory and U.S. feminism, "Found Footage: Feminism Lost in Time," argues that *If These Walls Could Talk 2* tells the story of lesbian feminism as a "forward march from Boston Marriages to Lavender Menace to Lesbian Baby Boom" in which, with a baby on the way, the final segment is able to proudly proclaim "that the historical battle for acceptance and regeneration has been won."[2] For Heller, the story of lesbian progress told by *If These Walls Could Talk 2* is less a celebration of gay pride in the queer commodity culture present than a symptomatic expression of a general cultural anxiety concerning the ability of feminism to reproduce itself in the late twentieth and early twenty-first century. In Heller's reading, the film's deployment of "found footage" at the beginning of each segment works to situate the narrative of lesbian progress within the context of a remembered feminist past. Archival images of 1950s hegemonic femininity, followed by film footage of women's liberation and gay pride marches from the 1970s and split screen headshots of famous public feminists from the 1970s through the 1990s, frame the film's story of increasing acceptance and integration of lesbians into American social life as a story about feminism and its successes. The anxiety in this story, for Heller, is most dramatically on show in the film's final segment when the "success" of feminism morphs into a narcissistic embrace of "the democratizing order of consumer culture and commodity fetishism."[3] While the found footage deployed in the film reveals an apparent desire to remember feminism and its achievements, at the same time it also works to place feminism in the past—as a preface to a present that has no more need of politics or social movements.

As in the first *If These Walls Could Talk* film,[4] each of the three segments of the story takes place in the same house—its physical metamorphosis from one inhabitation to another acting as a synecdoche for the transformations in historical and political context that structure the story the film wants to tell. And as with the first film, the house also acts as a symbol of continuity and containment for the story the film tells of women's expanding economic and social power. If, as the second film suggests, lesbians can now reproduce, then it also wants to quickly assure its viewers that their desire to go forth and multiply will not mean a proliferation of dark and shady bars filled with freaks and "unwanted beings"—a movement out into the world and beyond the four walls of a family home—but, rather, a proliferation of all-American suburban domestic coupledom.[5] Although in the first segment the deprivations of a pre-Stonewall, closeted existence reveal the social and legislative need for a feminist politics, the second segment reveals a feminist politics out of control and unable to deliver on its promise to fight for "women's equal rights with men."[6] Set in 1972, the second segment details the explosive tensions between a group of lesbian feminist students and their radical feminist counterparts, with Chloë Sevigny as the butch, motorcycle-riding love interest further complicating the scene by acting as a catalyst for the breakdown of woman-identified sisterhood in Michelle Williams's lesbian feminist household. It is only when Kal and Fran occupy the house, now transformed back into a more affluent version of the closeted couple's home of the first story, that lesbians —and indeed women in general—are seen as confident users and occupiers of public spaces and institutional power. The anxiety expressed in the film concerning feminism is, then, more precisely an anxiety about the usefulness and place of feminist politics in women's lives. The conflicts and displaced contradictions and antagonisms of the second segment overwhelm the containment strategy and progressive narrative of the film as a whole. And it is in this segment, I would suggest, that the film's "remembering" of (second-wave) feminism is most acutely and problematically put on display.

Still, it is important to emphasize that *If These Walls Could Talk 2* is a rare example of a mass-cultural attempt to engage in an active remembering of the women's liberation movement. Rarer still is the film's attempt to narrate the story of the social and cultural effects of lesbian feminism on U.S. postwar history. Other mass-media films and TV shows about lesbians in the 1990s and 2000s have tended to suppress the connection between lesbianism and feminism in favor of a *Sex and the City*–like celebration of economically powerful, consumer driven, sexual and social pleasure seekers.[7] Lesbianism in these films and TV shows is usually presented as a lifestyle option among many others that comes with its own aesthetic style, favorite clothing brands, music, coffee houses, and professions (museums and philanthropic organizations seem to be big career options in TV lesbian land) but decidedly not its own history. Or lesbianism is simply one version of the romantic plotline that organizes any "chick film" narrative: girl meets girl after she meets boy or vice versa.[8] Films like *Miss Congeniality*, released in 2000, as well as its sequel, *Miss Congeniality 2: Armed and Fabulous* from 2005, do something more interesting in the sense that, under the guise of being generic screwball comedies, they quite deliberately invoke memories of second-wave feminism in order to resolve the discord caused by the political protests of an earlier era. In these two films, the second wave is "remembered" through a retelling of some of its most significant mass-mediated events and internal conflicts—a remembering that, while demanding recognition of feminism's achievement in carving out more public space and social opportunities for women, also deflects our attention away from the eventfulness of the movement itself.

In this final chapter I want to look at how women's liberation, as a movement and a counterpublic sphere that was also, at the same time, the name given for a diverse proliferation of feminisms during the late 1960s and early 1970s, gets remembered today. I track how memories of women's liberation circulate between the supracultural domain of the mass media and the subcultural domains of academic feminism and queer studies. Specifically, I look for the ghost of the feminist-as-lesbian in films, newspaper articles, and academic essays that either invoke or directly engage in a remembering of the women's liberation movement. My choice of texts may seem idiosyncratic in the sense that they include an HBO movie, a Hollywood studio film, newspaper articles from the UK and the online magazine *Salon.com*, and three theoretical essays by U.S. feminist and queer scholars. Yet I bring them together here because, with the exception of two essays from the 1980s, all of the texts appeared in and around 2000, and all of them, despite the diversity of genres they deploy and audiences they engage, are concerned in some way or another with remembering the women's liberation movement. My intention is to think through some of the complicated ways in which memories of the second wave, and women's liberation more particularly, are not simply transmitted but actively produced through a meeting, or "entangling," of the U.S. national public sphere and the counterpublic sphere of U.S. feminisms.[9] Too often critics look in one place or the other—the mass-mediated cultural imaginary of the U.S. national public sphere or the subcultural imaginary of feminist movements and/or academia—failing as a consequence to track the ways in which the feminist imaginaries of specific groups or movements are bound up in, and not simply in opposition to, the national public sphere. Marginal publics and subcultures are always entwined with dominant ones, and indeed they feed off each other, as Anne Cvetkovich's and Judith Halberstam's recent work on queer and lesbian public cultures and subcultures attests.[10] It is one of the contentions of this chapter that the whiteness of women's liberation is remembered as an inevitable, or naturalized, historical effect precisely because our memories of the movement are produced out of this entanglement.

By attending to the entanglement of feminist, queer, and mass-mediated memories of women's liberation, I want to track the process of condensation through which the multiplicity of women's liberation is transformed into a story that is taken for granted and largely unquestioned in the present. In particular, I am interested in how women's liberation becomes incorporated into a larger narrative about American feminism that works to cover over, or diminish, its eventfulness and unknowability in the present. Whether it is the projection of a multiracial ideal of U.S. female citizenry in a Hollywood film from 2000, or the claiming of the girl figure for late twentieth-century feminist and queer theory in a queer studies essay from the same year, women's liberation is not remembered as an event on its own terms but as an object against which present-day social or theoretical conflicts or concerns are either resolved or interrogated. Conversely, I track the appearance of the feminist-as-lesbian in these rememberings as a figure that disrupts the attempt to stabilize the relationship between past and present, as in the films I examine, or as in the case of the academic essay from 2000, the desire to make women's liberation exist outside the time of its political and theoretical concerns. In this chapter, then, the feminist-as-lesbian figures the contested and unsettled nature of the relationship between the past and the present of women's liberation, and she demands an accountability toward the eventfulness of the movement as something unfinished and beyond the capacity of any one story or account to know or apprehend it in the present. Finally, it is my hope that by following the feminist-as-lesbian as a ghost of women's liberation, new memories of the movement—memories that will enable less limiting and more surprising articulations of our attachments and disattachments to the unsettling eventfulness of that time—will be produced.

POLITICS, PUBLICS, AND MEMORY

In her recent paradigm-altering excavation of the affective life of the American public sphere, Lauren Berlant argues for a theoretical distinction between what she defines as an "intimate public sphere" and a counterpublic one.[11] For Berlant, drawing upon the work of Nancy Fraser and Michael Warner, the concept of the counterpublic presumes a neatness of criteria that "underdescribes the dynamics of indirection and mediation" through which a public manifests itself (8). In Fraser's terms, a counterpublic is defined by its marginal and subordinate position relative to a dominant public sphere, and it can be divided into "strong" and "weak" versions depending on whether the public is a "decision making" one that addresses itself primarily to state institutions or an "opinion making" one that engages largely in cultural production.[12] Relative to its perceived strength or weakness, a counterpublic for Fraser and Warner is always either imminently or actually political in how it articulates its relation to a dominant public sphere.[13] Berlant's critique of Fraser's and Warner's work focuses on their underlying assumption of a direct causal relationship between social antagonisms and the production of counterpublics. For Berlant, too many different things are "over-enmesh[ed]" into one as a consequence of this assumption: a counterpublic is made when a group is definable by its nondominant social position, its historical subordination, its cultural specificity, its alternativeness, and its antagonistic relation to "a dominant paradigm" (7–8). Instead, Berlant proposes a more nuanced understanding of the relationship between social antagonisms and the production of publics. What needs to be taken more into account, in her view, are the mediations and obfuscations of consumer capitalism and the mass-mediated national public sphere, both of which engender myriad and "imprecise" practices of identification and imagined belonging for people that often operate in contradictory relation to complex "environments of living" (9).

Berlant's term for conceptualizing this less obviously antagonistic practice of collective public activity is the *intimate public*, which she defines as a public "that foregrounds affective and emotional attachments located in fantasies of the common, the everyday, and a sense of ordinariness, a space where the social world is rich with anonymity and local recognitions, and where challenging and banal conditions of life take place in proximity to the attentions of power but also squarely in the radar of a recognition that can be provided by other humans" (10). The primary example of an intimate public for Berlant is "women's culture," the "first mass cultural intimate public in the United States," and one that has been closely bound up in the making of the U.S. national public sphere since at least the mid-nineteenth century (viii). The intimate public of women's culture is, according to Berlant, distinguished by its assumption of a common femininity for American women across social divisions and a corresponding presumption of a need not only to communicate that commonality but also to find mutual recognition and satisfaction in it. Because U.S. women's culture traffics in fantasies of the normal and the ordinary, it cultivates investments in conventional forms of femininity that are presented—in narrative and image— as identities of a national as well as gendered belonging for women, even if those conventions can be tracked across borders. National and gender identifications are shaped by processes of social differentiation, such that whiteness and bourgeois-ness are evoked as the often implicit ideals of a national gendered belonging. Women's culture can be pleasurable, according to Berlant, precisely because its promise of normality and belonging offers relief from the difficulties and stresses of living in a world riven by social antagonisms and made alienatingly complex by the technologies of late capitalism. In Berlant's theoretical elaboration, the intimate public sphere of U.S. women's culture is, by definition, more indeterminate than a counterpublic sphere, tends to be generated by commodity culture rather than simply as the result of an exclusion from the dominant public sphere, and is saturated with the genres of affective belonging rather than, as the concept of the counterpublic tends to presume, "political taxonomies" (9). Central to Berlant's distinction between counterpublics and intimate publics, then, is their divergent relations to the political: although it is possible for an intimate public to be "mobilized as counterpublicity," they are usually generated against the political or, in Berlant's terms, as a "*relief from the political*" (10). It is this "juxtapolitical" relation between intimate publics and politics that marks the crucial point of analysis for Berlant, for it is in this densely complex and proximate relation between women's culture and politics that the reasons for why women stay "attached to disaffirming scenarios of necessity and optimism in their personal and political lives" are to be found (2).

Women's liberation, as a protest movement that understood the intimately public domain of hetero-domesticity as one of its primary battlegrounds in the fight to transform perceptions of women's capabilities and possibilities, was a counterpublic sphere that acted on and in the intimate public sphere of women's culture. And in this sense, the movement exemplifies one of Berlant's major claims: that the relationship between the counterpublic sphere of feminist politics and the intimate public sphere of women's culture is more complicated and convoluted than the neatness of the conceptual paradigms might suggest. In becoming a political movement, women's liberation drew upon, and saw its objects in, the intimate public spheres of mass-mediated representations of women, as well as in the everyday experiences of women's ordinary, "private" lives. It was precisely "the affective and emotional attachments located in fantasies of the common, the everyday, and a sense of ordinariness" (10) that were both the source of feminist collectivity and belonging in women's liberation and also the grounds of its political struggle. Women's liberation was, and was not, distinct from women's culture. Rather than "a nosy neighbor" (x), then, as Berlant herself describes the relationship of feminism to the intimate public sphere of women's culture, women's liberation was more like its naughty offspring or "demented child," to echo an accusation directed at the women's liberation movement in 1970.[14]

To think of women's liberation in this way reveals what Christopher Castiglia has called "the false purity of a spatial differentiation" between "sub- and national cultures."[15] Women's liberation was not simply oppositional in its relationship to the dominant paradigms of American cultural and social hegemony, it was also implicated in them—just as the cultural imaginings and social norms of American society were enfolded into the fantasies and practices of resistance that formed women's liberation as a movement and a public. I want to invoke the full range of the meaning of *to implicate* here: *to implicate* means to "intertwine; to wreathe, twist, or knit together"; it also means "to involve (a person) in a charge," and "to involve, or include (a person) in the operation of something; to affect or cause to be affected in the act of something."[16] If we substitute a collectivity for a person in the above definition, then we can think of women's liberation as not only entangled in or intertwined with the national public sphere—and the mass-mediated intimate public sphere of women's culture in particular —but also as *involved* in it. To be involved in something carries the double weight of being both invested in and affected by it. In struggling against the dominant "genres" of femininity in the U.S. national public sphere, women's liberation revealed its interest in those genres and the sense of national belonging they engendered, and in wanting something from the nation the movement was also affected—"charged"—by the genres of femininity through which American women were interpellated as belonging, or not, to the nation.[17]

I want to suggest that this involvement of the subcultural world of women's liberation in the supracultural domain of U.S. women's culture generated the shorthand notations, or figures and objects, around which memories and narrative accounts of the movement have been produced. From the incitement of the burning bra image used to denote the Miss America protest in 1968 to the emergence of the feminist-as-lesbian figure during the tumultuous events of 1970, the most arresting memory images of women's liberation were forged in the mix of the movement's entanglement with, and involvement in, the mass media and intimate public sphere of women's culture. This entanglement also accounts for the close familiarity between the "man-hating, ball-busting, selfish, hairy extremist," identified by Susan J. Douglas as the stereotypical feminist figure of U.S. mass culture, and the "flannel shirt androgyne[,] closeminded, antisex puritan[,] humorless moralist[,] racist and classist ignoramus[,] essentialist utopian" identified by Bonnie Zimmerman as the representative stereotypical figure for lesbian feminism in U.S. academic feminism.[18] They are similar figures because they emerge from the same contested battleground of the women's liberation movement; they are an effect of the collapse of the political into women's culture that marks the distinctiveness of women's liberation as a form of protest in the late 1960s and early 1970s.[19]

The questions I ask in this chapter are: What are these figures and objects of women's liberation doing in the present? How does their circulation between the supracultural domain of U.S. mass culture and the subcultural domains of U.S. academic feminism shape particular memories and accounts of women's liberation in the present? And how do they configure a particular relation to the feminist past that also enacts a forgetting of what was confusing and unrepresentable during the tumultuous years of women's liberation's emergence onto the national scene? In order to pursue these questions I utilize a methodology I call, borrowing from Avery Gordon, looking for the ghosts of women's liberation.[20] Figures like the feminist-as-lesbian, forged as they were in the eventfulness of women's liberation's entangled confrontations with the intimately public and publicly private social worlds of American heteronormativity, transgress the borders between sub- and supracultural publics. This discursive homelessness is, in turn, a sign that the figure is a ghostly rather than simply iconic remainder of the past of women's liberation. She haunts rather than occupies the U.S. feminist present because her signification exceeds our rational, schematic, and orderly accounts of women's liberation—she operates outside the "official" histories and formalized memories of the movement. And as a ghostly remainder of women's liberation's entanglement in, and confrontation with, the sociocultural hegemonies of the U.S. national public sphere, the feminist-as-lesbian is also a kind of clue for what remains unrepresentable or unknowable about the movement's struggle for social presence and political power. Looking for the ghost of the feminist-as-lesbian, then, requires a symptomatic reading of cultural production across the "false purity" of the borders that separate subcultures from mass cultures. It also requires looking for resemblances, repetitions, and echoes between one textual remembering of women's liberation and another. Reading these textual echoes as clues for what remains culturally and politically illegible about the movement in the present allows us to "imagine what was lost that never even existed" about women's liberation—a political and ethical task for feminism and its possible futures.[21]

CONGENIAL MEMORIES

In many ways 2000 is a convenient near present moment for tracking collective memories of women's liberation.[22] In the perception that they mark the end of something, fin-de-siècle eras encourage the creation of collective cultural memories that, in Andreas Huyssen's terms, are "an attempt to secure continuity of time—a relationship between past present and future that orients and situates us in the present."[23] In a related argument, Huyssen also notes that in the late twentieth century the production of collective memory cannot be separated from the commodification and spectacularization of the past: "public media memories," orientated toward national cultures but produced through globalizing technologies, are, in Huyssen's view, the primary form of collective remembering in late twentieth-century nation-states.[24] The commodification and spectacularization of collective cultural memories of women's liberation, in conjunction with the perception that the century's end generated a decisive shift in the historical relation of one era of feminism (or postfeminism) with another, is evident in a number of mass-cultural films that came out in and around 2000. The two that I focus on—If These Walls Could Talk 2 and Miss Congeniality—are films that, unlike many of their contemporaries, engage in direct invocations of women's liberation and attempt, in Dana Heller's words, to "intercept and interact" with less commodified and more localized memories of the movement.[25] In my readings of the films I want to suggest that the discursive homelessness of the feminist-as-lesbian figure, as a ghostly remainder of women's liberation, disrupts their narrative function as mass-cultural texts; that is, the ghost of the feminist-as-lesbian appears in these films not so much as a historical character but as an un-narratable interruption of the imaginary resolution each film projects for the history of U.S. feminism.[26]

The crisis that must be resolved in If These Walls Could Talk 2, as in all progress narratives, takes place in the middle of the story it wants to tell. Set in 1972, the second segment of the film's three-part structure sets out to "remember" the conflicts over lesbianism in the early years of the second-wave women's movement as part of the process—a necessary cathartic moment—for the successful integration of lesbians into American social life. As the segment's opening montage of "found footage" depicting famous feminists and women's liberation marches from the 1970s fades from view, the scene switches to a shot of the house previously occupied, with studied respectability, by the elderly closeted couple of the first segment. As the camera focuses in through the hazy sunshine of a northern California morning, the house looks bedraggled and unkempt. A sheet with a peace sign hangs carelessly over the porch and the garden looks scruffy and neglected. In contrast to the carefully nurtured domesticity of the lesbian couple in the first segment, this house declares its occupants' disinterest in such homely pleasures. And as the four young women burst out of the house in their hippy outfits, offer an irreverent greeting to their "uptight" neighbor, and roar off in a dilapidated station wagon, the viewer is encouraged to witness their youthful unconcern for suburban proprieties as a sign of their disidentification from the norms of domesticated hetero-respectability. In this segment, the familial home as the site and symbol of social reproduction is constantly on the verge of being abandoned—by the young women who now carelessly occupy it and by what they, as characters in the film, are designed to invoke: memories of women's liberation's political challenge to heterosexuality and middle-class respectability.

The association of lesbian feminism with an ultimately self-destructive disregard for the forms of social and intimate life organized around heterosexual relations structures the story the second segment of the film wants to tell. In order for lesbian feminism's rejection of hetero-domesticity to be remembered as a necessary cathartic moment in a progress narrative of lesbian integration, it has to be seen as a temporary, albeit useful, aberration—a moment of misguided excess that nevertheless provided the opportunity for the social rehabilitation of lesbians into American social life.

From the very first scene, this remembering of lesbian feminism as a temporary aberration is enacted through a clash, not exactly of "reproductive systems," as Heller's reading of the film would have it, but between politics and romantic love. In this remembering of lesbian feminism, the home becomes the space in which love and politics are shown to be not simply incompatible but dangerously antagonistic. Politics has to happen elsewhere and in another time, as demonstrated by the fact that the only scenes of political action in the entire film are those found in the documentary footage at the beginning of each segment. As an effect of this displacement of the political, the home becomes the place of impossibility for lesbian feminism as shown by the breakdown of relationships in the house once Linda, the household's de facto leader, meets and falls in love with the not really so tough, young butch Amy in a local dyke bar. By making politics anterior to the domestic spaces of American social life, and to the history of feminism it wants to tell, the film "remembers" lesbian feminism as an idea and a constituency that was out of time and out of place.

In place of remembering lesbian feminism as a politics and women's liberation as an event, the film offers a more familiar compensatory narrative: girl meets "boy" and falls in love. This substitution of a form (the love story) for imagistic memories of the movement's eventfulness literally evacuates women's liberation from the scenes of its own history—a process enacted through the details, as well as the sequence, of the love story the segment tells. For instance, when Linda meets Amy at the local dyke bar it is as a consequence of a lack of social space for her lesbian feminist group. Rejected by the feminist collective on campus because of their public and political lesbianism, the four young housemates decamp from the slovenly comfort of their house and go looking for a place to be gay. The decision to visit the bar is also made, then, out of a feeling that staying in their house would not allow them to be gay either—at least not in a way that would be publicly recognized as a practice of living differently from the norm of hetero-domestic familial life. The privatized space of the house, like the radical feminist meeting on campus, cannot offer the lesbian feminists a space to be themselves, which is to say, gay *and* political. Conversely, as a space of friendship rather than coupledom, the house cannot offer the four housemates the prospect of love. They occupy the house like the students they are: as a temporary place of experimentation and pseudo-rebellion from the normative scripts of bourgeois life that they know, as privileged, middle-class women, they will eventually follow. The house is a place of relative freedom from the demands of capitalism and family life but also from dissatisfaction and alienation precisely because, like student houses in general, it cannot offer the young women a place to "be in love and have [their] freedom too," as Linda asserts is her desire at the beginning of the film. Here, student life becomes the social convention through which an affective memory of women's liberation is invoked as a temporary, occasionally fun, but ultimately dissatisfying rebellion against the ultimately far more desirable inevitability of bourgeois citizenship and romantic love. Rather than a politics that comes from the outside or that threatens from within, women's liberation is invoked as integral to the larger narrative sequence of women's increasing participation in the public and political life of America and, therefore, as something to be remembered fondly but indulgently as a wayward adolescent escapade in the continuing life project of American women becoming mature citizens.

If the house and the feminist meeting cannot offer the lesbian feminist friends a space to be gay and political, neither can the bar. When Linda meets Amy at the dyke bar, the dissatisfactions of her home life and political life give way to the acutely felt satisfactions of sexual desire and the prospect of falling in love. But if the bar offers the possibility of finding love, the story of "falling in love" cannot take place in the glare of its butch-femme spectacle. And so, rather than a space that would solve the problem of being both gay and political, the bar becomes the site of yet another displacement that enacts the narrative the film wants to tell. In this scene, the dyke bar operates less as an incitement to remember lesbian feminism's class and ideologically based rejection and judgment of butch-femme as role-playing mimicry and more as the mise-en-scène for women's liberation's (adolescent) rejection of romantic coupledom in general. We know this because the scene carefully sets out Linda's *and* Amy's difference from the dyke bar culture that surrounds them and because the terms of their romance are articulated not in the language of butch-femme but in the language of women's liberation—that is, in the language of self-authenticity and autonomy.

While Linda's difference from the scene is obvious—her hippie-ish attire, youthful good looks, and manifest curiosity all contributing to her adventurer and outsider status—Amy's difference is more subtly produced. Although she "fits in" with her smart, butch look of slicked back hair, slacks, shirt and tie, her aloneness coupled with the soft golden glow through which both she and Linda are shot make her stand out from the crowd of butch-femme couples in the bar. These couples, in their ill-fitting clothes, imperfect bodies, and worn faces, project the working-class world of mid-century butch-femme subculture and become, like the gloomy, ratty looking bar itself, the necessary contrast to not only the blandly unmarked faces of the young lesbian feminists sitting uncomfortably and disdainfully in their midst but also to the newness of the love affair between Amy and Linda. That Amy, like Linda, is untouched by the hard life reflected by the bar and its inhabitants is made more apparent when she admits to Linda that she doesn't really smoke, she just carries cigarettes around to "look tough." Looking tough, as opposed to actually being tough, creates the necessary distance between Amy as a desirable figure—for Linda and for all nice young (lesbian and not) women—and the butch dykes in the bar. Indeed, Amy's desirability as not really butch is further confirmed by Linda's later assertion that Amy is "not like that," meaning the butch-femme couples in the bar, and that her attractiveness is not about her butchness but about her not "need[ing] other people to define who she is." Here, the liberal bourgeois ideology of authentic subjectivity as something untouched or unmarked by social categories of distinction and subjugation becomes the stated ideal for all love affairs that the film projects over and against both the protopolitical subcultures of butch-femme and the politicization of love by women's liberation. And it is the distance between Amy and the butch-femme bar culture, which is nevertheless needed to signify her commitment to romantic coupledom, that allows the film to transform the role-playing of butch-femme culture into a re-presentation of the pleasure of conventional forms of romantic love in general.[27]

The love that Linda pursues becomes, in contrast to the political perspectives of both the university feminist collective and her lesbian feminist housemates, the route to a freedom expressed in the film as the ability to be "who you really are." Love, so the story goes, will overcome all: the rejection of the lesbian feminists by the feminist collective, the overt hostility of Linda's housemates to her new lover, and, finally, the need for a feminist movement at all. In organizing its memory of women's liberation through the familiar narrative of the love plot, the film absorbs the social and cultural anxieties provoked by women's liberation's challenge to the ideology of romantic love by transforming its contradictory and conflicted politicization of sexuality into a fight over object choice. The very real antipathy within women's liberation (and lesbian feminism) toward butch-femme sexuality is, as a consequence, re-remembered as a rejection of domesticated love by the movement, and butch-femme, in turn, gets rehabilitated into the soft focus—cream and beige—bourgeois future that is Kal and Fran. The resolution offered by the segment taking place in 1972, and *If These Walls Could Talk 2* as a whole, then, is for lesbians to find a love that lets them be true to themselves. The moral of this resolution is that for lesbians to find a home in American history and society they have to abandon politics—a solution to their social marginality imagined as reproductive domestic bliss in the final segment.

Conversely, memories of the political threat of lesbian feminism are displaced onto the figure of the angry black woman—in this case, Linda's housemate, Karen—a move that not only empties women's liberation of its political challenges to hetero-domesticity but also elides the historical presence of other kinds of feminism in the late 1960s and early 1970s, including black feminism. As the most articulate and vehement member of the lesbian-feminist household, Karen displays an overt hostility to Amy. Her afro, like her withering put downs, implicitly invoke memories of the black nationalist movement as the dangerous comparative outside to women's liberation's call for social transformation. And as an echo of the young Angela Davis's iconic radicalism, Karen also becomes a shorthand notation for the complex relations between black radicalism and radical feminism—relations that remain virtual and unexplored as memory in the film. As a figuring of black radicalism, Karen secures the boundaries between a more palatable form of lesbian feminism—the kind that can be accommodated within the conventions of romantic love and the national imaginary—and the other kind: the kind that, as Karen states at the beginning of the segment, can "wait till after the revolution" to find love.

The segment from 1972 ends with Linda and Amy passionately making out on the stoop of Amy's modest little house before going inside to have sex. Although the ending is, in one sense, another enactment of the overall narrative thrust of the film—that women's happiness and sense of freedom will come from their attachment to, and investment in, romantic couple-dom—it is also an ending that tends to suggest the fragility of the suturing of butch-femme and lesbian feminism in the film. In contrast to the coup-lings in the first and third segments of the film, the relationship between Amy and Linda seems improbable and transitory—a feeling engendered by the lack of a resolution in the segment between Linda's lesbian-feminist household and Amy's butchness. This failure to resolve the tensions be-tween lesbian feminism and butch-femme (and those between women's liberation and black, Chicana, and other feminisms of the era) are a result of the film's refusal to remember the politics of women's liberation as any-thing other than the vague call for "equal rights between men and women." Indeed, the lesbian feminists seem strangely out of place precisely because their reasons for being feminist—other than that they are lesbians—are never expressed. Instead, the segment attempts to enfold the pastness of women's liberation (and lesbian feminism) into the present of women's culture's market-driven, commodity-saturated, romantic coupledom. As a result, a form of lesbianism—the beige and cream kind—is folded into the national scripts of heteronormativity rather than viewed as a threatening deviation. But the segment's lack of a believable ending can also be read, symptomatically, as an effect of the film's failure to contain its memories of women's liberation within the conventions of the love plot. By having Amy and Linda go inside to have sex rather than, say, move in together (the missing U-Haul moment), the ending also suggests that, contrary to the film's progress narrative, the women's liberation movement was not simply or in retrospect about the historical continuity and reproduction of femi-nism. Rather, in its excessiveness, what at the time was called its fanaticism, its silliness, and its ridiculousness, the movement, in conjunction if not often in alliance with other feminist movements of the era, opened up mul-tiple and divergent lines of confrontation with the institutions and ide-ologies of a national heteronormativity. This multiplicity of eventfulness that generated women's liberation as a counterpublic and a movement also resists historical narration. There is no place and no single modality of time for women's liberation: it is, despite attempts to prove otherwise, a strangely homeless and storyless phenomenon, precisely because its challenge to the intimate public sphere of national heteronormativity remains affectively alienating to a mass-cultural public sphere that organizes genres of national belonging through the intimate and the domestic.

Miss Congeniality, as with *If These Walls Could Talk 2*, offers a narrative reworking of the pastness of women's liberation that incorporates memories of its revolt into a present no longer in need of a collective feminist movement. And, like *If These Walls Could Talk 2*, *Miss Congeniality* orchestrates its remembering of women's liberation through the mass-cultural clichés of American heteronormativity.[28] But whereas *If These Walls Could Talk 2* structured its story of feminist and lesbian progress as the successful integration of some (white and middle-class) lesbians into the national imaginary through the convention of romantic coupledom, *Miss Congeniality* organizes its retelling of the Miss America protest of 1968 through the genre of action comedy. The film tells the story of a lonely tomboy— Sandra Bullock's overly eager and reckless FBI Agent Hart—who, after going undercover at the Miss America Pageant not only saves the newly crowned Miss America from being blown up but also discovers the "liberating" pleasures of femininity. Although the film makes no direct references to the Miss America protest by women's liberation in Atlantic City in 1968, it is full of references to the event: Bullock's undercover agent enters the competition as Miss New Jersey, while Candice Bergen's vainglorious pageant director dismisses all critics of the pageant as "feminists [and] intellectuals, you know, ugly women" and attempts to implicate the Women's Liberation Front in her plot to blow up the pageant (as a protest at being fired). In the film's retelling of the Miss America protest, women's liberation's angry if humorous mocking of the pageant as a meat market and the contestants as sheep is transformed into a humorous but ultimately affectionate mocking of national femininity as cliché.[29] The use of humor allows an expansivity of affective resonance in the film—its play with the clichés of femininity projecting an ambivalence toward femininity and feminism that provides the possibility of their suturing at the end of the film through the figure of the now happily feminized, but still tough, Agent Hart.[30] As I'll discuss in more detail below, lesbianism literally appears as an interruption in the proceedings in a scene that restages the New York Radical Women's dramatic disruption of the pageant in 1968, when, during the televised finale, they unfurled a banner with women's liberation on it and started yelling.[31] But this time, the interruption takes place on the stage rather than in the audience, and the yell is more a declaration of achievement than revolt: that some thirty years after the women's liberation movement's protest lesbians too can "make it to the top ten" of America's most beautiful women.

That feminism is always already enfolded into the national imaginary in *Miss Congeniality* is signaled from the very beginning of the film, when, as the credits roll, we witness the trials and tribulations of a tough little girl whose successful attempt to save a boy from the playground bully only sees her rejected for being "a girl." As the little girl with the dweeby black glasses turns into Sandra Bullock wearing the same glasses while operating as an undercover agent in an FBI sting, the viewer is invited to make the retrospective link between a girl who can do the work of saving the nation and the woman who is doing it. The representational iconography of national security is everywhere in the opening scenes of the movie, from the Russian gangsters at the center of the sting to "the citizen" as the psychotic baddie Bullock's FBI team is also trying to catch. The film's playful if not particularly imaginative mimicry of the "good cop who saves the nation from harm" genre of action movies includes Bullock's character driving with hair-raising, high-speed dexterity through the streets of Manhattan only to arrive at a Starbucks, push to the front of the line wielding her badge, and make a large order for her FBI team waiting back at the office for their double-vanilla lattes. The joke—that women can play the tough hero but are often given the menial jobs instead—signals one of the primary messages of the film: that American women, given the opportunity fought for by feminists, can save the nation too.

Saving the nation includes, of course, saving women. And in a neat, if politically insidious reversal of the hero plot, Sandra Bullock's Agent Hart can only become the hero who saves Miss America after her own transformation into a hyper-feminine woman. The makeover scene, in which Agent Hart is taken into an aircraft hangar and worked on by multiple teams of cosmetic experts in order to make her presentable for her undercover role as Miss New Jersey, enacts the film's ambivalent attitude toward femininity. On the one hand, the ludicrousness of the scene—its "major operation" dramatization of the extensive procedures Agent Hart undergoes, from hair, skin, and nail cleaning to bikini waxing, teeth polishing, and starvation—suggests just how much work, and pain, women must go through to achieve an idealized form of femininity. On the other hand, the "success" of the makeover—at the end of the scene we witness the new "drop-dead gorgeous" Agent Hart emerge, surrounded by her team of experts, while the Commitments cover of "Mustang Sally" plays over the starstruck faces of her male FBI colleagues—revels in the effects a successful performance of femininity can have. And indeed, it is only after he has witnessed Agent Hart's successful transformation into a standardized beautiful woman that Benjamin Bratt's hunky FBI team leader takes Hart seriously—as an agent and as a potential love interest.

This ambivalence toward femininity becomes the emotional mechanism through which the film enacts its own "makeover" remembering of the Miss America protest. Rather than re-presenting women's liberation's objections to the pageant as a political protest against its classist and racist production of an idealized national femininity, the film privatizes the protest as a general internal struggle all women face in their desire or quest to become fully fledged citizens. That is, women's liberation's "tomboy" reluctance to participate in the forms and conventions of a national femininity is converted in the film into Agent Hart's personal struggle to realize the power of an American-made femininity that will not only attract men but offer her a way to participate as an "agent" of the nation. The rest of the film plays out this scenario of femininity as national agency: Agent Hart's transformation into Miss New Jersey not only allows her to discover the real baddie—Cathy Morningside, the pageant director, whose overzealous attachment to an idealized femininity is revealed as a selfish desire to be forever "queen" of America—but to form a communal friendship with "the girls" she is supposedly competing with but who she is in fact protecting. When Hart takes the pageant finalists out to a bar in order to determine whether the seemingly innocent Miss New Hampshire is in fact "the citizen," the scene quickly transforms into a generic girl-bonding moment with personal stories and the pleasures of an assumed commonality of experience overtaking the investigative pretext of the gathering. In this scene, the collectivity of feminist protest during the Miss America Pageant in 1968 is transformed in the present into an enactment of the intimately public pleasures of feminine bonding. Here, then, the retelling of the Miss America protest as a story about women finding common cause through their struggles with, yet attachments to, femininity substitutes the seductions of amnesia for memory: *Miss Congeniality* offers its viewers an invitation to forget the messy and potentially alienating difficulties of political protest—a forgetting that paradoxically depends on the signaling of what it is women are supposed to forget—in favor of a reinvestment in an idealized and privatized genre of femininity, one that promises women mutual recognition and understanding, desirable men who desire them, and a feeling of being wanted by the nation.

By the end of the film, the makeover of the Miss America protest into a feel-good story about female bonding is complete. With the obligatory expression of authentic feeling, Agent Hart renounces her previous disdain for the pageant and its contestants, declaring that she has come to realize that beauty queens are just "smart, terrific people trying to make a difference in the world." Instead of women's liberation's active challenging of the pageant as an institutional agent in the objectification and subjugation of women (which in turn depends upon the divisive disciplinary effects of gender normalization), Agent Hart "saves" it—from the excesses of an overly selfish and exclusively white investment in femininity, that is, Cathy Morningside, and from the tendency, expressed most vehemently by feminists, to take the pageant too seriously. In the happy ending offered by the film, American women can have their feminist feelings and be feminine too, so long as the all too serious work of maintaining and investing in an ideal femininity is covered over by a simultaneous refusal to investigate— that is, politicize—the larger social, economic, and cultural forces that traffic in, and benefit from, their investments.

Although the pageant finalists include black, white, Latina, and Asian American contestants, this presentation of diversity in the film serves less as a celebration of a contemporary multicultural inclusiveness and more as a signaling of women's culture's ability to absorb difference into a homogenizing norm of common femininity. In order to maintain the necessary vagueness of this pleasurable feeling of sameness in difference, the film displaces and condenses memories of the histories of racial and class exclusions in the production of an idealized femininity onto the figure of Miss Texas, the highly competitive white girl, "bitch" who everyone loves to hate. But it is the irruption of the lesbian's coming-out moment near the end of the movie that provides an opening in the film to mock its liberal fantasies of a present-tense celebration of an all-inclusive multicultural American femininity. When Miss New York, one of the three women of color finalists, rushes from the back of the stage to shout out to a startled audience and her adoring white girlfriend, "I just want all those lesbians out there to know, if I can make it to the top ten, so can you! Viva Brooklyn! Tina, I love you baby!" the women's liberation protest is echoed in form, if not in content. While in its content the shout can be interpreted as a celebration of a present-day inclusion of all women, including black and

Latina women and lesbians, into the privileged domains of an idealized femininity, the form of its irruptive force works against any sense of inclusion or incorporation. Instead, the shout signals a return of the repressed: the absent presence of a diverse and heterogeneous feminist revolt against classist and racist notions of normative femininity, publicly derided as lesbian and that, in the Miss America protest of 1968 and in countless other political protests, refused and contested the appeal of conventional forms of femininity.

The congenial memories of women's liberation produced by *If These Walls Could Talk 2* and *Miss Congeniality* work to enfold a beige and cream form of lesbian feminism into collective fantasies of a feminism that participates in, rather than challenges, the reproduction of an idealized national femininity. They also work to ensure that the pastness of women's liberation remains something distant and distinct from a "postfeminist" present that is presumed to offer all women greater access to the cultural, social, and economic capitals that will inevitably lead to their equality with men. As a consequence of these productive amnesias, women's liberation's revolt against middle-class respectability—although often ambivalent in its continuing attachments to the privileges of white femininity—is forgotten, along with the movement's politicizations of the intimate domains of hetero-domesticity and romantic coupledom. While it is bad enough that this forgetting of women's liberation deprives us in the present of a memory of the political challenges and eventfulness of the movement, it also does something even more perfidious in that we are left, instead, with a "memory" of women's liberation that tends to solidify its whiteness and middle-classness into a static, ahistorical unchangeability. That is, in making women's liberation both more palatable for the "intimate public sphere" of present-day, mass-mediated women's culture and also more distant from the present, these films enact a further naturalization of second-wave feminism as a white, middle-class women's cause that elides not only the heterogeneity of the women's liberation movement and its haphazard and ambivalent estrangements from white femininity but also the potentiality of its emergent moment—a moment that belonged neither to white women nor to women's liberation but to a multiplicity of women and feminisms. Yet the figure of the feminist-as-lesbian, in her narrative homelessness, disrupts the process of memory as reification in these films, reminding us, if we care to look, that there was something much less coherent, and palatable, about women's liberation and its challenges to the institutions and ideologies of a national heteronormativity.

MEMORIES ARE SUCH A DRAG

Another example of an active remembering of women's liberation from around 2000 can be found in "Packing History, Count(er)ing Generations," by the queer studies scholar Elizabeth Freeman.[32] Unlike the mass-cultural films discussed above, Freeman's audience is an academic one, and her primary objective is not to resolve the contradictions and tensions of the women's liberation era but to open up the problematic of time in order to disrupt the seemingly settled historical and theoretical relationships between radical feminism and the contemporary queer moment. In her desire to "drag" the queer present back toward "disavowed histories" of feminism, Freeman's project in "Packing History" was an influential precursor to the preoccupations of *Feeling Women's Liberation*, as I hope the following discussion will make clear. However, in my attempt to look for the ghostly figure of the feminist-as-lesbian across the supracultural and subcultural domains of the U.S. national public sphere and U.S. feminism respectively, I want to read Freeman's essay against the grain of its larger argument (with which I am largely in agreement). Instead, I read Freeman's exploration of her concept of "temporal drag" in relation to the history of radical feminism in order to track the way in which, despite her attempt to open up the pastness of radical feminism to a potentially disorientating "temporal transitivity," Freeman's essay ends up invoking the time of radical feminism largely through absence—an absence paradoxically signaled by the unexamined figure of the feminist-as-lesbian.

Freeman begins her essay with a story about an offended student who objected to Freeman's humorous characterization of lesbians as "potluck givers." Although Freeman, as a young graduate student teaching her first lesbian and gay studies class had, she states, made the joke against herself and her inability to inhabit "prevailing lesbian identity-forms," the student had felt that the joke was made against her obvious attachment to the sartorial style of lesbians who give potluck dinners. Freeman calls this a story about "anachronism with 'lesbian' as the sign of times gone by" (727). The student's identification as a lesbian (who gives potluck dinners) rather than as a riot grrrl or queer national, Freeman argues, disrupts "any easy assumptions about generations and register[s] the failure of the generational model to capture political differences" (727). The student's explicit identification as a lesbian meant that she exhibited, according to Freeman, a "crossing of time" that was evidence less "of postmodern pastiche" than a "stubborn identification with a set of social coordinates that exceeded her own historical moment" (728). That is, for Freeman, the student's identification revealed that political cultures and eras do not supplant each other in a neat linear way but coexist or infuse each other, complicating any simplistic commitment to political "progress" or evolvement.

Freeman's term for this time crossing is "temporal drag"—with all of "the associations that the word drag has with retrogression, delay, and the pull of the past upon the present" (728). The term is useful for Freeman because it allows her to complicate the "idea of horizontal political generations succeeding one another" (729), and, more specifically, it allows her to problematize the relationship between queer theory and politics and feminist history as articulated by a number of queer theorists: temporal drag, "as opposed to the queenlier kind celebrated in queer cultural studies, suggests the gravitational pull that 'lesbian' sometimes seems to exert upon 'queer.' In many discussions of the relationship between the two, it often seems as if the lesbian feminist is cast as the big drag, drawing politics inexorably back to essentialized bodies, normative visions of women's sexuality, and single-issue identity politics" (728). Here, Freeman is describing a representation of the relationship between *queer* and *lesbian* that has been used as an argument for the theoretical and political validity of queer theory (as opposed, if only implicitly, to women's studies) and, in conjunction, as an account of recent feminist history (the transition from "second wave" to "third wave" or the "postfeminist" era). The lesbian feminist, she notes, is often "cast as the big drag," the antiquated monster, of an essentialist identity politics. Queer in contrast, and drawing upon the work of Judith Butler, is understood as performative and is concerned with the doing of the new, the deviant, and the different. In this conception of the relationship between queer and feminist, the lesbian stands as a representational figure of past feminist errors and "wrong directions" within a broadly conceived contemporary queer present.

Yet, for Freeman, the conceptualization of queer, as narrowly defined by gender transitivity and the performance of the new as copy, brings with it the problematic tendency to actively forget or negate what has happened in the past. As a way of counteracting this propensity in queer theory,

Freeman argues that the notion of temporal drag offers us a way of articulating a "temporal transitivity" that doesn't leave behind "anachronisms" like feminism, in that it allows us to explore both the "pastness of the past" and "put pressure on the present," as her rich reading of Elizabeth Subrin's film about Shulamith Firestone, *Shulie*, reveals, while at the same time, it conjoins queer and feminist theoretical concerns with the performative and historicity respectively (728). Temporal drag also invokes, as Freeman makes clear, the "camp effect" of drag as the performance of a melancholic "resuscitation" of a beloved, lost object (732). For Freeman, this camp effect has to be understood within the terms of a "narrative, historicist model of 'allegorization'" in which the lost object is longingly brought to life through a transformative—allegorical—reanimation that is collective and world making rather than subject orientated (732). Indeed, Freeman reads Subrin's film *Shulie*, released in 1997 and a shot-by-shot remake of a documentary of the same name from 1967, not as a biographical resurrection of the young, not yet identified with radical feminism Shulamith Firestone, but as camp reanimation of a preradical feminist moment—one figured by the character Shulie. As the beloved lost object, Firestone isn't resuscitated as she was (an impossibility) but transformed into Shulie, a character that literally, but imperfectly (Kim Soss, the actress playing Shulie, wears an obvious wig and ill-fitting glasses and the ephemera of 1990s living is present on film, including the omnipresent Starbucks coffee cup), reenacts the Firestone of the earlier documentary. The pre–women's movement, pre-representative figure of radical feminism, Shulamith Firestone, is reanimated in the queer present disrupting the temporal order through which we read queer as "post"-radical feminism. The temporal disorientation goes a step further in that what has passed, radical feminism, is now in the film's reenactment of a prehistory of the women's liberation movement, what hasn't even begun. For Freeman, therefore, Subrin's reanimation of Firestone not only makes apparent the "pastness of the past," it also produces—reanimates—the "social coordinates" of Firestone's prefeminist moment (the contingencies of her present time as captured in the documentary from 1967) in such a way as to make those coordinates "available" to us "in a different way": what is now queer is the prehistory of radical feminism (735).

I like the concept of temporal drag precisely because it suggests a disorientating relation to the past and makes apparent the "out-of-jointness" of the feminist present. The sense of the past as a burden, as something that bothers us in the present and pulls us backward, also suggests the drag of "reading along the grain" of the archive of women's liberation with its discomforting strangeness or, conversely, its all too familiar limitations. But at the same time, Freeman's notion of temporal drag as a camp reanimation of past events or figures relies too much on a relationship to the past that is enacted through love or, more precisely, longing. In Freeman's formulation of a "queer desire for history," the past is brought to life through "conjecture, fantasy, overreading, revision, and a seemingly myopic focus on ephemera," as she writes elsewhere of the queer fascination with history.[33] This "touching" between one historical era and another that marks so much of the recent work on queer historiography is also apparent in *Shulie*, as Freeman makes clear in noting that Subrin's identification with the young Firestone as a "very smart, middle-class, Jewish female artist" is a motivating factor in her desire to remake the documentary from 1967 (731). In contrast, to have a haunted relationship with the past is precisely to engage with what has been resisted, feared, or ignored about the past that we want to claim as feminist or queer in the present. While the resuscitation of lost objects from the collective feminist or queer past may produce a different way of thinking and relating to that past, it would not, it seems to me, produce the opening necessary for an accountability toward what was difficult and less desirable about that past. As Freeman rightly asserts, we need to trouble the neat linearity of the idea that one "horizontal" generation hands over, intact and complete, its feminist legacy to another, but we also need to confront the complicated entanglements of a feminist and/or queer past in the social and cultural regimes of normalization from which they emerged.

We see the presence of a ghost, revealingly, in Freeman's essay. While she begins with an account of how the figure of the lesbian often acts as a drag on contemporary queer theory and politics, as the figure representative of the "bad" old days of essentialist identity politics—the bad old days of women's liberation and lesbian feminism—by the end of her essay the lesbian has disappeared altogether. As an "angelface" of radical feminist history, neither the character Shulie, in the film *Shulie*, nor the real historical subject Shulamith Firestone performs, I would argue, as a sign of the "not yet" lesbian feminist (732). Rather, as Freeman points out, the film performs a temporal drag that opens up the "prehistory" of radical feminism to the now of "postfeminism." The moment of "political possibility" for Freeman lies precisely in the time before the battle lines between lib-

eral, radical, and lesbian feminism were drawn and political identities calcified. It is in this pre–women's movement moment, which Freeman reads
through the figure of "the girl" as the movement's childhood time of vulnerability, experimentation, unknowingness, and contingency, that the potentiality of the disruptive and "messy" energy of radical feminism is to be
found. Missing from this look back at the feminist past is the event of
women's liberation itself: the moment when radical feminism exploded
into public view and when lesbian feminism and radical feminism emerged
as (at least) two distinct and sometimes mutually hostile forms of "second-
wave" feminism. Here, the lesbian feminist acts not so much as a drag on
Freeman's questioning of the temporal ordering of feminist history but as a
haunting absence. As a founding member of the Redstockings and the New
York Radical Feminists, both radical feminist groups, Firestone was never
identified with lesbian feminism nor, to my knowledge, did she ever come
out as a lesbian during her time in the women's liberation movement.[34]
The absence of this part of Firestone's history allows Freeman to elide the
distinction between lesbian feminism and radical feminism in her reading
of *Shulie*. The effect of this elision, ironically, is the absence of any reckoning with the lesbian as a figure of women's liberation, the very figure Freeman invoked at the beginning of her essay. Rather, the figure of the lesbian
feminist is present yet elsewhere in Freeman's exploration of the recent
feminist past: too late for 1967, prehistory, and too early for 1997, posthis-
tory, she becomes the necessary signifier for a feminist moment that is
absented from Freeman's search for the political possibilities of a relationship between queer performativity and feminist history.

The look backward that enacts queer as the untimely and the transgressive depends on the production of an alternative stabilized temporality—be
that history or heterosexuality—that can often work to cover over, or at
least leave unexplored, the involvements of the queer and the deviant in the
hegemonic and the dominant. As Jasbir Puar, among others, has argued,
there is nothing consistently and inherently subversive about queer theory
or politics, and in fact, in its focus on the transgressive and the untimely,
American queer studies has tended to narrate "its own sexual exceptionalism" as simultaneously distinct from and superior to other forms of sexual
expression or ways of being—a practice that secures a certain privilege of
unknowing for queer theory in a way that mimics rather than confronts the
privileges of unknowing in heteronormative national cultures.[35] In positing
"the girl" figure of queer and feminist public cultures of the 1990s as a

vehicle for accessing the untimeliness of Subrin's look back at radical feminism, Freeman narrates her own version of queer as sexual exceptionalism. In deploying the metaphor of childhood as an expression of an anti- or preidentitarian moment of unruly experimentation and unformed-ness for feminism, Freeman implicitly relies on an assumption that the moment of women's liberation was a "grown-up" time of settled identities and formalized sexualities. As the symptomatic sign of this assumption, the lesbian-as-feminist figures a continuation of a memory of radical feminism as identitarian and essentialist. As a consequence Freeman's temporal drag, while opening up the pastness of the pre–women's movement moment to the queer present, enacts a further stabilization of *radical feminism* and *lesbian feminism* (read: white, middle class, lesbian) as static terms against which *queer* can move. In effect, then, and in the name of temporal transitivity, the time of women's liberation becomes an empty homogeneous time in Freeman's essay in order to allow a queer look backward that need not confront the movement's messy, implicated attempts to refuse the privileges and comforts of white femininity. Yet I would suggest that it is the movement's inadequate and ambivalent revolt against the norms of national heteronormativity that continue to shape and infuse contemporary queer interrogations of sex and sexuality. The question for the present is: How might this refusal of a queer look back at women's liberation enable the continuation of white, middle-classness—undercover as it were—as a default position of privilege within queer theory?

THE RETURN OF KATE MILLETT

If the figure of the feminist-as-lesbian remains an unexplored but necessary sign in Freeman's temporal drag on radical feminist history, we can read a flurry of articles about Kate Millett in the mainstream and online press in the late 1990s as evidence of the figure's "return" as a ghost of that history. The articles appeared in 1998 and 1999, on both sides of the Atlantic, and were concerned with the forgotten state of the women's liberation movement and of Kate Millett in particular. The articles were inspired by a long and angry essay by Millett that appeared in the summer of 1998 for the feminist magazine *On the Issues*, in which, using the example of her own experiences after the demise of the women's liberation movement, Millett draws attention to the economic and emotional plight of former second-wave activists.[36]

Millett frames her discussion in terms of the problems facing aging feminist women who live alone or have lived unconventional lives and, as a result, are financially and socially vulnerable. Describing her futile attempts to secure a teaching position in a women's studies department—the only possibility being an adjunct position that would pay her per the course—Millett wonders, "what is wrong with me. Am I 'too far out' or too old? Is it age? I'm 63. Or am I 'old hat' in the view of the 'new feminist scholarship'?" Her future, she tells us, holds only "bag-lady horrors." Her books are all out of print, and anything she writes now "has no prospect of seeing print"—her only source of income coming from her ability to work her Christmas tree farm in upstate New York.[37] Yet her own difficulties, she tells us, pale in comparison to those of other women from the beginnings of the women's liberation movement:

> Recently a book inquired Who Stole Feminism? I sure didn't. Nor did Ti-Grace Atkinson. Nor Jill Johnston. We're all out of print. We haven't helped each other much, haven't been able to build solidly enough to have created community or safety. Some women in this generation disappeared to struggle alone in makeshift oblivion. Or vanished into asylums and have yet to return to tell the tale, as has Shula Firestone. There were despairs that could only end in death: Maria del Drago chose suicide. So did Ellen Frankfurt. And Elizabeth Fischer, founder of *Aphra*, the first feminist literary journal.[38]

Millett's portrait is of a "generation" of women who, having risked the promised, if not always actual, safety of conventional life for a feminism they believed would transform society, have been left to "struggle alone in makeshift oblivion"; their dreams of a new society now lost, while a younger generation of feminists occupy tenured positions in women's studies departments and further their careers by rewriting the feminist past for their own professional benefit.[39]

Millett's account of her generation's plight is an interested story, one that exaggerates and simplifies.[40] The six people she mentions besides herself do not make up a generation, nor can their experiences stand as exemplary for all the women who were active in the second wave in all its different array of feminist movements, groups, and political alignments. Nor can the conversation Millett's article engendered in the press stand as an accurate, or adequate, commentary on the state of feminism in the late twentieth and early twenty-first centuries in the United States and Britain.

And yet the media's reading of Millett's appearance in *On the Issues* as a sudden, surprising resurfacing into the public realm—as a ghost of the feminist past suddenly returning to haunt her old stomping ground—does, I think, tell us something of the way in which the eventfulness of the second-wave era has been remembered *and* forgotten since the various feminist movements of that time first exploded into public view more than forty years ago. What becomes clear as one reads the press articles on Millett's "return" is that a direct confrontation with the feminist actions and theories of the second-wave era is avoided. If Millett (re)appears in the press as a ghost from the feminist past, then it is precisely because her return signifies that which cannot be remembered but still haunts contemporary conceptions in the United States and Britain of who and what women's liberation was.

We see the haunting aspect of Millett's resurfacing, and the refusal to confront what her haunting evokes, most clearly in Maureen Freely's article "What Kate Did Next," published for the *Observer* newspaper in England (Millett's *On the Issues* article had appeared in abbreviated form in the *Guardian*, the *Observer*'s sister paper under the title "The Feminist Time Forgot").[41] Although the question Freely asks her readers—"why have these early activists become so desperately unfashionable, so tainted, that even women's studies programmes don't want to preserve them, if only as museum pieces?"—seems to invite comment on the kind of feminism the early activists practiced and articulated, the women she interviews all "insist" that the fate of Millett and her cohort has little to do with their feminism (2). For Anita Bennett, a founder of Female Liberation of Berkeley and one of the organizers of the Women's Strike for Equality in the summer of 1970, the problems many of the early activists experienced were rooted in "the larger context" of the political atmosphere of the 1960s. Many of the women in the women's liberation movement, she tells Freely, were also members of the antiwar and civil rights movements, and as a result, they were susceptible to red-baiting and FBI harassment that sometimes led to feminist activists losing their jobs, apartments, or even both. As a consequence of their vulnerability to state and police harassment, in conjunction with the emotional stress of activism generally, it is not surprising, Bennett notes, that some second-wave era feminists might succumb to feelings of isolation, depression, and suicide. Like activists in other protest movements of the 1960s, Millett and company's forgotten state, Bennett argues, is largely due to the widespread government crackdown on "radicals" in the 1970s (2). For Cora Kaplan, an American academic and feminist activist working and living in England, the problem of feminism's forgotten forebears is not as "dire" as Kate Millett would have us believe. Many activists from the early days of the second wave, Kaplan tells Freely, occupy influential academic posts (she cites Charlotte Bunch's chairing of Rutgers' Institute for Women's Studies as an example) and many, like herself, have remained actively engaged in feminism as it has changed over the years. Moreover, Kaplan suggests, it isn't so much the feminism of the early activists that young women object to today but the idea of the 1960s they are seen to represent. Kate Millett and company are out of fashion, not because of their "views on women, lesbianism and patriarchy," Kaplan asserts, but because they exude a particular style of political protest that, with cultural baggage attached, is regarded as naïve and inadequate for today's political and social realities (2).

Freely's interviews with Anita Bennett and Cora Kaplan effectively organize the heterogeneity of "second-wave" feminisms into a general, unitary historical account of the 1960s.[42] This homogenizing move leads Freely to argue that the problem of the forgotten activists of the second-wave era lies not so much in the effects of government repression of 1960s radicals, as Bennett is quoted as arguing, nor in the out-of-fashion state of the radicalism of the 1960s rather than second-wave feminist "views on women, lesbianism and patriarchy," as Kaplan is quoted as arguing, but in the general vicissitudes of history itself (2). Like the feminist generations before her own, Freely writes, Millett's generation was always going to experience "the temporary oblivion" suffered by one generation of political activists as the next emerges eager to claim the rightfulness of their particular creed. It is "a strange little pattern," Freely concludes, that tells us more about "human nature or the way history gets written than it tells you about feminism" (2).

Freely's rather easy and, ultimately, uninteresting conclusion, that it is simply the patterns of historical production that have condemned Millett and her peers to oblivion (a conclusion that evacuates history of any contingency or specificity), leaves unanswered the implicit question of why Millett, and those feminists mentioned in her *On the Issues* article, have been forgotten while others have not. After all, as Leslie Crawford in *Salon .com*, the online politics and arts magazine, writes in her response to Millett's article, other "star" feminists from the second-wave era still have their place in the zeitgeist.[43] People like Betty Friedan, Gloria Steinem, and

Germaine Greer, all one-time peers of Millett, continued to have a public visibility through the 1990s and beyond. As Crawford states, all three had books published by mainstream publishers in the 1990s. Biographies of Friedan and Greer appeared in 1998 and 1999 respectively, and Carolyn Heilbrun's biography of Steinem was published in 1995.[44] And all three remained occasional contributors to public discussions on the state and value of feminism (Germaine Greer more so in Britain than the United States).

Rather than locate the reasons for Millett's present-day obscurity in the general vicissitudes of history, Crawford finds them in the particularity of Millett's "ambivalent" persona. While Friedan was the "stately matriarch" and Steinem the "brassy babe," Millett was the "manic-depressive, married, bisexual, women's reformer, gay liberationist, reclusive sculptor, in-your-face activist, retiring Midwesterner, brassy New Yorker." She was, as Crawford summarizes, "far too conflicted and complicated a figure" to stay present in the zeitgeist (4). Crawford goes on to argue that Millett's stature as movement figurehead was laced with controversy from the very beginning. As "intensely as she was lionized," Crawford writes, "she was demonized." From Norman Mailer's description of her in his excoriating review of *Sexual Politics* for *Harper's* in 1970 as "the Battling Annie of some new prudery," to those in the movement who accused her of not being "gay enough," Kate Millett was always the site of conflicting messages about who she was and about what the movement stood for (4). But while Crawford locates Millett's persona and subsequent obscurity in the events surrounding her at the height of the women's liberation movement's most controversial and spectacular cultural and social visibility, this does not lead to a contemplation of the contested politics of the movement as a possible reason for Millett's forgotten state. Rather, the conflicts and ambivalences of Millett's persona are seen as merely personal characteristics, the "flaws" of a troubled psyche.[45] Indeed, the particularity of the controversy surrounding Millett in 1970, and the connection between that controversy and the feminism she was seen to represent and advocate, is precisely what is left unexplored in both Crawford's and Freely's articles.

Millett's difference from Friedan and Steinem does not lie, simply, in the comparative simplicity of their public personas in contrast to that of Millett but in what that simplicity transmits in the cultural politics of the national public sphere. The "stately matriarch" and the "brassy babe" are both stereotypical caricatures of accepted female roles: the mother and the alluring, seductive, single young woman. Both stereotypes are intrinsically heterosexual and neither disturb the hegemony of sex and gender norms in American society. And so, despite the relative radicalism of their actual politics, Friedan and Steinem both represent an image of feminism that does not bring into question the heteronormativity of American society. In contrast, the "ambivalence" of Millett's public persona comes precisely from the fact that she participated in and represented political and cultural practices that went beyond, and brought into question, that institution. Millett was not only the married, bisexual, lesbian of *Time* fame, she was also the author of the best-selling *Sexual Politics*, a book that transformed literary criticism by conceptualizing sexuality as a domain of social and cultural power, called for an end to monogamous heterosexual marriage, and proposed a sexual revolution that would, in effect, bring about the end of heteronormativity. In fact, Millett's controversial, ambiguous persona was precisely an effect of her views "on women, lesbianism and patriarchy." And it is for this reason, rather than simply a troubled psyche or the vicissitudes of history, I would argue, that she has been "forgotten," while Friedan and Steinem have not.[46]

On the one hand, then, as both Freely and Millett reveal through the stories they tell, the women's liberation movement has been remembered not as a contested historical phenomenon with effects in the present but as an "object" constructed by interested parties attempting to situate themselves in a historical narrative, which explains the meaning of their particular form or interpretation of feminism. In addition, these memories are produced—as story, cliché, or stereotype—in order to transform women's liberation into something always already known and familiar. Women's liberation becomes the "real" feminism that johnny-come-latelies deny or denigrate in their eagerness to assert their own brand of feminism (the story told in Millett's article), or it becomes the vanquished other of a feminism that has "moved on" with the swells and eddies of time (the story told in Freely's article).[47] In both accounts, women's liberation is awarded an originary significance that simultaneously prevents any real historical exploration of what that significance might be. Instead, the movement is encrypted as something that is over but that nevertheless operates as a purposefully opaque "object" wielded by interested parties in their constructions of a singular feminist past.

On the other hand, Crawford's article suggests something of what is being forgotten in popular and feminist public memories of the women's liberation movement. Rather than understand Millett's ambivalent persona to be an effect of personal "turmoil"—as another example of the privatization of women's liberation's political protest—as Crawford does, we could read it more as an effect of the ambiguousness of the politics of the movement itself. Women's liberation haunts us today precisely because of its lack of coherence and unity and because of the challenges it made, among other things, to the intimate public sphere of a proper femininity— challenges that are not yet over. If the women's liberation movement often represented its political goals as a fight for legislative, social, and economic rights, it also simultaneously engaged in a contestation of the cultural and symbolic spheres of the intimate public of women's culture. In its challenging of the ideas and representations of *woman*, as an idealized form of femininity nevertheless made to appear ordinary, women's liberation and the women who acted in its name took the risk of becoming strange in relation to gender and sex norms. It is this risk taking, and the social and cultural eccentricities it produced, that gets evoked in the media's reading of Millett's "return" to the public realm. As a "far too conflicted and complicated" figure, Millett operates as a remainder of the unsettling and unsettled threat the movement posed—for feminists as well as nonfeminists—to the mass-mediated class and raced norms of femininity that produced the heteronormative social imaginary of the U.S. public sphere.

If the lesbian, or feminist-as-lesbian, often acts, as Freeman suggests, as the "big drag" on contemporary feminist and queer politics, as an unwanted reminder of the bad old days of essentialism and identity politics, it is because she operates, I would argue, as a screen memory—a "whiting out," to emphasize the racial connotations of Terry Castle's term for the derealization of lesbianism in modern culture—of the more complex and contingent politics of the early women's liberation's revolt against the lure of white, middle-class respectability. The ambiguity of Millett's public persona suggested an estrangement from white femininity, as well as a lack of fixity in the explorations of sexuality and gender in the early years of the women's liberation movement more generally. Her complex public persona refused any absolute or simple sexual or political identity. Indeed, rather than augmenting the emergence of identity politics, and of "lesbian feminism" as a discrete political position within the women's liberation movement, the controversies surrounding Millett in 1970 and the contradictoriness of her (various and shifting) public personas signaled an undoing, a potential disassemblement of gender and sexual subjectivities in the

United States in the mid-twentieth century. As one of the more public examples of the risk-taking inventiveness and active changeability of many women in the early years of the second-wave era, Kate Millett challenged the image of *woman* as an anchoring sign for the sociocultural production of heterosexuality in U.S. public cultures. It is this challenge that has been de-realized through the hypervisibility of the feminist-as-lesbian figure in cultural memories and historical accounts of the movement in the late twentieth and early twenty-first century. Lesbianism, for Millett and for others in the early years of the women's liberation movement, as we have seen, was not necessarily an identity to be celebrated as a thing in itself, nor was it simply an "issue" among others within the larger political project of feminism (an idea that reasserts the centrality of *woman* for feminism as well as for the heteronormative national imaginary). Rather, it was something closer to what we now call *queer*—a practice of subverting existing social identities and of anticipating future forms of social and sexual life.

"SOMETHING TO BE DONE"

Now I would like to turn to two essays, both by well-known American feminist thinkers, in order to trace the beginnings of the "something to be done" signaled by the flickering and continuing presence of the feminist-as-lesbian figure in popular, feminist, and queer memories of women's liberation. That ghosts call on us to do something is an ethical imperative taken from Avery Gordon, who deploys the above phrase as an incitement to confront the haunting ways in which the past is alive and has an effect on a present that mostly tries to ignore its presence.[48] As Gordon writes, the ghosts that haunt us are the specters of lost or buried possibilities from a painful, often violent past:

> The willingness to follow ghosts, neither to memorialize nor to slay, but to follow where they lead, in the present, head turned backwards and forwards at the same time. To be haunted in the name of a will to heal is to allow the ghost to help you imagine what was lost that never even existed, really. That is its utopian grace: to encourage a steely sorrow laced with delight for what we lost that we never had; to long for the insight of that moment in which we recognize, as in Benjamin's profane illumination, that it could have been and can be otherwise.[49]

But even here, although Gordon is calling upon her readers to look backward as well as forward and toward a past that is too complex and often too painful to apprehend fully, there is also the trace of a romantic desire to be seduced by the past: to "feel a steely sorrow laced with delight" when looking backward runs the risk of too quickly substituting the pleasures of imagining otherwise for an active questioning of how the past is used and related to in the present.

Unlike Gordon, then, whose focus in *Ghostly Matters* was on providing a method of redress for the social and political crimes of state-sponsored violence in the Dirty War of Argentina and the Reconstruction period in the United States, my reckoning with the eventfulness of women's liberation is less interested in healing—on finding justice for the wounds of the past—than on returning to the movement's moment of invention in order to bring into question the ways in which its eventfulness has been bequeathed to us in the present. By attending to the ways in which the categories, terms, and figures of the movement have been constructed, claimed, and naturalized, for example, opens up its "discursive productions of social and historical reality as complex, contradictory processes" that demand our scrutiny.[50] Rather than seduction, the past of women's liberation demands a confrontation with—and an accountability toward—its messy involvements in the public and social domains of proper femininity.

The two essays I read in this section, in their different ways, are attempts to confront the elisions and displacements in feminist theoretical and cultural work concerned with the political protests of women's liberation, and both essays are concerned with the ways in which lesbianism figures in those elisions or displacements. In this sense they are both examples of an attempt to look for, rather than follow, the ghosts of the recent feminist past.[51] The two essays—Teresa de Lauretis's "The Essence of the Triangle" and Adrienne Rich's "Compulsory Heterosexuality and the Lesbian Continuum"—bookended the 1980s and were highly influential in marking the theoretical and conceptual parameters of a period of intense disagreement and conflict within the diverse publics of U.S. feminisms. The 1980s witnessed a decisive breaking down of any lingering illusions of a homogeneous feminist movement within the remaining cohorts of the predominantly white women's liberation movement. The 1980s was also the decade that put to rest the comforting fantasy of feminism's oppositional innocence in relation to power, sexuality, and mainstream culture and politics. As a response to this breaking down of an imaginary consensus concerning the central aims and objects of American feminism, the 1980s also saw a series of what Katie King calls "interested stories" sediment into a dominant narrative of second-wave feminism.[52] These stories tended to secure that narrative by manufacturing a decisive break between the era of second-wave feminism, or women's liberation, and what came after it. As told through these interested stories, the break happened in myriad ways: through the so-called sex wars, through the essentialism versus poststructuralism debate, through the so-called emergence of minority feminisms, both racial and postcolonial (*so-called* because it is an erroneous, and contested, though widespread chronology that situates minority feminisms as having happened *after* the women's liberation movement), and through the academicization of feminism. Returning to Rich's and de Lauretis's essays offers us a way—one way—of approaching something of what was being buried, silenced, or tidied up in the production of these stories, and what, as a consequence, is left unexplored about the continuities, as well as the disjunctures, between the time of women's liberation and the present.

In "The Essence of the Triangle" Teresa de Lauretis takes what she calls a "more discerning look" at the essentialism versus poststructuralist debate in Anglo-American feminist theory in the late 1980s.[53] For de Lauretis, "essentialism" is present in Anglo-American feminist theory, not for its analytic usefulness but because it operates as a sign for a feminist Other that cannot be directly or openly addressed. In order to make this argument, de Lauretis reads two much discussed Anglo-American feminist texts from her contemporary moment—Linda Alcoff's "Cultural Feminism versus Poststructuralism: The Identity Crisis in Feminist Theory" and Chris Weedon's *Feminist Practice and Poststructuralist Theory*—and traces the way each conjures up the specter of "essentialism" in order to dismiss it from the ranks of "good" feminist theory.[54] Essentialism is used in both texts, de Lauretis argues, as a simplistic and reductive representation of *cultural feminism,* a term most often used to designate radical and/or lesbian feminist theory (of which Adrienne Rich, Mary Daly, and Susan Griffin are the primary representatives), and serves as the "straw woman" against which a more "sophisticated" theoretical practice is promoted. Although de Lauretis argues against the hierarchy of theoretical positions this move invokes, her primary concern is with what is elided in the act of ordering in both texts. Her question is: What "motivates" these theorists to typologize and "brand" different feminisms "along an ascending scale of theoretico-political sophistication where essentialism weighs heavy at the lower end" (4)? In other words, what is unacknowledged or avoided in the act of setting up and then dismissing a constructed feminist other?

In order to answer this question de Lauretis switches her perspective by looking at the work of the Italian feminist group Libreria delle Donne di Milano. By looking to another feminist practice of thought, de Lauretis hopes to offer a defamiliarizing perspective, one in which the texts of "cultural feminism" and poststructuralism have been read genealogically rather than taxonomically, and one in which the history and particular location of the feminists involved was understood as constitutive of the group's particular practice of feminist theorizing. For de Lauretis, the particularity of Libreria delle Donne di Milano's feminist theorizing lies in the group's "practice of sexual difference," which had emerged not out of an ahistorical, metaphysical understanding of sexual difference as an innate or natural difference between men and women but out of the "particular location, the social and political situatedness" of the group as Italian feminists in a sex-segregated society (13). Following Luce Irigaray's work on sexual difference, the Italian group understood this difference not in the binaristic terms of Beauvoir's "Self/Other" dichotomy, in which both terms are defined through the "standard" of one, but in terms of an irreducible, yet to be articulated difference that remains virtual to the practice of feminist theorizing. By analyzing Libreria delle Donne di Milano's written historicization of their emergence as a material and discursive entity, de Lauretis traces the way in which the group produced a "female genealogy or female symbolic" through the creation of a conceptual and discursive space that was distinct from the masculine political discursive spaces they were operating within (23). With the creation of a "symbolic community" and the production of particular figures (notably the "symbolic mother") who act as forms of mediation between a virtual world of women not defined in relation to *woman* and the symbolic order of the masculine-dominated society they are writing within, the group created a "different production of reference and meaning" between and for women rather than in relation to men (27). This "symbolic community" of women, de Lauretis writes, is "at once discovered, invented, and constructed" by the group rather than revealed or uncovered (13).

For de Lauretis, the example of Libreria delle Donne di Milano, despite its overly maternalist and desexualized enactment of a female symbolic space (and de Lauretis is critical of the collective for these proclivities), shows us how feminist theories emerge out of the particular sociohistorical contexts of the women who produce them or what, borrowing from Walter Benjamin, de Lauretis calls the particular "'state of emergency' we find ourselves in" as women in a world made by and for men (27). De Lauretis also sees, in the genealogical work of the Italian group, a more active and productive relationship to history, one that does not categorize the history of Italian feminism but looks to the past as a generative force in the constitution of a specific, time-and-space-bound conception of sexual difference, which then becomes the basis for expressing a particular way of being feminists in the world. The poststructuralism versus essentialism debate in Anglo-American feminist theory, and the construction of a "phantom" essentialism in particular, in contrast, reveals a refusal on the part of the feminist theorists involved to confront the contingencies of their sociohistorical situation as women, and as feminists, in a world that has already named them as such. This refusal leads de Lauretis to suggest at the end of her essay "that what motivates the suspicion, on the part of Anglo-American feminists, of a feminist essentialism, may be less the risk of essentialism itself than the further risk which that entails: the risk of challenging directly, the social symbolic institution of heterosexuality" (32). Taking the risk of essentialism seriously, therefore, becomes, on the one hand, a challenge to feminists to be more attuned to—haunted by—the sociocultural limits and experiential realities of the hand that history has (differently) dealt them. On the other hand, it becomes a call for feminists to reorient their remembering of the "second-wave" feminist claim of an "essential difference" of women as less an assertion of some natural innate being-ness of women and more as a potentiality, a radical project of reimagining the social and cultural domains—a reimagining that is part of the process of constituting "new social spaces" and new "forms of community" through which women will enact new subjectivities. I would also add that, in her challenge to take "the risk of essentialism seriously," that is, to take the risk of challenging the "social symbolic institution of heterosexuality," de Lauretis is also arguing that feminists need to be haunted by the possibilities latent within the reimaginings of lesbianism in the early years of the women's liberation movement.

"The something to be done" in de Lauretis's confrontation with a phantom essentialism is evident in the way she reads feminist theory genealogically as a practice, a *doing* of feminism rather than as simply a reflection upon, or contemplation of, feminism's political goals. Whereas in Elizabeth Freeman's essay the figure of the lesbian operates as a sign of a feminist past that could not be dragged into the present, in de Lauretis's essay the notion of essentialism can be read symptomatically in Anglo-American feminist theory as another manifestation of the ghostly presence of the feminist-as-lesbian that conjures up a screen memory of a particular form of feminism that is then condemned or dismissed as "wrong." In both cases feminist theory is doing something other than, or in addition to, what it states it is doing. Feminist theory doesn't just present an argument, a body of intellectual work, it also produces silences, repressions, and affects that reappear symptomatically, as "ghosts," in other feminist work. As something to be done in our looking for the ghosts of women's liberation, then, we might read the feminist-as-lesbian as a figure through which a virtual world of nonheterosexuality was glimpsed in Anglo-American feminist theory and, paradoxically, as a figure through which the "stakes, indeed the affective investments that feminism may have in the heterosexual institution," are also glimpsed (33). The ghostliness of the feminist-as-lesbian figure as tracked by de Lauretis in Anglo-American feminist theory lies precisely in the contradictory mix of a simultaneous investment by American feminism in virtual and actual forms of nonheterosexuality and in the sociocultural norms of a white, bourgeois, national femininity. That is, what remains to be explored about the pastness of women's liberation is less the fact of its white middle-classness and its—relative and partial—failure to move toward the other of normative femininity but how that failure manifested itself in the movement's struggles with and against its own conditions of possibility.

Adrienne Rich's "Compulsory Heterosexuality and the Lesbian Continuum" has been the subject of controversy and contest in Anglo-American feminist theory since it was first published in 1980—surely a sign of its affective power as well as theoretical influence on the emergent field of Anglo-American feminist theory. In response to the essay's reception by feminist critics after it was first published in *Signs* in 1980, Rich republished the essay in her collection *Blood, Bread, and Poetry: Selected Prose, 1979–1985*, along with a foreword, in which she explained her reasons for writing the essay, and an afterword, in which she printed correspondence between herself and Ann Snitow, Christine Stansell, and Sharon Thompson, the editors of the *Powers of Desire* anthology in which the essay had also appeared and who had communicated to her certain misgivings about it.[55] An analysis of the foreword and afterword, in conjunction with an analysis of the essay itself, reveals not only the terms of the debate between Rich and her critics to be ones in which heterosexuality and lesbianism play a central part but also the stakes involved for a feminism that would confront its own investments in heteronormativity.

In the foreword, Rich offers the following explanation for why she wrote "Compulsory Heterosexuality and Lesbian Existence": "I wanted to suggest new kinds of criticism, to incite new questions in classrooms and academic journals, and to sketch, at least, some bridge over the gap between lesbian and feminist." She goes on to state that "at the very least," she wanted "feminists to find it less possible to read, write, or teach from a perspective of unexamined heterocentricity" (1986, 24). Rich's formulation of her motives for writing the essay reveal neither an "essentialist" nor a "separatist" perspective but, rather, a questioning of the "object and field of analysis" of feminist theory, as de Lauretis would say. More particularly, Rich poses the problem of an "unexamined heterocentricity" in relation to a larger question: How can feminist theory ask new questions of the world and the experiences of those people identified and living their lives as women? In asserting the need for a critique of "heterocentricity," Rich isn't arguing so much for a right way to be feminist or against "bad" feminists, but she is, rather, arguing for "new kinds of questions," questions that will lead to a critical appraisal of those aspects of our existence as women that have remained, so far, "unexamined."

Rich's explanation of her reasons for writing "Compulsory Heterosexuality and Lesbian Existence" is consistent with her published responses to the questions posed by the editors of *Powers of Desire*. As the questions from Snitow, Stansell, and Thompson make clear, their primary concern with the essay was Rich's conception of a "lesbian continuum," and her use of the notion of "false consciousness" as a way to describe women's continued participation in heterosexuality. The lesbian continuum, they wrote, implies the reduction of different experiences to "sameness" (female friendship = lesbianism; penetration = rape), while false consciousness implies that straight women suffer from "wrong" thinking when they sleep with men (1986, 69). For Snitow, Stansell, and Thompson, the explanatory power of Rich's essay is weakened by her collapse of distinct realms of experience and her assumption of a simplistic dichotomy between "good feminism" (lesbian feminism) and "bad feminism" (straight feminism). Yet, for Rich, the criticisms put forward by the three editors miss (purposefully?) the larger point of her essay. In their eagerness to address the problematic nature of notions like false consciousness, they evade rather than confront Rich's central argument: that feminists need to find ways to theorize and explain the ways in which women are coerced into their dominated state, what Rich terms the "real, identifiable system of heterosexual propaganda" (1986, 79). Notions like lesbian continuum and false consciousness, while perhaps not adequate to the task she has set for them, should, Rich argues, first of all be recognized as attempts to theorize what has "glided so silently into the foundations of our thought": the unexamined "assumption of female heterosexuality" (1983, 182).

Like de Lauretis, Rich understands her essay, and by implication all works of feminist theory, to be generative rather than descriptive. Concepts like the lesbian continuum, therefore, should be read not as an attempt to describe the historicity of the experiential reality of women, or indeed of lesbians, but as an attempt to produce that historicity. As feminist interlocutors conducting a genealogy of the feminist past (whereby the collectivity of feminism is in the process of being constructed rather than assumed), the questions to address to Rich's text would not be "is this feminism?" or "is this lesbianism?" but rather what are the forms of relationship and belonging being articulated in Rich's idea of lesbianism and how do they, and how don't they, help us to think differently about feminism, women, and their place in the world? Reading "Compulsory Heterosexuality and Lesbian Existence" as a generative act of making feminist thought transforms the meaning and usefulness of the essay, despite what for many might be its problematic content. While Rich's evaluation of "good" sex as full of "mutuality and integrity" and "bad" sex as lacking emotion (1983, 185–86), for example, can be read as ahistorical and/or antimaterialist assumptions in the essay, her notions of "lesbian existence" and "lesbian continuum" nevertheless provide us with a means to conceptualize a "female symbolic space" that is both temporally contingent and historically constituted.

Rich defines *lesbian existence* as the "fact of the historical presence of lesbians and our continuing creation of the meaning of that existence," and the *lesbian continuum* as the presence of "woman-identified experiences" throughout history that may or may not include sexual relations (1983, 186). As Rich herself writes, to assert the existence of lesbians and to promote a lesbian continuum is "to take the step of questioning heterosexuality" as a natural or given phenomenon. This questioning, while requiring great "intellectual and emotional work," not to mention "courage," will result in "a freeing-up of thinking, the exploring of new paths, the shattering of another great silence" (1983, 186). That is to say, Rich does not assert lesbian existence and a lesbian continuum as a known phenomenon or premeditated path of idealized relationships between women but as a "leap" into the unknown. Yet, as Rich also writes, that leap should not take place over the "tasks and struggles of here and now," over the "actualities within which women have experienced sexuality," but through a careful "intellectual and emotional" working through of them (1983, 182) and through an investigation and drawing upon the history of women, specifically the history of "women who—as witches, *femme seules*, marriage resisters, spinsters, autonomous widows, and/or lesbians—have managed on varying levels not to collaborate" (1983, 180).

Rich's conceptions of lesbian existence and a lesbian continuum, then, have more to do with a "community" of women that is "at once discovered, invented and constructed," to use de Lauretis's words, than it has to do with the claiming of the innate being-ness and sameness of women. Although we might pause over the idealization of community for feminism here, especially considering more recent feminist critiques of the term as exclusionary and disciplinary in its dependence upon a fantasy of belonging, the emphasis of Rich's assertions are on the production of an association rather than on the revelation of sameness.[56] As Rich writes, the idea of a lesbian continuum allows us to "connect" instances of woman identification that are "diverse" and "disparate." The key word here is *connect*. Rich does not argue for an equivalence between different episodes, places, and times of woman-identified experience but for the production of a relationship between them; the fact of lesbian existence is always bound to "our continuing creation of the meaning of that existence" (1983, 195). It is up to us as feminists to articulate and make connections between different women in different times and places. And it is through such work that feminists will create a "female symbolic space" that is articulated in resistance to the dominant symbolic space—the space of heteronormativity.

In her conception of the lesbian continuum, Rich works with and elaborates upon the refashioning of lesbianism that formed a part of the feminist project(s) of the early women's liberation movement. She reorientates lesbianism as a practice of transformation in which the invention and creation of new relationships, new collectivities, and new social, cultural, and political bonds between women are produced as possible routes to a different future. Moreover, she understands that this future difference will come from resisting the lure of heterosexuality as a socio-symbolic institution and from women becoming strange in relation to the norms of social categorization in their particular historically bound sociocultural contexts.

Witches, *femme seules*, spinsters, the mythic mannish lesbian, bulldaggers, butch-femme couples, and, I would add, the feminist-as-lesbian are all specters of resistance in Rich's construction of a feminist "symbolic space." And although the lesbian continuum may not continue to open up what Deleuze and Guattari call "lines of flight" into a nonheterosexual, nonwhite feminist future—a testament perhaps to the way certain concepts become too burdened, too sticky with the historicity they were produced by—it also forms part of the archive of an active feminist resistance to the normal and the same.[57] In addition, the genealogical relationship to the feminist past promoted by de Lauretis, and exemplified in concepts like the lesbian continuum, allows us to look for the figure of the feminist-as-lesbian, as glimpsed in the "return" of Kate Millett, for example, within the context of a history of feminist resistance to, and challenges of, the socio-symbolic space of heteronormativity. By reincorporating her into the ongoing, expansive, and diverse elaboration of a feminist symbolic space, the figure of the feminist-as-lesbian becomes a sign of the possibilities—unrealized as well as realized—of women's liberation. She becomes a sign, for example, of that movement's complex challenge to heterosexuality as a sociocultural institution, a sign of that movement's resistance to the claims of the normal, the mainstream, and the legitimate. She becomes a sign of how, in the early years of the women's liberation movement, a significant collectivity of women became consciously, actively, and visibly strange in relation to the sociocultural norms of their particular moment. And while the resistance to the normal may have hardened, for some, into narrowly defined and exclusionary political and social identities, the "affective and relational virtualities" they opened up for feminism continue to reverberate in the present.[58]

THE POLITICS OF MEMORY AND
FEELING HISTORICAL

The whole allure of the book, the reason it's interesting, is because these things really happened.—ALISON BECHDEL IN HILLARY CHUTE, "An Interview with Alison Bechdel"

The relation of the present to the past is most often figured through idealizations and demonizations of particular epochs or individuals on the one hand, and reparations and apologies for past wrongs on the other. . . . We might ask what this figuring covers over, defers, or symptomizes in the present. How does it elide the most difficult questions about the bearing of the past on the present?—WENDY BROWN, *Politics Out of History*

In this book I have read along the grain of the archive of women's liberation in order to render problematic the ways in which the movement has been accounted for and remembered in the present. By tracking the transmission of meaning and emotion through the phrases and terms from the past of women's liberation to the present of mainstream, feminist, and queer relations to that history, I have attempted to attend to the complex and contingent eventfulness of the movement without entombing it in a didactic demand that it be recognized as the origin for present feminist concerns. More particularly, I have returned to what was, for many feminist activists and scholars of the women's liberation movement, the defining circumstances of the movement's emergence as a distinct feminist movement, namely the widespread media coverage and public discord that constituted the movement's upsetting eruption into the national public sphere in 1970, in order to offer a critical history of the production of women's liberation as a white women's feminist movement. While I have argued that those events produced the figure of the feminist-as-lesbian through which the women's liberation movement is largely known and remembered in the present, I have also attempted to demonstrate a method of relating to the past that does not depend on making an authoritative claim to a history or on the futuritial community-building pleasures of a disjunctive touching between one historical era and another: neither a claim to history nor a desire for history but, rather, an attempt to highlight the deeply historically implicated relations between the two. Indeed, my turn to what Wendy Brown calls "the politics of memory" is designed to foreground the contested nature of feminist histories and their inevitable connections to, and entanglements in, other histories—those other histories include the New Left, gay liberation, and Black Power movements, as well as the majoritarian history of postwar American mass culture, but it might also have included the histories of political movements and events beyond the imagined community of the United States. Now I want to expand, briefly, on the distinction I make between an accountability toward the past and the desire for history. I do so in order to illuminate what such different approaches to the past might do for queer and feminist studies and their relationship to the events of the gay and women's liberation movements— events that shaped the conditions of possibility for queer and feminist subcultures and studies in the United States today. I end with a short reading of Alison Bechdel's *Fun Home: A Family Tragicomedy*, which I hope will stand as an example of the generative potential of approaching events like women's liberation as neither just "feminist" nor "queer" but both and more.

An accountability toward the past rather than the desire for history. The *rather than* in this sentence is meant to invoke two related things: a different, but not opposite, way of relating to the past and a divergence of critical emphasis. In other words, the distinction I am making here is not between what we might call, for convenience's sake, queer and feminist historiography but between different kinds of investments in the past— investments that have no direct line to one particular identity formation or academic field. Still, we could think of these divergent investments as the effects of disciplinary imperatives—the paradigms of thought that shape fields like queer theory, for example, and make them something distinct from other fields, including feminist theory. But we might also think of them as responses to different political demands and "historical emergencies"—as the effects of the contingencies of social location and historical moment. To have an investment in the past suggests something beyond or in addition to an exclusively cognitive or "expert" relation to it. How we might *use the past* and how we are accountable to it are, as the above formulation suggests, as much questions about desire and fantasy as they are about political affiliation and/or (inter)disciplinary location and expertise.

In his highly influential study of emotion as productive of a specifically queer historicality, Christopher Nealon writes about the institutional and conceptual tensions between queer theory and gay and lesbian studies as the effects of a contrasting relationship to history. Drawing upon Lisa Duggan's identification of a "disciplinary problem" between a history-based gay and lesbian studies and the more literary queer studies, as well as Michael Warner's observation of the different methods at work in the two fields—historical for gay and lesbian, psychoanalytical for queer—Nealon summarizes the differences between the two projects this way: "queer theorists, determined to write a story of the origins of homosexuality, assign themselves to understanding the (logically, if not temporally) 'presocial' intersection of matter and language in the figure of sexuality and therefore tend to produce "radical" understandings of homosexuality—that is, theories that locate homosexuality at the very margins or origins of culture itself. . . . Historians of U.S. lesbian and gay sexuality, meanwhile, engaged in the project of capturing lost information about past queer lives, place the objects of their study firmly within the realm of the cultural, as articulate—if contingent—historical forms."[1]

For Nealon, this divergence of *interest* in the historical produces a question that illuminates the political stakes of the debate between gay and lesbian studies and queer theory and, I might add, between feminist and queer approaches to the past: "is homosexuality most potent as a force for social change when it is inarticulate, unconscious, and acting as a threat to representation? Or when it clothes itself in specific historical and political forms, which pose challenges to particular arrangements of power and authority?" (18). Nealon's solution to this question is to "return to history," not in order to continue the (gay and lesbian) project of finding and claiming lost information about queer life but to write a historiography of what "is proto-historical in homosexuality, desire" (20). For Nealon, the answer to the above question is to return to the past for what it anticipates—desires—for the future. It is in the future anterior of the imaginative relations of past queer lives to history that Nealon locates a specifically queer historicality, what he calls a desire to "feel historical," and with which he suggests queerness as a politics of prolepsis: as a "mode of address, as a set of relations, lived and imagined, that are perpetually cast out ahead of our 'real,' present-tense" (180). To return to history is to go in search of those imaginative reachings in order to ponder their emergent possibilities for queer ways of living as well as for what might be their sometimes problematic appropriations of other forms of marginalized experience. To feel historical, then, refers to two things at once: the creative, if constrained by context, attempts of queers to fashion out of historical analogy forms of personhood and collectivity beyond the heteronormativity of present-tense social convention, and the affective force of historical uncertainty and unknowability that such future-anterior desires produce for queers in the present.

Nealon's calls for a less possessive, as in less identity or individual based, form of queer sexuality and politics and less "punishing" relations to the queer past resonates widely in contemporary queer theory and has led to a host of closely aligned studies and theoretical innovations in the field.[2] Carolyn Dinshaw's *Getting Medieval: Sexualities and Communities, Pre- and Postmodern* is perhaps the most exemplary text of this queer desire for history and, like Carla Freccero's later *Queer/Early/Modern*, offers one of the most sustained arguments for a queer historiographical method. In the following paragraphs I want to read these texts in relation to each other in order to tease into view what, when looked at from the perspective of feminist history, and of the history of second-wave feminism in particular, this approach to history can and cannot do. In other words, my critique, if we want to call it that, has less to do with objecting to the aspirations of this approach than with noting its partiality. I want to suggest that an emphasis on the "productive potentiality of queerness as a set of historical possibilities and relations" tends not to be as interested in an ethics of accountability toward the past, and it has often led to an assumption of queerness as desirable—as a body, scenario, or text we want to touch—rather than leading to investigations of what might be the undesirable effects of specific historical constellations of queerness. It seems to me that this problem becomes especially acute when we return to the recent past of movements like the women's and gay liberation movements. As explicitly political formations, the gay and women's liberation movements made claims and acted in ways that exceeded the intentionality of its actors, which continue to have political, social, and cultural effects in the present. That is, the messy, compromised inventiveness of a movement like women's liberation has left us with a past we might not always want to touch, even if, at the same time, it has also bequeathed to us a set of historical possibilities and relations not fully realized in the present. To return to the anticipatory force of a movement like women's liberation, then, can only be part of a response to its eventfulness; an accountability to what has materialized in its name—to what "really happened"—must also, it seems to me, form part of an ongoing, open-ended response to the movement and its eventfulness.

Of course, as a medievalist, Carolyn Dinshaw does not return to the recent past of the new social movements of the 1960s and 1970s, though her return to late fourteenth- and early fifteenth-century England is, in part, concerned with drawing out the links between discourses of "sexual irregularities" and the political and religious heresies of the time.[3] Indeed, as a medievalist, Dinshaw's elaboration of a specifically queer relation to history depends on making connections with those who, to use her beautiful phrase, "elude resemblance" (21). It is the charge of partial recognition from such elusive resemblances that becomes, for Dinshaw, the affective impulse for making queer histories. The affective relations that make queer histories are not, then, for Dinshaw as for Nealon, evidential barometers of queer ways of being. Rather, they are heuristic devices that enable—through the touching, or inhabitation of, a figure from the past in the present—a re-imagining of what was and might be possible for queers.

The figure through which Dinshaw makes her argument for queer affective relations across time is Michel Foucault, who operates in the text, along with Roland Barthes, as a kind of queer father with whom and against which Dinshaw fashions her project. It is through their—creative and affective—relationships to the past that Dinshaw lays claim to her desire to make queer relations with the past. The Foucault of Getting Medieval is above all a tactician: rather than write histories, Dinshaw argues, Foucault returns to the past to use it. His vision of the premodern in the History of Sexuality, Volume One, for example, which at first glance seems "merely nostalgic, idealized, totalized" is in fact, according to Dinshaw, a "serious ethical and political vision of a future that is not straitened by modern sexuality" (15). This tactical use of the past becomes, for Dinshaw, the political impulse of her "disaggregative project"—it enables the making of relations across time that do not insist upon a causal narrative of historical progress or negate the indeterminate nature of past phenomena. A tactical use of the past offers, instead, a "fictioning" of history in order to "fiction a politics not yet in existence" (205).[4]

These fictioning relations are affective because they depend on the partial recognitions of the historian and scholar looking back at the past and desiring something other than what is legible in the present. They are creative because they recognize "the historical past as a vibrant and heterogeneous source of self-fashioning as well as community building" (142). Dinshaw's refusal to read Foucault's relationship to the early modern period as "merely nostalgic" is a rejection of a certain diminishment of history in both queer and mainstream political domains, as well as an attempt to foreground the productive force of the affective in the writing of history. Like Nealon, who positions himself as a "hermeneutic friend" to the gay and lesbian artists and writers he reads in *Foundlings*, Dinshaw finds in Foucault's affective attachment to forgotten or discarded pasts a certain pleasure—the erotic charge, if you will, of historical complicity.

The criticisms that have been made about such queer historical relations, including those of Lee Edelman, perhaps their most influential critic, have tended to focus on its "utopian paradigm"—its belief in better other worlds or tomorrows for queers. I do not want to rehearse Edelman's criticisms or the quite vociferous push back by a number of queer theorists in response to his polemic—those arguments are well represented elsewhere.[5] Rather, I mention them in order to highlight Dinshaw's anticipation of them in *Getting Medieval* and as a way of foregrounding what, for me, is a slightly different problem, what I have been describing as the (ahistorical) assumption that propels this desire for history: that the productivity of queerness is always desirable or to put it even more emphatically, and therefore provocatively, that queerness, unlike feminism, is a desire that is always desirable.[6] I want to make this argument in relation to Dinshaw's reading of Foucault's short essay "Lives of Infamous Men." Nealon, too, mentions this essay (according to his notes, it was suggested to him by Dinshaw), and it tends to serve, along with Foucault's introductions to *Pierre Rivière* and *Herculine Barbin*, as a quintessential example of the queer historical impulse.[7]

"Lives of Infamous Men," as Dinshaw notes, opens with Foucault recounting how his chance discovery of brief fragments of "real existences" usually lost to documentation had left him feeling an "intensity" he could not easily explain. This feeling of intensity becomes, for Dinshaw, the affective impulse of a queer relationality across time. Rather than identification or a reading into the past a likeness that supports an understanding of the self (or group) in the present, Dinshaw reads the intensity Foucault feels as a Deleuzian difference that, on the one hand, separates him from the lives he glimpses through these fragments and, on the other, offers the possibility of "a very desubjectified connectedness between his life and those infamous ones" (137). This connectedness is, for Dinshaw, the promise of queer community: a community "constituted by nothing more than the connectedness (even across time) of singular lives that unveil and contest normativity" (138). Drawing upon the real existence of the fourteenth-century prostitute, John/Eleanor Rykener, Dinshaw offers her own example of what such a connectedness might look like: "John/Eleanor Rykener could perhaps have been in such a collection of infamous people, and mine would be the anthologizing body feeling the vibration from the document, crossing time, religion, nation, sexuality, in making a relation to that incommensurable creature who haunts the normative fourteenth-century London household, even as I haunt the (very different) normative household in current United States culture" (138). As with the shock Foucault feels when confronted with the "words and lives" of his collection of socially marginalized figures from late sixteenth- and early seventeenth-century France, the vibration Dinshaw feels when reading the deposition of John/Eleanor Rykener is due to his/her strangeness, his/her incommensurability in relation not just to the fourteenth-century normative household but to Dinshaw's (post)modern life.

There is a desire at work here—in Foucault's original essay and in Dinshaw's reading of it—to arrest the queer historical project at the moment when the queer historian "touches" the lives of others. Foucault's reluctance to move away from his fascination with his own affective responses to the documents he finds, and Dinshaw's attempt to extend that fascination into a practice of relating to the past, suggests an investment in what Nealon calls the *thereness* of the future anterior of queer imaginings. This is the desire for history—the pleasure of queer affective relations across time: they provide the "relics" that enable our desiring as something pleasurable and the imagining of queer existences and worlds outside the constraints of our sociopolitical present. The "strange poems" that mark the "real existences" of Foucault's "infamous men," along with Dinshaw's reading of the textual remainders of John/Eleanor Rykener and Margery Kempe, fascinate precisely because they, like Chaucer's fictional Pardoner, evade cate-gorization and illuminate the perversity of so-called normal life. This is queerness as historical subversion and outsider-ness, and the pleasures of "touching" it, of lingering in the thereness of its possibilities, are, as Din-shaw rightly asserts, necessary for the fashioning of queer selves and com-munities in the present.

But it seems to me that this use of the past also runs the risk of burying distant others under the weight, not of our condemnation or indifference but of our desire. That is, as Judith Butler suggests in her critique of Fou-cault's reading of Herculine Barbin's journals, the queer desire for history can often turn the lives of others into what Barbin himself/herself feared: the "playthings" of someone else's "impossible dream."[8] And what gets left out, as Butler goes on to insist in her examination of the "constitutive contradiction" of Foucault's "anti-emancipatory call for sexual freedom," is the ambivalence of a queerness—or a feminism for that matter—that is always already implicated in the norms it exposes.[9] Butler's rejection of Foucault's propensity, in texts like "Lives of Infamous Men" and his intro-duction to *Herculine Barbin*, to romanticize the marginal lives of distant others as part of his desire for a non-modern, non-bourgeois sexuality, is instructive when directed toward a past, like that of women's liberation, which is too near to our present moment and too enmeshed in contempo-rary debates and practices of nonnormative sexuality. There is not enough estranging distance between 1970 and 2012 for the kinds of projective in-vestments both Foucault and Dinshaw direct toward the premodern. And for these reasons, the past of women's liberation makes a different kind of demand: one that would have us confront and interrogate its all too present presence in the contemporary moment. Rather than a—desirable—strange-ness, the past of women's liberation, precisely because of its nearness and seeming familiarity, provides a more difficult legacy in the present.

Butler's reservations in relation to Foucault's (and by implication Din-shaw's) queer historical impulse resonate in many ways with Carla Frec-cero's turn to spectrality as a mode of queer relationality with the past. And Freccero's reading of current theoretical preoccupations with ghosts as evidence, not just of "a certain collective longing about the past and the future" but as "a way of calling and being called to historical and ethical accountability," suggests the switch in critical emphasis that I have at-tempted to demonstrate in *Feeling Women's Liberation*.[10] Rather than the active, tactile relationship to the past Dinshaw advocates for, Freccero posits "a suspension, a waiting, an attending to the world's arrivals," that, in its "passivity," is also queer (109). Freccero's understanding of queer spectrality as a passive attentiveness to the past can be linked to Stoler's "reading along the grain" of the archive, and both have influenced my return to the women's liberation archive. Both are methods of relating to the past that resist what Freccero describes as "the retrospectivity of *either* triumphant *or* melancholic modern narratives" (104). Rather than using the past, a passive attentiveness provides a space for a critical curiosity and accountability toward what is neither especially appealing nor alluring about the past. It allows for an engagement with what has been done, as well as what has been desired or anticipated in the past.

Freccero's turn to haunting and the ghostly as a way to conceptualize a queer relationship to the past, in its attempt to foreground an ethical responsibility to the past, marks a departure from Nealon's and Dinshaw's emphasis on the uses of history for queer community building in the present. Yet Freccero's insistence on calling this haunted relationship to the past *queer* (the passivity she calls queer could, after all, just as well be called feminine)[11] suggests an investment in an idea of queerness that is not historical in the sense Benjamin meant but bound to the present-day of queer theoretical concerns.[12] That is, queerness operates in *Queer/Early/Modern* as a form of desire that cannot, finally, be called to account for its own historical contingency. We find this ahistorical desirability of queerness most on display in Freccero's reading of Jean de Léry's *History of a Voyage to the Land of Brazil* (1578). Freccero reads this text as haunted and locates Léry's openness to the ghosts of the Tupi Indians, which he met as part of a French religious and colonial expedition to Brazil in 1556, in his minoritarian subject position as a Protestant preacher during the French religious wars of the late sixteenth century. It is Léry's estrangement from the politico-religious present of his time and place that "allows" Léry to be haunted by the ghosts of his Brazilian adventure (90). Freccero's term for this haunting is *penetrative reciprocity*, a "becoming-object for an other subject," that produces the joy or ecstasy of self-annihilation (102). The inspiration for this term is Leo Bersani and queer psychoanalytical theory in general:

> This image of penetrative reciprocity thus delineates a different subjectivity from the one informing Goldberg's conquerors, and it suggests the "self-shattering" impulse or *jouissance* Leo Bersani describes

as distinctive and resistive in male "homosexual" subjectivity. Bersani, indeed, muses that "same"-sex desire might be what permits the possibility of a reciprocity that resists the annihilative effacement of the other. "Can a masochistic surrender," he asks, "operate as effective (even powerful) resistance to coercive designs?" If identification with the indigenous other man is experienced by conquerors as threatening, in need of radical and thus violent obliteration for difference to be produced—and if this is, in the context of the European—New World encounter, a "normative response"—then we might say that Léry's text enacts instead a "sodomitical subjectivity" (to adapt Kaja Silverman's term), a perverse, "masochistic" identification with the other that he has come . . . to resemble. (99–100)

We might call Freccero's notion of penetrative reciprocity radical in the sense that Nealon uses it to define psychoanalytically inspired theorizations of homosexuality. But we might also call it idealistic—especially when used to define a queer subjectivity that becomes "elsewhere than as an imperial avatar in the new world" (102). Freccero's Léry, in other words, comes dangerously close to representing the kind of essentialized (queer rather than feminist) "standpoint" from below or from the margins that Donna Haraway warned us against in 1991. In Freccero's reading of Léry, queerness becomes a subject position that becomes a way of relating to the past that then comes to stand for the radical or subversive possibilities of queerness across time. This process of association is the effect, I would argue, of a desire for queerness as desirable, with Léry as the "relic" that incites that desire—the desire for the *thereness* of queerness.

The problem is we can't stay *there*, as Nealon acknowledges and as Dinshaw and Freccero do too. The *thereness* of the future anterior of past presents leads you elsewhere: to a reckoning with the racial and racist fantasies of Nealon's early and mid-twentieth century white writers, to the gender asymmetries of early and postmodern homosexualities in Dinshaw's text, and to the violences of French colonialism, at home and abroad, in Freccero's book. That is, so-called queer histories interact with and are produced out of their relations to—their involvement in—other histories; and how we get to use a term like *queer* to name these historical moments and relations, even while also emphasizing their indeterminate nature, is only possible because of the "naming effect" of historical coagulations of queerness—like those that emerged out of the women's and gay liberation movements and became, variously, queer theory, queer studies, queer sub-cultures. An accountability to these histories—the historicity of the material effects of *queer* as a term, like *feminist*, that is, in Tani Barlow's terms, *catachrestic*, demands a moving in and out of what is designated queer, or feminist, about them.[13] It demands, to follow Barlow's adaptation of Alain Badiou's "ethics of truths," "an open-ended fidelity to the event"—in this case the (re)emergence of the possibility of feminist and queer critical and political practice, which is to say the event of gay and women's liberation—that provokes "a sustained investigation of the situation," not in order to impose once and for all a defining interpretation of those movements and their meaning in the present but to "induce" a new ethical subject that can only exist as an effect of the investigation.[14]

A different relationship to the past, one with a critical emphasis on the contested nature of conflicting and seemingly incommensurate claims to that past in the present, comes out of recent work in memory studies and, in particular, those on the Holocaust. And it is perhaps not surprising that scholars of the Holocaust have had to confront the ways in which claims to a history and to the establishment of "proper," in the sense of "in the right name," relations to the past have led to intense struggles over who can make those claims and how to go about fashioning those relations. Indeed, the debates within memory studies about the historical and political use of the Holocaust and its relationship to other contested histories—of European colonialism, Israeli foreign policy after 1967, and the history of U.S. slavery, for example—serve, it seems to me, as illuminating counterexamples to queer theory's desire for history.

A focus on the production of memory and accounts of the past in the present, as Michael Rothberg argues in his recent *Multidirectional Memory*, investigates the connections between claims to (or desire for) a history and the production of an identity in the present. Rejecting the uniqueness model of identity-based claims to the past, as well as the corresponding criticism of memory studies as contributing to the conservatism of identity politics, Rothberg argues that claims to memory and identity are "necessary and inevitable" in order for different groups to claim social presence or undertake political action. But at the same time, those claims to memory and identity, rather than the result of a righteous or essentialist relation to the past, should be understood as emerging out of an "open-ended field of articulation and struggle" in the present.[15] Identities, in other words, are produced through active attempts to remember and relate to the past, and the study of memory becomes a way to historicize not just a relation to the past but what is being claimed through such a relation in the present. And so, rather than dismiss claims to particular memories and identities as "tainted" by exclusivity, Rothberg argues for an understanding of memory as "multidirectional"—as the product of "negotiation, cross-referencing, and borrowing" that "encourages us to think of the public sphere as a malleable discursive space in which groups do not simply articulate established positions but actually come into being through their dialogical interactions with others" (5).

Rothberg's notion of multidirectional memory is an important corrective to what he calls "competitive memory," with its false claims to the uniqueness of singular pasts, and it provides us with a way of conceptualizing the messy *involvements*—or, in his terms, "historical relatedness"—of different, even conflicting, claims to the past. But most importantly, perhaps, by focusing on the production of collective memory as multidirectional, Rothberg reminds us of the ethical implications of an accountability, in the present, to the pasts we claim as "ours"—that we give a name to—but that are, inevitably, connected to and involved in pasts that are claimed in relation to some other name or collectivity. Rothberg, in other words, engages in what Wendy Brown defined as the politics of memory: a persistent questioning of the "way the past is remembered or disavowed," which enacts a "responsibility" between generations and in relation to the present tense of political and ethical concerns (150). In this book and in relation to the contested histories of women's liberation and the so-called second wave of feminism more generally, my intention was to enact that responsibility by pursuing such questions.

With that intention in mind, I want to end with a remembering of women's liberation that is also a queer desire for history. My turn to Alison Bechdel's comic memoir, *Fun Home: A Family Tragicomic*, published in 2006, is not meant simply as a reiteration of what much of the already considerable and often excellent critical response has said about the book.[16] In fact, I first encountered *Fun Home* the way most of its readers did: somewhat haphazardly. Whether as a fan of Bechdel's syndicated comic serial *Dykes to Watch Out For* or through a friend's recommendation or simply by browsing a bookshop, most readers—like me—did not read *Fun Home*, at least initially, with a scholarly project in mind. Even for those of us who participate—somewhat haphazardly—in lesbian and queer publics and subcultures, the book's mainstream publisher and popular appeal (it has made an appearance on the *New York Times* best-seller list) make it difficult to fit the book into an exclusively queer, lesbian, or feminist public sphere. Indeed, the book's appeal to a whole variety of audiences—from dykes and queers, to book reviewers in mainstream publications like the *New York Times*, to comic aficionados, to, well, my mother—is precisely what makes it so interesting as an object of cultural and personal memory. Part of my interest here in *Fun Home*, then, lies in its status as a cultural object that cuts across the "false purity" of the distinctions between subcultures and national public cultures, as well as those between queer and feminist history. *Fun Home* both exhibits and brilliantly exploits the entanglement of feminist, lesbian, and queer subcultures with mass and "high" cultures in a way that opens up the complexities of their involvement with each other.

In its pointed and artful mixing up of things that are usually kept apart— high and low culture, straight and gay, lesbian and feminist and (male) queer, the past and the present, the visual and the written—*Fun Home* exemplifies the aesthetic, historiographical, and political potential of what Ann Cvetkovich calls the "insurgent genre" of the graphic narrative.[17] As a "hybrid . . . mass cultural art form," to use Hillary Chute's and Marianne DeKoven's definition, the graphic narrative's difference from exclusively written or filmed memoirs lies precisely in its "cross discursive" use of verbal and visual languages—a mixture that democratizes it as an art form by opening up multiple points of entry for the reader.[18] But just as importantly, the graphic narrative's hybrid form also brings the reader's attention to the "contested border" between word and image in a way that constantly brings into view the unsettling gap between the evidence of experience and the array of its possible meanings.[19] In my reading of *Fun Home*, I want to explore how Bechdel offers us a practice of relating to the past that, in its excessive attention to overlooked or ordinary detail and its obvious artifice, vividly illustrates the paradox that historical truth can only be grasped around its edges and through artifice—through the creation of a form in which to tell it or apprehend it. The details of a life, of a past event, and indeed of a social movement provide the material to make memories—the stories, narratives, and objects that give meaning to the present in relation to a past. But in their very detailed nature they also prevent us from ever settling on one story or account. If Bechdel's memoir revels in its own artifice, then it is not simply or only because it allows her to imagine what might have been otherwise about her father's life, it is also because it gives Bechdel a method and a form, a route backward to the details of a past that will forever elude her ability to really know it precisely because "it really happened." A fastidious attention to detail for Bechdel reveals not so much the truth of her father's life, or indeed of her own life, but its unassimilability into one story or, indeed, one gesture of (queer) revolt—a refusal of representational coherence that also prevents us from too easily settling on clear distinctions between fact and fiction, convention and subversion, queer and straight, the past and the present. Instead, through her crossing back and forth between narrative and image, through her obsessive attention to detail, and through the creativity of her form of remembrance, Bechdel invites her readers to contemplate "the complexity of loss," to borrow her paraphrasing of Proust, when confronting a past that, in its materiality and excess, escapes our ability to know it, even when, and especially when, it is making claims on us.[20]

The figure that dominates *Fun Home*, and around which Bechdel crafts her memoir of growing up in a small Pennsylvania town in the 1960s and 1970s, is Bechdel's father. Bruce Bechdel's death in 1980, when Alison Bechdel was still a college student is, as Cvetkovich writes, "the unrepresentable trauma to which the text insistently returns."[21] But the mystery of his death —the uncertainty as to whether it was an accident or suicide—also becomes the aporetic epicenter of Bechdel's explorations of the past and her relationship with her father. As Cvetkovich goes on to write, Bruce Bechdel's death is "the point of departure for the more diffuse narrative of his sexuality, which encompasses not only his attraction to young men but also his devotion to literature and home restoration, his emotionally volatile relation to his wife and children, and his artistic ambitions."[22] The diffuseness that Cvetkovich identifies is, I would argue, an effect of Bechdel's fidelity to "what really happened." The profusion of detail she amasses cannot be contained or fixed by her artful "managing" of it through drawing and a densely layered narrative full of literary references and allusions. Rather, her compulsive collecting of material and desire to make connections—through which, as Cvetkovich rightly argues, Bechdel "crafts new archives of history and memory"—simultaneously makes the artificiality of that production apparent as something distinct from a past it can only invoke or suggest.[23] Like the maps Bechdel draws to show the topographic parameters of her father's provincial life in Beech Creek, Pennsylvania, to the "centerfold" photograph she carefully redraws of a young man who was probably her father's lover, it is the artifice of Bechdel's attention to detail that accentuates the complex and productive relation between the remainders of her father's life and the range of their possible meaning in the present. Bechdel's memoir becomes like the house her father so lovingly restores: an affective repository that both reveals and conceals the past. The question isn't so much if these walls could talk but how these walls speak of the many possibilities of artifice as a route back toward the elusiveness of "what really happened."[24]

I want to attend to the complexity of the past and its loss in Bechdel's memoir by concentrating on her re-remembering of lesbian feminism and, by extension, women's liberation, for it is in the promise of her archival method as a way to look back at the movement that I am most interested here. Although a number of the memoir's critics have discussed the literary references and allusions that illuminate and complexify the story Bechdel tells, very few, with the exception of Ann Cvetkovich, have paid much attention to the book's equally "dense proliferation of lesbian and feminist texts." Indeed, for Cvetkovich, "one of Fun Home's charms is that it claims a relatively unapologetic relation to the lesbian feminist culture within which Alison came out."[25] It is charming because it is unexpected: the linkages Bechdel draws between her own burgeoning lesbian feminism and her father's queerness undercut, as Cvetkovich notes, the more settled and routine memories of second-wave feminism, and of lesbian feminism in particular, as a woman-identified or "matriarchal" movement. In addition, Bechdel's identifications with various styles of butchness in the text are not posited in an explicitly antagonistic relation to her growing political and sexual consciousness as a lesbian feminist; on the contrary, and perhaps because Bechdel tends to draw the convergences between her butchness and lesbian feminism rather than write them, they remain suggestively indeterminate in their meanings. For Cvetkovich, the surprising connections Bechdel makes between her father's queerness, her butchness, and her lesbian feminism exemplify the "temporal drag" of a "queer temporality" that "refuses narratives of progress."[26] And while I don't disagree with this conclusion, it too quickly passes over the details of the densely textured "network of transversals," to use another of Fun Home's Proustian phrases, that Bechdel detects as the productive indeterminacy of her past (102).

Most of the visual signifiers and literary references to lesbian feminism in Fun Home appear in the last chapter, "The Antihero's Journey." The chapter opens with a series of panels illustrating the bicentennial celebrations in New York City and ends with a drawing depicting "the tricky reverse narration" that would have her father posthumously catching a young Alison as she "leapt" into her own queer future (232). The mid-1970s sets both the scene for the linkages Bechdel makes between her own queerness and that of her father's and also provides her with the cultural artifacts—the objects of transfer—through which she forges those connections. Prevalent among these artifacts are the lesbian and gay books she draws either in neat stacks in her college dorm room or being discovered by a bookish young Alison in the library. Drawings of gay and lesbian texts had appeared earlier, in chapter three, when Bechdel first returns to the events that had affectively and effectively conjoined her coming out with her father's death. These earlier drawings act as a foreshadowing of the connections Bechdel will make in the last chapter, and they invoke lesbian feminism as integral, rather than marginal or incidental, to the story of intergenerational queerness she tells. Indeed, the atmosphere of a very gay 1970s— as depicted in the drawings of young men lounging and cruising in the shadows of the tall ships that mark the bicentennial celebrations—reverberate backward to these earlier references, connecting lesbian feminism to the sexual libertarianism of the city's gay male subculture of the 1970s in ways that make it, like the social world of the Village Alison wanders around in youthful wide-eyed wonderment, seem full of erotic possibility.

Books, as Bechdel illustrates throughout her memoir, were not only vital tools for understanding her parents and the atmosphere of her childhood, they were also the preferred conduit for expressions of intimacy and identification between an adolescent Alison and her father, as the panel of drawings showing the "novel" exchange of intimacy between Alison and her father in his high school English class reveal (199). Bechdel's reading of her father's manic, dazzling, and often frightening presence through F. Scott Fitzgerald's *The Great Gatsby*, for example, like her childhood confusions of the Addams family house's "dark, lofty ceilings, peeling wallpaper, and menacing horsehair furnishings" with her own home, draw out the complicated, intertwined connections between fact and fiction through which both her childhood and her father become readable (35). The books her parents read are the interpretive devices for Bechdel's speculations on their hidden desires and disappointments and for the elusive atmosphere of unsaid and unknown things that permeated her childhood. But books also operate as conduits of feeling, mediating projections and identifications between Bechdel and her father that open up for each of them, if in incommensurate ways, the social worlds and public fantasies through which they orientate themselves as desiring beings and social actors. In *Fun Home*, books are not, or not only, evidence of a common culture, they are also vehicles of exchange that enable a proliferation of queer and lesbian connections that echo across the illusory coherence of our distinctions between past and present, feminist and queer, gay and lesbian, private and public.

The stacks of lesbian and lesbian-feminist texts drawn by Bechdel include such classics as *Lesbian/Woman*, *The Well of Loneliness*, *Rubyfruit Jungle*, and *Desert of the Heart*, but it is Kate Millett's *Flying* that acts as a densely intertextual nodal point of queer exchange between Bechdel and her father. Bechdel draws Alison first discovering *Flying* in a local library on one of her last visits home from college before her father's death. The moment of discovery comes out of a desire to escape—from having to write a paper for her philosophy of art class but, more pressingly, from the unhappy atmosphere of her parents' collapsing marriage. The book's "eye-catching silver-and-hot-pink cover" (217) becomes a distraction from her mother's revelations about her father's turbulent "hidden" life—his affairs, the time he contracted body lice when out on his own on a trip to New York, "the shop-lifting, the speeding tickets, the lying, his rages" (216). In contrast to the shock of her mother's revelations, the "avalanche pace and shame-less name dropping" of *Flying* offered a much more public—eye-catching—declaration of queerness (218). And it is not hard to speculate how *Flying*'s stories of Millett's downtown bohemian life, her crazy feminist cohort, famous friends, sexual experimentation, and artistic milieu could become an alternative imaginary world for Bechdel, one far from the sadness of her parents' frustrated provincial life in Beech Creek, Pennsylvania. For a young Alison, Millett seemed to be "a latter-day Colette, with the libertine aristocrats exchanged for conceptual artists and radical feminists" (217). The memory of women's liberation here, then, offers us a different set of details—both personal and cultural—that link the movement to Colette's Paris of the 1920s and its cosmopolitan mixing of sexual and artistic experimentation. But more particularly, and within the context of Alison's near simultaneous discovery of the joys of cunnilingus and *Flying*, "radical feminism" also becomes a scenario of escape from the "sucking Charybdis of [her] family," with its pervasive atmosphere of sexual shame, to the liberating "Scylla of [her] peers," with its promise of a more open and public form of sexual and artistic expression (213). Through the particularity of Bechdel's memories of *Flying* as a mediating text for her own coming out as a lesbian, a different kind of affective history of lesbian feminism is produced—one that reminds us of the women's liberation movement's erotic possibilities and the sense of excitement and wonder that infused its sexual and social revolt.

But if *Flying* provides Bechdel with a fantasy scenario of lesbianism as an escape from family life into a "cult of friendship," to use Kate Millett's term for her sexual and social experimentations in the early 1970s, it also acts as a link backward—toward her father and the kind of queer life he had led.[27] The link is enacted in the form of a gift when Alison, "in an eloquent unconscious gesture" that mirrored "his own Trojan Horse gift of Colette," leaves *Flying* for her father to return to the library (224). Her father's frank admiration of Millett in a subsequent letter to Alison is apparent in his mimicking of Millett's writing style in *Flying* as well as his appreciation of her sexual (and literary?) courage: "I'm flying high on Kate Millett. Started reading it the day you left. It just pulls you in. God, what Guts" (224). The gift Bechdel offers her father here is a glimpse into an imagined future of sexual and artistic liberation that, as he poignantly recognizes in his letter, will be Alison's rather than his. In this memory, lovingly conjured up by Bechdel through her painstaking reproduction of her father's letter, *Flying* becomes a conduit for an exchange between Bechdel and her father about the lost possibilities and virtual potentiality of their "shared predilection" (222). Through the mediating text of *Flying*, the social world of feminist sexual and social experimentation Millett obsessively documents becomes the scene for her father's projections of what-if and Alison's identifications with her father's queerness, and as a result the rich social, sexual, and cultural potentiality of the movement is glimpsed as something virtual to its historicity and as productive of queer and lesbian futures still in the making, rather than as a set of known achievements—as something over and done with.

The lost and virtual possibilities for a shared queerness that the exchange of texts between father and daughter enacts, reverberates across the dense intertextuality of *Fun Home*. Millett's use of the Icarus myth in *Flying* as a metaphor for the sexual, psychic, and social risks of her feminist politics, ricochets through Bechdel's use of the same metaphor—via James Joyce's *Ulysses*—to illuminate her father's less public risk-taking, though equally dramatic, fall to earth, as well as her own leap into sexual difference. And indeed, Millett's struggles with her queerness and Bechdel's father's struggles with his are hauntingly evoked through the correspondences between their lives: their close proximity in age (Millett was born in 1934, Bruce Bechdel in 1936); their lower-middle-class, provincial Catholic upbringing; their manic depression; their creativity. Out of these correspondences—made available to us through the profusion of detail in Millett's *Flying* and Bechdel's *Fun Home*—other kinds of historical and intergenerational connection are made possible, ones that, in allowing us to imagine otherwise also, and just as importantly, illuminate the dense and contradictory social and cultural processes out of which queer and feminist lives are crafted as something contrary to the conventional and the normal. Simply put, Bechdel offers a different account and a different context for reading *Flying*, one that opens up the complexity of its historical moment to new affects in the present.

The memories of women's liberation crafted by Bechdel in *Fun Home* are partial in their detail. The subjectivity with which she returns to the 1960s and 1970s leaves us with little access to the tumultuous eventfulness of the civil rights and Black Power movements and their complex involvements in the women's and gay liberation movements. Similarly, the "shared predilection" she draws between her lesbianism and her father's queerness shapes a memory of their convergence that does little to disturb their whiteness. The productive proliferation of connections between texts, images, and personal memory in *Fun Home* provides us with a feminist and queer archive that is singular, and therefore limited, in its detail. But it is precisely this singularity of collected and arranged detail that allows us to make links between the accounts of lesbian feminism and a queerness it offers and those that belong to others. The work of the archivist as scholar, as distinct from the archivist as artist, is to continue to make those links and to remain attentive to the historical detail that will better enable us to be surprised by a feminist past that continues to infuse and shape the present. Being attentive to the detail of "what really happened" during the emergence of women's liberation will not result in a defining story of the movement, but it does provide an opening for an accountability toward the particularity of the production and consumption of different claims to the feminist past. It might also lead to the discovery of new image memories of the movement, new stories, and new lines of flight into a feminist future that, partly as a consequence of our discoveries, will look and feel very different from women's liberation. The allure of "what really happened," as Alison Bechdel illustrates so vividly in *Fun Home*, lies precisely in its capacity to draw us backward to a past that confounds and eludes us while simultaneously providing arresting images and found objects that can incite new concepts, new ways of life, and new narratives of explanation in the present. I would like to end on the paradox of remembering that Bechdel leaves us with: How can calling attention to the details of women's liberation's emergence, by following the shape of our image memories of the movement back to its beginnings, not only return us to the elusive complexity of the movement's eventfulness but make the feelings that fuel and transmit those memories seem a little less obvious, a little less inevitable or natural? Can we feel women's liberation differently?

NOTES

INTRODUCTION

Around 1970

1 Throughout *Feeling Women's Liberation*, the term *women's liberation* is deployed in two ways: to designate the historical specificity of the predominantly white, middle-class radical feminist movement of the late 1960s through the early 1970s and as an echo of the way in which it became the magical phrase through which the ideas and images of the women's movement and feminism were conjured in general during the late 1960s and early 1970s. I use *second wave* less as a descriptive term for the myriad feminist movements of the era, including the black and Chicana feminist movements that emerged at the same time as the women's liberation movement, than as a placeholder for a term that would better invoke the highly contested, diverse, and energetic explosion of feminisms during this time.

2 For an analysis of the increased media coverage of the women's movement from the late 1960s through 1970, see Howell, *Reflections of Ourselves*. A search on the *New York Times* database for articles with the term *women's liberation* found 3 articles in 1968, 23 in 1969, and 329 in 1970, with the figures for post-1970 tapering off from 288 in 1971 to 125 in 1974. Conversely, a search for articles with the term *feminists* peaked in 1974 with 147, compared to 58 in 1970 and less in the last two years of the 1960s. I think that the opposite trajectories of these two terms is indicative of the way in which the women's liberation movement became a singular media event of feminism in 1970.

3 See Brownmiller, *In Our Time*, 152, 136–66. See also Davis, *Moving the Mountain*, 106–20; Rosen, *The World Split Open*, 296–308.

4 See Davis, *Moving the Mountain*, 121–29.

5 The *New York Times* covered the ERA exhaustively throughout 1970 and had front-page coverage of the Strike for Equality. The zap action by the Lavender Menace and the sit-in at the *Ladies' Home Journal* also received extensive coverage by the *Times* and other national news venues—something I analyze in detail in chapter 1.

6 Echols ends chapter five of *Daring to Be Bad*, "The Eruption of Difference," with these words: "In some respects, the emergence of lesbian-feminism

edged the movement closer to cultural feminism. Its emphasis on a female counterculture and its essentialist arguments about female sexuality were quintessential cultural feminism. . . . In fact, cultural feminism's ascendance within the movement is in large measure attributable to the turmoil created by lesbianism and class" (241).

7 Ryan, *Feminism and the Women's Movement*, 49–51. See also Springer, *Living for the Revolution*, especially chapter four, "Black Women's Issues as Feminist Issues," 88–112; Roth, *Separate Roads to Feminism*, 12–14. Roth is less interested in tracking intramovement conflict over sexuality, but she does note the tensions over "heterosexism" in the early years of the Chicana, black, and white women's liberation movements.

8 Thanks to Robyn Wiegman for pointing out that *Sexual Politics* is often referred to as one of the first, if not the first, explicitly feminist dissertations to come out of the U.S. academy and certainly the first to be published to such widespread attention.

9 Marie-Claude Wrenn, "The Furious Young Philosopher Who Got It Down on Paper," *Life*, September 4, 1970, 22; "Who's Come A Long Way Baby?," *Time*, August 31, 1970, 4.

10 "Women's Lib: A Second Look," *Time*, December 14, 1970, 50. See also Martha Shelley, "Women's Liberation Media Star," *Come Out*, 1970–71, n.p., and quoted in Gever, *Entertaining Lesbians*, 83–84.

11 Sinfield, *The Wilde Century*, 125.

12 You can access a short documentary of the Town Hall event—*Town Bloody Hall*, by Chris Hedegus and D. A. Pennebaker (1979)—on YouTube. Like Millett, Jill Johnston was also a public figure around which media and movement discord over lesbianism circulated in the early 1970s. Unlike Millett, Johnston was not closely associated with women's liberation, and her eccentric approach to political speech and action made her a figure of suspicion for many feminist activists in the movement. Although Johnston did join the Gay Liberation Front and wrote the highly influential and idiosyncratic polemic on lesbian feminism *Lesbian Nation* (1973), she did not achieve the same iconic status as a feminist lesbian as Millett did in 1970. For more on Johnston as a famous lesbian in the early 1970s, see Gever, *Entertaining Lesbians*.

13 Judith Butler's *Gender Trouble*, first published in 1990, has become one of the markers for a discordant break between queer and feminist theory from the late 1980s on. See Butler's preface to the 1999 edition for her account of how the book was meant as a critique of the "pervasive heterosexual assumption in feminist literary theory" in the late 1980s and how it was met with hostility by some feminist theorists. Gayle Rubin's "Thinking Sex" is regarded as one of the first theoretical essays to make a clear distinction between the work of feminist theory and sexuality studies, what would become queer

theory. Rubin's essay and the rest of the *Pleasure and Danger* collection, of course, grew out of the notorious Barnard Conference of 1982 in which radical feminists and antipornography feminists clashed in public demonstrations outside the conference site and in hostile attacks in print. The Barnard Conference also figures as a precipitating event in the split between feminist and queer theory, which, as Lisa Duggan among others has noted, has had disciplinary effects within the academy. See Duggan, "The Discipline Problem." See also Scott, *Women's Studies on the Edge*, for discussion of some of the institutional and disciplinary histories that have effectively made women's studies distinct from, and quite often antagonistic toward, queer, ethnic, and postcolonial studies.

14 See for example, DuPlessis and Snitow, *The Feminist Memoir Project*; Rosen, *The World Split Open*; and Baxandall and Gordon, *Dear Sisters*.

15 Dinshaw, *Getting Medieval*. See also, Freeman, "Queer Temporalities"; Cvetkovich, *An Archive of Feelings*; Halberstam, *In a Queer Time and Place*; and Love, *Feeling Backward*.

16 Stoler, "Colonial Archives and the Arts of Governance," 92.

17 Ibid.

18 Ibid., 85.

19 Ibid., 86.

20 This is especially remarkable because Evans is careful to point out the power and authority of black women, such as Ruby Doris Smith Robinson, and their political influence on younger black and white women in SNCC. In Evans's account the example and leadership of the black women leaders in SNCC politicizes many of the young white women in the organization. In a sense, then, this politicization happens, and then the politicizers must disappear only to later reappear and become re-politicized (Evans, *Personal Politics*, 84).

21 Echols, *Daring to Be Bad*, 5.

22 Katie King defines the term *cohorts* as a group defined by their particular "generational and physiological investments in their local object" (*Theory in Its Feminist Travels*, 6). While I use the term in King's sense, I also apply it more generally to the different groups and collectivities constitutive of women's liberation.

23 Although Flora Davis, in *Moving the Mountain*, locates the beginnings of the movement in a variety of "origins," including political legislation in the early 1960s, the "first wave" of feminism from the late nineteenth and early twentieth centuries, and the civil rights movement, she falls into the same narrative trap as Evans and Echols. Dividing the book into three sections, Davis's history follows a now familiar trajectory: "Part One: the Second Wave Begins: Reinventing Feminism"; "Part Two: the Movement Divides and Multi-

plies"; "Part Three: Confronting the Political Realities." Her asides to the reader—"at least in retrospect, the second wave appears to have been just one, highly complex movement from the beginning" (70)—are an admission that telling the story of the movement from any one perspective inevitably leads to a misleading portrayal, and they stand as important qualifiers to the overall narrative thrust of her history. The abundance of detail Davis offers in her account of the movement, and the multiple reasons she gives for its rise to prominence, allows for the complexity of the movement's constituency and aims to come through, despite the constraints of her narrative structure.

24 DuPlessis and Snitow, *The Feminist Memoir Project*, 15.

25 Ibid., 3.

26 A comparison with Susan Brownmiller's memoir *In Our Time* might be useful here. Brownmiller was an active member of the movement from the late 1960s, and her involvement in actions, like the takeover of the *Ladies' Home Journal* offices and the rape speak-out at Columbia University in 1970, makes her account a compelling one. Yet, paradoxically, her refusal to admit the subjectivity of her memoir—that her account is necessarily partial and incomplete—compromises her claim that the memoir should be read as a history of the movement. Similarly, *The Feminist Memoir Project*, by the simple fact of who is included in the group of memoirists (or who wrote their piece in time for the publishing deadline), can only be a partial and incomplete account of the second-wave era of feminist movements.

27 Guy-Sheftall, "Sisters In Struggle," 490.

28 This phrase comes from Michel Foucault, *The History of Sexuality*, 11.

29 Rosen, *The World Split Open*, xiv.

30 See, for example, Scott, *Gender and the Politics of History*, for an acute diagnosis of the dual dangers of feminist history. Either you fall into the trap of naturalizing gender, leading to ahistorical assumptions about women's lives across time and space, or conversely, the category of "women" is subsumed into generalized forms of social or cultural history, such that the problems of female labor are those of the capitalist system and the particularity and contingency of female labor across time and space remains unaccounted for.

31 Davis, *Moving the Mountain*, 15–16.

32 Ibid., 366–67.

33 For example, Davis writes in her introduction, "this is an activist's history" (9).

34 Katie King, *Theory In Its Feminist Travels*, 124.

35 Ibid., 125.

36 This term comes from Millett, *Flying*, 14. I discuss *Flying* in more depth in chapter 4.

37 Brown, *Politics Out of History*, 140.

38 Ibid., 147.

39 See especially Tani Barlow's work on the event of women as a marker of modernity in her essay " 'What is a poem?' History and the Modern Girl." See also Pratt, "In The Event"; and Sewell, *Logics of History*, especially chapters seven and eight, "A Theory of the Event: Marshall Sahlin's 'Possible Theory of History' " and "Historical Events as Transformations of Structures," 197–270. Although Sewell's understanding of what constitutes a historical event tends to rely on the already established assumptions of what counts historically (state- and nation-based political actions and processes), his engagement with cultural anthropology helps him to define the event in terms of the problematics of change over time and the social and historical effects of that change for historians. See also Badiou, *Manifesto for Philosophy* and *Being and Event*.

40 Unlike the later reincarnation of the feminist-as-lesbian figure, during the early twentieth century the representative power of the lesbian was limited, especially in relation to feminism. As Laura Doan argues, knowledge of lesbianism was "never common" before the obscenity trial of *The Well of Loneliness* in England in 1928 (*Fashioning Sapphism*, xiv). And even after the trial, representations of lesbianism rarely referenced feminism (certainly not through the figure of Hall herself). See also Smith-Rosenberg, "Discourses of Sexuality and Subjectivity," for the (limited) representative power of the female invert within scientific and medical discourses on feminism in early twentieth-century American culture. See Cott, *The Grounding of Modern Feminism*, for an analysis of the emergence of feminism and its relation to changing conceptions of female sexuality in the United States in the early twentieth century.

41 Douglas, *Where the Girls Are*, 7; Zimmerman, "Confessions of a Lesbian Feminist," 163.

42 Zimmerman, "Confessions of a Lesbian Feminist," 163.

43 See Silver, *Virginia Woolf Icon*, for an argument about how the cultural iconicity of a famous figure is a product of border crossing between high and low, academic and popular, commercial and scholarly domains. Silver makes her argument in relation to Virginia Woolf and suggests that Woolf's symbolic transitivity since her death in 1941 is an effect of her ability to project and elide multiple meanings and affects of modernity. Woolf's iconicity is dependent, of course, on her fame and her transformation into a commodity, and for that reason her hypervisibility operates in a very different way from that of the feminist-as-lesbian: no one figure, including Kate Millett, became famous enough to transform the feminist-as-lesbian into an icon, and the style of feminist protest she invokes has yet to be translated

into a commodified form. Indeed, the feminist-as-lesbian's estrangement from commodification adds to her ghostliness in the contemporary moment.

44 Gordon, *Ghostly Matters*, 17.

45 For a fascinating discussion of the antagonisms and caricaturizations of feminism in some queer theory and in some feminist theory, see Wiegman, "Heteronormativity and the Desire for Gender," 91.

46 Foucault, "Nietzsche, Genealogy, History," 83–84.

47 This phrase is inspired by Maurice Halbwachs's *On Collective Memory*, and, in particular, his understanding of the way in which social thought is transmitted through figures, like the mother, who are at once both general and notional. See especially his chapter "The Collective Memory of the Family," 54–83.

48 In an interview with Paul Rabinow, Foucault argues that in the 1960s certain fields of human practice and experience, like madness and sexuality, became sites of political and social contestation that brought into question their intelligibility. As a consequence, different ways of thinking about these experiences, as well as different "acts and practices" constitutive of them, developed. See Foucault, "Polemics, Politics, and Problematizations," 113–19. See also Warner, "Styles of Intellectual Publics," for a helpful reading of Foucault's conception of "problematization." As Warner argues, problematization for Foucault does not simply mean "to complicate" or an "intellectual tangle" but "the practical horizon of intelligibility within which problems come to matter for people. It stands for both the conditions that make thinking possible and for the way thinking, under certain circumstances, can reflect back on its own conditions" (154).

49 This is Terry Castle's term for the impalpability of the lesbian in modern culture. I'm using it in Castle's sense but I'm also using it to make explicit the racialization of the de-realization of lesbianism Castle tracks through modern literature and film. See Castle, *The Appparitional Lesbian*, 28.

50 Jaggar, "Love and Knowledge," 151.

51 Berlant, *The Female Complaint*, viii–ix.

52 Here, I'm borrowing the phrase an "archive of feelings" from Cvetkovich, *An Archive of Feelings*.

53 One possible link between Butler's more psychoanalytic and linguistic notion of performativity and its delineation in social theory is with the French sociologist Pierre Bourdieu and his work on habitus. See Bourdieu, *Outline of a Theory of Practice*, for his extensive definition of habitus as the field of dispositions, practices, classificatory schemes, and feelings through which social actors reproduce the social (78–87). See also Bourdieu, *Practical Reason*, for a very helpful series of essays that cover the range of Bourdieu's the-

oretical and sociological enterprise. A more recent study of the ontology of race, and in particular of whiteness, is Saldhana's *Psychedelic White*. Other work on whiteness studies includes Frankenberg's *The Social Construction of Whiteness* and her edited volume *Displacing Whiteness*. See also Dyer, *White*, for an analysis of the production of whiteness as norm in mass culture.

54 This is Tani Barlow's term and is used by her to denote proper nouns or neologisms that, in their contingent particularity, provide access to the heterogeneity of their historical moment (*The Question of Women in Chinese Feminism*, 15).

55 See, for example, Zerilli, *Feminism and the Abyss of Freedom*, whose return to the writings of Monique Wittig and the Italian Feminist group Libreria delle Donne di Milano, among others, in order to argue for an understanding of feminist theoretical work as a political practice that inaugurates "figures of the newly thinkable," has influenced my thinking about how to return to women's liberation. See also Enke, *Finding the Movement*; Hemmings, *Why Stories Matter*; Distelberg, "Mainstream Fiction, Gay Reviewers, and Gay Male Cultural Politics in the 1970s"; and Ross, *May '68 and Its Afterlives*.

56 Ahmed, *The Cultural Politics of Emotion*, 5. There has been a relative explosion of feminist, queer, and cultural studies work on affect and emotion in the last ten years. Jasbir Puar offers a very neat summary of the two main orientations of this work: the "technoscience criticism" of, for example, Brian Massumi, Michael Hardt and Antonio Negri, and Patricia Ticineto Clough; and the "queer theory on emotions and tactile knowings" work of theorists like Sara Ahmed, Eve Sedgwick, and Ann Cvetkovich. The former orientation has a more philosophical genealogy, from Deleuze and Guattari through Henri Bergson to Baruch Spinoza, while the queer theory orientation utilizes conceptual paradigms from the cultural studies work of Raymond Williams and psychoanalysis. Of course, such neat distinctions, as Puar also notes, do not account for the productive intermingling of both orientations in the work of feminist theorists like Elizabeth Wilson and Lauren Berlant. The divergence between the technoscience critics and the queer emotionalists, to coin a phrase just for this comparison, centers on the definition of affect as autonomous from emotion and the semiotic or semantic. Brian Massumi has offered one of the most emphatic arguments for "the autonomy of affect," drawing upon neuropsychological and biopsychological studies on the physiological and biological production of sensation to claim an ontological status for affect independent of cognition. Emotions, in contrast, are the codified and conventionalized forms of captured affects. We can recognize and read emotions precisely because they are always already culturally specific forms of feeling. For Massumi and other technoscience critics, the importance of maintaining a distinction between affect and emo-

tion is both analytic and political. Analytically, it opens up what Massumi calls "the middle terms" of the "body—(movement/sensation)—change" relationship that organizes much of the theoretical preoccupations of feminist and cultural theory. Politically, it opens up the question of the potentiality and possibility for social change by drawing attention to what is virtual to the social rather than what has been. See Massumi, *Parables for the Virtual*, 1, 88–89. See also Puar, *Terrorist Assemblages*, 207, 206–11; Clough, *The Affective Turn*; Hardt and Negri, *Empire*.

Sara Ahmed offers her own genealogy for scholarship on emotion and affect, arguing that most of it can be separated into two broadly conceived models. The "inside out" model derives from psychological conceptions of subjective interiority, while the "outside in" model derives from anthropological and sociological conceptions of the emotions as "social and cultural practices" (*The Cultural Politics of Emotion*, 9). Although Ahmed agrees with the sociologists—that the emotions are "social and cultural practices"—she argues that both models often assume a separation or distinction between inside and outside (that the subject is conceptually distinct from the social) that is misleading in terms of what emotions "do." See also Rosaldo, "Toward an Anthropology of Self and Feeling," for a similar reading of emotions as social processes. Rosaldo's anthropological approach does not necessarily deviate from psychological understandings of affect as biological sensations. But she would argue with the (psychological) notion that affect originates in the body and then becomes social through cultural interpretation. She, like Ahmed, argues against the dichotomous separation between biology/natural and social/manufactured that this formulation assumes. Ahmed's and Rosaldo's positions are not dissimilar to Sylvan Tomkins's understanding of the difference between affect and emotion, as Sedgwick and Frank present in *Shame and Its Sisters* and Sedgwick discusses in *Touching Feeling*. While, for Tomkins, there are "innate activators of affect" that are universal (interest, startle, fear, anger, distress, joy, laughter), those affects do not have specific "objects" (Sedgwick, *Touching Feeling*, 99). For Tomkins, as Sedgwick repeatedly asserts, "any affect may have any object," and this lack of (pre)determination "is the basic source of complexity of human motivation and behavior" (ibid.). Here, the difference between the queer emotionalists and the technoscience critics lies not so much in their understanding of the distinction, or not, of affect from emotion than in their respective fields of analysis. For Massumi and Hardt and Negri, for example, their field is the social, at its most broadly conceived and abstract. For scholars like Sedgwick and Ahmed, the field is the cultural, at its most textual and discursive. In *Feeling Women's Liberation* my main objects of analysis are textual, and my reading of them as artifacts of the rhetorical invention of a political movement means that the emphasis will be on how they register and circulate emotion rather than affect. However, I also want to maintain the necessity of the distinction between affect and emotion, if only to signal when and where rhetorical objects and figures are productive of affects not yet captured by emotion.

57 Ahmed, *The Cultural Politics of Emotion*, 44.

58 Gross, *The Secret History of Emotion*, 61.

59 Ibid., 171.

60 Baxandall and Gordon, *Dear Sisters*, 1.

61 Halbwachs, *On Collective Memory*, 189.

62 Ibid., 53.

63 Ibid., 61.

64 Huyssen, "Present Pasts," 28.

65 Berlant, *The Female Complaint*, x.

66 Ibid., 10.

67 I will use the term *image memory* interchangeably with shorthand notation in order to suggest that the figure is also *a sight*. I also want the term to act as an echo of Walter Benjamin's notion of "imagistic memories" ("Theses on the Philosophy of History") that, in Wendy Brown's words, "survive into the present and through their creation, also resist the present" in that they interrupt historical narratives of progress rather than confirm them (*Politics Out of History*, 157).

68 Cornell, "Rethinking the Time of Feminism," 148.

ONE

Lady Protestors to Urban Guerrillas

1 "Women's Lib: A Second Look," *Time*, December 14, 1970, 50.

2 Millett, *Sexual Politics*, 31. Millett posits patriarchy as the central organizing structure of society, defining it as a "political institution" that is a "social constant" running "through all other political, social, and economic forms" (31). I discuss *Sexual Politics* in more depth in chapter 3.

3 See Millett, *Flying*, 15; Brownmiller, *In Our Time*, 150. I will discuss what Millett actually said and circumstances of her declaration in more detail at the end of the chapter.

4 "Women's Lib," 50.

5 See Irving Howe, "The Middle-Class Mind of Kate Millett," *Harper's*, December 1970, 110–29.

6 "Women's Lib," 50.

7 Ibid.

8 Helen Lawrenson's "The Feminine Mistake," *Esquire*, January 1971, 83, 146–47, 153–54, is another damning article on women's liberation.

9 "Women's Lib," 50.

10 The excessiveness of the response to Millett and *Sexual Politics* was also noted at the time by some commentators. See Phyllis Jacobson, "Kate Millett and Her Critics," *New Politics* (Fall 1970), http://newpolitics.mayfirst .org/node/294.

11 Eve Sedgwick's analysis of the productive force of silence in discourses of sexuality is articulated through her readings of texts from the late nineteenth century and early twentieth century. Although I am arguing here that some of the silences prevalent in the early twentieth century are no longer intelligible in the mid- to late twentieth century, I am not arguing that there are no silences in our contemporary and near contemporary discourses on sexuality. One of my questions in this chapter is why the silences of the early twentieth century—mostly articulated through notions of female asexuality and middle-class propriety—were no longer able to contain the relation of lesbianism to feminism in the mid-century. See Sedgwick, *Epistemology of the Closet*, 4–5.

12 Echols, *Daring to Be Bad*, 94.

13 See, for example, "The Liberation of Kate Millett," *Time*, August 31, 1970, 19; and Marie-Claude Wrenn, "The Furious Young Philosopher Who Got It Down on Paper," *Life*, September 4, 1970, 22. I discuss these portraits in detail in chapter 4.

14 Berger, *Ways of Seeing*, 46.

15 Ahmed, *The Cultural Politics of Emotion*, 44.

16 Ibid., 45.

17 Huyssen is quick to make clear that all memories, personal and collective, are in a sense, "imagined." Memory works retrospectively and through representation. We cannot retrieve past events in their entirety; instead, memory articulates a relation to the past through a representation (creative and partial) of what happened. Huyssen is using the term *imagined* to highlight the mediated nature of cultural memories produced through the mass media, which have no root in the social experiences of particular groups even though they might refer to those experiences. See Huyssen, *Present Pasts*, 17.

18 Warner, *Publics and Counterpublics*, 89.

19 See Berlant, "The Subject of True Feeling," and *The Queen of America*, for a reworking of the concept of the national public sphere in relation to postwar notions of American citizenship. For Berlant, the imagined community of the "U.S. present-tense" is produced through privatized notions of citizenship that situate national belonging in terms of "personal acts and values, especially acts originating in or directed toward the family sphere" (*The Queen of America*, 5). The nationness of postwar U.S. culture, in other words, is

imagined through a "we," rendered in individualist and ahistorical terms, that negates the histories of social and political struggle.

20 Anderson, *Spectres of Comparison*, 57. See also Anderson, *Imagined Communities*.

21 Gitlin, *The Whole World Is Watching*, 3.

22 Habermas, *Structural Transformation in the Public Sphere*, 40.

23 McCarthy, introduction to *The Structural Transformation of the Public Sphere*, xii.

24 Here my argument draws upon work by feminist media scholars who have questioned Gitlin's understanding of the mass media's relationship to the New Left as a dichotomous confrontation between opposing interests. For example, Bernadette Barker-Plummer argues in her analysis of second-wave media strategies that "social movements are social constructions that are created and maintained through communication practices across time." That is, social movements are formed through the complex interaction of political cohorts and groups with the media rather than simply "framed" by them. Where my argument differs from much of the feminist media studies scholarship is in my focus on the ways in which this interaction between feminist groups and the mass media is also the site for the production of image memories of feminism that exceed the "rational" discourse through which feminism is translated and communicated by the media. My interest is less on the relative political effectiveness of movement strategies toward the media and more on the potentiality of the affective productivity of their interaction. See Barker-Plummer, "News as a Political Resource," 309. See also Ashley and Olson, "Constructing Reality"; Bradley, *Mass Media and the Shaping of American Feminism*; and Van Zoonen, "The Women's Movement and the Media." A more recent analysis of the "media imaging" of feminism from women's liberation to the contemporary era can be found in Hinds and Stacey, "Imaging Feminism, Imaging Femininity." Although Hinds and Stacey's study concentrates on the British press, their analysis of "the uneven and multiple significations of media imaging of feminism" (155) from 1968 to 2000 closely resembles my approach to the print media's coverage of women's liberation in the United States. Where our projects differ is in my focus on the emergence of women's liberation as an event that the media initially struggled to find a coherent response to. Hinds and Stacey, in contrast, are more interested in tracking the uneven and multiple media constructions of feminist figures over time. In other words, Hinds and Stacey are interested in patterns and preoccupations in the media coverage of feminism over a relatively long period of time, while I am interested in the explosive moment when new patterns and preoccupations were in the process of being figured out.

25 See Miller, *Democracy Is in the Streets*, 330. The Port Huron Statement is quoted in full as an appendix, 329–74.

26 This is John Durham Peters's definition of the mass media in "Seeing Bifocally," 77.

27 The Port Huron Statement, as quoted in Miller, *Democracy Is in the Streets*, 329.

28 *The movement* was an umbrella term used in the late 1960s to refer to the interrelated student, antiwar, civil rights, and emerging Black Power and women's liberation movements. The term is also evidence of an imagining that could incorporate discrete social groups and interests into a collectivity defined by "unseeable totalities," like the threat of nuclear war or structural racism.

29 DeKoven, *Utopia Limited*, 130.

30 The Port Huron Statement, as quoted in Miller, *Democracy Is in the Streets*, 329.

31 Warner, *Publics and Counterpublics*, 75.

32 Joseph, *Waiting 'Til the Midnight Hour*.

33 This dynamic echoes an earlier one between black and women's suffrage in the nineteenth century, as Davis herself argues in *Women, Race, and Class*.

34 See Brownmiller, *In Our Time*, 152, 136–66. See also Davis, *Moving the Mountain*, 106–20; and Rosen, *The World Split Open*, 296–308.

35 See Davis, *Moving the Mountain*, 121–29.

36 The *New York Times* covered the ERA exhaustively throughout 1970, something I will analyze later in this chapter.

37 "The Liberation of Kate Millett," *Time*, August 31, 1970. The August article was one of a few that profiled Millett in the summer of 1970 as a leader and "master" theorist of the women's movement, albeit in a slightly mocking and condescending tone.

38 The *New York Times* is the most comprehensively indexed newspaper and, therefore, more readily available for survey reviews of news trends—another reason for my focus on the paper. My sample of the *New York Times*'s coverage of the movement includes articles from all sections of the newspaper that appeared between January 1 and December 31, 1970. My search terms, initially through Lexis-Nexis and then through the *New York Times*'s own digital archives, were *women's liberation, women's liberationists, radical feminism,* and *radical feminists,* and I looked at more than 180 articles in total, not counting those from other sources. Although I will not be looking at television coverage of the movement, Susan Douglas offers an introductory discussion on the subject. Her account of the television coverage of the movement corresponds with my analysis of the *New York Times*'s coverage. Both formats utilized the tropes of middle-class femininity and respectabil-

ity to situate movement women as "outsiders" and irrational fanatics. See Douglas, *Where the Girls Are*, 139–61. See also Spigel and Curtin, *The Revolution Wasn't Televised*, for essays on television as a medium for both representing and incorporating the ideas of the new social movements in the 1960s.

39 Gitlin, *The Whole World Is Watching*, 299. Due to the subsequent diversification of news sources through the emergence of new media technologies, the paper's role as a national barometer for newsworthy events and developments, although still significant, is less prominent today than it was in 1970.

40 In his appendix on sources and methods, Gitlin discusses the way in which the *New York Times* plays an important part, through the reporting of leads and leaks, in the way the U.S. government communicates its policies and actions. He goes on to state that the *New York Times* "sets agendas, generating and certifying issues in government, business, intellectuals, professional, and academic circles throughout the country" (*The Whole World Is Watching*, 299).

41 Gornick quoted in Brownmiller, *In Our Time*, 138.

42 Howell, *Reflections of Ourselves*, 42.

43 The Women's Strike for Equality on August 26, 1970, was front-page news in the *New York Times*. *Newsweek*, *Time*, and *Life* also had cover stories on the movement in 1970.

44 "Carswell Called Foe of Women's Rights," *New York Times*, January 30, 1970, 20.

45 In their article on the print media's framing of the movement, Laura Ashley and Beth Olson note that a primary "delegitimizing" technique was to put quotation marks around the words used by the feminists themselves. See Ashley and Olson, "Constructing Reality," 263.

46 Ibid.

47 However, Ervin's tactic backfired when he called on Leo Kanowitz, a law professor at the University of New Mexico, who then informed the committee that he had "changed his mind" and was now in favor of the amendment. See Eileen Shanahan, "Equal Rights: Who Is against It and Why?," *New York Times*, September 13, 1970, 6.

48 Ibid.

49 Ibid.

50 See Rosen, *The World Split Open*, for an extensive account of the founding of NOW and the organization's criticisms of the EEOC. NOW's founding members included union representatives as well as former EEOC commissioners like Aileen Hernandez. In its first statement of purpose NOW made the argument for equality between the sexes on the basis that the United States should provide social welfare, like child care and pregnancy leave, that

would support women at work and home. Women, the statement goes on to assert, "should not have to choose between family life and participation in industry or the professions" (NOW "Statement of Purpose," as quoted in Rosen, *The World Split Open*, 79).

51 See Meyerowitz, *Not June Cleaver*. Meyerowitz challenges the dominance of the Cold War domestic ideology paradigm for understanding women's experiences in the postwar years, and she makes the argument that in the 1950s there were various constituencies of women who not only lived in a way that was very different from the domestic ideal but actively campaigned for social change. The essays in the book demonstrate this argument through their focus on working-class, immigrant, and minority women's political activities and social experiences.

52 Chafe, *The American Woman*, and as quoted in Rosen, *The World Split Open*, 19.

53 See, for example, Richard D. Lyons, "Women Forcing Colleges to Give Job Data to U.S.," *New York Times*, November 8, 1970, 1, 64; "Women Lawyers Cite Obstacles," *New York Times*, December 9, 1970, 65; Marilyn Bender, "Women's Lib Bearish in Wall St.," *New York Times*, October 11, 1970, 147.

54 Robert Sherrill, "That Equal-Rights Amendment—What Does It Mean?" *New York Times Magazine*, September 20, 1970, 26.

55 Ibid., 100.

56 Ibid., 26.

57 Ibid., 98, 101.

58 A subsequent editorial in the paper described the feminist protests in Congress during the ERA hearing as henpecking. See "The Henpecked House," *New York Times*, August 12, 1970, 40.

59 Ibid., 173, 175.

60 It is this figure, of course, that Betty Friedan attempts to demythologize in *The Feminine Mystique* and that Elaine Tyler May analyzes in *Homeward Bound: American Families in the Cold War Era*. Joanne Meyerowitz, in her introduction to *Not June Cleaver*, challenges both Friedan's and May's tendency to equate the ideology of domesticity with the realities of women's lives in postwar America. Meyerowitz's complicating of the political and social landscape of the 1950s, and her displacing of the domestic ideal from the forefront of historical studies of this period, suggests, rightly, that the representations of women during the postwar decades were both inadequate and erroneous in their uniform depiction of women. Yet, it is worth noting that Friedan, long a labor activist before she wrote *The Feminine Mystique*, was no doubt well aware of the diversity of American women's lives, and her decision to write about middle-class white women and the domestic ideal was probably not simply a capitulation to the ideology she was attempting to challenge but more a recognition that the space for political and social re-

sistance was as much in the realm of the spectacle of a society, transformed by the mass media and especially television, as it was in, for example, union organizing. While it is necessary today to complicate the history of women in the postwar decades, it is also necessary to note that the manner in which political communities were imagined changed in the postwar decades, and this change, in turn, produced different tactics and strategies of resistance.

61 Numerous profiles of Angela Davis, along with daily news updates on her fugitive status, appeared in the mainstream press in 1970. The profiles and news reports on Davis usually began by describing her as a "young, black militant" and included a drawing or picture featuring what became iconic images of Davis with an Afro and sunglasses. See for example, Steven V. Roberts, "Angela Davis: The Making Of a Radical," *New York Times*, August 23, 1970, E5; Steven V. Roberts, "Angela Davis: Flight but Not Fight Is Over," *New York Times*, October 18, 1970, E6. See also, "Angela Davis: Black Revolutionary," *Newsweek*, December 1970.

62 Alice Echols argues that the term *women's liberation* was used as early as 1967 by women in SDS and was favored over *feminism* or *women's rights* because it participated in the leftist vernacular of the New Left, refused a middle-class, bourgeois idea of feminism, and also linked the movement to national liberation movements in colonized countries. See Echols, *Daring to Be Bad*, 53.

63 Carl Davidson quoted in Echols, *Daring to Be Bad*, 40–41.

64 See Rothberg, *Multidirectional Memory*. Rothberg's understanding of collective memory as "multidirectional" is especially helpful here in tracking the ways in which the new social movements of the 1960s engaged in a practice of "cross-referencing" and "borrowing" of other memories and historical events in the production of a distinct political identity (11). Through such borrowings a term like *guerrilla* travels in the 1960s—from its historical origins in the Napoleonic Wars and contemporary national liberation struggles in South America and Africa, to the student and Black Power protest movements in the United States and Europe—and in the process it conjures up various historical events and crises, connecting the seemingly unconnected wars of nineteenth-century Europe and the American revolutionary and civil wars of the eighteenth and nineteenth centuries with the protest movements and liberation struggles of the 1960s.

65 "The Henpecked House," *New York Times*, August 12, 1970, 40.

66 Rosen, *The World Split Open*, 92.

67 See Davis, *Moving the Mountain*, 116; and Rosen, *The World Split Open*, 93. According to both Davis and Rosen, depending on the source (organizers, media, or police) anywhere from ten to over fifty thousand women marched in New York alone. While in Chicago it was reported that approximately five thousand people turned up for a rally on the day.

68 Rosen, *The World Split Open*, 93.

69 "The Liberated Woman," *New York Times*, August 27, 1970, 34.

70 Ibid.

71 Grace Lichtenstein, "Feminists Demand 'Liberation' in *Ladies' Home Journal* Sit-In," *New York Times*, March 19, 1970, 5.

72 See Brownmiller, *In Our Time*, 36–37.

73 Diedre Carmody, "General Strike by U.S. Women Urged to Mark 19th Amendment," *New York Times*, March 21, 1970, 21.

74 In Robert Sherrill's article on the ERA battle in Congress, Shirley Chisholm, among others, is quoted as saying that the ERA's benefits would be "social and psychological" rather than "economic." In other words, it is in the realm of everyday social life and the cultural imaginary that the ERA would most benefit women, due to the fact that it would enable them to think and act beyond the conventions and expectations of traditional femininity. Sherrill, "That Equal-Rights Amendment—What Does It Mean?," 27.

75 The definition of *apprehension* in the *Oxford English Dictionary* includes the "act of seizing upon," "grasping," and "arresting" an image or object; "laying hold of the senses" through "conscious perception"; and "the representation to oneself of what is still future"; "anticipation" as well as "fear as to what may happen; dread."

76 "Leading Feminist Puts Hairdo before Strike," *New York Times*, August 27, 1970, 30.

77 Grace Lichtenstein, "For Most Women, 'Strike' Day Was Just a Topic of Conversation," *New York Times*, August 27, 1970, 30.

78 Linda Charlton, "Women March Down Fifth in Equality Drive," *New York Times*, August 27, 1970, 1, 30.

79 Judy Klemesrud, "It Was a Great Day for Women on the March," *New York Times*, section 4, August 30, 1970, 4.

80 "Reds' Pamphlets Discuss Feminists," *New York Times*, May 10, 1970, 62.

81 Paul Delany, "Panthers Weigh New Constitution," *New York Times*, September 7, 1970, 13; Paul Delany, "Panthers Reconvene in Capital to Ratify Their Constitution," *New York Times*, September 8, 1970, 57.

82 Will Lessner, "New Left Groups in Session Here," *New York Times*, July 19, 1970, 33. There were a number of conferences and meetings organized across the movement in 1970 that were attempts to shore up faltering coalitions between white radical groups and the Black Power movement. Gay liberation and women's liberation also participated in these meetings, although they were effectively marginalized by the male leadership of the New Left and Black Power movement. Full of a heterosexist macho posturing though they may have been, these meetings were also remarkable for their attempt to imagine a movement that could incorporate the diverse agendas of people of

color revolutionary nationalism, anticolonial liberation, and gay and women's liberation. See Echols, *Daring to Be Bad*, 222–24; and Joseph, *Waiting 'til the Midnight Hour*, 252–54.

83 Charlayne Hunter, "Many Blacks Wary of 'Women's Liberation' Movement in U.S.," *New York Times*, November 17, 1970, 17, 47.

84 Helen H. King, "The Black Woman and Women's Lib.," *Ebony*, March 1971.

85 Linda Charlton, "The Feminine Protest," *New York Times*, August 28, 1970, 20.

86 Helen Dudar, "Special Report: 'Women's Lib: The War on Sexism,'" *Newsweek*, March 23, 1970; Ruth Mehrtens Galvin et al., "Who's Come a Long Way Baby?," *Time*, August 31, 1970; Sophy Burnham, "Women's Lib: The Idea You Can't Ignore," *Redbook*, September 1970; "Women's Liberation, Women's Liberation Issue," *Ladies' Home Journal*, August 1970.

87 Marilyn Bender, "The Women Who'd Trade in Their Pedestal for Equality," *New York Times*, February, 4, 1970, 30; Susan Brownmiller, "'Sisterhood Is Powerful': A Member of the Women's Liberation Movement Explains What It's All About," *New York Times Magazine*, March 15, 1970.

88 Enid Nemy, "Centenarian Recalls Suffragette Days," *New York Times*, May 18, 1970, 36; Marilyn Bender, "Liberation Yesterday—The Roots of the Feminist Movement," *New York Times*, August 21, 1970, 29.

89 "Julie Eisenhower Calls Feminists Too Strident," *New York Times*, April 12, 1970, 78; Joan Cook, "She Takes a Stand against Liberation," *New York Times*, September 28, 1970, 50.

90 Douglas, *Where the Girls Are*, 7.

91 Bender, "The Women Who'd Trade in Their Pedestal for Equality," *New York Times*, February, 4, 1970, 30.

92 Ibid.

93 Brownmiller, "'Sisterhood Is Powerful,'" 130.

94 Paul Wilkes, "Mother Superior to Women's Liberation," *New York Times Magazine*, November 29, 1970.

95 For a rich discussion of Foucault's notion of biopower in relation to the cultural and social production of gendered bourgeois identities through technologies of sex and discourses of race, see Stoler, *Race and the Education of Desire*, 8.

96 Sharon Howell in *Reflections of Ourselves* observes that discussions about gender, and the woman's role in particular, changed markedly in the 1960s. Heavily influenced by the civil rights movement, the discourse about gender relations shifted from one that deployed predominantly biological metaphors to one that was explicitly sociological and political (52–58). Works like Erving Goffman's *Stigma: Notes on the Management of Spoiled Identity* (1963) and Mary McIntosh's "The Homosexual Role" (1968), for example,

understood identity as a social and cultural process that situated people in relation to each other, rather than as a mark of authentic beingness. See DeKoven's *Utopia Limited* for an expansive analysis of the epistemic shift from modern to postmodern thought in the 1960s. DeKoven argues that while the 1960s marked the emergence of postmodern philosophical and political discourses, those discourses emerged not as a break from modernist ones but in an uneasy, imbricative, relation to them.

97 Lionel Tiger, "Male Dominance? Yes, Alas. A Sexist Plot? No," *New York Times Magazine*, October 25, 1970, 136.

98 Morton Hunt, "Up against the Wall, Male Chauvinist Pig!," *Playboy*, May 1970.

99 Ibid., 207.

100 Ibid., 95–96.

101 Ibid., 96.

102 Ibid., 206.

103 Susan L. Peck, "Letters," *New York Times Magazine*, March 29, 1970, 6.

104 Jean Stafford, "Topics: Women as Chattels, Men as Chumps," *New York Times*, May 9, 1970, 24.

105 Judy Klemesrud, "The Lesbian Issue and Women's Lib," *New York Times*, December 18, 1970, 47.

106 See Penn, "The Sexualized Woman"; and Freedman, "'Uncontrolled Desires.'" As Penn and Freedman reveal, by the 1960s there was a near "national hysteria concerning the perceived epidemic of sexual psychopathology" (Penn, "The Sexualized Woman," 364). Part of that near hysteria included lurid and sensationalistic accounts of lesbian underworlds by pulp fiction writers and journalists, and popular "scientific" accounts of female homosexuality that emphasized the subterranean deviancy of lesbian desire.

107 A number of feature articles on homosexual subcultures appeared in news magazines during the 1960s. See D'Emilio, *Sexual Politics, Sexual Communities*, 138 (especially footnote 24). One of the more popular exposés of lesbian subcultures was Jess Stearn's *The Grapevine*, which appeared in 1964. Frank Caprio's *Female Homosexuality: A Psychodynamic Study of Lesbianism* is perhaps the most well-known and popular psychological study of lesbianism from that era. Although originally published in the 1950s, it was reprinted throughout the 1960s. See also Klaich, *Woman + Woman*. Klaich described Caprio's study as "widely read and widely quoted" (98).

108 In her analysis of the "sexualized woman" in postwar America, Donna Penn situates the lesbian as the site of a concerted effort by medical and cultural authorities to "contain" female sexuality by making her, like the prostitute, a sexual outlaw. The lesbian, according to Penn, was a prominent part of the "politics of contamination" that animated the discourses of sexuality

through which the postwar, bourgeois self was constructed by popular and institutional discourses. Conjured in relation to a gallery of social outcasts who threatened to intrude upon the inviolable middle-class body, the postwar lesbian's sexuality manifested itself as uncontrolled appetite. Her dangerousness lay in her seductive desire for "innocent" women who would, normally, be the recipients of male attention and desire. While the portrait of the lesbian as sexual predator was an attempt on the part of medical and cultural authorities to fortify the borders surrounding "normal" female sexuality, it also revealed the centrality of sexuality and desire to lesbian subcultures, as Penn asserts. See Penn, "The Sexualized Woman," 361–63.

109 Radner and Luckett, *Swinging Single*, 2.

110 This is something Radner makes clear in her introduction (*Swinging Single*, 3). Moreover, she links the new sexualities of the 1960s to a consumer industry that, in its promotion of self-improvement "goods," depended upon and therefore actively promoted the gender divide. Helen Gurley Brown was the editor of *Cosmopolitan* and, therefore, at the wheel of an advertising machine expressly devoted to the promotion of the gender divide.

111 Radner and Luckett, *Swinging Single*, 2.

112 Stearn, *The Grapevine*, 2–5 (emphasis added).

113 Caprio, *Female Homosexuality*, 7.

114 Ibid., 132.

115 In the early years of the homophile movement, activists were more concerned with gaining respectability, which meant minimizing the differences between heterosexuals and homosexuals. In the 1960s, with leaders like Barbara Gittings in Daughters of Bilitis and Frank Kameny in the Mattachine Society, an increasingly radical activism came to the fore and was intent on claiming the right to be homosexual, as well as the right to express homosexuality publicly. See D'Emilio, *Sexual Politics, Sexual Communities*, 223–39.

116 The Buffalo community charted by Davis and Kennedy was predominantly working class, and although white and black lesbians lived largely segregated lives, there was a limited amount of interracial dating and socializing. See also Leslie Feinberg's fictionalized account of the Buffalo community in *Stone Butch Blues*, and for an account of the lesbian bar scene in New York in the 1950s, see Audre Lorde's *Zami: A New Spelling of My Name*.

117 Millett, *Flying*, 15.

TWO
"Goodbye to All That"

1 Abbott and Love, *Sappho Was a Right-On Woman*, 114.

2 Radicalesbians, "The Woman Identified Woman," 240.

3 See Echols, *Daring to Be Bad*, 214. See also Ann Snitow as quoted in Echols, *Daring to Be Bad*, 219.

4 Ibid., 215.

5 Rosen, *The World Split Open*, 168.

6 Abbott and Love, *Sappho Was a Right-On Woman*, 132. In particular, Abbott and Love understand Millett's outing by *Time* as a moment when many within the movement were forced to confront their own prejudices toward lesbianism: here was a respected and nationally recognized "leader" of the movement suddenly being transformed before their eyes into a sexual and social outcast.

7 Brownmiller, *In Our Time*, 136–66; Echols, *Daring to Be Bad*, 241; Jay, *The Lavender Menace*, 145; Rosen, *The World Split Open*, especially chapter five, "The Hidden Injuries of Sex," 143–95; Ryan, *Feminism and the Women's Movement*, 49–51. Like Abbott and Love, Karla Jay's memories are those of someone who participated in the events she describes. As a member of the Lavender Menace and longtime activist in gay and lesbian and feminist groups, it is not surprising that Jay's memory of the zap action at the Second Congress to Unite Women would be that it was a signature event. However, Susan Brownmiller, like Ruth Rosen and Alice Echols, was neither a participant nor a member of the audience at the zap action (though she was an active participant in women's liberation at the time), but she also locates the events of 1970 as key in the history of women's liberation. For Brownmiller, their significance lies more in the role the press played in the movement's development rather than in the strategic and ideological importance of lesbianism to feminism. Part of my argument in this chapter is that you cannot separate the two: the role of the media in the movement's self-presentation was intrinsic to the growing significance of lesbianism within the movement.

8 See Echols, *Daring to Be Bad*, 203–42; Jay, *The Lavender Menace*, 137–46.

9 See Abbott and Love, *Sappho Was a Right-On Woman*, 125–30; Davis, *Moving the Mountain*, 262–63.

10 Abbott and Love, *Sappho Was a Right-On Woman*, 131. In her account of the rise of black feminist organizations in the late 1960s, Kimberly Springer makes the point that, although there was tension around lesbian membership within black feminist organizations, it did not tend to result in the expulsion of lesbian members, nor did it erupt into the counterpublic sphere of black feminism in the way that it did for the predominantly white women's liberation movement. One exception to this, according to Springer, was the Third World Women's Alliance's West Coast chapter, which did force out a number of lesbian members in the early 1970s. See Springer, *Living for the Revolution*, 131–33.

11 Radicalesbians, "The Woman Identified Woman," *Berkeley Tribe*, November

6, 1970, 5; and unidentified authors, "Gay Sisters Demand," *Berkeley Tribe,*
November 13, 1970, 7.

12 Breines, "What's Love Got to Do with It?," 1103.

13 See the Redstockings, "Manifesto." It reads: "We identify the agents of our oppression as men. Male supremacy is the oldest, most basic form of domination. All other forms of exploitation and oppression (racism, capitalism,
imperialism, etc.) are extensions of male supremacy: men dominate women,
a few men dominate the rest." The Chicago Women's Liberation group had issued their manifesto in 1968 in "Toward a Radical Movement" by Heather
Booth, Evi Goldfield, and Sue Munaker (position paper from the Lesbian
Herstory Archives, subject files: "Women's Lib"). It reads: "For justice to
come to black people there must be black economic and political self-
determination. For an end to militarism there must be an end to control of
society by business which profits only with the suppression of national wars
of independence. For the true freedom of all women, there must be restruc-
turing of the institutions which perpetuate the myths and the subservience of
their social situation." The Redstockings position remained essentially the
same throughout 1970. By 1972 the Chicago group's position had expanded to
include an analysis of lesbianism, although this was done within the context
of a socialist feminist perspective. See "Lesbianism and Socialist Feminism: A
Position Paper of the Chicago Women's Liberation Union. Written by the
Gay Women's Group of the CWLU and Adopted by the CWLU at Its Annual
Membership Conference, November, 1972" (from "Women's Liberation Files:
Position Papers," the Women's Collection, Northwestern University).

14 Jay, *The Lavender Menace,* 66.

15 For a historical account of Chicana feminism, see Blackwell, "Contested
Histories: Las Hijas de Cuauhtemoc, Chicana Feminisms, and Print Culture
in the Chicano Movement, 1968–1973"; and Garcia, *Chicana Feminist
Thought.* For a sociological analysis of the emergence of black feminist orga-
nizations out of the Black Power and civil rights movements, see Springer,
Living for the Revolution.

16 According to Beverly Guy-Sheftall in her preface to *Words of Fire,* this may
have had to do with a general reluctance on the part of black women to "air
dirty linen" in a public sphere in which their stories were not recognized or
heard (xvi).

17 Berlant, *The Female Complaint,* 11.

18 My "method" for tracking the emotional work of the texts I look at is indebted
to Sara Ahmed's work on the performativity of texts in the production of emotions as social relations. See Ahmed, *The Cultural Politics of Emotion.*

19 Ahmed, *The Cultural Politics of Emotion.* 176.

20 Quoted in full in Abbott and Love, *Sappho Was a Right-On Woman,* 124. See

also Judy Klemesrud, "The Lesbian Issue and Women's Lib," *New York Times*, December 18, 1970, 47, for a partial quote of the statement.

21 Abbott and Love, *Sappho Was a Right-On Woman*, 125.

22 Cornell, "Rethinking the Time of Feminism," 148.

23 Foucault, "Nietzsche, Genealogy, History," 83.

24 Ibid., 81, 88.

25 For a discussion of Foucault's concept of "problematization," see Warner, *Publics and Counterpublics*, 154.

26 Sedgwick, *Epistemology of the Closet*, 86–87.

27 See "Toward a Radical Movement" by Heather Booth, Evi Goldfield, and Sue Munaker (position paper from the Lesbian Herstory Archives, subject files: "Women's Lib"); and Baxandall and Gordon, *Dear Sisters*.

28 See Seidman, "Identity Politics in a 'Postmodern' Gay Culture," 106–11.

29 Of course it also has something to do with gay men, who in the words of Mark Jordan are castigated for their "non-masculinity" rather than for having sex with other men. See Jordan, "Making the Homophile Manifest," 200.

30 This was a conclusion also being reached at this time by the leadership of the lesbian organization Daughters of Bilitis (DOB). By 1970 the editorial pages of the DOB's magazine, the *Ladder*, were full of articles drawing the connections between women's liberation and the plight of lesbians. See Gene Damon, "Women's Liberation Catches Up to the Ladder"; and Rita Laporte's "The Undefeatable Force," *Ladder*, August–September 1970, 4–5.

31 This is Katie King's term for the way in which lesbianism became the dominant signifier of contest and change in the early women's liberation movement. See King, *Theory in Its Feminist Travels*, 125.

32 Echols, *Daring to Be Bad*, 220.

33 Rosen, *The World Split Open*, 173.

34 Echols, *Daring to Be Bad*, 226.

35 See Myron and Bunch, *Lesbianism and the Women's Movement*, for essays by the Furies and other early lesbian feminist groups.

36 Nicholson, *The Second Wave*, 3.

37 Ronell, "The Deviant Payback: The Aims of Valerie Solanas," 4.

38 Morgan's rewriting of "Goodbye to All That" in the context of the campaign for the Democratic nomination for president in 2008 is one of many echoes of women's liberation in the present.

39 Morgan, "Goodbye to All That," 269.

40 Ahmed, *The Cultural Politics of Emotion*, 172–78.

41 Morgan is not shy in outing the actions of powerful men like Krassner, who she accuses of "buying" a prostitute for a friend and for suggesting a "rape-in" action against legislators' wives as part of the movement's antiwar protests. Morgan, "Goodbye to All That," 271.

42 Ahmed, *The Cultural Politics of Emotion*, 174.

43 Ibid., 271.

44 Gross, *The Secret History of Emotion*, 76.

45 Morgan, "Goodbye to All That," 275.

46 Solanas, SCUM *Manifesto*, 77.

47 Ronell, "The Deviant Payback: The Aims of Valerie Solanas," 17.

48 I use Walter Benjamin's concept of profane illumination here to suggest that women's liberationists were, like the early twentieth-century surrealists of Benjamin's study, attempting to "win the energies of intoxication for the revolution" by bringing "to the point of explosion . . . the immense forces of 'atmosphere' concealed" in commonsense, everyday ways of knowing and being in the world. Morgan's invocation of Solanas's SCUM *Manifesto* is just one example, I argue, of the ways in which women's liberationists attempted to "shatter" the "habit" of thinking, feeling, and knowing what we can call, variously, "heterosexism," "heteronormativity," "sexism," and so on. As we will see in chapter 3, there is a haunting similarity between the words (albeit translated) Benjamin uses to define a "profane illumination" and the Radicalesbian's drawing of the figure of the lesbian. See Benjamin, "Surrealism: The Last Snapshot of the European Intelligentsia," 189, 182; and also Gordon, *Ghostly Matters*, for a discussion of the usefulness of Benjamin's concept for historiographical projects concerned with confronting the "lingering" presence of the past (204–5).

49 Solanas, SCUM *Manifesto*, 61, 71, 76.

50 Ibid., 76.

51 Ibid., 61.

52 Ibid.

53 Ibid., 76.

54 See, for example, Baxandall and Gordon's introduction to *Dear Sisters* in which, as part of their analysis of the historical effects of cultural misconceptions of the second wave, they point to the media's predilection for a "few crazies" as a reason for the lack of studies and historical memory of the movement's political effectivity (1–2). See also Heller, "Shooting Solanas," for a discussion of the ambivalent responses to the film about Solanas, *I Shot Andy Warhol*, in the feminist press.

55 Heller, "Shooting Solanas," 165.

56 Ronell, "The Deviant Payback," 16.

57 Patricia Haden, Donna Middleton, and Patricia Robinson, "A Historical and Critical Essay for Black Women," 317. All subsequent citations will appear parenthetically in the text.

58 Friedan, *The Feminine Mystique*, 1, 16.

59 See Hesford and Diedrich, "Introduction," for a discussion of the utility of *against* as a method of interpretive conjuncture.

60 The phrase *pulp sexology* comes from Annamarie Jagose. For her discussion

of the proliferation of mass-marketed paperbacks devoted to making visible the sexual underworlds of midcentury America, see Jagose, *Inconsequence*, 122–45. Jagose argues that, contrary to their stated intention of making perverse subcultures like lesbianism visible in order to quarantine them from the rest of society, these studies tended to exacerbate the difficulty of telling the difference between gay and straight by finding actual or potential perverse behavior everywhere they looked.

61 Horowitz, *Betty Friedan and the Making of* The Feminine Mystique, 202.
62 Meyerowitz, "Beyond the Feminine Mystique," 251–52.
63 Ibid., 232.
64 Ibid., 250–51.
65 See chapter thirteen of *The Feminine Mystique*, "The Forfeited Self," in which Friedan engages in a detailed discussion of A. H. Maslow's work. For a discussion of the influence and relationship of "the new psychology" to second-wave feminism, see Gerhard, *Desiring Revolution*, 83–85.
66 See Friedan, *The Feminine Mystique*; and Gerhard, *Desiring Revolution*, 83–84.
67 Friedan, *The Feminine Mystique*, 299, quoting Rollo May.
68 Ibid., 324.
69 Ibid., 322, 319, 361.
70 Ibid., 263.
71 Ibid., 265, 178.
72 Horowitz, *Betty Friedan and the Making of* The Feminine Mystique, 203.
73 Meyerowitz, "Beyond the Feminine Mystique," 252.
74 Gordon, *Ghostly Matters*, 204–5.

THREE
Becoming Woman Identified Woman

1 Millett, *Sexual Politics*, xi.
2 Ibid., 31.
3 See, Christopher Lehmann-Haupt, "He and She—I" and "He and She—II," *New York Times*, August 5 and 6, 1970, 30 and 31; Irving Howe, "The Middle-Class Mind of Kate Millett," *Harper's*, December 1970, 110–29; and Norman Mailer, "The Prisoner of Sex," *Harper's*, March 1971, 41–92. I briefly discuss these reviews in chapter 4.
4 Kaplan, "Radical Feminism and Literature," 16.
5 See Foucault, *The History of Sexuality*, especially part five, "Right of Death and Power over Life," 133–60.
6 Millett, *Sexual Politics*, 31.
7 Foucault, *The History of Sexuality*, 103. Foucault's skeptical response to sexual liberation was most famously articulated in *The History of Sexuality*, first

published in France in 1976 and in the United States in 1978. Foucault had been an interested observer of the Black Power, women's, and gay liberation movements in the United States and had read many of the manifestoes and position papers they produced. The argument Foucault makes in *The History of Sexuality* was a forceful rejection of the "repressive hypothesis" of sexuality as a biological or psychological life force forever facing more or less sophisticated attempts to contain or repress it. In contrast, Foucault argued that the late eighteenth and early nineteenth century saw a significant shift in the discursive regimes of sexuality as bourgeois society attempted to secure for itself the power to discipline bodies and regulate populations. Sexuality, for Foucault, was not a desire that emanated from bodies but a set of discourses and practices produced historically and subject to change depending on the ordering mechanisms of particular epochs and societies. To claim liberation through an unconventional sexuality was not, for Foucault, as many counterculture, feminist, and gay activists in the 1960s and 1970s proposed, a break or disruption of the hegemonic discourses of sexuality in the mid to late twentieth century but was, rather, another enactment of it. See also Stoler, *Race and the Education of Desire*, for an incisive reading of Foucault's historicization of sexuality within the context of European colonial expansion; and Macey, *The Lives of Michel Foucault*, for Foucault's interest in the Black Power, gay, and women's liberation movements.

8 For Bourdieu the "specific ontology" of social categories lies in the "two-way relationship" between the objective structures of state policy and legislation and the subjective structures of everyday living or habitus—the field of dispositions, practices, classificatory schemes and feelings. See "The Family Spirit," 67–69.

9 Ibid., 68.

10 As well as Robin Morgan's *Sisterhood Is Powerful*, see also the collection of gay liberation position papers and essays in Jay and Young, *Out of the Closets: Voices of Liberation*.

11 Gross, *The Secret History of Emotion*, 233.

12 Foucault, *The History of Sexuality*, 157.

13 See Roth, *Separate Roads to Feminism*; and Springer, *Living for the Revolution*.

14 Roth's analysis of the relationship between "parent" movements and their feminist offspring is especially helpful in mapping out the similarities and differences between black, Chicana, and white feminist responses to the highly charged masculinist rhetoric at work in the New Left, black nationalist, and Chicano movements of the late 1960s.

15 Springer, *Living for the Revolution*, 46.

16 Brown, *Politics Out of History*, 3.

17 Ibid., 4.

18 Foucault, "Friendship as a Way of Life," 115.

19 Scott, "The Evidence of Experience," 88–89.

20 Bourdieu, "The Family Spirit," 68.

21 "'The Personal Is Political': Origins of the Phrase," WMST-1, http://user pages.umbc.edu/~korenman/wmst/pisp.html. Of course, if we want to be really pedantic, we can trace the ideas that inspired this phrase to a whole range of twentieth-century political and philosophical thinkers. However, as a couple of contributors to the WMST-1 discussion note, it was during the second-wave era that this phrase became a concept.

22 Carol Hanisch, "New Introduction to 'The Personal Is Political,'" The 'Second Wave' and Beyond, forum hosted by Sheri Barnes, Judith Ezekiel, and Stephanie Gilmore (Alexander Street Press), http://scholar.alexanderstreet .com/pages/viewpage.action?pageId=2259.

23 Ibid.

24 The suggestion that consciousness raising is just therapy would be echoed in later criticisms of the practices of feminism and women's studies.

25 See DeKoven, Utopia Limited, for a similar argument. Although DeKoven is concerned with the emergence of the postmodern during the 1960s rather than women's liberation, my reading of the relationship between the New Left and women's liberation owes a debt to her analysis of that era. See especially her chapter, "Personal and Political," 249–69.

26 See Miller, Democracy Is in the Streets, 329–74.

27 Many of the ideas in the Port Huron Statement echoed those in the civil rights movement, including the championing of informal grassroots politics and the notion of a "beloved community" as an ideal for collective action and social solidarity.

28 DeKoven, Utopia Limited, 123, 124–25.

29 Quoted in Miller, Democracy Is in the Streets, 374.

30 Ibid.

31 Hanisch, "New Introduction to 'The Personal Is Political.'"

32 Quoted in DeKoven, Utopia Limited, 133.

33 Hanisch, "New Introduction to 'The Personal Is Political.'"

34 See Echols, Daring to Be Bad, 139–202; Rosen, The World Split Open, 143–95; and Gerhard, Desiring Revolution, 81–116.

35 See Laura X, "On Our Sexual Liberation," Position Papers, Women's Collection, Northwestern University—please note that this paper was initially presented at the Breaking the Shackles of Women Conference, University of California, Berkeley, January 30–31, 1970; Marge Piercy, "The Grand Coolie Damn," 473–92; and Katz, "Smash Phallic Imperialism," 257–61.

36 Firestone, The Dialectic of Sex, 6–7.

37 Evans, *Personal Politics*, 88.

38 Springer, *Living for the Revolution*, 24.

39 Evans, *Personal Politics*, 89.

40 See Washington, "We Started from Different Ends of the Spectrum," 238–40.

41 Hayden and King, "Sex and Caste," 237.

42 Ibid., 235.

43 Washington, "We Started from Different Ends of the Spectrum," 238.

44 Barbara Smith, as quoted in Springer, *Living for the Revolution*, 57.

45 Springer, *Living for the Revolution*, 47–48.

46 We can perhaps map this field through a comparative reading of the way in which black and white feminist groups and theorists during the early second-wave era, while often using the same rhetoric and theoretical language, actually produce quite distinct analyses of their position as women and starkly different conclusions about what to do about it. For example, Toni Cade, in the introduction to *The Black Woman* in 1970 writes: "If we women are to get basic, then surely the first job is to find out what *liberation for ourselves* means" (7; emphasis added). And in her essay, "On the Issue of Roles" in the same volume, Cade calls for the eradication of the "fictions" of masculine and feminine roles and writes: "What are we talking about when we speak of revolution if not a free society made up of *whole individuals*" (105). Similarly, yet speaking to a different feminist cohort, the editors of the feminist newspaper *off our backs* wrote in their debut edition that the newspaper was "for all women fighting for the liberation of their lives," and that "women need to be free of men's domination to find their real identities, redefine their lives, and fight for the creation of a society in which they can lead decent lives as human beings" ("Dear Sisters," *off our backs*, February 27, 1970, 2). Unlike Friedan's idea that a woman's autonomy would be achieved through equal access to the public sphere, implicit in both Cade's and *off our backs*'s articulation of women's liberation is the idea that some form of separation or independence from men is necessary, and that autonomy will be achieved through the transformation of society and the eradication (rather than limitation to the domestic sphere) of gender roles. Rather than the successful career woman with a happy marriage, the autonomous woman envisioned by Cade and the editors of *off our backs* would discover herself through a revolution in the relationship between men and women. The difference between *The Black Woman* and *off our backs* lay not so much in the assertion of autonomy as one of the primary goals of feminism but how each imagined that autonomy. For Toni Cade and Frances Beal, autonomy was understood relationally: it would come from a "rewriting" of the relationships between black men and women and from an effective utiliza-

tion of the "resources" of the black community (Beale, "Double Jeopardy," 100). For the editors of *off our backs*, autonomy was imagined in terms of a freedom from relationships with men that were seen as inhibiting and constraining rather than potentially supportive. The autonomous woman imagined in the *off our backs* editorial was less a subject acting within a sociocultural context, in order to reform or transform it, and more a subject who had, somehow, freed herself from that context altogether.

47 Susan Brownmiller, "Sisterhood Is Powerful," *New York Times Magazine*, March 15, 1970, 140.

48 See Smith-Rosenberg, "Discourses of Sexuality and Subjectivity," for the historical emergence and cultural construction of the lady in lavender figure.

49 As Alice Echols notes, the Furies may not have been the most representative group of lesbian feminists in 1971–72 but they were the most influential, largely because they published their own newspaper. The Furies began publishing their newspaper the *Furies* in January 1972. The inaugural issue included Ginny Berson's "The Furies" and Charlotte Bunch's "Lesbians in Revolt," both of which set out, in very dogmatic terms, the theoretical paradigms for lesbian feminism. See Echols, *Daring to Be Bad*, 228–41; and Myron and Bunch, *Lesbianism and the Women's Movement*.

50 Gerhard's *Desiring Revolution* offers a clear and detailed account of the Barnard conference, placing it within the contemporary context of the rise of the New Right and as part of the longer historical trajectory of twentieth-century American feminisms. Gerhard describes the swirl of hostility and conflict that marked the confrontation between the conference organizers, some of the speakers, and the hastily formed Coalition of Women for a Feminist Sexuality and against Sadomasochism, which had campaigned against the conference's emphasis on "sexual pleasure" and picketed the opening day. See also Vance, *Pleasure and Danger*, for a collection of essays inspired by the conference.

51 Scott, "Fantasy Echo," 287.

52 Ibid., 289.

53 Smith-Rosenberg, "Discourses of Sexuality and Subjectivity."

54 Ibid., 267.

55 Newton, "The Mythic Mannish Lesbian."

56 See Cott, *The Grounding of Modern Feminism*; and Schwarz, *Radical Feminists of Heterodoxy*. Although Richard Von Krafft-Ebing and Havelock Ellis both wrote quite explicitly of the connection between "sexual inversion" in the female and feminism, they did so within a more exclusive medico-scientific discourse and through anonymous case studies. As such, their work functioned more as part of the suggestion and inference surrounding the first wave of feminism rather than as vehicles for a direct exposé of femi-

nism's supposed inherent lesbianism. See Krafft-Ebing, *Psychopathia Sexualis*; and Ellis, *Psychology of Sex*. As Smith-Rosenberg writes, although by the turn of the century a medico-scientific discourse was busily constructing the New Woman as a feminist with, at the very least, latent homosexual tendencies, no publicly recognized feminist leader was "directly attacked as a lesbian" ("Discourses of Sexuality and Subjectivity," 272).

57 For an account of the inability, or refusal, on the part of both commentators and feminists themselves during the first decades of the twentieth century to speak of sexual desire between women, see Cott, *The Grounding of Modern Feminism*, 41–45; and Judith Schwarz, *Radical Feminists of Heterodoxy*, 36–39. In her history of the Heterodoxy club, Schwarz argues that, although the club included same-sex couples and women who had love affairs with other women, it became increasingly concerned with advocating companionate heterosexual marriage as both a sign and a vehicle for a successful feminism. In its early years, the club had what Schwarz calls a much more "open-ended" belief in "sexual and economic freedom." But even here women's desire for other women was submerged within a general rhetoric of "sexual freedom" (39).

58 Of course, many self-identified female inverts and mannish women were active in or associated themselves with feminism in the early twentieth century. My argument here is that the actual or potential association of the mannish lesbian with feminism was eclipsed by her cultural legibility as a sexual invert and isolated individual. Esther Newton's discussion of Radclyffe Hall and her fictional alter ego, Stephen Gordon, in "The Mythic Mannish Lesbian" illustrates my point. In focusing on Radclyffe Hall and Stephen Gordon as her primary examples of the mannish lesbian, Newton locates the representation of lesbian sexual desire in the figure of the lonely Lothario whose successful seduction of women only leads to the painful knowledge that she will, inevitably, lose her lover to men and the heterosexual contract. In the tragedy of not having been born a man, Stephen Gordon is almost an antifeminist figure. And, contrary to Newton's claim that Radclyffe Hall was a self-identified feminist, Diane Souhami, in her biography of Hall, asserts that after a brief flirtation with the Suffragettes, Hall was quite vociferous in her opposition to feminism; she much preferred to be identified with the men of her class and standing in society than she did with other women. See Souhami, *The Trials of Radclyffe Hall*. It is interesting to note that Carroll Smith-Rosenberg and Esther Newton had initially written a paper together on what became, separately, "Discourses of Sexuality and Subjectivity" and "The Mythic Mannish Lesbian." The reason for this separation, according to the brief published explanations offered by the authors themselves, was that Smith-Rosenberg wanted to focus on the reasons

why a collective association could not be maintained over a generational shift in the feminist movement in the early twentieth century, while Newton wanted to focus on why a particular class and generation of women fashioned themselves as mannish lesbians. In other words, the decision to write separate essays seems to me to be symptomatic of the impasse I have been outlining between politics and sexuality in modern feminism—an impasse based less on the incompatibility of different forms of female sexuality with feminism as a political project and more the result of a historiographic and analytic inability to track the movement of women from one public sphere to another. Nan Enstad provides a historical argument for this observation in "Fashioning Political Identities." See also Smith-Rosenberg, "Discourses of Sexuality and Subjectivity," 532n1; and Newton, "The Mythic Mannish Lesbian," 536–37 (acknowledgments).

59 The paper has had a varied circulation and publication history. Koedt first presented the paper at the first national women's liberation conference in Chicago, Thanksgiving weekend 1968. Section one then appeared in the women's liberation newspaper *Notes from the First Year* in 1969, and it was printed in its entirety in *Notes from the Second Year* in 1970. It also traveled widely, becoming an influential essay for women's liberation movements in Australia and the United Kingdom, for example, as well as in the United States. The essay is also one of the most anthologized of the movement. See Koedt, Levine, and Rapone, *Radical Feminism*, 198, for publication details. In my discussion of "The Myth of the Vaginal Orgasm," I will refer to the version published in *Radical Feminism* and all subsequent citations will appear parenthetically in the text.

60 Here, Koedt is quoting from one of her scientific sources, G. Lombard Kelly.

61 Koedt's example of the violent suppression of female sexuality is the problematic example of clitoridectomy, which then becomes associated with "backward societies" and allowed to stand in comparison with the supposedly more sophisticated, psychological tortures American society inflicts on women and their sexuality (206). This kind of "discursive colonialism" continues to haunt Anglo-American feminism. In Koedt's essay, the presumption of a temporal distinction between Western women and Third World women invokes—as a political ideal—sexual liberation for American women as a sign of their superiority over non-Western women. See Mohanty, "Under Western Eyes."

62 See also, Koedt, "Lesbianism and Feminism." The essay first appeared in 1971 in *Notes from the Third Year*.

63 Koedt, "Loving Another Woman," 88. The interviewee remains anonymous, a testament perhaps to the discomfort at this time of publicly identifying as

a lesbian, even in the women's liberation movement. In my discussion of "Loving Another Woman," I will refer to the version published in *Radical Feminism* and all subsequent citations will appear parenthetically in the text.

64 For accounts of Atkinson's media notoriety and controversial position in women's liberation, see Echols, *Daring to Be Bad*; Rosen, *The World Split Open*; and Brownmiller, *In Our Time*. Atkinson's high regard for her own messianic qualities, and her theoretical combinations of existentialist philosophy, Marxism, and what we might call a Solanasesque politics of refusal, meant that she was often an unnerving figure for many in women's liberation. But her fearless refusal to recognize the proprieties of political speech (most infamously in her call on feminists at a women's liberation meeting to support a recently arrested, adulterous, and violent mafia boss in his battle against the state) often created the kinds of absurdist moments that illuminated, if only fleetingly, the absurdities of the so-called normal world.

65 Although Atkinson was certainly one of the first "nonlesbians" in women's liberation to articulate a relationship between feminism and lesbianism, one of the earliest and most publicized papers on the relationship between feminism and lesbianism was Martha Shelley's "Notes of a Radical Lesbian," which was originally published in *Come Out: A Liberation Forum for the Gay Community* in 1969 and republished in Robin Morgan's anthology, *Sisterhood Is Powerful* in 1970. From 1968 to 1969, Shelley had been the president of the New York chapter of the Daughters of Bilitis (DOB). Frustrated with the chapter's modest ambitions to be a support group rather than a political-activist group, Shelley left the organization in 1969 to help form the Gay Liberation Front and take a more active role in the women's liberation movement. Shelley's frustrations were echoed elsewhere in the DOB at this time. The organization's magazine, the *Ladder*, had, by the late 1960s, become the site of a conflict within the DOB as a whole over the role of the organization: should it remain a social and educational group whose main goal was to "integrate the homosexual into society," as an editorial from the magazine in 1963 declared, or should the organization actively fight for social transformation and women's liberation, as the editorials by Gene Damon and Rita Laporte asserted in a 1970 edition (*Ladder*, January 1963, 4; and *Ladder*, August–September 1970, 4–5)? Members of the DOB, including Damon and Laporte as well as Del Martin, would become active participants in the women's liberation movement, and the connections they made between lesbianism and the need for feminism formed part of the enactment of a lesbian feminist politics in the women's movement. For a history of the DOB and Martha Shelley's involvement, see D'Emilio, *Sexual Politics, Sexual Communities*, 92–107, 210. See also Martin and Lyon's *Lesbian/Woman*.

66 Atkinson, *Amazon Odyssey*. Atkinson's op-ed, although rejected by the *New York Times*, was published in Jill Johnston's *Village Voice* column on March 30, 1972.

67 See King, *Feminist Theory in Its Travels*, 125–26, for an account of how Atkinson's views on lesbianism were taken up, quoted, and misquoted in the movement's initial explorations of the meaning and place of lesbianism in radical feminist politics.

68 Atkinson, "Lesbianism and Feminism: Justice for Women as 'Unnatural,'" in *Amazon Odyssey*, 86. All subsequent citations from this essay will appear parenthetically in the text.

69 Like many position papers from the second-wave movement, "The Woman Identified Woman" appeared in many forms and in a variety of publications. The paper was originally distributed by the Lavender Menace at the Second Congress to Unite Women in May 1970 and published by the Radicalesbians in *Notes from the Third Year* in 1971. It has subsequently been anthologized in a variety of publications, including *Radical Feminism* in 1973 and Linda Nicholson's collection of second-wave feminist theory, *The Second Wave: A Reader in Feminist Theory*. In my research in the Women's Collection at Northwestern University and the Herstory Archives in Brooklyn, I came across a number of different forms of the paper—some with no identifying publication information. Like much of the theoretical output of the early years of women's liberation, the paper would have been distributed along networks of different feminist groups and organizations, through personal relationships, and through alternative press releases. Its publication history, therefore, reveals only a limited view of its actual distribution among feminist and nonfeminist groups. My reading of the paper refers to the edition anthologized in Koedt, Levine, and Rapone, *Radical Feminism*. All citations of the paper will appear parenthetically in the text.

70 Gordon, *Ghostly Matters*, 204–5.

71 Echols, *Daring to Be Bad*, 215–16.

72 Nicholson, *The Second Wave*, 147–48.

73 Rosen, *The World Split Open*, 167–69.

74 Baxandall and Gordon, *Dear Sisters*, 107.

75 Halberstam, *Female Masculinity*, 134–39.

76 Both Sidney Abbott and Barbara Love were members of the Radicalesbians at the time of the Second Congress to Unite Women in May of 1970, and in fact some of the rhetoric from "Woman Identified Woman" appears almost verbatim in *Sappho Was a Right-On Woman*.

77 See DeKoven, *Utopia Limited*; and Fredric Jameson, "Periodizing the 1960s."

FOUR

Fear of Flying

1 Millett, *Flying*, 14. All subsequent citations from *Flying* will appear parenthetically in the text. My title for this chapter gestures to Erica Jong's novel
of the same name, published in 1973, in which the heroine's struggle to attain
a measure of sexual and social liberation is presented within the heteronormative terms of her conflicted feelings for men, marriage, and motherhood.
My title is also meant to indirectly refer to Lauren Berlant's essay "The Female Complaint," in which she first defines the complaint as the paradig-
matic form of female public utterance and identifies Jong's novel as one
example of this form. For Berlant, the female complaint, as a genre of
women's culture, allows for the expression of disappointment while maintaining a fidelity to the world—of marriage, romantic love, motherhood,
men—that is the subject of complaint. To complain, in other words, becomes a way to manage ambivalence and to alleviate the pain of what is
often unresolvably difficult about everyday life—in such a way that we can
remain invested in the cultural narratives and scenarios of sexual and social
fulfillment. I have not come across any explicit reference by Millett to Jong's
novel and so can only speculate that she meant her book as a riposte to
Jong's unexamined heterosexism and as an assertion of the political possibilities of taking the risk of separating from the comforts of normative femininity. See Jong, *Fear of Flying*. See also Berlant, "The Female Complaint."

2 According to an undated speech by Millett on "The Story of *Flying*," the
book came in a "flood" with most of it written over the summer of 1971 and
a first draft completed by January 1972. See the Kate Millett Papers, FL 6,
Sallie Bingham Center for Women's History and Culture, David M. Rubenstein Rare Book and Manuscript Library, Duke University.

3 Ibid.

4 Reviews in the American press were overwhelmingly negative, ranging from
Larry McMurtry's vehement dismissal of the book as "trivial, atrociously
written, and very dull" in "The Literary Scene" (publication details unknown, review found in the Kate Millett Papers, FL 6, the Sallie Bingham
Center for Women's History and Culture, David M. Rubenstein Rare Book
and Manuscript Library, Duke University) to Elinor Langer's response to
Flying in "Confessing" for *Ms.* in December 1974. All expressed horror at the
mass of material in *Flying* and complained about Millett's apparent un-
willingness to exclude anything from her "documentary." Barbara Gold's review, "The Cost of Making It in the Movement," *Baltimore Sun*, July 28,
1974, was a rare exception. In Gold's view, *Flying* was a compelling "cry of
agony" that was impossible to hear unless you had also participated in the

movement and knew the kind of life it created. See also Kolodny, "The Lady's Not for Spurning," for an analysis of the American reviews of *Flying*. The UK reviews were less condemnatory. Juliet Mitchell, Lorna Sage, and A. S. Byatt all reviewed *Flying* for national publications, and though they had mixed reactions to the book (with Byatt the closest in her criticisms to those voiced in the American press), they recognized its experimentalism and ambition. See Juliet Mitchell, "Women in Love," *New Statesman*, June 13, 1975, 781–82; Lorna Sage, "What Kate Did Next," *Observer Review*, June 15, 1975; A. S. Byatt, "Misuses of Egoism," *Times*, June 16, 1975. The difference between the American and UK responses to *Flying* is, no doubt, the result of a complex array of cultural incongruities between the two—a testament to the ways in which political movements with international ambitions and transnational manifestations are also experienced, thought, felt, and remembered in national terms.

5 Kolodny, "The Lady's Not for Spurning," 241. Kolodny is referring to the autobiographical tradition beginning with St. Augustine through Rousseau, Goethe, Benjamin Franklin, and Henry Adams. Jane Wilson, "Sexual Apologetics," *New York Times Book Review*, June 23, 1974.

6 The "unconventional loves" is Kate Millett's phrase and comes from her response to Elinor Langer's review of *Flying* in *Ms.* See Kate Millett, "The Shame Is Over," *Ms.*, December 1975. Elinor Langer, "Confessing," 71. See also Wilson, "Sexual Apologetics."

7 This is also Annette Kolodny's reading of the critics' response to *Flying*. See "The Lady's Not for Spurning," 238–41.

8 See Juhasz, "Towards a Theory of Feminist Autobiography." See also Lauret, *Liberating Literature*. Like Kolodny, Juhasz and Lauret examine *Flying* within the context of a feminist practice of writing that emerged in relation to, and out of, the women's liberation movement.

9 Sturken, *Tangled Memories*, 7.

10 In a number of interviews during 1970, Millett often refers to not being able to get an academic job commensurate with her qualifications. Her temporary position as non-tenure track faculty at Barnard ended in 1968–69, when she was fired for actively supporting the student occupation of the administrative building at Columbia University. Millett's frustration at not being able to secure a permanent academic job echoes throughout the personal testimonies and polemics of women who became active in women's liberation. See, for example, the personal stories of Sheila Tobias and Annis Pratt in Howe, *The Politics of Women's Studies*, 29–38, 80–92.

11 Barlow, *The Question of Women in Chinese Feminism*, 9. Barlow's intellectual history of twentieth-century Chinese feminism inspired me to rethink the

problem of writing about *Flying* as a text that was an attempt by Millett to write herself into a different—feminist and queer—future. Barlow's imaginative and rigorous determination to "write the destabilized histories" of "women," as a category made and remade through the investments of various groups of Chinese women at different moments during the twentieth century, helped me to orientate my reading of the historical documents of women's liberation as texts that were not simply knowing political responses to a known world but acts of invention that can be read today as material evidence of the struggle to enact "women's liberation" as a set of ideas, some of which became truisms of and for the movement, and some which did not.

12 See Oliver, *Witnessing*, for a discussion of the difference between the performative (the saying) and the constative (the said) that produces the tension of witnessing as history-in-the-making (93).

13 Eng and Kazanjian, *Loss*, 4.

14 See Millett's own account of her reception by some movement members following the success of *Sexual Politics* in *Flying*, 58–59. See also Brownmiller, *In Our Time*, 148–51; and Martha Shelley, "Women's Liberation Media Star," *Come Out*, 1970–71.

15 Millett's relative openness with the media in the summer of 1970 (she agreed, after all, to be interviewed at her home and have pictures taken of her with Yoshimura) also added to her role as women's liberationist star of 1970. Yet, on the other hand, as Millett reveals in *Flying*, her control over what the journalists wrote and what pictures they used for their articles was minimal. See *Flying*, 15.

16 See Horowitz, *Betty Friedan and the Making of* The Feminine Mystique, for an account of Friedan's work in the labor movement prior to her reincarnation as the "housewife" author of *The Feminine Mystique*. Friedan's past as a labor activist was one she was careful not to draw attention to while president of NOW.

17 Millett writes, "My face on the cover. They asked me whose picture they should use the week of the women's march. I said no one woman but crowds of them. . . . I could explain it was a trick, a portrait painted from a photograph without my knowledge or permission" (*Flying*, 17).

18 "Whose Come a Long Way Baby?," *Time*, August 31, 1970, 16.

19 Ibid., 19.

20 "The Liberation of Kate Millett," *Time*, August 31, 1970, 19.

21 Ibid.

22 Marie-Claude Wrenn, "The Furious Young Philosopher Who Got It Down on Paper," *Life*, September 4, 1970, 22.

23 Ibid. Although *Time* called her the "Mao-Tse-tung" of women's liberation,

Marilyn Bender in the *New York Times* had called her the "Karl Marx of New Feminism" back in July. See Marilyn Bender, "Some Call Her the Karl Marx of New Feminism," *New York Times*, July 20, 1970, 30.

24 Ibid.

25 Ibid.

26 Mary Russo, drawing upon the work of Bakhtin and Peter Stallybrass and Allon White, examines the female grotesque as a figure of ambivalence. As "the open, protruding, extended, secreting body, the body of becoming, process and change," the grotesque woman works to undo the borders between normative femininity and what has been abjected from that ideal. In Russo's reading, the grotesque woman does not function as an "opposite" to ideal femininity but rather as an uncanny transformation of it. She exceeds rather than denies the norm, and she transgresses rather than rejects the boundaries within which femininity is drawn. I read the media profiles of Kate Millett in 1970 through this idea of the grotesque. See Russo, *The Female Grotesque*, 8.

27 Mary Russo uses the concept of "error" as a way of talking about the possibilities brought about when groups and social movements take "the risk" of acting in excess of the normal. To be in error, therefore, is to be in excess of the processes of standardization, which make and remake the normal. See Russo, *The Female Grotesque*, 12.

28 Marie-Claude Wrenn, "The Furious Young Philospher Who Got It Down on Paper," 22.

29 Quote from Millett, *Flying*, 434.

30 See Joseph, *Waiting 'til the Midnight Hour*, for a discussion of the effects of Nixon's presidency on the fragmentation of the Black Power movement and the New Left in the early 1970s, especially the last two chapters, "Dark Days, Bright Nights" and "Dashikis and Democracy."

31 See Millett, *Sita*, and the Kate Millett Papers, LBT 6, Sallie Bingham Center for Women's History and Culture, David M. Rubenstein Rare Book and Manuscript Library, Duke University.

32 The relationship between Millett's manic depression, political activism, and artistic creativity remains suggestively enigmatic in this chapter. How do we account for the political and social productivity of so-called manic depression or bipolar disorder, while also remaining attentive to the details of particular embodiments of its psychic and social effects? The biologizing paradigms that have come to dominate public discussions of mental illness leave little room for an exploration of their social and political productivity, and in relation to women and people of color, diagnoses of depression or other forms of mental illness are too often used to foreclose a more expansive examination of social and economic subjugation and resistance. Millett would later go on to write an account of her experiences of institutionaliza-

tion in the 1970s and 1980s in *The Loony Bin Trip*. Much of that book is explicitly hostile to her forced institutionalizations and medications, but her overreliance on the libertarian paradigms of the antipsychiatry movement leaves her unable to offer a compelling account of her experiences of madness as something other than the result of betrayal—by friends, family, and lovers, as well as by the medical establishment. The recent resurgence of interest in Felix Guattari's political activism and therapeutic work at La Borde clinic in France in the 1960s and 1970s, along with his collaborations with the philosopher Gilles Deleuze, among others, can be interpreted as part of a widespread—interdisciplinary and multifield—attempt to reimagine and reconceptualize the links between politics, social change, madness, and biosocieties. Much of this work challenges the contemporary hegemony of the biomedical model of psychiatry but does not, as with the antipsychiatry movement, deny the existence of a sociobiological phenomenon we call madness. See, for example, Deleuze and Guattari, *Anti-Oedipus*; Foucault, *History of Madness* and *Madness and Civilization*; and more recently, Martin, *Biopolar Expeditions*; and Metzl, *The Protest Psychosis* and *Prozac on the Couch*.

33 Wilson, "Sexual Apologetics," 1.

34 Ibid., 2–3.

35 Ibid., 2–3, 3.

36 Langer, "Confessing," 71, 69, 70, 71.

37 Ibid., 70, 71.

38 Ibid.

39 Millett, "The Shame Is Over," 27–28.

40 See, for example, Chris Bearchell's review of *Flying* in *Body Politic* (Toronto, Canada), July–August, 1975, 24–27; Marsaili Cameron, "Coming Out from the Inside," *Gay News* (London), no. 74, June 1975; and Marsaili Cameron and Denis Lemon, "Interview: Coming Out—That Made All the Difference," *Gay News* (London), no. 75, July 1975, 17–18. Along with the more positive reviews of *Flying* in the gay press, Millett also received a substantial number of letters from readers (including an elderly male Lothario who saw his younger self in Millett), which often expressed a rapturous admiration for her frankness concerning lesbian sex. A few of these letters, some by married women, were also love letters to Millett. For fan letters and a collection of alternative and mainstream reviews of *Flying*, see Kate Millett Papers, FL 6, Sallie Bingham Center for Women's History and Culture, David M. Rubenstein Rare Book and Manuscript Library, Duke University.

41 Butt, *Between You and Me*, 12.

42 Ibid., 105.

43 Ibid., 43–44.

44 Millett, "The Shame Is Over," 26.

45 Ibid., 27.

46 Ellen Willis, foreword to Alice Echols, *Daring to Be Bad*, x.

47 See Echols, *Daring to Be Bad*; Rosen, *The World Split Open*; Jay, *Tales of the Lavender Menace*; Brownmiller, *In Our Time*.

48 See Kathie Sarachild, "Feminist Consciousness Raising and Organizing (outline prepared for a Lake Villa Conference workshop, 11/27/68)," Women's Liberation Movement Position Papers, Women's Liberation File, Lesbian Herstory Archives, Brooklyn, New York.

49 Sarachild, "Feminist Consciousness Raising and Organizing."

50 Jay, *Tales of the Lavender Menace*, 57, 62.

51 This is Meaghan Morris's term for a practice of feminist intellectual work in which "experience" is used to question historical truths (rather than used as a stamp of personal authority; i.e., "this has happened to me, therefore it is true for everyone"). See Morris, *Too Soon, Too Late*, xxii.

52 Quote from Millett, *Flying*, 14.

53 Kolodny, "The Lady's Not for Spurning," 241.

54 Ahmed, *The Cultural Politics of Emotion*, 104, 105.

55 Sedgwick, *Touching Feeling*, 37.

56 Quote from Millett, *Flying*, 159.

57 In a future echo of Millett's predicament, Lessing, after winning the Nobel Prize for Literature in 2007, would later describe the fame and notoriety that comes with the Nobel Prize as taking away her writing. Lessing's comments return us to Millett's earlier attempts to write against fame.

58 Quote from Millett, *Flying*, 127.

59 Quote from ibid., 130.

60 Foucault, "Friendship as a Way of Life," 137.

61 Breines, "What's Love Got to Do with It?," 1105, 1099.

62 As Breines writes, "Most black feminists tell of racism in the women's movement. They recount being ignored or objectified by white women." And, she notes, "for African Americans, 'loss' [as it relates to the promise of the social movements of the 1960s and of the civil rights movement in particular] would be more accurately employed to refer to the demise of racial justice rather than to the ideal of integration." For Breines, the "puzzle" of accusations of racism has to be untangled by reading and responding to—witnessing—the very different reactions of black and white feminists to the early years of women's liberation. See Breines, "What's Love Got to Do with It?," 1096 and 1099.

63 This is Avery Gordon's phrase. See *Ghostly Matters*, 16.

64 Quote from Millett, *Flying*, 338.

FIVE

Looking for the Ghosts

1 Here I am of course referring to Elizabeth Lapovsky Kennedy and Madeline Davis's groundbreaking oral history study of midcentury working-class lesbian communities in Buffalo, New York, *Boots of Leather, Slippers of Gold: The History of a Lesbian Community*. The highly stylized butch-femme gender contrast suggested by the book's title, and practiced by the working-class lesbians interviewed by Kennedy and Davis, is precisely not what Kal and Fran are designed to invoke. The style they perform is a commodified middle-classness that is less overtly sexualized so that it can include, in its generalizing ideality, all vaguely "normal" Americans.

2 Heller, "Found Footage," 86.

3 Ibid., 91.

4 *If These Walls Could Talk* came out in 1996 and tackled the historical repercussions of Roe v. Wade. Starring Sissy Spacek, Demi Moore, and Cher, the film was directed by Nancy Savoca.

5 The phrase "unwanted beings" comes from Radclyffe Hall's *The Well of Loneliness*. Hall uses the term to describe the feeling of rejection and social abjection that is the lot of the "congenital invert" (203). My use of it here was inspired by Heather Love's discussion of Hall in *Feeling Backward: Loss and the Politics of Queer History*. Love's call for a queer look backward, "a disposition towards the past" that is about "embracing loss" and "risking abjection" (30) rather than mining history for the celebratory story of overcoming failure or defeat, is closely aligned to my looking back at women's liberation as a complicated and unsettling event that, in its failures as well as its successes, tells us something about the difficulties of becoming feminist.

6 As articulated by one of the straight feminists in the second segment, the "real" feminist issue during the era of the second wave was "equal rights" between men and women.

7 I am thinking here of Showtime's *The L Word* (2003–9) as well as HBO's *Sex and the City* (1998–2004), and also films such as *Kissing Jessica Stein* (2002) and *Puccini for Beginners* (2007).

8 Both *Kissing Jessica Stein* and *Puccini for Beginners* are examples of this kind of film. Other lesbian romance "chick films" include *Imagine Me and You* (2005) and *Saving Face* (2004).

9 *Entanglement* is Marita Sturken's term for the relationship between history as "official" national discourse and cultural memory as a more informal practice of defining and naming collectivities. I am using it in a slightly different sense: as a way to articulate the relationship between dominant and mar-

ginal forms of collective cultural memory. See Sturken, *Tangled Memories*. See also Lipsitz, *Time Passages*, for an extended discussion of the ways in which U.S. national collective memory and popular culture are "peculiarly linked" (vii).

10 See Cvetkovich, "In the Archives of Lesbian Feelings" and *An Archive of Feelings*. See also Halberstam, *In a Queer Time and Place*. In her work on the queer and lesbian archive, Cvetkovich details the practices of collecting through which queer archivists of the gay experience draw upon popular culture in order to fashion their own affective worlds and histories. The point Cvetkovich's (and Halberstam's) work makes is that the relationship between queer and mainstream culture is circular and, in the affects it produces, densely imbricated rather than simply oppositional.

11 Berlant, *The Female Complaint*. All future references to *The Female Complaint* will be cited parenthetically in the text.

12 Fraser, "Rethinking the Public Sphere," 24.

13 Ibid.; and Warner, *Publics and Counterpublics*.

14 Judy Klemesrud, "The Lesbian Issue and Women's Lib," *New York Times*, December 18, 1970, 47.

15 Castiglia, "Sex Panics, Sex Publics, Sex Memories," 167.

16 See the *Oxford English Dictionary* (OED online).

17 Berlant's conceptualization of femininity as a genre is richly suggestive of the mix of fantasy and form through which women are encouraged to inhabit femininity. In Berlant's terms, femininity as a genre is "a structure of conventional expectation that people rely on to provide certain kinds of affective intensities and assurances" (*The Female Complaint*, 4).

18 Douglas, *Where the Girls Are*, 7; Zimmerman, "Confessions of a Lesbian Feminist," 163.

19 See Jameson, "Periodizing the Sixties," and *Postmodernism, or, the Cultural Logic of Late Capitalism*, for an argument concerning the decisive shift to the cultural domain in the production and enactment of the political in the new social movements of the 1960s.

20 Gordon's phrase is slightly different, resulting in a different methodological, and critical, emphasis: she "follows the ghosts" (*Ghostly Matters*, 22). To look for the ghosts (of the feminist past), rather than to follow them, suggests the need to argue for their importance to feminism as a form of historical memory—something that, for many complicated reasons (including, most prominently, the desire by feminist historians to make manifest a history that is often forgotten), might be resisted by many feminists. After all, part of the long struggle of feminism has been to demand not just a political but also a cultural and historical presence that is as "real" as any other social movement or political event. My argument here is that in order to make

manifest the presence of feminism historically, culturally, and socially, we have to confront the ways it has been made to disappear—even when, and perhaps especially when, feminists have participated in the disappearing.

21 Gordon, *Ghostly Matters*, 57.

22 Numerous essays, journal special issues, and edited collections appeared in the late 1990s and early 2000s attempting to address the state of feminism and its possible future directions. Instead of an exhaustive list (an exhausting and impossible idea) see, for example, Scott, *Women's Studies on the Edge*; Howard and Allen, "Feminisms at a Millenium"; Bronfen and Kavka, *Feminist Consequences*; Wiegman, "Feminisms, Institutionalism, and the Idea of Failure" and "Academic Feminism against Itself."

23 Huyssen, "Present Pasts: Media, Politics, Amnesia," 35.

24 Ibid., 29.

25 Heller, "Found Footage," 88.

26 Fredric Jameson's analysis of the function of mass culture in late capitalist societies is helpful here: for Jameson, mass culture is not an "empty distraction or 'mere' false consciousness," as many Marxist cultural critics have tended to assume, but rather it is "a transformational work on social and political anxieties and fantasies which must have some effective presence in the mass cultural text in order subsequently to be 'managed' or repressed" (Jameson, "Reification and Utopia in Mass Culture," 141).

27 Along with Berlant's *The Female Complaint*, see also Shumway, *Modern Love*; Kipnis, *Against Love*; and Seidman, *Romantic Longings*, for extended discussions of the social history of modern love as a central organizing paradigm for capitalist expansion and the privatization of the public sphere in the United States in the twentieth century.

28 Here I am drawing upon feminist and Marxist cultural critiques of the cliché as a vehicle for the enactment of conventional thought as collective memory. In Haug et al.'s *Female Sexualization*, for example, the cliché is "the linguistic means by which we [women] are socialized into heteronomy" (62). And in *The Female Complaint*, Lauren Berlant defines the cliché as "the main genre of displacement central to securing a place for normative love in U.S. popular culture" (179). To use cliché, as the German Marxist feminist collective in Haug's book notes, is to "pass sentence" on ourselves by literally writing or speaking ourselves into the conventions of femininity. Berlant, in comparison, is eager to track the cultural productivity of the cliché for women: the way it can enable women to feel attached to the conventions of femininity and alleviate them of the burden of their own social and psychic complexity (see especially, chapter five: "Remembering Love, Forgetting Everything Else," in *Now Voyager*, 169–205).

29 For accounts of the Miss America protest, see Echols, *Daring to Be Bad*;

Rosen, *The World Split Open*; the Redstockings' website, www.redstockings
.org; and the PBS American Experience film *Miss America* (www.pbs.org).

30 The affective dissonance of the film—its lack of a clear target for its humor—
may account for the overwhelmingly negative response by mainstream media and film critics, many of whom found its campy mocking of gender stereotypes annoying and its humor "sitcom-like." Interestingly, not one critic
(that I could find) thought or knew to mention the film's obvious references
to the Miss America protest. In fact few of the reviews mentioned feminism
at all. A. O. Scott, for example, in his review of the film for the *New York
Times*, preferred to associate the film with other recent releases, including
Crouching Tiger, Hidden Dragon, Girlfight, and *Charlie's Angels*. According to
Scott, all of these films suggested a present moment "intoxicated with female
machismo"—one apparently in no need of referencing feminism. See A. O.
Scott, "Operation Ugly Duckling," *New York Times*, December 22, 2000;
A. O. Scott, "Tough, Frosted, Must Be Empowerment," *New York Times*,
November 3, 2000.

31 Rosen, *The World Split Open*, 160.

32 Freeman, "Packing History, Count(er)ing Generations." All further references to this essay will be cited parenthetically in the text.

33 Freeman, "Queer Temporalities," 159–76.

34 Alice Echols's detailed analysis of the rise of radical feminism from 1967 until
1975 includes coverage of Firestone's activities as a founder of the Redstockings and the New York Radical Feminists (NYRF). Echols never identifies
Firestone as a lesbian or lesbian feminist. Indeed, both the Redstockings and
NYRF had, according to Echols, a "strong 'presumption of heterosexuality'"
running through their politics—at least during Firestone's time. Moreover,
Firestone dropped out of the women's movement entirely in the fall of 1970,
before lesbian feminism became a coherent political standpoint and largely
as a result of the tumultuous and chaotic fighting between the myriad radical feminist groups proliferating at the time (Echols, *Daring to Be Bad*, 147).
Yet, Freeman suggests that Firestone did eventually become a lesbian: "Finally, Shulie's status as not-yet-identified (as 'adult woman,' as 'feminist,' as
'lesbian,' as the representative or symbol of a complete movement) allows
Subrin a point of entry into the contemporary moment in terms other than
'post'" ("Packing History," 742).

35 Puar, *Terrorist Assemblages*, 22.

36 Millett, "Out of the Loop and Out of Print: Meditations on Aging and Being
Unemployable," *On the Issues* 7, no. 3 (1998): 38. *On the Issues* was a feminist
quarterly print magazine published from 1983 to 1999. It is now available
online at www.ontheissuesmagazine.com. Merle Hoffman, the founding editor and owner of the magazine, is the CEO of Choices, a for profit women's

medical center based in Long Island City. Hoffman was active in the women's liberation movement and has long been a feminist activist on reproductive issues and domestic violence.

37 Although at the time of writing the article this may have been true, in 2001 Millett's book on her mother, *Mother Millett*, was published by Verso, and in 2000 the University of Illinois Press reissued a number of Millett's books, including *Sexual Politics, The Loony-Bin Trip*, and *Sita*.

38 Millett, "Out of the Loop and Out of Print," 38.

39 Ibid., 41.

40 I am indebted here to Katie King's conceptualization of feminist history as a constantly constructed "object" that produces interested stories in the present. See King, *Theory in Its Feminist Travels*.

41 Maureen Freely, "What Kate Did Next," *Observer*, January 3, 1999, 2. All future references to this article will be cited parenthetically in the text.

42 I am using *general* here in the way Berlant reorientates its meaning in *The Female Complaint*. There she defines generality as "an experience of social belonging that is embodied and has qualities" in opposition to the universal, which is defined philosophically and/or topographically (284n9). In contrast to the universal as an abstraction, the general is a collective and conventional feeling that is culturally constituted. Much like Benedict Anderson's concept of the nation as an imagined community, generality is produced through the creation and dissemination of cultural emotions, genres, and conventions.

43 Leslie Crawford, "Kate Millett, the Ambivalent Feminist," *Salon*, June 5, 1999, http://www.salon.com/people/feature/1999/06/05/millet. All future references to this article will be cited parenthetically in the text.

44 See Horowitz, *Betty Friedan and the Making of the Feminine Mystique*; Wallace, *Germaine Greer*; and Heilbrun, *Education of a Woman*.

45 This personalization can be seen most revealingly in Crawford's inclusion of "manic-depressive" in her description of Millett's contradictoriness, even though Millett was not diagnosed with manic depression till the mid-1970s, after the moment Millett first became famous and controversial. Crawford's assumption of mental illness as an organic problem also forecloses speculation concerning the possible relationship between Millett's illness, the politics of radical feminism, and her public outing as lesbian in 1970.

46 I might add that Ti-Grace Atkinson has also suffered historical oblivion for the same reason: like Millett, Atkinson's overt disidentification with heterosexuality, marriage, and romantic love in general was one of the reasons why she was regarded by the mainstream media, and by many in the movement, as too extreme and therefore too ridiculous to be taken seriously. My contention here is that this kind of dismissal was precisely an effect of Millett's

and Atkinson's actions and politics: by so flagrantly renouncing the appeal of white femininity, they made themselves, as white, middle-class women, look absurd rather than dangerous.

47 Freely, "What Kate Did Next," 3.

48 Gordon, *Ghostly Matters*, 168, 183. Gordon, in turn, borrows the phrase from Michel de Certeau, as she acknowledges. See de Certeau, *The Writing of History*, 101.

49 Gordon, *Ghostly Matters*, 57.

50 Scott, "The Evidence of Experience," 93.

51 Clare Hemmings's *Why Stories Matter: The Political Grammar of Feminist Theory* offers a more elaborate methodological and theoretical argument for reading feminist theory this way.

52 King, *Theory in Its Feminist Travels*, 124.

53 De Lauretis, "The Essence of the Triangle, or Taking the Risk of Essentialism Seriously," 1–39. All future references to this essay will be cited parenthetically in the text.

54 See Weedon, *Feminist Practice and Poststructuralist Theory*; and Alcoff, "Cultural Feminism versus Post-structuralism." While de Lauretis is impatient with Weedon's understanding of essentialism as the unsophisticated precursor to poststructuralism, her critique of Alcoff's exploration of the differences between the two is much more positive and partial. For de Lauretis, the main problem with Alcoff's essay lies in her "agonistic frame of argumentation" that unnecessarily distorts her examination of different conceptions of feminism by forcing them into two coherent camps, which, in turn, depend upon the provision of a "missing premise" (in the case of cultural feminism, an "innate female essence") that then provides the reason for their coherency as distinct feminist camps (de Lauretis, "The Essence of the Triangle," 12).

55 See Rich, "Compulsory Heterosexuality and the Lesbian Continuum," in *Powers of Desire: The Politics of Sexuality* (1983), 177–89; and Rich, "Compulsory Heterosexuality and the Lesbian Continuum," *Blood Bread and Poetry: Selected Prose, 1979–1985* (1986), 23–75. All subsequent references to these versions of Rich's essay will be made parenthetically in the text, and the references will include the year of publication for the sake of clarity.

56 See, for example, Joseph, *Against the Romance of Community*, for a thoughtful engagement with poststructuralist and feminist thought on the ideal of community and its continuing appeal for political groups and movements, despite widespread understanding of its exclusionary and disciplinary effects.

57 See Deleuze and Guattari, *A Thousand Plateaus*.

58 Here I am echoing Michel Foucault's assertion that homosexuality is neither a

state of being nor a fixed identity but a historical occasion for the forming of new social bonds and worlds. See Foucault, "Friendship as a Way of Life," 138.

EPILOGUE
The Politics of Memory

1 Nealon, *Foundlings*, 17. All subsequent references will appear parenthetically within the text. See Duggan, "The Discipline Problem: Queer Theory Meets Lesbian and Gay History"; and Warner, "Introduction," *Fear of a Queer Planet*, vii–xxxi.

2 A preliminary list would include Eng and Kazanjian, *Loss*; Cvetkovich, *In the Archive of Lesbian Feelings*; Love, *Feeling Backward*; Muñoz, *Cruising Utopia*; and Freeman, "Queer Temporalities."

3 Dinshaw, *Getting Medieval*, 6. All future references will be cited parenthetically in the text.

4 Dinshaw cites an interview with Foucault in which he makes this point: "I am well aware that I have never written anything but fictions. . . . One 'fictions' history on the basis of a political reality that makes it true, one 'fictions' a politics not yet in existence on the basis of a historical truth" (Foucault, "The History of Sexuality," cited in Dinshaw, *Getting Medieval*, 193).

5 See, for example, Muñoz, *Cruising Utopia*; and Freeman's introduction to "Queer Temporalities."

6 For example, Dinshaw ends *Getting Medieval* with an appeal to the critical scrutiny feminism can provide for queer historical relations. In Dinshaw's reckoning, it is feminism that teaches us to "consider carefully" any claims to a self-apparent act or transparent surface, for it is feminism that reminds us of the gender asymmetries that lead to different acts having different "values and effects," depending on who is acting and under what circumstances (204). As a political project and critical approach distinct from queer theory, feminism operates in Dinshaw's book not as its own desire but as the voice that questions and troubles the desire of the queer historical impulse: "And we can insist that such a project of disaggregation be specifically informed and guided by feminist analyses and goals of transforming the 'social relations within which sexuality is organized and articulated'" (206).

7 Foucault, *Pierre Rivière, Having Slaughtered My Mother, My Sister, and My Brother* and *Herculine Barbin, Being the Recently Discovered Memoirs of a Nineteenth-Century French Hermaphrodite*.

8 Barbin cited in Butler, *Gender Trouble*, 105.

9 Butler, *Gender Trouble*, 97.

10 Freccero, *Queer/Early/Modern*, 69. All future references will be cited parenthetically in the text.

11 See, for example, Daniel Gross's discussion of the rhetorical deployment of
passivity in the English Civil War as a way to "mobilize 'man's' feminine soul
for broadly political purposes" (*The Secret History of Emotion*, 104).

12 "Historicism contents itself with establishing a causal connection between
various moments in history. But no fact that is a cause is for that very reason
historical. It became historical posthumously, as it were, through events that
may be separated from it by thousands of years. A historian who takes this
as his point of departure stops telling the sequence of events like the beads
of a rosary. Instead, he grasps the constellation which his own era has
formed with a definite earlier one" (Benjamin, "Theses on the Philosophy of
History," 263). See also Dinshaw, *Getting Medieval*, 17, for a discussion of the
same passage.

13 In *The Question of Women in Chinese Feminism*, Barlow explains her use of
catachresis as an historiographical concept this way: "Conventionally, catachresis refers to a particular misuse of a proper noun, where the term's referent is, theoretically or philosophically speaking, inadequate. A historical
catachresis is my way of taking advantage of the ellipsis and making its analytic inadequacy a positive value. When reconsidered as *historical* catachresis, ubiquitous, descriptive, proper nouns become legible repositories of
social experience" (1). My point is simply that *queer*, like *feminist*, acts like a
proper noun with an inadequate referent when used in relation to a theoretical field or critical or political practice. If, to echo Eng, Halberstam, and
Muñoz's formulation, queer is a "political metaphor without a fixed referent"
in "What's Queer About Queer Studies Now?" (1), then it is also an access
point for historical coagulations of political and social experience. The ines-
capable slippage between the use of *queer* as both noun and verb points to
the paradox that animates queer studies today: the claiming of a name, an
identity, for a practice of investigation, political mobilization, and world and
academic field making that is predicated on the valorization of an anti-
identitarian, subjectless critique.

14 See Barlow "'What is a poem?'" See also Michael Rothberg's taking up of
Badiou's *Ethics* in *Multidirectional Memory*, 267–308.

15 Rothberg, *Multidirectional Memory*, 4 and 21. All future references will be
cited parenthetically in the text.

16 Just for starters, see Whitlock and Poletti, "Autographics," especially Julia
Watson's contribution to the special issue, "Autographic Disclosures and Ge-
nealogies of Desire in Alison Bechdel's *Fun Home*"; Abrams and Kacandes,
"Witness," especially Ann Cvetkovich's contribution to the special issue,
"Drawing the Archive in Alison Bechdel's *Fun Home*." See also Chute and

DeKoven, "Graphic Narrative," especially Hillary Chute's interview with Bechdel, "An Interview with Alison Bechdel"; and Nancy K. Miller, "The Entangled Self: Gender Bondage in the Age of Memoir."

17 Cvetkovich, "Drawing the Archive in Alison Bechdel's *Fun Home*," 112.

18 Chute and DeKoven, "Graphic Narrative," 769. The term *graphic narrative* is theirs, and they use it to connote the range of narrative forms in graphic texts.

19 Ibid.

20 Bechdel, *Fun Home: A Family Tragicomic*, 120. All future references will be cited parenthetically in the text.

21 Ann Cvetkovich, "Drawing the Archive in Alison Bechdel's *Fun Home*," 112.

22 Ibid., 112–13.

23 Ibid., 122.

24 Thanks to Lisa Diedrich for encouraging me to think about the role of artifice in Bechdel's memoir.

25 Ann Cvetkovich, "Drawing the Archive in Alison Bechdel's *Fun Home*," 124.

26 Ibid.

27 Millett, *Flying*, 266.

BIBLIOGRAPHY

Abbott, Sidney, and Barbara Love. *Sappho Was a Right-On Woman*. New York: Scarborough Press, 1977.

Abrams, Kathryn, and Irene Kacandes, eds. "Witness." Special issue, *Women's Studies Quarterly* 36, nos. 1–2 (spring–summer 2008).

Ahmed, Sara. *The Cultural Politics of Emotion*. New York: Routledge, 2004.

Alcoff, Linda. "Cultural Feminism versus Post-structuralism: The Identity Crisis in Feminist Theory." *Signs: Journal of Women in Culture and Society* 13, no. 3 (1988): 405–36.

Anderson, Benedict. *Imagined Communities: Reflections on the Origin and Spread of Nationalism*. Revised edition. London: Verso, 1991.

——. *Spectres of Comparison: Nationalism, Southeast Asia and the World*. London: Verso, 1998.

Ashley, Laura, and Beth Olson. "Constructing Reality: Print Media's Framing of the Women's Movement, 1966 to 1986." *Journalism and Mass Communication Quarterly* 75, no. 2 (summer 1998): 263–77.

Atkinson, Ti-Grace. *Amazon Odyssey*. New York: Links, 1974.

Badiou, Alain. *Being and Event*. New York: Continuum, 2007.

——. *Manifesto for Philosophy: Followed by Two Essays, "The (Re)turn of Philosophy Itself" and "Definition of Philosophy."* SUNY Series, Intersections: Philosophy and Critical Theory. New York: SUNY Press, 1999.

Barker-Plummer, Bernadette. "News as a Political Resource: Media Strategies and Political Identity in the U.S. Women's Movement, 1966–1975." *Critical Studies in Mass Communication* 12 (September 1995): 306–24.

Barlow, Tani E. *The Question of Women in Chinese Feminism*. Durham, NC: Duke University Press, 2004.

——. "'What is a poem?' History and the Modern Girl." Paper presented at the Feminist Theory Workshop, Duke University, March 20–21, 2009. Published in David Palumbo-Liu, Bruce Robbins, and Nirvana Tahnouki, eds., *Immanuel Wallerstein and the Problem of the World: System, Scale, Culture* (Durham, NC: Duke University Press, 2011), 155–83.

Baxandall, Rosalyn, and Linda Gordon. *Dear Sisters: Dispatches from the Women's Liberation Movement*. New York: Basic, 2000.

Beale, Frances. "Double Jeopardy: To Be Black and Female." In Cade, *The Black Woman*, 100.

Beauvoir, Simone de. *The Second Sex*. Translated by H. M. Parshley. New York: Penguin, 1953.

Bechdel, Alison. *Fun Home: A Family Tragicomic*. New York: Mariner, 2007.

Benjamin, Walter. "Surrealism: The Last Snapshot of the European Intelligentsia." In *Reflections: Essays, Aphorisms, Autobiographical Writings*, edited by Peter Demetz, translated by Edmund Jephcott, 177–92. New York: Harcourt Brace Jovanovich, 1978.

——. "Theses on the Philosophy of History." In *Illuminations*, edited by Hannah Arendt, translated by Harry Zohn, 253–64. New York: Schocken Books, 1969.

Berger, John. *Ways of Seeing*. London: British Broadcasting Corporation and Penguin, 1972.

Berlant, Lauren. "The Female Complaint." *Social Text* 19–20 (autumn 1988): 237–59.

——. *The Female Complaint: The Unfinished Business of Sentimentality in American Culture*. Durham, NC: Duke University Press, 2008.

——. *The Queen of America Goes to Washington City: Essays on Sex and Citizenship*. Durham, NC: Duke University Press, 1997.

——. "The Subject of True Feeling: Pain, Privacy, and Politics." In *Feminist Consequences: Theory for the New Century*, edited by Elisabeth Bronfen and Misha Kavka, 126–60. New York: Columbia University Press, 2001.

Blackwell, Maylei. "Contested Histories: Las Hijas de Cuauhtemoc, Chicana Feminisms, and Print Culture in the Chicano Movement, 1968–1973." In *Chicana Feminisms: A Critical Reader*, edited by Gabriela F. Arredondo, Aída Hurtado, Norma Klahn, Olga Nájera-Ramírez, and Patricia Zavella, 59–89. Durham, NC: Duke University Press, 2003.

Bourdieu, Pierre. "The Family Spirit." *Practical Reason: On the Theory of Action*. Stanford, CA: Stanford University Press, 1998.

——. *Outline of a Theory of Practice*. Cambridge: Cambridge University Press, 1977.

——. *Practical Reason*. Stanford, CA: Stanford University Press, 1998.

Bradley, Patricia. *Mass Media and the Shaping of American Feminism, 1963–1975*. Jackson: University of Mississippi Press, 2003.

Breines, Wini. "What's Love Got to Do with It? White Women, Black Women, and Feminism in the Movement Years." *Signs: Journal of Women in Culture and Society* 27, no. 4 (summer 2002): 1095–133.

Bronfen, Elizabeth, and Misha Kavka, eds. *Feminist Consequences: Theory for the New Century*. New York: Columbia University Press, 2001.

Brown, Wendy. *Politics Out of History*. Princeton, NJ: Princeton University Press, 2001.

Brownmiller, Susan. *In Our Time: Memoir of a Revolution*. New York: Dial Press, 2000.

Butler, Judith. *Gender Trouble: Feminism and the Subversion of Identity*. New York: Routledge, 1990.

——. *The Psychic Life of Power: Theories in Subjection*. Stanford, CA: Stanford University Press, 1997.

Butt, Gavin. *Between You and Me: Queer Disclosures in the New York Art World, 1948–1963*. Durham, NC: Duke University Press, 2005.

Cade, Toni, ed. *The Black Woman*. New York: Signet Press, 1970.

Caprio, Frank. *Female Homosexuality: A Psychodynamic Study of Lesbianism*. New York: Citadel Press, 1954.

Castiglia, Christopher. "Sex Panics, Sex Publics, Sex Memories." *boundary 2*, no. 27 (2000): 149–75.

Castle, Terry. *The Apparitional Lesbian: Female Homosexuality and Modern Culture*. New York: Columbia University Press, 1993.

Chafe, William. *The American Woman: Her Changing Social, Economic, and Political Roles, 1920–1970*. New York: Oxford University Press, 1972.

Chute, Hillary. "An Interview with Alison Bechdel." In Chute and DeKoven, "Graphic Narrative," 1004–15.

Chute, Hillary, and Marianne DeKoven, eds. "Graphic Narrative." Special issue, *Modern Fiction Studies* 52, no. 4 (2006).

Clough, Patricia Ticineto, ed. *The Affective Turn: Theorizing the Social*. Durham, NC: Duke University Press, 2007.

Connerton, Paul. *How Societies Remember*. Cambridge: Cambridge University Press, 1989.

Cornell, Drucilla. "Rethinking the Time of Feminism." In *Feminist Contentions: A Philosophical Exchange*, edited by Seyla Benhabib, Judith Butler, Drucilla Cornell, and Nancy Fraser, 145–56. New York: Routledge, 1995.

Cott, Nancy F. *The Grounding of Modern Feminism*. New Haven: Yale University Press, 1987.

Cvetkovich, Ann. *An Archive of Feelings: Trauma, Sexuality, and Lesbian Public Cultures*. Durham, NC: Duke University Press, 2003.

——. "Drawing the Archive in Alison Bechdel's *Fun Home*." In Abrams and Kacandes, "Witness," 111–28.

——. "In the Archives of Lesbian Feelings: Documentary and Popular Culture." *Camera Obscura* 49 (2002): 106–47.

Davis, Angela Y. *Women, Race, and Class*. New York: Vintage, 1983.

Davis, Flora. *Moving the Mountain: The Women's Movement in America Since 1960*. Chicago: University of Illinois Press, 1999.

Davis, Madeline D., and Elizabeth Lapovsky Kennedy. *Boots of Leather, Slippers of Gold: The History of a Lesbian Community*. New York: Penguin, 1993.

de Certeau, Michel. *The Writing of History*. Translated by Tom Conley. New York: Columbia University Press, 1988.

DeKoven, Marianne. *Utopia Limited: The Sixties and the Emergence of the Postmodern*. Durham, NC: Duke University Press, 2004.

Delany, Samuel R. *The Motion of Light in Water: Sex and Science Fiction Writing in the East Village, 1957–1965*. New York: Arbor House and William Morrow, 1988.

de Lauretis, Teresa. "The Essence of the Triangle, or Taking the Risk of Essentialism Seriously: Feminist Theory in Italy, the U.S., and Britain." *differences* 1, no. 2 (1989): 1–39.

Deleuze, Gilles, and Felix Guattari. *Anti-Oedipus: Capitalism and Schizophrenia*. Translated by Robert Hurley, Mark Seem, and Helen R. Lane, with a preface by Michel Foucault. Minneapolis: University of Minnesota Press, 1983.

——. *A Thousand Plateaus: Capitalism and Schizophrenia*. Translated and with a foreword by Brian Massumi. Minneapolis: University of Minnesota Press, 1987.

D'Emilio, John. *Sexual Politics, Sexual Communities: The Making of a Homosexual Minority in the United States, 1940–1970*. Chicago: University of Chicago Press, 1983.

Derrida, Jacques. *Specters of Marx: The State of the Debt, the Work of Mourning, and the New International*. Translated by Peggy Kamuf. New York: Routledge, 1994.

Dinshaw, Carolyn. *Getting Medieval: Sexualities and Communities, Pre- and Postmodern*. Durham, NC: Duke University Press, 1999.

Distelberg, Brian J. "Mainstream Fiction, Gay Reviewers, and Gay Male Cultural Politics in the 1970s." GLQ 16, no. 3 (2010): 389–427.

Doan, Laura. *Fashioning Sapphism: The Origins of a Modern English Lesbian Culture*. New York: Columbia University Press, 2001.

Douglas, Susan J. *Where the Girls Are: Growing Up Female with the Mass Media*. New York: Times Books, Random House, 1994.

Duggan, Lisa. "The Discipline Problem: Queer Theory Meets Lesbian and Gay History." GLQ 2, no. 3 (1995): 179–91.

DuPlessis, Rachel Blau, and Ann Snitow. *The Feminist Memoir Project: Voices from Women's Liberation*. New York: Three Rivers Press, 1998.

Dyer, Richard. *White: Essays on Race and Culture*. London: Routledge, 1997.

Echols, Alice. *Daring to Be Bad: Radical Feminism in America, 1967–1975*. Minneapolis: University of Minnesota Press, 1989.

Ellis, Havelock. *Psychology of Sex*. 2nd edition. New York: Harcourt Brace Jovanovich, 1978.

Eng, David L., Judith Halberstam, and José Esteban Muñoz, eds. "What's Queer about Queer Studies Now?" Special issue, *Social Text* 23, nos. 3–4 (fall–winter 2005).

Eng, David L., and David Kazanjian, eds. *Loss: The Politics of Mourning.* Berkeley: University of California Press, 2003.

Enke, Anne. *Finding the Movement: Sexuality, Contested Space, and Feminist Activism.* Durham, NC: Duke University Press, 2007.

Enstad, Nan. "Fashioning Political Identities: Cultural Studies and the Historical Construction of Political Subjectivities." *American Quarterly* 50, no. 4 (1998): 745–82.

Evans, Sara. *Personal Politics: The Roots of Women's Liberation in the Civil Rights Movement and the New Left.* New York: Vintage, 1979.

Feinberg, Leslie. *Stone Butch Blues.* Ithaca, NY: Firebrand, 1993.

Firestone, Shulamith. *The Dialectic of Sex: The Case for Feminist Revolution.* New York: Farrar, Straus and Giroux, 2003.

Foucault, Michel. "Friendship as a Way of Life." In *Ethics, Subjectivity, and Truth: The Essential Works of Michel Foucault, Volume One, 1954–1984,* edited by Paul Rabinow, 135–40. New York: New Press, 1997.

——. *Herculine Barbin, Being the Recently Discovered Memoirs of a Nineteenth-Century French Hermaphrodite.* Translated by Richard McDougall. New York: Pantheon Books, 1980.

——. *History of Madness.* New York: Routledge, 2006.

——. "The History of Sexuality." Interview with Lucette Finas, translated by Leo Marshall. In *Power/Knowledge: Selected Interviews and Other Writings, 1972–1977,* edited by Colin Gordon, 183–90. New York: Pantheon, 1980.

——. *The History of Sexuality: An Introduction, Volume One.* New York: Vintage Press, 1990.

——. *Madness and Civilization: A History of Insanity in the Age of Reason.* New York: Vintage, 1988.

——. "Nietzsche, Genealogy, History." In *The Foucault Reader,* edited by Paul Rabinow, 76–100. New York: Pantheon, 1984.

——. *Pierre Rivière, Having Slaughtered My Mother, My Sister, and My Brother.* Translated by Frank Jellinek. Lincoln: University of Nebraska Press, 1982.

——. "Polemics, Politics, and Problematizations: An Interview with Michel Foucault." In *Michel Foucault: Ethics, Subjectivity and Truth,* edited by Paul Rabinow, translated by Robert Hurley, 113–19. New York: New Press, 1997.

Frankenberg, Ruth, ed. *Displacing Whiteness: Essays in Social and Cultural Criticism.* Durham, NC: Duke University Press, 1997.

——. *The Social Construction of Whiteness: White Women, Race Matters.* Minneapolis: University of Minnesota Press, 1993.

Fraser, Nancy. "Rethinking the Public Sphere: A Contribution to the Critique of

Actually Existing Democracy." In *The Phantom Public Sphere*, edited by Bruce Robbins, 1–32. Minneapolis: University of Minnesota Press, 1993.

Freccero, Carla. *Queer/Early/Modern*. Durham, NC: Duke University Press, 2006.

Freedman, Estelle. "'Uncontrolled Desires': The Response to the Sexual Psychopath, 1920–1960." *Journal of American History* 74 (June 1987): 83–106.

Freeman, Elizabeth. "Packing History, Count(er)ing Generations." *New Literary History* 31, no. 4 (2000): 727–44.

——, ed. "Queer Temporalities." Special issue, *GLQ* 13, nos. 2–3 (2007): 159–76.

Friedan, Betty. *The Feminine Mystique*. New York: Dell, 1975.

——. *It Changed My Life: Writings on the Women's Movement*. New York: Random House, 1976.

Garcia, Alma, ed. *Chicana Feminist Thought*. New York: Routledge, 1997.

Gerhard, Jane. *Desiring Revolution: Second-Wave Feminism and the Rewriting of American Sexual Thought, 1920–1982*. New York: Columbia University Press, 2001.

Gever, Martha. *Entertaining Lesbians: Celebrity, Sexuality, and Self-Invention*. New York: Routledge, 2003.

Gitlin, Todd. *The Whole World Is Watching: Mass Media in the Making and the Unmaking of the New Left*. Berkeley: University of California Press, 1980.

Goffman, Erving. *Stigma: Notes on the Management of Spoiled Identity*. New York: Simon and Schuster, 1963.

Gordon, Avery. *Ghostly Matters: Haunting and the Sociological Imagination*. Minneapolis: University of Minnesota Press, 1997.

Gross, Daniel M. *The Secret History of Emotion: From Aristotle's Rhetoric to Modern Brain Science*. Chicago: University of Chicago Press, 2006.

Guy-Sheftall, Beverly. "Sisters in Struggle: A Belated Response." In DuPlessis and Snitow, *The Feminist Memoir Project*, 485–92.

——, ed. *Words of Fire: An Anthology of African-American Feminist Thought*. New York: New Press, 1995.

Habermas, Jurgen. *Structural Transformation in the Public Sphere: An Inquiry into a Category of Bourgeois Society*. Translated by Thomas Burger and with an introduction by Thomas McCarthy. Cambridge, MA: MIT Press, 1989.

Haden, Patricia, Donna Middleton, and Patricia Robinson. "A Historical and Critical Essay for Black Women." In *Voices from Women's Liberation*, edited by Leslie B. Tanner, 316–24. New York: Signet, 1971.

Halberstam, Judith. *Female Masculinity*. Durham, NC: Duke University Press, 1998.

——. *In a Queer Time and Place: Transgender Bodies, Subcultural Lives*. New York: New York University Press, 2005.

——. "Shame and White Gay Masculinity." In Eng, Halberstam, and Muñoz, "What's Queer about Queer Studies Now?," 219–33.

Halbwachs, Maurice. *On Collective Memory*. Edited, translated, and with an introduction by Lewis A. Coser. Chicago: University of Chicago Press, 1992.

Hall, Radclyffe. *The Well of Loneliness*. New York: Anchor, 1990.

Hardt, Michael, and Antonio Negri. *Empire*. Cambridge, MA: Harvard University Press, 2000.

Haug, Frigga, et al. *Female Sexualization: A Collective Work of Memory*. London: Verso, 1999.

Hayden, Casey, and Mary King. "Sex and Caste: A Kind of Memo." In Evans, *Personal Politics*, 235–37.

Heilbrun, Carolyn G. *Education of a Woman: The Life of Gloria Steinem*. New York: Ballantine, 1996.

Heller, Dana. "Found Footage: Feminism Lost in Time." *Tulsa Studies in Women's Literature* 21, no. 1 (spring 2002): 85–98.

——. "Shooting Solanas: Radical Feminist History and the Technology of Failure." In *Feminist Time against Nation Time: Gender, Politics, and the Nation-State in an Age of Permanent War*, edited by Victoria Hesford and Lisa Diedrich, 151–68. Lanham, MD: Lexington, 2008.

Hemmings, Clare. "Telling Feminist Stories." *Feminist Theory* 6, no. 2 (2005): 115–39.

——. *Why Stories Matter: The Political Grammar of Feminist Theory*. Durham, NC: Duke University Press, 2011.

Hesford, Victoria, and Lisa Diedrich. "Introduction: Thinking Feminism in a Time of War." In *Feminist Time against Nation Time: Gender, Politics, and the Nation-State in an Age of Permanent War*, edited by Victoria Hesford and Lisa Diedrich, 1–21. Lanham, MD: Lexington, 2008.

Hinds, Hilary, and Jackie Stacey. "Imaging Feminism, Imaging Femininity: The Bra-Burner, Diana, and the Woman Who Kills." *Feminist Media Studies* 1, no. 2 (2001): 153–77.

Hirsch, Marianne, and Valerie Smith. "Feminism and Cultural Memory: An Introduction." *Signs: Journal of Women in Culture and Society* 28, no. 1 (2002): 1–19.

Horkheimer, Max, and Theodor Adorno. *Dialectic of Enlightenment*. New York: Continuum, 1982.

Horowitz, Daniel. *Betty Friedan and the Making of* The Feminine Mystique*: The American Left, the Cold War, and Modern Feminism*. Amherst: University of Massachusetts Press, 2000.

Howard, Judith A., and Carolyn Allen, eds. "Feminisms at a Millennium." Special issue, *Signs: Journal of Women and Culture in Society* 25, no. 4 (2000).

Howe, Florence, ed. *The Politics of Women's Studies: Testimony from Thirty Founding Mothers*. New York: Feminist Press, CUNY, 2000.

Howell, Sharon. *Reflections of Ourselves: The Mass Media and the Women's Movement, 1963 to the Present.* New York: Peter Lang, 1990.

Huyssen, Andreas. "Present Pasts: Media, Politics, Amnesia." *Public Culture* 12, no. 1 (2000): 21–38.

——. *Present Pasts: Urban Palimpsests and the Politics of Memory.* Stanford, CA: Stanford University Press, 2003.

Jaggar, Alison M. "Love and Knowledge: Emotion in Feminist Epistemology." In *Gender/Body/Knowledge: Feminist Reconstructions of Being and Knowing,* edited by Alison M. Jaggar and Susan R. Bordo, 145–71. New Brunswick, NJ: Rutgers University Press, 1989.

Jagose, Annamarie. *Inconsequence: Lesbian Representation and the Logic of Sexual Sequence.* Ithaca, NY: Cornell University Press, 2002.

Jameson, Fredric. "Periodizing the 1960s." *Social Text,* "The 60s without Apology," no. 9/10, (spring–summer 1984): 178–209.

——. *Postmodernism, or, the Cultural Logic of Late Capitalism.* Durham, NC: Duke University Press, 1994.

——. "Reification and Utopia in Mass Culture." *Social Text* 1 (winter 1979): 130–48.

Jay, Karla. *Tales of the Lavender Menace: A Memoir of Liberation.* New York: Basic Books, 1999.

Jay, Karla, and Allen Young eds. *Out of the Closets: Voices of Gay Liberation.* Twentieth Anniversary Edition, with a foreword by John D'Emilio. New York: New York University Press, 1992.

Jong, Erica. *Fear of Flying.* New York: Signet, 1974.

Jordan, Mark D. "Making the Homophile Manifest." In Radner and Luckett, *Swinging Single,* 181–205.

Joseph, Miranda. *Against the Romance of Community.* Minneapolis: University of Minnesota Press, 2002.

Joseph, Peniel E. *Waiting 'til the Midnight Hour: A Narrative History of Black Power in America.* New York: Henry Holt, 2006.

Juhasz, Suzanne. "Towards a Theory of Feminist Autobiography: Kate Millett's *Flying* and *Sita;* Maxine Hong Kingston's *The Woman Warrior.*" In *Women's Autobiography: Essays in Criticism,* edited by Estelle Jelinek, 221–37. Bloomington: Indiana University Press, 1980.

Kaplan, Cora. "Radical Feminism and Literature: Rethinking Millett's *Sexual Politics.*" *Sea Changes: Essays on Culture and Feminism.* London: Verso, 1986.

Katz, Sue. "Smash Phallic Imperialism." In Jay and Young, *Out of the Closets,* 259–61.

King, Katie. *Theory in Its Feminist Travels: Conversations in U.S. Women's Movements.* Bloomington: Indiana University Press, 1994.

Kipnis, Laura. *Against Love: A Polemic.* New York: Pantheon, 2003.

Klaich, Dolores. *Woman + Woman: Attitudes Towards Lesbianism*. New York: William Morrow, 1974.

Koedt, Anne. "Lesbianism and Feminism." In *Radical Feminism*, edited by Anne Koedt, Ellen Levine, and Anita Rapone, 246–58. New York: Quadrangle, 1973.

———. "Loving Another Woman—Interview." In *Radical Feminism*, edited by Anne Koedt, Ellen Levine, and Anita Rapone, 85–93. New York: Quadrangle, 1973.

———. "The Myth of the Vaginal Orgasm." In *Radical Feminism*, edited by Anne Koedt, Ellen Levine, and Anita Rapone, 198–207. New York: Quadrangle, 1973.

Kolodny, Annette. "The Lady's Not for Spurning: Kate Millett and the Critics." In *Women's Autobiography: Essays in Criticism*, edited by Estelle Jellinek, 238–59. Bloomington: Indiana University Press, 1980.

Krafft-Ebing, Richard von. *Psychopathia Sexualis*. 12th edition, 1886–1903. New York: Paperback Library, 1965.

Lauret, Maria. *Liberating Literature: Feminist Fiction in America*. London: Routledge, 1994.

Leys, Ruth. *Trauma: A Genealogy*. Chicago: University of Chicago Press, 2000.

Lipsitz, George. *Time Passages: Collective Memory and American Popular Culture*. Minneapolis: University of Minnesota Press, 1990.

Lorde, Audre. *Zami: A New Spelling of My Name*. Watertown, MA: Persephone, 1982.

Love, Heather. *Feeling Backward; Loss and the Politics of Queer History*. Cambridge, MA: Harvard University Press, 2007.

Macey, David. *The Lives of Michel Foucault*. New York: Pantheon, 1993.

Martin, Del, and Phyllis Lyon. *Lesbian/Woman*. San Francisco: Bantam, 1972.

Martin, Emily. *Biopolar Expeditions: Mania and Depression in American Culture*. Princeton, NJ: Princeton University Press, 2007.

Massumi, Brian. *Parables for the Virtual: Movement, Affect, Sensation*. Durham, NC: Duke University Press, 2002.

May, Elaine Tyler. *Homeward Bound: American Families in the Cold War Era*. New York: Basic, 1988.

McCarthy, Thomas. Introduction to *Structural Transformation in the Public Sphere: An Inquiry into a Category of Bourgeois Society*, by Jurgen Habermas, xi–xiv. Translated by Thomas Burger. Cambridge, MA: MIT Press, 1989.

McClintock, Anne. *Imperial Leather: Race, Gender, and Sexuality in the Colonial Contest*. New York: Routledge, 1995.

McIntosh, Mary. "The Homosexual Role." In *Forms of Desire*, edited by Edward Stein, 25–41. New York: Routledge, 1990.

McRobbie, Angela. *The Aftermath of Feminism: Gender, Culture and Social Change*. London: Sage, 2008.

Metzl, Jonathan M. *The Protest Psychosis: How Schizophrenia Became a Black Disease*. Boston: Beacon, 2009.

——. *Prozac on the Couch: Prescribing Gender in the Era of Wonder Drugs*. Durham, NC: Duke University Press, 2003.

Meyerowitz, Joanne. "Beyond the Feminine Mystique: A Reassessment of Postwar Mass Culture, 1946–1958." In Meyerowitz, *Not June Cleaver*, 229–62.

——, ed. *Not June Cleaver: Women and Gender in Postwar America, 1945–1960*. Philadelphia: Temple University Press, 1994.

Miller, James. *Democracy Is in the Streets: From Port Huron to the Siege of Chicago*. Cambridge, MA: Harvard University Press, 1994.

Miller, Nancy K. "The Entangled Self: Gender Bondage in the Age of Memoir." *PMLA* 122, no. 2 (2007): 537–48.

Millett, Kate. *Flying*. New York: Simon and Schuster, 1990.

——. *The Loony-Bin Trip*. New York: Simon and Schuster, 1990.

——. *Sexual Politics*. New York: Ballantine Books, 1978.

——. *Sita*. New York: Ballantine Books, 1977.

Mohanty, Chandra Talpade. "Under Western Eyes: Feminist Scholarship and Colonial Discourses." *Feminist Review* 30 (autumn 1988): 65–88.

Morgan, Robin. "Goodbye to All That." In *Voices From Women's Liberation*, edited by Leslie B. Tanner, 268–76. New York: New American Library, 1970.

——, ed. *Sisterhood Is Powerful: An Anthology of Writings from the Women's Liberation Movement*. New York: Vintage, 1970.

Morris, Meaghan. *Too Soon, Too Late: History in Popular Culture*. Bloomington: Indiana University Press, 1998.

Muñoz, José Esteban. *Cruising Utopia: The Then and There of Queer Futurity*. New York: New York University Press, 2009.

——. *Disidentifications: Queers of Color and the Performance of Politics*. Minneapolis: University of Minnesota Press, 1999.

Myron, Nancy, and Charlotte Bunch, eds. *Lesbianism and the Women's Movement*. Baltimore: Diana Press, 1975.

Nealon, Christopher. *Foundlings: Lesbian and Gay Historical Emotion before Stonewall*. Durham, NC: Duke University Press, 2001.

Newton, Esther. "The Mythic Mannish Lesbian." In *Hidden from History: Reclaiming the Gay and Lesbian Past*, edited by Martin Bauml Duberman, Martha Vicinus, and George Chauncey Jr., 281–93. New York: Signet Classic, 1989.

Nicholson, Linda, ed. *The Second Wave: A Reader in Feminist Theory*. New York: Routledge, 1997.

Oliver, Kelly. *Witnessing: Beyond Recognition*. Minneapolis: University of Minnesota Press, 2001.

Penn, Donna. "The Sexualized Woman: The Lesbian, the Prostitute, and the

Containment of Female Sexuality in Postwar America." In Meyerowitz, *Not June Cleaver*, 358–81.

Peters, John Durham. "Seeing Bifocally: Media, Place, Culture." In *Culture, Power, Place: Explorations in Critical Anthropology*, edited by Akhil Gupta and James Ferguson, 75–92. Durham, NC: Duke University Press, 1997.

Piercy, Marge. "The Grand Coolie Damn." In Morgan, *Sisterhood Is Powerful*, 473–92.

Pratt, Lloyd, ed. "In The Event." Special issue, *differences* 19, no. 2 (2008).

Puar, Jasbir K. *Terrorist Assemblages: Homonationalism in Queer Times*. Durham, NC: Duke University Press, 2007.

Radicalesbians. "The Woman Identified Woman." In *Radical Feminism*, edited by Anne Koedt, Ellen Levine, and Anita Rapone, 240–45. New York: Quadrangle, 1973.

Radner, Hilary, and Moya Luckett, eds. *Swinging Single: Representing Sexuality in the Sixties*. Minneapolis: University of Minnesota Press, 1999.

Redstockings. "Manifesto." In *Sisterhood Is Powerful*, edited by Robin Morgan, 598–602. New York: Vintage, 1970.

Rich, Adrienne. "Compulsory Heterosexuality and the Lesbian Continuum." *Blood Bread and Poetry: Selected Prose, 1979–1985*, 23–75. New York: W. W. Norton, 1986.

——. "Compulsory Heterosexuality and the Lesbian Continuum." In *Powers of Desire: The Politics of Sexuality*, edited by Ann Snitow, Christine Stansell, and Sharon Thompson, 177–89. New York: Monthly Review Press, 1983.

——. "Compulsory Heterosexuality and the Lesbian Continuum." *Signs: Journal of Women and Culture in Society* 5, no. 4 (1980): 631–60.

Ronell, Avital. "The Deviant Payback: The Aims of Valerie Solanas." In Solanas, SCUM *Manifesto*, 1–34. New York: Verso, 2004.

Rosaldo, Michelle. "Toward an Anthropology of Self and Feeling." In *Culture Theory: Essays on Mind, Self, and Emotion*, edited by Richard Sweder and Robert Levine, 137–57. Cambridge: University of Cambridge Press, 1984.

Rosen, Ruth. *The World Split Open: How the Modern Women's Movement Changed America*. Revised edition. New York: Penguin, 2001.

Ross, Kristin. *May '68 and Its Afterlives*. Chicago: University of Chicago Press, 2002.

Roth, Benita. *Separate Roads to Feminism: Black, Chicana, and White Feminist Movements in America's Second Wave*. Cambridge: Cambridge University Press, 2004.

Rothberg, Michael. *Multidirectional Memory: Remembering the Holocaust in the Age of Decolonization*. Stanford, CA: Stanford University Press, 2009.

Rubin, Gayle. "Thinking Sex: Notes for a Radical Theory of the Politics of Sexuality." In *Pleasure and Danger: Exploring Female Sexuality*, edited by Carole S. Vance, 267–319. London: Routledge and Kegan Paul, 1984.

Russo, Mary. *The Female Grotesque: Risk, Excess, and Modernity*. New York: Routledge, 1994.

Ryan, Barbara. *Feminism and the Women's Movement: Dynamics of Change in Social Movement Ideology and Activism*. New York: Routledge, 1992.

Saldhana, Arun. *Psychedelic White: Goa Trance and the Viscosity of Race*. Minneapolis: University of Minnesota Press, 2007.

Schwarz, Judith. *Radical Feminists of Heterodoxy: Greenwich Village, 1912–1940*. Norwich, VT: New Victoria, 1986.

Scott, Joan W. "The Evidence of Experience." In *Feminist Approaches to Theory and Methodology: An Interdisciplinary Reader*, edited by Sharlene Nagy Hesse-Biber, Christina K. Gilmartin, and Robin Lydenberg, 79–99. New York: Oxford University Press, 1999.

——. "Fantasy Echo: History and the Construction of Identity." *Critical Inquiry* 27, no. 2 (winter 2001): 284–304.

——. *Gender and the Politics of History*. Revised edition. New York: Columbia University Press, 1999.

——. *Women's Studies on the Edge*. Durham, NC: Duke University Press, 2008.

Sedgwick, Eve Kosofsky. *Epistemology of the Closet*. Berkeley: University of California Press, 1990.

——. *Touching Feeling: Affect, Pedagogy, Performativity*. Durham, NC: Duke University Press, 2003.

Sedgwick, Eve Kosofsky, and Adam Frank. *Shame and Its Sisters: A Silvan Tomkins Reader*. Durham, NC: Duke University Press, 1995.

Seidman, Steven. "Identity Politics in a 'Postmodern' Gay Culture." In *Fear of a Queer Planet: Queer Politics and Social Theory*, edited and with an introduction by Michael Warner, 105–42. Minneapolis: University of Minnesota Press, 1993.

——. *Romantic Longings: Love in America, 1830–1980*. London: Routledge, 1991.

Sewell, William H., Jr. *Logics of History: Social Theory and Social Transformation*. Chicago: University of Chicago Press, 2005.

Shumway, David. *Modern Love: Romance, Intimacy and the Marriage Crisis*. New York: New York University Press, 2003.

Silver, Brenda R. *Virginia Woolf Icon*. Chicago: University of Chicago Press, 1999.

Sinfield, Alan. *The Wilde Century: Effeminacy, Oscar Wilde, and the Queer Moment*. New York: Columbia University Press, 1994.

Smith-Rosenberg, Carroll. "Discourses of Sexuality and Subjectivity: The New Woman, 1870–1936." In *Hidden from History: Reclaiming the Gay and Lesbian Past*, edited by Martin Bauml Duberman, Martha Vicinus, and George Chauncey Jr., 264–80. New York: New American Library, 1989.

Solanas, Valerie. *SCUM Manifesto*. With an introduction by Avital Ronell. London: Verso, 2004.

Souhami, Diane. *The Trials of Radclyffe Hall*. London: Weidenfeld and Nicholson, 1998.

Spencer, Robyn Ceanne. "Engendering the Black Freedom Struggle: Revolutionary Black Womanhood and the Black Panther Party in the Bay Area, California." *Journal of Women's History* 20, no. 1 (spring 2008): 90–113.

Spigel, Lynn, and Michael Curtin, eds. *The Revolution Wasn't Televised: Sixties Television and Social Conflict*. New York: Routledge, 1997.

Springer, Kimberly. *Living for the Revolution: Black Feminist Organizations, 1968–1980*. Durham, NC: Duke University Press, 2005.

Stearn, Jess. *The Grapevine: A Report on the Secret World of the Lesbian*. New York: Doubleday, 1964.

Stoler, Ann Laura. "Colonial Archives and the Arts of Governance: On the Content in the Form." In *Refiguring the Archive*, edited by Carolyn Hamilton, Verne Harris, Michele Pickover, Graeme Reid, Razia Saleh, and Jane Taylor, 83–100. Norwell, MA: Kluwer Academic, 2002.

———. *Race and the Education of Desire: Foucault's History of Sexuality and the Colonial Order of Things*. Durham, NC: Duke University Press, 1995.

Sturken, Marita. *Tangled Memories: The Vietnam War, the Aids Epidemic, and the Politics of Remembering*. Berkeley: University of California Press, 1997.

Tanner, Leslie, ed. *Voices from Women's Liberation*. New York: Signet, 1971.

Trouillot, Michel-Rolph. *Silencing the Past: Power and the Production of History*. Boston: Beacon, 1995.

Vance, Carole, ed. *Pleasure and Danger: Exploring Female Sexuality*. London: Pandora, 1983.

Van Zoonen, L. "The Women's Movement and the Media: Constructing a Public Identity." *European Journal of Communication* 7, no. 4 (1992): 453–76.

Wallace, Christine. *Germaine Greer: Untamed Shrew*. London: Faber and Faber, 1999.

Warner, Michael, ed. *Fear of a Queer Planet: Queer Politics and Social Theory*. Minneapolis: University of Minnesota Press, 1993.

———. *Publics and Counterpublics*. New York: Zone, 2002.

Washington, Cynthia. "We Started from Different Ends of the Spectrum." In Evans, *Personal Politics*, 238–42.

Watson, Julia. "Autographic Disclosures and Genealogies of Desire in Alison Bechdel's *Fun Home*." In Whitlock and Poletti, "Autographics," 27–58.

Weedon, Chris. *Feminist Practice and Postructuralist Theory*. Oxford: Basil Blackwell, 1987.

Whitlock, Gillian, and Anna Poletti, eds. "Autographics." Special issue, *Biography* 31, no. 1 (winter 2008).

Wiegman, Robyn. "Academic Feminism against Itself." *NWSA Journal* 14, no. 2 (2002): 18–37.

———. "Feminisms, Institutionalism, and the Idea of Failure." *differences* 11, no. 3 (1999–2000): 107–36.

———. "Heteronormativity and the Desire for Gender." *Feminist Theory* 7, no. 1 (2006): 89–103.

Woolf, Virginia. *Three Guineas*. New York: Mariner Books, 1963.

Zerilli, Linda. *Feminism and the Abyss of Freedom*. Chicago: University of Chicago Press, 2005.

Zimmerman, Bonnie. "Confessions of a Lesbian Feminist." In *Cross-Purposes: Lesbians, Feminists, and the Limits of Alliance*, edited by Dana Heller, 157–68. Bloomington: Indiana University Press, 1997.

INDEX

Castiglia, Chris, 213, 308n15

Castle, Terry, 238, 274n49

Ceballos, Jacqueline, 5

Certeau, Michel de, 312n48

Chicago Women's Liberation Union (CWLU), 83–84, 91, 289n13

Chicana feminism, 3, 84, 119, 221, 269n1, 270n7, 289n15, 293n14

Chisholm, Shirley, 5, 284n74

Chute, Hillary, 249, 261, 314–15n16, 315n18

civil rights movement, 8, 39, 45, 49, 120, 121–22, 126, 129–30, 179, 201, 234, 271n23, 285n96, 289n15, 294n27, 306n62; *See also* black freedom movements

Clough, Patricia Ticineto, 275–76n56

Cold War, 33, 37; cultural paranoia of, 26, 76; domestic ideology of, 48–49, 57, 58, 74, 78, 120, 282n51, 282n60

collective memory, 21–23, 31, 33, 52, 215, 260, 283n64, 308n9, 309n28. *See also* Halbwachs, Maurice; subcultural memory

colonialism, 20, 36, 46, 258, 259

"Compulsory Heterosexuality and the Lesbian Continuum" (Rich), 240–41, 244–48, 312n55

consciousness raising, 56, 84, 94, 122, 123, 129, 130, 141, 179–81, 188, 294n24, 316nn48–49

Cornell, Drucilla, 24, 88, 277n68, 290n22

Crawford, Leslie, 235–38, 311n43, 311n45

Cvetkovich, Ann, 210, 261–63, 274n52, 275n56, 308n10, 313n2, 314–15nn16–17, 315nn21–23, 315nn25–26

Daughters of Bilitis (DOB), 77, 142, 287n115, 290n30, 299n65

Davis, Angela, 3, 39, 53, 220, 280n33, 283n61

Davis, Flora, 11–12, 269nn3–4, 271–72n23, 272nn31–33, 280nn34–35, 283n67, 288n9

Davis, Madeline, 77, 287n116, 307n1

Decter, Midge, 27

Dekoven, Marianne, 37, 123, 153, 261,

280n29, 286n96, 294n25, 294n28, 294n32, 300n77, 314–15n16, 315n18

De Lauretis, Teresa, 240–48, 312nn53–54

Deleuze, Gilles, 248, 255, 304–5n32, 312n57; on affect, 275n56

D'Emilio, John, 77, 286n107, 287n115, 299n65

Diedrich, Lisa, 291n59, 315n24

Dinshaw, Carolyn, 252–58, 271n15, 313nn3–4, 313n6, 314n12

disidentification, 2, 30, 134, 189, 194; from norms of hetero-respectability, 101, 103, 104, 216, 311n46; with women's liberation, 126

Doan, Laura, 273n40

Douglas, Susan J., 14–15, 214, 273n41, 280–81n38, 285n90, 308n18

Duggan, Lisa, 261, 270–71n13, 313n1

Dunbar, Roxanne, 72

DuPlessis, Rachel Blau, 9, 11, 271n14, 272n24

Echols, Alice, 3, 8–9, 11, 30, 82, 94, 147, 269n6, 271n21, 271n23, 278n12, 283nn62–63, 284–85n82, 288nn3–4, 288nn7–8, 290n32, 290n34, 294n34, 296n49, 299n64, 300n71, 306nn46–47, 309n29; on Shulamith Firestone, 310n34

Edelman, Lee, 254

Ellison, Ralph, 15

emotion: economies of, 16, 19–20; rhetorical deployment of, 96–97. *See also* feelings

Empire (Hardt and Negri), 275–76n56

Eng, David, 303n13, 313n2, 314n14

Equal Rights Amendment (ERA), 3, 40, 46–53, 56–57, 84, 281n47, 282n58, 284n74

essentialism, 119, 150; perception of (in relation to second-wave feminism), 15, 76, 121, 238; problem of (for feminist theory), 241–44, 312nn53–54

Evans, Sara, 8, 11, 126, 129, 271n20, 271n23, 295n37, 295n39. *See also* civil rights movement

gay liberation, 25, 37, 38, 65, 76, 79, 83, 87, 93, 117, 130, 131, 156, 160, 180, 187, 188, 192, 193, 198, 236, 250, 252, 258–59, 267, 284n82, 292–93n7, 293n10

Gay Liberation Front, 168, 270n12, 299n65

Genet, Jean, 115, 165

Gerhard, Jane, 292nn65–66, 294n34, 296n50

ghosts, 59, 239–40, 256–57; "following the ghosts" (Gordon), 308–9n20; looking for the ghosts of women's liberation, 15, 159, 209, 211, 214–16, 227, 230, 232, 234, 244, 273–74n43

Gitlin, Todd, 34–36, 37, 38, 279n21, 279n24, 281nn39–40

"Goodbye to All That" (Morgan), 85, 96–100, 102–4, 105, 106, 112, 120, 125, 153, 290nn38–39, 290n41, 291n45, 291n48

Gordon, Avery, 15, 147, 214–15, 239–40, 274n44, 291n48, 292n74, 300n70, 306n63, 308–9nn20–21, 312nn48–49

Gordon, Linda, 21, 150, 271n14, 277n60, 290n27, 291n54, 300n7

Grapevine (Stearn), 76, 286n107, 287n112

Greer, Germaine, 5, 236

Gross, Daniel, 20–21, 98, 117, 277nn58–59, 291n44, 293n11, 314n11

grotesque: female grotesque, 206, 304nn26–27; Millett as feminist grotesque, 159, 168–69, 304n26

Guattari, Felix, 248, 304–5n32, 312n57; on affect, 275n56

Guevara, Che, 54

Guy-Sheftall, Beverly, 9–10, 11, 272n, 289n16

Habermas, Jurgen, 35, 46, 279n22

Haden, Patricia, 104–5

Halberstam, Judith, 150, 210, 271n15, 300n75, 308n10, 314n13

Halbwachs, Maurice, 19, 22–23, 52, 274n47, 277nn61–63

Hall, Radclyffe, 188, 273n40, 297n58, 307n5

Hanisch, Carol, 121–22, 123–24, 294nn22–23, 294n31, 294n33

Hayden, Casey, 126–30, 295nn41–42

Hearst, Patty: kidnapping of, 169

Heilbrun, Carolyn, 236, 311n44

Heller, Dana, 103, 207, 216–17, 291nn54–55, 307nn2–3, 309n25

Hemmings, Clare, 275n55, 312n51

Herculine Barbin (Foucault), 254, 256, 313nn7–8

heteronormativity, 59, 75, 80, 101, 113, 128, 147, 186, 215, 221–22, 227, 232, 237, 245, 247–48, 252, 274n45, 291n48. See also sex-caste system; sexuality

hetero-respectability. See respectability

"A Historical and Critical Essay for Black Women" (Haden, Middleton, and Robinson), 104–5, 291n57

history: "fictioning" of (Dinshaw), 254, 313n4; production of, 2; "queer desire for" (Dinshaw), 6, 13, 230, 252, 256, 260

History of Sexuality Volume One: Introduction (Foucault), 118, 253, 272n28, 292n5, 292–93n7, 293n12, 313n4

Hoffman, Merle, 310–11n36

homophile organizations, 49, 77, 287n115, 290n29. See also Daughters of Bilitis; Mattachine Society

Horowitz, Daniel, 107, 292n61, 292n72, 303n16, 311n44

Howe, Irving: review of Sexual Politics (Millett), 26–27, 78, 277n5, 292n3

Howell, Sharon, 43, 269n2, 281n42, 285n96

Hunt, Morton, 71–72, 107, 286nn98–102

Hunter, Charlayne, 65, 285n83

Huyssen, Andreas, 22, 33, 215, 277n64, 278n17, 309n23

If These Walls Could Talk (film), 307n4

If These Walls Could Talk 2 (film), 206–9, 216–22, 226

image memory, 17, 24, 76, 77, 79, 157; definition of, 277n67

Jaggar, Alison M., 18, 274n50

Jagose, Annemarie, 292n60

Meyerowitz, Joanne, 107–8, 282n51, 282n60, 292nn62–64, 292n73

Middleton, Donna, 104–5

Miller, Henry, 4, 115, 165, 168

Miller, James, 280n25, 280n27, 280n30, 294n26, 294nn29–30

Miller, Nancy K., 314–15n16

Millett, Kate, 4–5, 31, 53, 67, 82, 112; experimentation with life, 174, 190, 192, 195, 196, 198, 199, 203–5, 265, 266; and gay liberation, 25, 87, 160, 189–90, 193, 236; mainstream media profiles of, 159–69; manic depression of, 170, 267, 304–5n32, 311n45; as the Marx of feminism, 164–65, 303–4n23; Neel's portrait of, 161–64; outed by *Time*, 13, 16, 25–28, 71, 78–79, 85, 87–88, 92, 142–43, 155–57, 169, 174–75, 182–84; public presentation of self, 158, 160, 171, 176–77, 187, 193, 204–5, 235–38; as queer, 238–39; relationship to Fumio Yoshimura, 79, 160, 163, 177, 181, 192, 196, 197–98, 203; relationships with men and women of color, 199–203; resurfacing in the 1990s, 232–39. See also *Flying*; *Sexual Politics*

Miss America protest (1968), 2–3, 5, 17, 30, 36, 61, 214, 309–10n29; retelling in *Miss Congeniality*, 222–26, 310n30

Miss Congeniality (film), 209, 216, 222–26

Miss Congeniality 2: Armed and Fabulous (film), 209

Mitchell, Juliet, 301–2n4

Morgan, Robin, 86, 161. See also "Goodbye to All That"; *Sisterhood Is Powerful*

Morris, Meaghan, 306n51

Muñoz, Jose, 313n2, 313n5, 314n13

"Myth of the Vaginal Orgasm" (Koedt), 135–42, 145, 152, 178–79, 298nn59–61

National Black Feminist Organization (NBFO), 9, 12

National Organization for Women (NOW), 3, 44, 48, 57, 61, 63, 65, 82, 83, 303n16; founding of, 281–82n50; politi-cal platform in 1970, 84; upheaval over lesbianism in, 3, 83

Nealon, Christopher, 251–55, 257–58, 313n1

New Left, 2, 31, 37, 39, 49, 55–56, 65, 85–86, 95, 119, 122–23, 126, 130, 179, 250, 283n62, 294n25, 304n30; alternative media networks of, 115; hetero-rhetoricism of, 96; mass media and, 35–36, 279n24; sexism of, 96–100, 102–3, 105–6, 125, 153, 284n82, 293n14; theories of, 121. See also Morgan, Robin: "Goodbye to All That"; Students for a Democratic Society

new social movements, 253; borrowings from earlier historical events, 283n63; politics of, 34, 36–37, 91, 308n19; representations of, 280–81n38; rhetoric of, 95, 119, 129, 153, 293n14; violence against, 78. See also black freedom movements; civil rights movement; New Left; women's liberation movement

Newton, Esther, 134, 135, 296n55, 297–98n58

Newton, Huey P., 39

New Woman: figure of, 133–34, 135, 136, 296–97n56

New York Radical Feminists (NYRF), 231, 310n34

Nixon, Richard M., 169, 304n30

Oliver, Kelly, 303n12

performativity, 18–19, 159, 231, 274n53, 289n18

"personal is political," 117–32, 135, 153, 294nn21–23, 294n31, 294n33; origins of the phrase, 121–22, 294n21. See also Hanisch, Carol; Sarachild, Kathie

Piercy, Marge, 125, 294n35

poststructuralism, 116, 241–43, 312n54

Powers of Desire (Snitow, Stansell, and Thompson), 244–45, 312n55. See also "Compulsory Heterosexuality and the Lesbian Continuum"

"problem that has no name." See *Feminine Mystique, The* (Friedan)

psychoanalysis, 136, 146, 251, 257–58, 274n53, 275n56

Puar, Jasbir, 231, 275–76n56, 310n35

public cultures, 2, 5, 210, 231, 239, 261

"pulp sexology" (Jagose), 107, 146, 292n60

"queer desire for history" (Dinshaw), 6, 13, 230, 252, 256, 260

queer spectrality, 256–57

queer studies, 6, 15, 209, 231, 251, 259, 314n13

queer theory, 2, 5, 210, 228–32, 250–51, 252, 259–60, 270–71n13, 274n45, 275n56, 313n1, 313n6. *See also* "queer desire for history"

race, 8, 15, 32–33, 38–39, 51, 64, 73, 78; performativity of, 18–19. *See also* women's liberation movement: racism of

racism, 24, 36, 39, 44–46, 49, 53, 56, 59, 104–5, 113, 127, 280n28, 289n13, 306n62. *See also* women's liberation movement: racism of

Radicalesbians, 81, 131. *See also* Abbott, Sydney; Lavender Menace; Love, Barbara; "Woman Identified Woman"

"reading along the grain" (Stoler), 6, 13, 118, 119, 230

Redstockings, 60, 65, 83–84, 231, 289n13, 309–10n29, 310n34

respectability, 70, 73, 76, 78, 80, 156, 163, 195, 216–17, 286n115; discourse of, 33, 42; refusal of, 59, 100, 102, 169, 226, 238

Rich, Adrienne, 240–41, 244–48, 312n55

Robinson, Patricia, 104–5

Robinson, Ruby Doris Smith, 129, 271n20

Rodman, Craig, 117

Ronell, Avital, 96, 100, 103, 290n37, 291n47, 291n56

Rosen, Ruth, 3, 10–11, 21, 57, 94, 150, 269n3, 271n14, 272n29, 280n34, 281–82n50, 282n52, 283–84nn66–68, 288n5, 288n7,

290n33, 294n34, 299n64, 300n73, 306n47, 310n29, 310n31

Roth, Benita, 3, 270n7, 293nn13–14

Rothberg, Michael, 259–60, 283n64, 314nn14–15

Rubin, Gayle, 270–71n13

Russo, Mary, 206, 304nn26–27

Ryan, Barbara, 3, 270n7, 288n7

Sage, Lorna, 301–2n4

Sappho Was a Right-On Woman (Abbott and Love), 82–83, 88, 152, 287n1, 288nn6–7, 288nn9–10, 289–90nn20–21, 300n76

Sarachild, Kathie, 122, 179, 306nn48–49

Scott, Joan Wallach, 10, 121, 132–33, 270–71n13, 272n30, 294n19, 296nn51–52, 309n22, 312n50

SCUM Manifesto (Solanas), 81, 96, 99–105, 106, 109, 112, 143, 291n46, 291nn48–53

Second Congress to Unite Women (1970), 3, 81–83, 131, 139, 147, 288n7, 300n69, 300n76. *See also* Lavender Menace

Sedgwick, Eve Kosofsky, 28, 183, 275–76n56, 278n11, 290n26, 306n55

self-fashioning, 37, 136, 158, 254. *See also* Millett, Kate: public presentation of self

Sex and the City (TV series), 209, 307n7

sex-caste system, 127–28, 130, 147. *See also* heteronormativity

sexology, 134. *See also* pulp sexology

sexuality: normative, 192; site of reproduction of social power, 4, 84, 114–17, 125–26

Sexual Politics (Millett), 3–4, 25–26, 40, 114–18, 125, 156–57, 159–60, 168, 171, 182, 185, 190, 236, 237, 270n8, 277n2, 278n10, 292nn1–2, 292n6, 303n14, 311n37

Shanahan, Eileen, 42, 46–48, 49, 56, 281n47

Shelley, Martha, 117, 270n10, 299n65, 303n14

Sherrill, Robert, 50–57, 60, 282nn54–57, 284n74

shorthand notation, 17, 19–24, 94, 106, 117, 153, 174, 214, 220, 277n67. *See also* feminist-as-lesbian figure; image memory

Shulie (Subrin), 229–31, 310n34. *See also* Firestone, Shulamith

Sinfield, Alan, 4, 270n11

Sisterhood Is Powerful (Morgan) 3, 40, 115, 293n10, 299n65

Smith, Barbara, 129, 295n44

Smith-Rosenberg, Carroll, 133–35, 273n40, 296n48, 296nn53–54, 296–97n56, 297–98n58

Snitow, Ann, 9, 11, 82, 244–45, 271n14, 272n24, 288n3

Solanas, Valerie, 85, 87, 99, 153, 290n37, 291n47, 291nn54–56; Solanesque politics of refusal, 98, 113, 299n64. See also *scum Manifesto*

Springer, Kimberly, 3, 119, 126, 129, 270n7, 288n10, 289n15, 293n13, 293n15, 295n38, 295nn44–45

Stafford, Jean, 73, 286n104

Stearn, Jess, 76, 286n107, 287n112

Steinem, Gloria, 87, 235, 236–37

Stoler, Ann Laura, 7, 257, 271nn16–19, 285n95, 292–93n7

structure of feeling, 123

Student Nonviolent Coordinating Committee (SNCC), 8, 84, 119, 126; women in, 84, 129–30, 271n20

Students for a Democratic Society (SDS), 55; Port Huron Statement, 36–37, 122–24, 280n25, 280n27, 280n30, 294n27; women in, 129, 283n62

Sturken, Marita, 157, 302n9, 307–8n9

subcultural memory, 6–7

Symbionese Liberation Army, 169

"temporal drag" (Freeman), 227–30, 232, 263

Third World liberation struggles, 39, 54, 77; figure of the Third World revolutionary, 73

Third World women, 298

Third World Women's Alliance, 64, 84, 129, 288n10

Tiger, Lionel, 27, 51, 71, 286n97

Tobias, Sheila, 302n10

Town Bloody Hall (documentary film), 270n12

Trilling, Diana, 5

urban guerrilla fighter: women's liberationist as, 39, 42, 50–51, 54–56, 69, 73, 78, 105, 283n64

Warhol, Andy, 99, 175, 177, 291n54

Warner, Michael, 33–34, 211, 251, 274n48, 278n18, 280n31, 290n25, 308n13, 313n1

Washington, Cynthia, 129, 295n40, 295n43

Weathermen, 39, 55

Weedon, Chris, 241, 312n54

whiteness, 42, 78, 200, 202, 267, 275n53; historicization of, 17–19; problem of naturalization of, 2. *See also* women's liberation movement: whiteness and middle-classness of

Wiegman, Robyn, 270n8, 274n45, 309n22

Willis, Ellen, 178, 306n46

Wilson, Elizabeth, 275n56

Wilson, Jane: review of *Flying* in *New York Times Book Review*, 171–72, 174–75, 178–79, 302nn5–6, 305nn33–38

Wittig, Monique, 275n55

"Woman Identified Woman" (Radicalesbians), 139, 145–51, 287n2, 288n11, 300n69, 300n76

women of color feminism, 1, 9, 11–12, 104–5, 126

women's culture (Berlant), 22–23, 212–14, 221, 225, 226, 301n1

women's liberation movement: accusation of exhibitionism of, 58–59, 171, 172; archive of, 2, 6–14, 21, 86, 95, 257; black women and, 65, 126, 285n84; as historical event, 2, 14–19; gay-straight split in, 94–95, 154; lesbianism in, 4, 12–13,

68, 74–77, 88–90; memoirs of, 3, 9, 272n26; origin story of, 7–8, 12; politics of self-transformation of, 124, 205; racism of, 11, 17, 23, 24, 126–30, 306n62; rhetoric of, 2, 17, 18, 20–21, 43, 84, 85, 95–96, 117, 276–77n56, 295n46, 300n76; spectacle-ization of, 50; universalizing vs. minoritizing views of, 90–91; whiteness and middle-classness of, 2, 17–19, 78, 112, 118, 126, 150, 154, 158, 180, 210, 212, 226, 267. *See also* feminist-as-lesbian figure; sexuality; urban guerrilla fighter

women's rights movement: nineteenth-century, 133–34, 280n33

Women's Strike for Equality, 3, 57, 61–64, 65, 234, 281n43

Woolf, Virginia, 52, 100, 273n43

X, Laura, 117, 125, 294n35

Yoshimura, Fumio. *See* Millett, Kate: relationship to Fumio Yoshimura

Young, Allen, 117, 293n10

Young Lords Party, 55, 65

Zerilli, Linda, 275n55

Zimmerman, Bonnie, 15, 214, 273nn41–42, 308n18